Political Economy of Africa
Selected Readings

Edited and introduced by
DENNIS L. COHEN and JOHN DANIEL

LONGMAN

LONGMAN GROUP LIMITED
London and New York

Associated companies, branches and representatives
throughout the world

First published 1981

British Library Cataloguing in Publication Data
The political economy of Africa.
    1. Africa—Economic conditions—1945–
    I. Cohen, D.
    II. Daniel, J.
    330.9'6'03   HC502

ISBN 0 582 64285 X (paper)
        64284 1 (cased)

    Printed in Hong Kong by
Sing Cheong Printing Co Ltd

Contents

iii

Acknowledgements

We are grateful to the following for permission to reproduce copyright material:

African Studies Association of the United States for Stephanie Urdang's article 'Fighting Two Colonialisms: the Women's Struggle in Guinea-Bissau' pp. 29–34 in *African Studies Review* Vol XVIII, No. 3, December 1975; Cambridge University Press for Samir Amin's article 'Underdevelopment and Dependence in Black Africa—Origins and Contemporary Forms' in *The Journal of Modern African Studies* Vol X, No. 4, December 1972; Frank Cass & Co Ltd for part one of Terisa Turner's article 'Commercial Capitalism and the 1975 Coup' from pp. 168–179 *Soldiers and Oil: The Political Transformation of Nigeria* edited by Keith Panter-Brick, 1978; Chama Cha Mapinduzi, Tanzania for pp. 1–8 from *TANU Guidelines on Guarding, Consolidating and Advancing the Revolution of Tanzania and of Africa* by the Tanzania African National Union; Rex Collings Ltd and the editor, Gavin Williams, for pp. 28–54 of the article entitled 'Nigeria: a Neo-Colonial Political Economy' by Gavin Williams from *Nigeria: Economy and Society* edited by Gavin Williams; Institute of Race Relations for Sam Mhlongo's article 'An Analysis of the Classes in South Africa' from *Race and Class* Vol XVI, No. 3, 1975; the author, Albert Memmi and Viking Press Inc for pp. 79–104 and pp. 119–141 from *The Colonizer and the Colonized*, translated by Howard Greenfeld copyright © 1965 by The Orion Press Inc, All rights reserved. Reprinted by permission of Viking Penguin Inc; Penguin Books Ltd for pp. 343–352 from *Unity or Poverty: The Economics of Pan-Africanism* by Reginald H. Green and Ann Seidman (Penguin African Library, 1968) and pp. 196–206 'The Guerilla Perspective' from *South Africa—No Middle Road* by Joe Slovo in *Southern Africa: The New Politics of Revolution* by Basil Davidson, Joe Slovo and Anthony R. Wilkinson (Pelican Books, 1976) © Basil Davidson, Joe Slovo, Anthony R. Wilkinson, 1976 reprinted by permission of Penguin Books Ltd; Review of African Political Economy for pp. 1–11 from article entitled 'The Multinationals in Africa' by the editors of the *Review of African Political Economy* No. 2, 1975 and pp. 41–48 from John Saul's article 'African Peasants and Revolution' in *Review of African Political Economy* No. 1, 1974; the editor, Professor T. Shanin for 'African Peasantries' by John Saul and Roger Woods in *Peasants and Peasant Societies* pp. 103–13 edited by T. Shanin and published by Penguin Books Ltd, 1971; South African Labour Bulletin for the article '"The Labour Aristocracy in Africa"; Introduction to an unfinished Controversy' by Peter Waterman in *South African Labour Bulletin* Vol 2, No. 5, 1975; United Nations for *The Meaning of Black Consciousness in the Struggle for Liberation in South Africa* by Ranwedzi Nengwekhulu, paper circulated by the United Nations Centre Against Apartheid, Department of Political and Security Council Affairs, July 1976; the University of Dar es Salaam for pp. 317–337 from the article 'The Internationalization of Capital and Labour' by Folker Fröbel, Jürgen Heinrichs, Otto Kreye and Osvaldo Sunkel, which originally appeared in *The African Review* Vol 4, No. 3, 1974.

Whilst every effort has been made, we are unable to trace the copyright owner of 'The Arusha Declaration' by the Tanzania African National Union. This statement of TANU policy was passed by the TANU delegates conference held in Arusha in 1967, and we would appreciate any information which would enable us to do so.

Preface

This collection of essays is the product of a number of years of experience in selecting, editing and using collections of articles and excerpts from longer works in the teaching of African politics. The present volume represents the culmination of efforts by the editors to produce an effective instrument for this purpose.

Previous editions were produced in 1973, 1975 and 1977 for purely local use by students in the institutions where the editors taught. Each successive revision has seen large-scale changes in the contents of the volume, and has reflected changes in the perspectives of the editors.

In terms of theoretical framework, we have moved from an eclectic approach, to an attempt at balancing opposed views on African political development, to an approach more committed to the use of a form of analysis which is generally labelled dependency theory. This is not to imply that a clear, uniform point of view is adopted by the authors of all the work contained in the book. Within the general category of dependency theory many different tendencies—theoretical, methodological, empirical and political—exist, and are represented here. Nevertheless, a broad, common framework is discernable in the work that follows.

The volume as it now stands is divided into four parts. The first presents the general structure of dependency within the international capitalist system of production and exchange, concentrating on its historical development and the international politico-economic mechanisms through which it is maintained in Africa.

The second part focuses on the internal structures within dependent areas which maintain and facilitate their dependency, namely the social classes produced as a result of the dependent mode of production, and the state structures which manage the system.

The third part deals with the cultural aspects of dependency, ie. the ideas that justify, explain and underlie dependent relations, as well as those which seek to change them, and the structures of socialisation by which these ideas are communicated.

The final part presents several ideological statements that are representative of the major strategic choices facing dependent African states seeking a path to development today. In one sense the choice between these strategies will be the product of the processes described in the earlier sections. Dialectically, this choice will in turn determine the rate and direction of change of these processes.

Each part of the book is introduced by a brief discussion, by the editors, of the articles included, as well as a bibliography of selected readings. While many of the readings included in the bibliographies will be applicable more widely, they are subdivided thematically to be of particular assistance to student readers.

In conclusion, we wish to thank the scholars whose work we have included in this volume; J.E. Bardill of the National University of Lesotho, who cooperated in producing an earlier version; Professor David Kimble, Vice-Chancellor of the University of Malawi, and Dr Yash Tandon of Dar es Salaam University, whose encouragement and constructive criticism have been a continuing aid to our development; and, most importantly, the students we have taught in

Ghana, Uganda, Lesotho, Botswana and Swaziland, who provided the challenge
to which this book is a partial response.

DENNIS L. COHEN
Maiduguri, Nigeria

JOHN DANIEL
Kwaluseni, Swaziland

Part One
The Development of Dependency

Introduction and Select Bibliography

DENNIS L. COHEN

The selections included in this section discuss the development of the key international mechanisms of dependency. The theory of dependency, as presented here, is an attempt to explain, understand and ultimately change the differences in levels of development between the various areas of the international capitalist system. These differences in the structures of production, exchange and accumulation between the developed capitalist states on the one hand, and the underdeveloped capitalist states on the other, are seen as resulting not from natural differences in productivity between different areas, nor from differences in technological and cultural levels in these areas, but from:

(1) the early development of capitalist relations of production in Western Europe, resulting, by the sixteenth century, in capitalism having become the dominant mode of production in that area;

(2) capitalism's need to expand the area from which its factors of production are drawn, within which its products are exchanged and surpluses realised and accumulated, and to which their reproduction, at high rates of profit, can be directed;

(3) the linking together of areas in which different levels of production, based on different modes of production, prevail, through the expansion and domination of capitalist production, and its exploitation of less developed areas;

(4) the operation of the law of uneven and combined development through the relations of exchange between areas of different levels of development, which extends and expands the differences as surplus value is transferred from less to more advanced areas, while the less developed modes of production are preserved as sources of cheap raw materials and labour and as protected markets for the more advanced areas, rather than being transformed themselves into the more advanced mode of production;

(5) the establishment, in most cases, of direct political control by the wealthier states over the poorer areas through various systems of colonialism;

(6) the creation, in the politically dominated and economically exploited areas, of their own dependent class structure, dominated by an international bourgeoisie, generally externally located, and including various small, comprador social strata which come increasingly to exercise neo-colonial, local management functions in the dependent areas, as well as the mass of small peasants and urban workers, whose labour is the source of the surplus value upon which the whole system is built;

(7) the development of a culture of dependency, ie. a set of attitudes, norms and ideas that facilitate the dominance of the less advanced (peripheral or satellite) areas, by the more advanced (centre or metropolitan) ones, encouraging assimilation for the comprador groups and submissiveness for the peasant and proletarian masses.

1

The first selection, 'The Internalisation of Capital and Labour', by Folker Fröbel, Jürgen Heinrichs, Otto Kreye and Osvaldo Sunkel, criticises capitalist development strategies and characterises capitalist development as being based upon the separation of the workers from the means of production, the concentration of capital in the hands of the bourgeoisie, and the progressive immiserisation of the workers. The authors discuss the phased development of the structure of dependency through the primitive accumulation of slavery and the use of forced labour in mines and plantations; the colonial phase of unequal exchange relations between the coloniser, supplying expensive manufactured commodities, and the colonised, supplying cheap food and raw materials; and the neo-colonial phase, when industrialisation becomes important in dependent areas under the domination of metropolitan-controlled multinational corporations making use of cheap labour reserves in the dependent areas. The resulting phase of increased transnational integration of production and an international division of labour is seen as the dominant present tendency.

The authors deny the possibility of independent, capitalist development for the dependent areas, and see only a limited possibility of assistance for them from the developed socialist world. Their conclusion, while pessimistic in the short run, points to the proletarianisation of larger and larger segments of dependent populations, and the internationalisation of their domination, interests and, finally, of their struggles as the force that can eventually challenge the system.

Samir Amin's 'Underdevelopment and Dependence in Black Africa—Origins and Contemporary Forms', presents an application of the theory of capitalist, dependent development more specifically to the African context. He analyses the developing relationship between Western capitalism and Africa on the basis of four phases. In the pre-mercantile period trade was limited and relations were not substantially unequal. In the mercantile period, 1600–1800, after the establishment of capitalist hegemony within several Western European states, the slave trade was the dominant form of relation, helping to produce the acceleration of European production. The bulk of the nineteenth century saw the more complete integration of Africa into international capitalism through 'legitimate' trade, as Africa became a significant source of cheap raw materials for European industrialisation. Finally, the colonial period from 1800 to 1960 saw the completion of this process with the emergence in Africa of areas providing different types of surpluses for European capitalism:

(1) the 'labour reserve' areas of Southern and East Africa, where mining and settler agriculture required large supplies of cheap labour which could only be produced through extensive repression and control over the indigenous population;

(2) the 'trading areas' of West Africa and part of East Africa, where the pre-colonial mode of production was distorted and made to serve capitalist needs through peasant production of cheap raw materials exchanged for more expensive consumer goods;

(3) the area of 'concessions' in Central Africa, where internal systems of control were replaced by plantations owned by large European producing companies.

Amin's analysis focuses on both sides of this process of the development of underdevelopment, the simultaneous development of Europe and underdevelopment of Africa.

'Nigeria: a Neo-colonial Political Economy', by Gavin Williams, extends

Amin's historical analysis by focusing on the contemporary structures—economic, social and political—of post-colonial neo-colonialism. Independence is seen by Williams as an opportunity for extending the process of integrating the new state—in this case Nigeria—into the global capitalist system.

Foreign exploitation is multilateralised and multinational corporations are presented with lucrative incentives for investment; industrialisation begins with the local manufacture of import substitutes; an indigenous bourgeoisie is given greater scope for development; and, above all, the state plays a commanding role in initiating, protecting and subsidising these processes.

Williams emphasises the consequences of these changes for the class structure. The indigenous bourgeosie, he argues, is able to use the state to bring about capitalist expansion and appropriate the surplus value created by workers and peasants, but it does this in collaboration with foreign capital. The exploitation of peasants and small producers is stepped up; and they respond to this by active revolt. Urban workers, far from being a passive labour aristocracy, have also intervened forcefully in politics to advance their class interests.

His analysis concentrates on the role of the Nigerian state in failing to resolve these class conflicts, as well as intra-bourgeois struggles over individual and community shares in the spoils of capitalist development. The latter conflicts he regards as central to the military *coup* and civil war of the 1960s. The military/bureaucratic regime of the 1970s is seen as trying to enforce greater cohesion on the ruling class in order to institutionalise the rules defining class relations of domination and exploitation. Indigenisation decrees, increased producer prices for peasants, the concession of wage increases to workers, the expansion of education, and the restructuring of federal-state relations, are all seen as attempts along these lines. Nevertheless, Williams is pessimistic about the capacity of the Nigerian state to succeed in this undertaking, faced with the intractable problems of unbridled competition for scarce resources. Despite its focus on Nigeria, this analysis is of general relevance.

The final selection in this part is the editorial on multinational corporations that introduced the second issue of the *Review of African Political Economy* (1975). The editors of the *Review*, while recognising that multinational corporations (MNCs) retain a national base in their ownership and control, see the expansion of their activities as the most important recent development in the continuing integration of the international capitalist system. Concentrating on MNC activities in dependent areas, they see these as further enlarging dependency through the following mechanisms:

(1) bringing local capital under foreign control through joint government–MNC enterprises;

(2) transferring surpluses from dependent to dominant areas through profits, dividends, royalties, transfer-pricing, over-invoicing, trademark and copyright fees, management contracts, etc.;

(3) retarding national development through the use of inappropriate technology;

(4) inflating profits through monopoly marketing privileges;

(5) distorting the pattern of local development through investing in areas of benefit to the centre investor, not necessarily to the periperhal area.

They also go into some detail on the relationship between MNCs and the neo-colonial state, how this can affect the latter's policies, both domestic and foreign, and how the nationalisation of such foreign enterprises has through continued minority control and management contracts often simply given the

MNCs greater access to state power, rather than bringing them under the effective control of the state.

Like Fröbel, *et.al.*, at the beginning of this section, the editors of the *Review* look to the internationalisation of labour in response to the internationalisation of capital, in the form of the creation of international trade unions, as a significant source of challenge to the increasing domination of multinational corporations over dependent states.

Select Bibliography

1 Dependency Theory

Samir Amin, *Accumulation on a World Scale: A Critique of the Theory of Underdevelopment*, Monthly Review Press, New York and London, 1974.

————, *Un-Equal Development: An Essay on the Social Formations of Peripheral Capitalism*, Monthly Review Press, New York and London, 1976.

Paul A. Baran, *The Political Economy of Growth*, Marzani and Mansell, New York, 1957.

———— and Paul M. Sweezy, *Monopoly Capital*, Penguin, 1968, esp. chapter 7.

Henry Bernstein, 'Underdevelopment and the Law of Value: A Critique of Kay', *Review of African Political Economy*, 6, May–August 1976.

Michael Barratt Brown, *After Imperialism*, Merlin Press, London, 1970, esp. Part One.

————, *Essays on Imperialism*, chapters 1 and 2, Spokesman Books, Nottingham, 1972.

Nikolai I. Bukharin, *Imperialism and World Economy*, Monthly Review Press, New York and London, 1973 (first edition published by International Publishers, Moscow, in 1929).

Christopher Chase-Dunn, and Richard Rubinson, 'Toward a Structural Perspective on the World-System', *Politics and Society*, 7, 4, 1977.

Arghiri Emmanuel, *Unequal Exchange*, Monthly Review Press, New York and London, 1972.

André Gunder Frank, *Latin America: Underdevelopment and Revolution. Essays in the Development of Underdevelopment and the Immediate Enemy*, Monthly Review Press, New York and London, 1969.

————, *On Capitalist Underdevelopment*, Oxford University Press, London, 1975.

————, *World Accumulation, 1492–1789*, The Macmillan Press, London, 1978.

————, *Dependent Accumulation and Under-Development*, The Macmillan Press, London, 1978.

Folker Fröbel, Jürgen Heinrichs, and Otto Kreye, 'The Tendency Towards a New International Division of Labor', *Review*, I. 1, Summer 1977.

Barry Hindess and Paul Q. Hirst, *Pre-Capitalist Modes of Production*, Routledge and Kegan Paul, London and Boston, 1975.

Stephen Hymer, 'Robinson Crusoe and the Secret of Primitive Accumulation', *Monthly Review*, 23, 4 (1971).

Geoffrey Kay, *Development and Underdevelopment: A Marxist Analysis*, The Macmillan Press, London, 1974.

Tom Kemp, *Theories of Imperialism*, Dobson Books, London, 1967.

V.G. Kiernan, *Marxism and Imperialism*, Edward Arnold, London, 1974.

V.I. Lenin, *Imperialism, the Highest Stage of Capitalism: A Popular Outline*,

Foreign Languages Press, Peking, 1969 (first edition published in Petrograd in 1917).

George Lichtheim, *Imperialism*, Praeger, New York, 1971.

Rosa Luxemburg, *The Accumulation of Capital: An Anti-Critique*, Monthly Review Press, New York and London, 1972 (first edition published in 1913).

Harry Magdoff, *The Age of Imperialism: The Economics of US Foreign Policy*, Monthly Review Press, New York and London, 1969.

Ernest Mandel, *Marxist Economic Theory*, Merlin Press, London, 1968, esp. chapter 13.

Karl Marx, *Pre-Capitalist Economic Formations* (edited by E.J. Hobsbawm), Lawrence and Wishart, London, 1964.

————, *Surveys from Exile: Political Writings*, Penguin, 1973, Vol. 2, pp. 301–33 on India and China.

————, *The First International and After: Political Writings*, Penguin, 1974, Vol. 3, pp. 158–71 on Ireland.

Kenzo Mohri, 'Marx and "Under-development"', *Monthly Review*, 30, 11, April 1979.

D.W. Nabudere, *The Political Economy of Imperialism*, Zed Press, London, 1977.

Roger Owen and Bob Sutcliffe eds., *Studies in the Theory of Imperialism*, Longman, London, 1972.

Anne Phillips, 'The Concept of Development', *Review of African Political Economy*, 8, January–April 1977.

Paul M. Sweezy, *The Theory of Capitalist Development*, Monthly Review Press, New York and London, 1970, esp. Part Four.

I. Wallerstein, 'Three Paths of National Development in Sixteenth Century Europe', *Studies in Comparative International Development*, 7, 2 (1972).

————, *The Modern World-System: Capitalist Agriculture and the Origins of the European World Economy in the Sixteenth Century*, Academic Press, New York and London, 1974.

2 Development of Dependency in Africa

Edward A. Alpers, 'Re-thinking African Economic History', *Kenya Historical Review*, I, 2 (1973).

————, *Ivory and Slaves in East Central Africa: Changing patterns of international trade in the late nineteenth century*, Heinemann, London, 1975.

E.A. Brett, *Colonialism and Underdevelopment in East Africa: The politics of economic change, 1919–1939*, Longman, London, 1973.

Catherine Coquery-Vidrovitch, 'Research on an African mode of production', in Peter Gutkind and Peter Waterman eds., *African Social Studies: A Radical Reader*, Monthly Review Press, New York and London, 1977.

Basil Davidson, *Black Mother: A Study of the Precolonial Connection between Africa and Europe*, Longman, London, 1961.

Philip Ehrensaft, 'The Political Economy of Informal Empire in Pre-Colonial Nigeria, 1807–1884', *Canadian Journal of African Studies*, 6, 3 (1972).

Maurice Godelier, 'Infrastructures, Societies and Histories', *New Left Review*, 112, November–December 1978.

Rhoda Howard, *Colonialism and Underdevelopment in Ghana*, Croom Helm, London, 1978.

Stephen Hymer, 'Economic Forms in Pre-Colonial Ghana', Yale University Economic Research Center Discussion Paper, 1969.

E.D. Morel, *The Black Man's Burden*, Monthly Review Press, New York and London, 1969 (first published in 1920).

Robin Palmer and Neil Parsons eds., *The Roots of Rural Poverty in Central and Southern Africa*, Heinemann, London, 1977.

Ronald Robinson and John Gallagher with Alice Denny, *Africa and the Victorians: The Climax of Imperialism*, Macmillan, London, 1961.

Walter Rodney, *How Europe Underdeveloped Africa*, Tanzania Publishing House, Dar es Salaam, 1972.

Jean Suret-Canale, *French Colonialism in Tropical Africa: 1900–1945*, Hurst, London, 1971.

Wallerstein, 'The Three Stages of African Involvement in the World-Economy', in Peter C.W. Gutkind and I. Wallerstein eds., *The Political Economy of Contemporary Africa*, Sage Publications, California, 1976.

Eric Williams, *Capitalism and Slavery*, Andre Deutsch, London, 1964, (first published in 1944).

3 Neo-Colonialism

Samir Amin, *Neo-Colonialism in West Africa*, Penguin, 1973.

Giovanni Arrighi and J.S. Saul, *Essays on the Political Economy of Africa*, Monthly Review Press, New York and London, 1973.

Henry Bernstein, ed., *Underdevelopment and Development: The Third World Today*, Penguin, 1973.

Bonnie Campbell, 'Neo-Colonialism, Economic Development and Political Change: Cotton Textile Production in the Ivory Coast', *Review of African Political Economy*, 2, 1975.

D.L. Cohen, and M.A. Tribe, 'Suppliers' Credits in Ghana and Uganda: An Aspect of the Imperialist System', *Journal of Modern African Studies*, 10, 4 (1972).

Arghiri Emmanuel, 'White Settler Colonialism and the Myth of Investment Imperialism', *New Left Review*, 73, May–June 1972.

———, 'Myths of Development versus Myths of Underdevelopment', *New Left Review*, 85, May–June 1974.

K. Fann and D.C. Hodges eds., *Readings in US Imperialism*, Academic Press, New York, 1971.

Ruth First, *The Barrel of a Gun: Political Power in Africa*, Penguin, 1970.

Andre Gunder Frank, 'Long Live Transideological Enterprise! The Socialist Economies in the Capitalist International Division of Labor', *Review*, I, 1, Summer 1977.

Folker Fröbel, Jürgen Heinrichs, and Otto Kreye, 'Export-Oriented Industrialization in Underdeveloped Countries', *Monthly Review*, 30, 6, November 1978.

J. Galtung, 'A Structural Theory of Imperialism', *The African Review*, 1, 4 (1972).

———, 'The Lome Convention and Neo-Capitalism', *The African Review*, 6, 1 (1976).

Martin Godfrey and Steven Langdon, 'Partners in Underdevelopment? The Transnationalisation Thesis in a Kenyan Context', *The Journal of Commonwealth and Comparative Politics*, 14, 1 (1976).

R.H. Green and Ann Seidman, *Unity or Poverty? The Economics of Pan-Africanism*, Penguin, 1967.

R.H. Green, 'Political Independence and the National Economy: An Essay on the Political Economy of Decolonisation', in Christopher Allen and R.W. Johnson eds., *African Perspectives: Papers in the history, politics and economics of Africa presented to Thomas Hodgkin*, Cambridge University Press, 1970.

T. Hayter, *Aid as Imperialism*, Penguin, 1971.

Stephen Hymer, 'The Political Economy of the Gold Coast and Ghana', in G. Rannis ed., *Government and Economic Development*, Yale University Press,

New Haven and London, 1971.

Pierre Jalee, *The Pillage of the Third World*, Monthly Review Press, New York and London, 1968.

———, *The Third World in World Economy*, Monthly Review Press, New York and London, 1969.

Richard Joseph, 'The Gaullist Legacy: Patterns of French Neo-Colonialism', *Review of African Political Economy*, 6, May–August 1976.

Gavin Kitching, 'Modes of Production and Kenyan Dependency', *Review of African Political Economy*, 8, January–April 1977.

Colin Leys, *Underdevelopment in Kenya: The Political Economy of Neo-Colonialism*, Heinemann, London, 1975.

P. McMichael, J. Petras and R. Rhodes, 'Imperialism and the Contradictions of Development', *New Left Review*, 85, May–June 1974.

D.W. Nabudere, 'Generalised Schemes of Preference in World Trade', *The African Review*, 5, 3 (1975).

Kwame Nkrumah, *Africa Must Unite*, Heinemann, London, 1963.

———, *Neo-Colonialism: The Last Stage of Imperialism*, Thomas Nelson, London, 1965.

Peter O'Brien, 'Trademarks in Developing Countries', *Journal of Modern African Studies*, 14, 2 (1976).

Cheryl Payer, *The Debt Trap: The IMF and the Third World*, Penguin, 1974.

———, 'Third World Debt Problems: The New Wave of Defaults', *Monthly Review*, 28, 4 (1976).

Robert I. Rhodes ed., *Imperialism and Underdevelopment: A Reader*, Monthly Review Press, New York and London, 1970.

Stewart Smith, *US Neo-Colonialism in Africa*, Progress Publishers, Moscow, 1974.

Paul M. Sweezy, 'Socialism in Poor Countries', *Monthly Review*, 28, 5 (1976).

Tamas Szentes, *The Political Economy of Underdevelopment*, Akademia Kiado, Budapest, 1971.

E.A. Tarabrin ed., *Neo-Colonialism and Africa in the 1970s*, Progress Publishers, Moscow, 1978.

Clive Thomas, *Dependence and Transformation: The Economics of the Transition to Socialism*, Monthly Review Press, New York and London, 1974.

I. Wallerstein, 'Dependence in an Interdependent World: The limited possibilities of transformation within the capitalist world economy', *African Studies Review*, 12, 1 (1974).

Bill Warren, 'Imperialism and Capitalist Industrialization', *New Left Review*, 81, September–October 1973.

Gavin Williams, *Nigeria: Economy and Society*, Rex Collings, London, 1976.

4 Multinational Corporations

R.J. Barnet and R.E. Muller, *Global Reach: The Rise of Multinational Corporations*, Simon and Shuster, New York, 1974.

Pierre Bonté, 'Multinational Corporations and National Development: MIFERMA and Mauretania', *Review of African Political Economy*, 2, 1975.

Marcia M. Burdette, 'Nationalisation in Zambia: A Critique of Bargaining Theory', *Canadian Journal of African Studies*, 11, 3 (1977).

Andrew C. Coulson, 'Tanzania's Fertiliser Factory', *Journal of Modern African Studies*, 15, 1 (1977).

S. Cronje, M. Ling and G. Cronje, *Lonrho: Portrait of a Multinational*, Penguin, 1976.

Arghiri Emmanuel, 'The MNCs and inequality of development', *International*

Social Science Journal, 28, 4 (1976).

Norman Girvan, 'Multinational Corporations and Dependent Underdevelopment in Mineral Export Economies', *Social and Economic Studies*, 19, December 1970.

S. Hymer, 'The Internationalization of Capital', *Journal of Economic Issues*, 6, 1972.

J.J. Jorgensen, 'Multinational Corporations and the Indigenisation of the Kenyan Economy', *The African Review*, 5, 4 (1975).

Steven Langdon, 'The Political Economy of Dependency: Notes Towards Analysis of Multinational Corporations in Kenya', *Journal of East African Research and Development*, 4, 2 (1972).

————, 'Multinational Corporations, Taste Transfer and Underdevelopment: A Case Study from Kenya', *Review of African Political Economy*, 2, 1975.

John Loxley and J.S. Saul, 'Multinationals, Workers and Parastatals in Tanzania', *Review of African Political Economy*, 2, 1975.

G. Massiah, 'Multinational Corporations and a Strategy for Economic Independence', *The African Review*, 5, 4 (1975).

A.A. Said and L.R. Simmons eds., *The New Sovereigns: Multinational Corporations as World Powers*, Prentice-Hall, Englewood Cliffs, N.J., 1975.

Ann and Neva Seidman, 'United States Multinationals in South Africa', *Journal of Southern African Affairs*, 1, Special Issue, October 1976.

I.G. Shivji, 'Capitalism Unlimited: Public Corporations in Partnership with Multinational Corporations', *The African Review*, 3, 3 (1973).

Yash Tandon, 'The Role of Transnational Corporations and Future Trends in Southern Africa', *Journal of Southern African Affairs*, 2, 4 (1977).

C. Tugenhadt, *The Multinationals*, Penguin, 1973.

Terisa Turner, 'Multinational Corporations and the Instability of the Nigerian State', *Review of African Political Economy*, 5, January–April 1976.

United Nations Economic Commission for Africa, 'The Multinational Corporations in Africa', in C. Legum ed., *African Contemporary Record*, Rex Collings, London, 1972.

Raymond Vernon ed., *The Economic and Political Consequences of Multinational Enterprise: An Anthology*, Graduate School of Business Administration, Boston, 1972.

C. Widstrand ed., *Multinational Firms in Africa*, Scandinavian Institute of African Studies, Uppsala, 1975.

LONGMAN INC.
19 WEST 44TH STREET   NEW YORK, N.Y. 10036

FREE DESK OR EXAMINATION COPIES FOR

PROFESSOR THOMAS KARIS
CITY COLLEGE CUNY

043462 1 240
18720 051581

QTY.	NUMBER, AUTHOR, AND TITLE	SRC
01	64285X COHEN: POLITICAL ECONOMY OF AFRICA	

FREE

WE HOPE YOU WILL FIND TIME TO USE THE SPACE BELOW TO GIVE US YOUR OPINION OF THESE TITLES, AND TO LET US KNOW ABOUT YOUR PLANS FOR THEIR USE IN YOUR COURSES.

COMMENTS

MAY WE QUOTE YOU? YES ☐ NO ☐   FOLD, TAPE, AND MAIL

FOLD, TAPE, AND MAIL

||||||

BUSINESS REPLY MAIL
FIRST CLASS PERMIT NO. 50745, NEW YORK, N.Y.

FIRST CLASS POSTAGE WILL BE PAID BY

LONGMAN INC.
19 WEST 44th STREET
NEW YORK, N. Y. 10036

COLLEGE DEPARTMENT

1 The Internationalisation of Capital and Labour*

FOLKER FRÖBEL, JÜRGEN HEINRICHS,
OTTO KREYE and OWALDO SUNKEL

Conventional Development Theory and the Development of Capitalism

Conventional development theory

Theories of development—of the development of the capitalist mode of production—were implicit, essential elements of the classicist's study of political economy. They were the focus of analysis in the works of Karl Marx.[1]

In view of (1) the rapid growth of US and Western European industry and (2) the world-wide spread of capitalism (through which the industrial countries directed the creation of an international division of labour), neo-classical bourgeois economics departed from the assumption that capitalism has essentially solved its problems of growth and expansion. Since the 1870s, bourgeois theorists have dedicated themselves to the subjects of price mechanisms, the functioning of the market and allocation. According to the neo-classical equilibrium model, a maximum output will be achieved if the individual economic units act in an 'optimal' way within perfect markets. State intervention should be avoided unless such intervention is necessary to guarantee the conditions of perfect competition, that is, the perfect functioning of the market.

Since the 1920s, bourgeois economics has been obliged to devote itself mainly to the study of crisis situations in the countries with a highly developed capitalist mode of production: inflation, depression, unemployment, the breakdown of international economic relations. According to the (post-) Keynesian growth model—and in contrast to the classical equilibrium model—state intervention is not only desirable but necessary. Even though it is maintained that the market economy leads to an efficient intersectoral allocation, it is conceded that disequilibrium in the temporal allocation (consumption/investment) may occur and thus lead to cyclical unemployment and inflation. Through the intervention of the state, the increase in investment should be so controlled that, on the one hand, unemployment will be avoided and, on the other, the total income created guarantees a sufficient demand for the resulting increase in output.

Considering the now unrealistic assumption of perfect market conditions (given the oligopolisation of the market), and considering the continual appearance of crisis symptoms in the countries with state-regulated capitalism (unemployment, inflation, the international monetary crisis), it has become more and more doubtful whether bourgeois economics is in a position to study properly the development of capitalism.[2] These doubts have been strengthened from yet another side; since the 1950s and 1960s, heretic social scientists have begun to relate the issue to the term 'development of underdevelopment', the subject matter of their research.

* From *The African Review*, 4, 3 (1974), pp. 317–37.

Bourgeois economics, confronted with the symptoms of underdevelopment,[3] had only two analytical approaches: the neo-classical equilibrium model and the post-Keynesian growth model.[4] In each model, the size and the growth of an economy are measured with a global indicator, the Gross National Product (GNP), without making any assumption in the first instance about the relationships between (1) GNP per capita, (2) the prosperity of the majority of the population, and (3) 'development'. For as many countries as possible, the calculation of the GNP was first attempted and a listing of the countries according to their GNP per capita was made. The nations were arranged from the highest (USA, Western European countries, Canada, Australia, Japan) to the lowest (Latin American, Asian and African countries). Then, an arbitrary dividing line was drawn to separate 'developed countries' from 'developing countries'. Secondly, the list—which grossly showed the per capita production in a particular year—was interpreted as the representation of a cross-temporal development continuum. In other words, the implicit assumption was that there was one normal or average path to development which all countries in the past had followed, and which all countries were obliged to follow in the future, a process from a primitive, traditional, agricultural, low-productivity economy through a set of development stages to a developed capitalist economy and society, like that of the USA or Western Europe. Thirdly, the structural changes which accompanied the growth of the GNP per capita were investigated. For this purpose, the GNP per capita was conceived as the independent variable, and numerous other indicators were correlated with it: the rate of investment; the distribution of income; birth and death rates; the sectoral structure of production and employment; the degree of urbanisation; literacy rates; the number of students per teacher; and the number of inhabitants per doctor. As was to be expected, all these indicators changed at varying rates when the scale, according to the GNP per capita, was traversed from bottom to top at a steady speed. These varying rates were interpreted as structural changes necessary for the development of a country.

In this way, one arrived at so-called development strategies, some components of which were rising investment, general industrialisation, mechanisation and chemicalisation of agriculture, education, and medical care. These strategies represented an attempt to imprint the attributes of the developed capitalist countries directly on the so-called developing countries.[5] (Ignored was the fact that the developing countries could never pass through the same historical process that led to the social and economic structure, the political systems, and the culture of the developed capitalist countries. Moreover, it was precisely this process that had created the dependency of the developing countries on the developed countries.) In the last two decades, numerous incentives were provided: the supply of foreign capital, foreign manpower, foreign technology, foreign values, culture, ideology and weapons.

The decisive consequence of these strategies has been the further expansion of the capitalist mode of production on a world scale. The supposed goal of the strategies, however, had been to reduce the gap in the standard of living between the industrial nations and the developing countries through acceleration of growth in the GNPs of the latter. Although structural changes, contributing to the expansion of the capitalist mode of production, did take place in many developing countries, it has meanwhile also become clear that the income of the majority of the population in these countries has hardly risen. The distribution of income has actually become more unequal; unemployment and underemployment have grown. Social standards—nutrition, education, housing, health, social security—have on the whole not improved. Rather, for the vast majority of the (growing) population, conditions have become worse. In short, there has been an absolute and, probably as well, a relative increase in the number of people suffering from misery, and the foreign dependence of these developing countries has been deepened.[6]

The objection that those incentives have not yet been fully employed, or that a longer time is needed in order to yield any results for the improvement of the living conditions of the majority, is hardly valid. There are numerous countries in which such development strategies have clearly and openly succeeded according to measures of growth in the GNP—for example, Brazil, Kenya and Iran. In spite of this, the social situation of the majority of the population in these countries has until now not improved, but rather worsened. Moreover, nothing indicates that the 'postponed' consumption, which has been forced on the masses in the name of economic development, will lead to a significant rise of their living standards in the forseeable future. What is clear, however, as these development strategies are pursued, is that the mass of the population in the developing countries is becoming an internationally available reserve army of industrial labourers. The non-achievement of the strategies' objectives, reflected in the progressive immiserisation of the majority of the population in many countries, requires a critical reappraisal of the basic assumptions on which these strategies are based. Thus, from the perspective of the underdeveloped countries, it has become doubtful if the ruling bourgeois economic theory is in a position to adequately analyse the development of capitalism. Bourgeois economics has not been able to give an explanation for the stagnation in the standard of living that occurs in the face of observable economic growth. Even less can it explain the reproduction and deepening (within the developing countries) of the foreign dependence and the internal social inequalities. Finally, the task of understanding the history of the developing countries as a part of the whole capitalist development process was never even undertaken.

Towards a notion of capitalist development

Capitalist development is the production and (extended) reproduction of the capitalist mode of production, that is, the expansion and deepening of the relations of wage labour and capital through (1) the separation of direct producers from their means of production (especially from the land); (2) transformation of surplus value into capital; (3) concentration and centralisation of the means of production; (4) the rise in the number of wage labourers; and (5) the further development of productive forces.[7] Capitalist development, in this sense, is not a homogeneous process that evenly envelops a society. The process is both more restricted, in so far as it does not equally embrace the whole of a society, and more extensive, in so far as it simultaneously encroaches on other societies in search of capital, labour, raw materials and markets. Capitalist development in one region and in one economic sector has destructive effects on the pre-existing forces and relations of production in this region and in this sector and, as well, in their dependent regions and sectors. At the same time, such change in one region or sector works as a stimulant for the further development of productive forces and the establishment of capitalist relations of production in other sectors and regions. The progressive expansion of the relation of wage labour and capital—although an unequal development—is accompanied by both the liberation and the oppression of the labour force within the new social relations of production. The creation of the industrial reserve army is linked to the

11

progressive immiserisation[8] of a growing proportion of the population, for which the continual deterioration in the standard of living is only the visible expression. If one considers the capitalist development process from its international character and from its simultaneously destructive and constructive effects, the global picture of the development of the capitalist mode of production differs radically from the conventional view. Development, meaning the expansion of the wage labour/capital relation, occurs both simultaneously and interdependently within different regions and sectors. Development, in this sense, is at once (1) the partial destruction of pre-existing productive forces, (2) the creation of new forces of production, but only within the limits of realisation of capital, and (3) the destruction of pre-capitalist relations of production. The latter results in the reduction and decline of social security, which pre-capitalist relations of production have offered to some extent. Development, in this sense, is also immiserisation inside as well as outside the developing regions and sectors.

In the countries with a highly developed capitalist mode of production ('developed countries'), the working class—especially through the enforcement of national labour laws and at the expense of the people of less developed countries—has been able, more or less, to raise its standard of living, of course only within the limits of the wage labour/capital relationship and dependent on the booms and depressions of the realisation of capital. Seen on a world scale, the countries with a weakly developed wage labour/capital relationship (the so-called developing or underdeveloped countries) compose the great reservoir of the industrial reserve army. The self-contained contradiction of the capitalist mode of production manifests itself in the immiserisation of the mass of the world's population. For it is in the developing countries, with their almost total lack of organised labour, that the poor, and frequently even sinking, standard of living of the majority becomes apparent. The 'underdevelopment' of the developing countries is the result of the process of unequal development, thus, the result of the single, unitary process of capitalist development.

The Process of Unequal Capitalist Development

The development of the presently underdeveloped countries is determined by the development of capital in the already developed countries. The relationship between the two groups of nations has evolved in such a way that a large part of the economic surplus of the underdeveloped countries is transferred through a variety of mechanisms to the developed countries. The relationship between the two groups is one of dependency and domination. The functional relations are mediated most visibly through the process of capital accumulation and expansion of the big enterprises of the developed countries. The development of the socio-economic structure, which reproduces the relationship of dependency and domination, derives directly from the production and the extended reproduction of the capitalist mode of production. This is illustrated and proven in the historical analysis of the capitalist mode of production.[9]

The phase of primitive accumulation/exploitation

The formation phase in the development of the capitalist mode of production, the phase of primitive accumulation (ie. the transformation of non-capitalistically produced surpluses into capital and the separation of the direct producers from their means of production) represents for the underdeveloped countries the beginning of their inclusion in the capitalist development process. For these countries, it is the phase of primitive exploitation of people (slavery), nature and wealth on the one hand, and the creation of a latent wage labour force on the other. The accumulation of the world-wide available economic surplus, and its transformation into capital in some regions of the world, is experienced simultaneously as exploitation and disaccumulations in other regions of the world. The integration of the world into the accumulation process of Europe is executed in different ways, from military to commercial intervention. Relatively developed forces of production in handicraft, manufacture and agriculture are destroyed, surpluses are withdrawn from regional use, direct producers are separated from their means of production. Finally, the immiserisation of the masses, which is characteristic of the development of the wage labour/capital relationship, begins.

While the forces of production and capitalist relations of production quickly develop in the emergent industrial countries, only partial development of the capitalist mode of production occurs in the other countries, and this is limited to agriculture and mining. These branches develop as complementary suppliers of agricultural and mineral raw materials to European industries. While in this phase the relationship of wage labour and capital in the emergent industrial countries becomes the dominant one, it develops only partially in the other countries, responsive to the demands of capital reproduction in the industrial countries. The result: the origins of a latent wage labour force arise. But the submission of this labour by capital remains formal. Latent wage labour is not directly included in the specifically capitalist process of production.

Development of the capitalist mode of production in the developed countries and the formation of the requirements for capitalist production in the underdeveloped countries

In the phase of primitive accumulation/exploitation, the preconditions for an autonomously determined evolution and expansion of the capitalist mode of production were established in one region of the world. The current division of the world between developed and underdeveloped countries was set up in this first phase. Subsequently, the continued development of capitalism means the autonomous extended reproduction of the capitalist mode of production in the developed countries: concomitantly, development in the developing countries is determined by the development in the developed nations, creating all the conditions and requirements for (dependent) development of the capitalist mode of production in the developing countries.

Colonialism and unequal exchange

Of great importance for the development of capital in the industrial countries was the transformation of the rest of the world into suppliers of food and raw materials. This transformation made possible a considerably greater transfer of labour out of agriculture and into the industrial sector (within the developed countries) than the rise in agricultural productivity would have otherwise permitted. In contrast, the emergent capitalist sectors in the developing countries (for the most part export-oriented agricultural and mineral production) developed as dependent sectors, integrated into the international economy but horizontally non-integrated in their national economies. The national economies stagnated and remained as residual economies, with the function of providing the capitalist sectors with labour, securing its reproduction, and providing other inputs to the capitalist sectors. Thus, a continual transfer of economic potential from the indigenous economy to the capitalist sector occurred.[10] An essential part of the surplus from unequal internal exchange is transferred through unequal external exchange to serve both consumptive and productive consumption in the developed countries. The external dependence of the capitalist sector and the external control of foreign trade interact to determine the terms of trade.

This phase in the relations between underdeveloped and developed regions embraces a period of several hundred years. It began in Latin America around 1500, in India 200 years later and, for some parts of Africa, for the first time at the end of the nineteenth century, while other parts of Africa were already drawn into the process 100 to 300 years earlier. The result is well-known: tightly restricted regional and sectoral dependent capitalist development; immiserisation of the majority of the population in Latin America, Africa, and Asia;[11] and complex industrial development and improvement of the standard of living for the majority of the population in the industrial countries. For the industrial countries, it is also the period of national concentration and centralisation of capital, the creation of large industrial firms capable of world-wide expansion. While at the beginning of the period the developed sector of the developing countries was still partially controlled by domestic enterprises and foreign commercial houses, its further expansion came to be engineered by those big enterprises of the developed countries.

The beginning of dependent industrialisation

The extended reproduction—based on mining and agriculture—of the restricted capitalist sector in the underdeveloped countries led to a continually rising demand in this sector for industrial products, for both capital goods and consumer goods. The rising demand allows the importation of a portion of these finished products to be replaced by internal production. However, the import dependence of the developed sectors of the underdeveloped countries, although altered, is strengthened, not weakened, and foreign control is not diminished, but increased. (1) Domestic production in the manufacturing industries occurs above all in the field of consumption goods, since this is the sector in which market conditions permit first profitable investments. Thus, the previously imported foreign products come to form the model for production in domestic manufacturing. On one hand, the consumer habits of the portion of the population with purchasing power were formed through a foreign-controlled educational system, and on the other hand, not only modern technology, but even relatively simple products and procedures that could be developed autonomously, are monopolised by foreign business. For new investments, replacements of capital assets and additional infrastructure, imports become continually necessary. (2) International status on the protection of products and processes requires payment of royalties for patents and trade-marks in almost all fields in which domestic production is begun. (3) Since the foreign-controlled part of the developed sector is dominant not only in terms of technology but also in terms of finance and personnel, the largest part of new investment is joined to existing foreign firms. (4) These foreign enterprises—up to this point not participating in domestic manufacturing—see traditional export markets threatened by the policy of import restriction and replace their exports to the underdeveloped countries with domestic production in the underdeveloped countries. This last factor, in particular, leads to an increase of branch industries of foreign corporations in the underdeveloped countries.

The fact that government measures in the developing countries (protective duties, for example) have contributed to accelerated growth of domestic production, does not change the fundamental fact: capital—and, in this phase, that means essentially US and Western European capital—is only invested under conditions that satisfy its realisation needs. This so-called policy of import substitution, introduced in the Latin American countries in the first part of the twentieth century (and which has become the declared strategy of almost all underdeveloped countries since the end of World War Two), ie., the attempt to replace the importation of finished goods by domestic production through the adoption of political and economic measures such as protective tariffs, import quotas and foreign exchange monopolies, is contradicted by its own results. Indeed, it is inadequate to call this a phase of import substitution.

This type of growth in manufacturing requires the fulfilment of public functions to provide the inputs for production and to secure its process. For example, the educational system, up to this point essentially oriented to meet the limited needs of the colonial administrations, must be expanded and modelled after the example of the capitalist industrial countries in order to meet the rising demand of the growing industrial sector for qualified labour. Through the massive migration of the latent reserve army of the rural areas into the slums of the industrial centres, an actual reserve army of cheap labour is available. Thus, another requirement for industrial production is fulfilled. Labour from the underdeveloped countries directly enters the world labour market, from which international capital—according to its needs—may recruit it. With this internationalisation of the labour force, all preconditions for the beginning of the phase of world-wide production are fulfilled.

The phase of world-wide production
The world-wide expansion of capital—rapid growth of foreign capital in underdeveloped countries and even more rapid growth in the developed countries—has been accompanied by the international concentration and centralisation of capital. Concentration and centralisation take place in a horizontal (one economic sector), as well as in a vertical (inputs to final product) and trans-sectoral (conglomerates) direction. International concentration and centralisation of capital create a new agent in the process of unequal development: the multinational corporation, the form of individual capital that reproduces itself through world-wide production. This is the phase of the real and not just the formal creation of the world market, the market for goods, capital and labour. The international division of labour becomes, at the same time, a division of labour within the enterprise. The optimal realisation of capital determines whether production occurs at the location of labour (international transfer of capital) or at the location of capital (international transfer of labour). In the words of the Business International Corporation, world-wide production is the optimal utilisation of the joint assets of the corporation in contrast to the optimal utilisation of individual national units of the enterprise. For internationally concentrated and centralised capital the world has become an uninterrupted continuum, not only for the sale of products but also for the purchase of the factors of production. International firms recruit not only labour, materials and credit on a world-wide basis, but also manufacturing resources. In the short run, the world-wide production is organised around existing productive capacities; in the long run, the settlement of capital occurs wherever it can reap the greatest profits.[12]

15

The internationalised scope of the capitalist economy

A number of research projects and investigations into the internationalised scope of the world capital economy have been conducted. The results, to the extent that they are reliable, enable one to get an idea of the dimension and degree of concentration. Aggregated statistics are, for the most part, available from the 'Multinational Enterprise Project' of Harvard's Graduate School of Business Administration,[13] the US Department of Commerce,[14] certain US congressional committees,[15] and the Department of Economic and Social Affairs of the UN.[16]

The book value of all foreign investment (both in developed and in under-developed countries) was estimated to be 108.2 billion US dollars in 1967 and 165 billion in 1971. These figures represent a growth in US investment from 59.5 to 86 billion dollars, of British investment from 17.5 to 24 billion dollars, and of West German investment from 3 to 7.3 billion dollars.[17] In 1967 invest-ment in the underdeveloped countries represented 31.8 per cent of the total.[18] According to the US Tariff Commission, the actual value of foreign capital is quite different. They estimate the actual value of US foreign capital in 1971 to have been 203 billion dollars, of which 78 billion was in manufacturing industries alone.[19] In 1966 the number of foreign branch enterprises of US firms was estimated to be 23 000.[20] In 1967, 187 US corporations had branches in six or more countries or major shares in foreign firms (25 per cent or more). Of a total of 7 927 foreign branch industries and affilitates of these 187 firms, 2 397 were located in underdeveloped countries; 1 260 of these were in manufacturing industries.[21] By the end of 1969, West German firms had 2 916 links in foreign countries.[22] Between 1961 and 1971, 460 US corporations established 7 134 new branch firms, expanded 1 630 previously existing operations, and made 2 297 licensing agreements. From the total number (11 061) of new foreign activities of these 460 corporations, 2 763 occurred in the underdeveloped countries.[23]

The foreign expansion of productive capital is accompanied by an equally rapid expansion in the field of banking. Between 1965 and 1972, the number of foreign establishments of US banks rose from 303 to 1 009. By the end of 1972 West German banks had 103 foreign affiliates. The proportion of foreign deposits of the New York banks grew from 8.5 per cent in 1960 to 65.5 per cent in 1972.[24]

The degree of concentration of foreign capital is reflected in the following figures: 250 to 300 US corporations account for approximately 70 per cent of all US foreign investment. Eighty-two firms account for over 70 per cent of West German foreign investment, nine corporations alone controlling 37 per cent.[25] Concerning the degree of concentration of capital in the world economy (and not only its internationalised part), there is also some statistical evidence available. In 1971 sales of the 650 largest corporations of the world totalled 773 billion dollars. This figure represents approximately one third of the estimated Gross National Production of the world capitalist economy. A considerably larger portion of the total economy is under direct control of these 650 firms. Of these 650 firms, 16 together represent sales of 153.9 billion dollars, and from that group four firms account for 76.1 billion dollars in sales.[26] From the evidence on the concentration within individual countries, one can estimate that, at present, 1 000 to 2 000 corporations represent 75 per cent of the total industrial production in the capitalist world.[27] As an indication of how rapidly this concentration and centralisation has occurred, one can look at the manufacturing industry in the US. At the end of 1968, the largest 200 industrial corporations controlled over 60 per cent of the total assets in manufacturing. This proportion is greater than that which was controlled by the largest 1 000 firms in 1941.[28]

The internationalised scope of this production (based on estimates of the foreign content of the production of multinational firms, which totals 330 billion dollars[29]) must be estimated at a considerably greater volume. The internationalised scope of the economy stretches itself over a considerable part of foreign production and also over a considerable part of the domestic, but internationally integrated, production of corporations. Finally, taking into consideration the portion of the world economy which depends on foreign immigrant labour in the domestic economy, internationalised production can be estimated between 25 per cent and 33 per cent of total production.

Structure and operation

The (foreign) branch firms are typically integrated into the multinational corporation, which is in turn organised vertically (hierarchically), according to the planned division of labour for the whole corporation.[30] The size of the multinational corporation and the current level of productive forces allow the corporate headquarters to plan and make decisions about the activity of the whole corporation and each single branch firm in such a way that production and sales are increasingly organised within a strategy of long-term profit maximisation of the corporation on a world-wide scale (with the partial exception of the socialist countries). Necessary preconditions for internationalised production, as it is being realised through the operations of the multinational firms, are:

(1) the world-wide development of a potential free labour force (an international industrial reserve army);

(2) the existence of an international infrastructure that enables decisions about the location of production to be made independently of geographical distance; this entails the development of transport technology which provides cheap bulk transport between places of production and places of consumption (freighters, containerisation, air cargo), and international organisation and communication systems;

(3) the development of a technology which allows for the decomposition of complex working processes into simple units (Taylorism), so that the labour force can be cheaply trained to perform even in complex production processes;[31]

(4) an organisation of capital characterised by international concentration and centralisation of productive as well as financial capital, which especially supports the financing of foreign investment (national capital markets, international capital markets, association with local capital, internal financing, public subsidy);

(5) an international superstructure with formal expression in legal procedure and institutional cooperation (World Bank, IMF, OECD), which functions essentially by the coordinated action of units towards the world-wide activities of multinational corporations (financial and monetary policy, stabilisation policy, labour migration).

Since these preconditions have been essentially established by now, national firms are compelled by the force of international competition to operate on a world-wide basis or to disappear. The structure of the multinational firm enables the headquarters to realise the profit at the location which is optimal

17

for the company as a whole. For example, through intra-firm transfer pricing, the multinational corporation can prevent high profits accruing to any one branch from being heavily taxed. Thus, the firm is able to avoid sharing these high profits with private shareholders or foreign governments.[32]

Industrial relocation
Especially visible is the international transfer of production in the so-called *free production zones*,[33] as they have developed in recent years not only in East Asia (Hong Kong, Singapore, Taiwan, South Korea,[34] Philippines, Indonesia), but in Latin America (Mexico, Panama, Columbia) and Africa (Mauritius) as well. Free production zones are placed in developing countries as enclaves to allow the exploitation of the local labour force by foreign firms with a minimum of integration in the local national economy. The international firms are not only protected from customs, currency, import and export controls, but are also frequently given tax exemptions and investment incentives as well. Industrial infrastructure—energy, water, transportation, airports and seaports —are financed by the local economy. The payments to labour in these zones are on average so low that they may not even cover the cost of production and reproduction of the labour force.[35]

Transnational Capitalist Integration and National Disintegration

In the first two sections of this paper the process of development and under-development was seen to form a single whole, and it was shown how the productive forces, a relatively (although regionally very unequal) high average economy produces *of necessity transnational capitalist integration and national disintegra-tion*. The latest phase of this process, the phase of world-wide production, is no exception. The internationalised core area of the capitalist system is comprised of the whole of the multinational corporations, their contract firms, the international finance corporations, and the international infrastructure and super-structure. It is characterised by a high level of development of productive forces, a relatively (although regionally very unequal) high average standard of living of those integrated, and by relatively high rates of growth. In the disintegrated sector (the rest of the world with the exception of the socialist countries), the forces of production are only partially developed, the standard of living is relatively—and often absolutely (ie. based on a physiological minimum for subsistence)—low, the rates of growth are small or even negative. There are two unavoidable disintegrating effects of vertical transnational integration of the internationalised core area.

Repression of local economic activities
In the multinational firm, intra-firm cooperation has precedence over regional integration, the exploitation of the firm's capacity takes priority over the use of local and regional capacities. Thus, branch production works against not only the development of a complex economy, but, in addition, often leads to the repression of the remaining autonomous, indigenous production. Local technology and local innovations are replaced by licensed technologies; the concentration of research and techniques in the corporate headquarters strengthens the technological dependence.

Unequal intersectoral exchange and transfer abroad

Branch production, which occurs because of the availability of a cheap labour force in underdeveloped countries or regions, is a form of production in which the reproduction of the labour force is based to a large extent on the horizontally disintegrated but vertically integrated hinterland. A continual unequal exchange takes place between the two sectors (partial self-support of the labour force, low prices for agricultural products, care for the sick and disabled within the disintegrated sector, low wages, and high prices for the goods produced in the integrated sector). Profits of the branch industries are, for the most part, realised abroad. This occurs as much through intra-firm accounting as through visible profit transfers. For example, from total direct investment income of US branch industries abroad in 1970, 7.9 billion of 8.7 billion dollars were repatriated in the US; 4.1 billion of the total came from underdeveloped countries. The earnings on foreign investment in the underdeveloped countries are, on average, double that of investments in developed countries.[36]

This raises the question of whether the traditional model of more or less sovereign nation-states (with control over their national economies) must be replaced by the more realistic model of a threefold divided world: the transnationally capitalist integrated sector; the world-wide industrial reserve army; the socialist countries. The once dominant nation-states would be reduced to fossil relics that could be played against each other or formed into new units at the service of international capital (eg. the European Common Market).[37]

But this does not imply that the multinational firms have already renounced the functions of the nation-states. Three basic relationships must be distinguished: (1) the most important function of the state in the capitalist metropolitan countries is the protection and securing of the international capitalist relations of production; (2) the state in the dependent capitalist countries must, above all, provide labour force and inputs and services to industry; (3) the state in the socialist economies deals directly as an economic partner with the multinational corporations, and is thus involved directly in the realisation of multinational capital.[38] In general, it is still the function of the state to provide the basic services for the production of commodities. Such infrastructure is comprised of both material and social services: transport, communication, schools, military and police, the legal system, research and development, energy and water.[39] One might tentatively advance the thesis that multinational firms, given their size, are in a position to provide for each of these services themselves. Nevertheless, an attempt to provide all of the services internally would seriously impair the competitive position of any one firm. With the internationalisation of production and the international concentration and centralisation of capital, competition is not likely to diminish, but rather to be sharpened. Thus, the state is likely to maintain its role even within an expanded internationalised economy.

If the state (as the political system) is conceived as the (national) expression of the respective situation of the (international) class struggle, then the state can serve the interests of a class to the degree that this class is dominant. Therefore, it would be incorrect simply to place the state and the multinational corporations in contradiction to one another. More accurately, the two would only be antagonistic to the extent that the interests of the workers within a state are realised. (The national bourgeoisie are tending to become fully dependent on internationalisation of capital.[40]) In this way the state could be forced, as a consequence of the internationalisation of labour, to delegate partially its functions to international bodies, as it is already forced by the internationalisation of capital in regard to some of its functions.

Perspectives on the Internationalisation of Capital and Labour

In the first section of this paper we proposed the concept of capitalist development on which our subsequent discussion was based. By disposing of other theories, we elaborated and justified our own position. In the second section we sketched the formation and development of the capitalist mode of production, emphasising the relationship between the developed and underdeveloped countries. In the third and fourth parts we elaborated the most current phase of this process (namely, the internationalisation of capitalist production, the most visible expression of which is the activity of the multinational firm). In the final section we shall ask which possibilities for the further course of the capitalist system are likely to become probabilities. For the sake of clarity, the discussion will deal separately with the economic, social, and political aspects of this further development.

Economic trends

With world-wide production, the decisions on the location and the nature of production are determined by the realisation requirements of the capital of the multinational firms. The creation of a complex industrial structure in underdeveloped countries is not the optimisation criterion of these firms. In the course of profitable relocation and/or the establishment of new production units, a gradual industrialisation of the underdeveloped countries occurs. But such industrialisation is only an appendage to internationally organised production, and it is through this international complex that the possibilities and dimensions of national integration are determined. Especially in regard to production employing advanced technology, frequently only portions of complex production processes are transferred to countries with low wage rates. Research and development remain the domain of the central industrial countries and under the control of multinational firms. In the long run, one cannot exclude the possibility that the location of different producers (horizontally isolated but vertically integrated, for example, in the free production zones) could force the big firms to incorporate the realisation of more complex local production in their calculation of profit. That is, the expansion of vertically integrated branch firms may lead to a potential partially complex industrial structure in underdeveloped countries. However, the social utilisation of such a structure requires its socialisation.

For the economy in the developed capitalist countries, one can draw some tentative conclusions. But on the basis of economic trends alone, no clear forecast for the development of the total capitalist system can be made. Nearly all of the labour intensive manufacturing (ie. leather, textiles, electronic components) have been affected by industrial relocation to regions and countries with the lowest wage levels. The decomposition of complex working processes into simple parts—in connection with systematic planning and cooperation— reduces the largest part of the labour force to suppliers of low-level skills. Thus, at the same time, the necessity to organise production according to regional differences in labour skills is decreased. The speed and extent of industrial relocation remain difficult to predict, however, since they can be influenced by a multitude of factors: the utilisation of existing investment, subsidies, social and regional plans, strikes, and action by the labour unions. The change in the international division of labour, however, is already visible. Since it has become possible in manufacturing industries to produce any given product at any given place, and since it is possible to manufacture parts of one and the same commodity in different places, the national economies of the developed countries will also become relatively more dependent on the development of the world economy. The decisions on method and location of production lie with a small number of multinational firms. It becomes obvious that it will no longer be possible, not even as a first approximation, to analyse the economic development of even the developed capitalist societies on a national basis.

Social trends

The phase of world-wide production in the process of capitalist development has already had a significant effect on the social structure of the underdeveloped countries and regions: the creation of an industrial labour force—a proletariat. In several underdeveloped countries, a numerically significant and politically capable proletariat has existed for some time around the centres of the extractive industries (eg., in Chile). The systematic use of cheap labour will lead to a proletarianisation of a good portion of the population in other underdeveloped countries as well. Many difficulties, however, impede an effective organisation of the labour force in the underdeveloped countries: (1) the existence of a large, although regionally not inexhaustible, reserve army; (2) the outlawing and repression of strikes and active unions in many countries; (3) the possibility of a split between the active and potential labour force through the promotion of a labour aristocracy; and (4) the recruitment of large numbers of women for the labour intensive, export industries. It is known from the history of labour movements that women are more difficult to organise than men.

On the other hand, as we have already seen in Chile, such difficulties do not always hinder the effective organisation of labour nor hinder labour action for the good of the whole population. The attempt to bring to bear the interests of one's own group may force social and political transformations which result in the improvement of living conditions for a large part of the remaining population as well. Moreover, such a possibility could become more important in the future. A partial convergence of the interests of the labour force in the underdeveloped and the developed countries and regions seems imminent. The predictable reproletarianisation of a part of the middle class (due to the division of complex industrial procedures into elementary units) and the certain marginalisation of a part of the labour force in the developed countries (due to industrial relocation) are indicated by the first attempts of international labour strategies initiated by the unions of the developed countries. The major element of this strategy is the demand for world-wide equalisation of working conditions, especially the length of the work day and the wage level. The strategy is meant to counter the threat to jobs and the wage level within the developed countries caused by the internationalisation of production.[41] Negotiation with the corporate centres (and not with the local branch management) and the threat of strikes, coordinated at the level of the multinational corporation, represent the bargaining potential of the labour unions. The highly developed international organisation of capital in the multinational firms is beginning to create an international organisation of labour. The development of an international organisation of labour will be made more difficult, however, because of the world-wide extension of the stratification of the labour force: by wage levels, working conditions, nationality, sex, age, race and religion. For if the multinational capital creates the preconditions for the organisation of labour, it also furthers the fragmentation of the labour force. The strength and the precise moment of a challenge to an internationally organised proletariat will be essentially determined by how far labour itself is capable of overcoming this fragmentation and minimising its own tendency to trade unionist self-restriction.

Political trends

The political options of the governments of the underdeveloped countries which are striving to achieve a latent complex industrialisation within the capitalist system will remain very limited as long as these nations compete as suppliers of cheap labour. Some chance might be seen for countries that hold short-term monopolies in non-substitutable strategic materials, primarily oil, perhaps also copper. The repercussions of inter-state agreements among underdeveloped countries in the conflict with the multinational corporations are not clear (OPEC, CIPEC). But neither is it clear that this type of action can lead to successful, though dependent, industrialisation. A second exceptional case might be made for the few countries that have an especially large potential domestic market; it has already been mentioned how economic policy might contribute to a partially complex, if still dependent, industrial development.

Since only 'political stability' can guarantee the necessary 'favourable investment climate' for the long-term planning and investment profitability of multinational firms, 'politically stable' regimes—often dictatorships—are preferred: Taiwan, South Korea, the Philippines, Brazil, South Africa. 'Political stability' means unrestricted profit transfer, tax and customs exemptions, and the forbidding or limiting of labour organisation. Countries and governments that do not show willingness to cooperate will be put under pressure, through sanctions, as an example to others who might think of deviating from the expected behaviour (in Chile, for example, ITT, Kennecott, the stoppage of World Bank credit, the closing of foreign accounts, etc.)

In the developed countries the internationalisation of capital and labour will be accompanied to an even greater extent by sectoral and regional underdevelopment. Examples of such underdevelopment, proof of the general validity of the law of unequal development (that is, capitalistic development producing simultaneously development and underdevelopment), are Ireland, Mezzogiorno, the Swiss Jura, and the coal mining regions of Appalachia and the Ruhr. Since this trend intensifies the interest of workers in the affected industries to retain their jobs, the relocation of manufacturing in low-wage countries will be an important subject of the class struggle during the coming years. The effects of relocation can be countered to a certain extent through subsidies to those affected by changes in the sectoral structure of production, through social planning, and through limitation of the number of foreign workers. Such consistent planning does not seem likely, however, for it is doubtful, because of the decline in domestically-controlled investment, that the state will be able to provide the necessary means, other than through increased taxation of the dependent employed. Even less is it possible to predict whether the legislative attempts of labour unions in the developed countries to establish a 'code of good behaviour' for multinational corporations, and to limit the internationalisation of capital and labour, will succeed against the powerful lobbies of the multinational firms. (See the debates in the US of the International Trade and Investment Act of 1972, the so-called Burke-Hartke Bill.)[24]

Open questions

As has become clear in the preceding summary of trends in the internationalisation of labour and capital, we are sceptical about predictions (based on *nationally limited* analysis) of the breakdown of single capitalist economies or of the total capitalist system within the foreseeable future. Our own analysis, which takes the internationalisation of capital and labour as the most decisive current trend in the development of the capitalist system, justifies no definitive evaluation of further developments. The possible consequences of the existence of socialist countries for the development process of capitalist countries are not analysed. There is hardly any doubt that in single cases (Cuba, Vietnam, but not Chile), only the massive support of other socialist nations made the survival of these societies possible and allowed them to reorganise in the interest of the majority of their population. It is questionable, however, whether such concentrated support can generally be applied. The social reality of several socialist countries (indications of a new class society and the regulation of workers in many socialist countries, a trend studied with great interest by organisations of international capital), poses the question whether the masses of other countries would adopt, more or less unchanged, this model of socialism. Further, it is unclear whether the growing domestic social tensions in the developed countries (reflecting the lessened possibility of a pacification of the labour force because of industrial relocation and the declining possibilities for state subsidies) might be controlled by a strengthening of the repressive functions of the state and/or by a forced resource transfer out of the underdeveloped countries into the developed countries.

The role of the multinational firms as carriers of industrialisation to the underdeveloped countries and regions remains ambiguous. On one hand, the relocation of production into the underdeveloped countries changes nothing in that this partial industrial development is still a form of *dependent development*. At the same time, an *independent* capitalist development of the underdeveloped countries with the establishment of complex industry is impossible in the current phase of world-wide production. On the other hand, because of relocation and the partial industrialisation of the underdeveloped countries, a part of the now disintegrated labour force in these countries will of necessity become organised. In the long run, this will lead to the creation within the underdeveloped countries of a politically capable proletariat, partially integrated into the internationalised core areas. This development has three potential consequences: (1) a significant part of the population within the dependent industrial economies, as opposed to plantation agriculture and raw material economies, will thus be mobilised and organised, and become a force for economic, social and political development; (2) it seems possible that the proletariat in the underdeveloped countries, in fighting for their own interests, will of necessity simultaneously fight for the interests of the portion of the population in the disintegrated sector; (3) for the first time, internationalised capital is confronted with an internationalised labour force with at least partially identical interests.

Notes

1 See, for example, Winifried Vogt, 'Zur langfristigen ökonomischen Entwicklung eines kapitalistischen Systems', *Leviathan*, 2, 1973, pp. 161–88. Vogt gives an introductory summary of the history of the theories dealing with the long-term development of the capitalist system.
2 Winifried Vogt, 'Zur Kritik der herrschenden Wirtschaftstheorie', *Mehrwert*, 2, 1973, pp. 1–30.
3 Gunnar Myrdal, *The Challenge of World Poverty*, Pantheon Books, New York, 1970.

Chapter 1 refers to the political causes of the early disinterest and the post World War Two rise of interest among social scientists in this process.

4 The neo-classical growth models were first constructed in the late 1950s and advanced in the 1960s; their inclusion here, however, would not fundamentally alter our critique.

5 We employ here and elsewhere the misleading expression 'developing countries', the term used by the UN and in the literature on 'development strategies'.

6 In this short essay, it is not possible to treat this question thoroughly. We refer the reader to United Nations (Department of Economic and Social Affairs), *World Economic Survey, 1969–1970*, United Nations Publication, E.71.II.C.1., New York, 1971; United Nations (Department of Economic and Social Affairs), *1970 Report on the World Social Situation*, United Nations Publication, E.71.IV.13., New York, 1971.

7 Karl Marx, *Das Kapital. Erster Band* (1st ed. 1867, 2nd ed. 1873), in *Marx-Engels Werke*, 23 Dietz, Berlin GDR, 1972.

8 By immiserisation we mean, in general, dependence on the profit requirements of capital and all the consequences that follow.

9 Here, there is extensive documentation. The most recent works include: Samir Amin, *L'accumulation à l'échelle mondial*, Editions Anthropos, Paris, 1970; Arghiri Emmanuel, *Unequal Exchange*, Monthly Review Press, London, 1972; André Gunder Frank, 'Latin America and Africa in World Economic History', IDEP-IDS-IEDES-CLACSO Conference on Strategies for Economic Development, Africa Compared with Latin America, Dakar, 4–17 September 1973 (IDEP/ET/CS/2347-27); and Osvaldo Sunkel and Pedro Paz, *El subdesarrollo latino-americano y la teoria del desarrollo*, Siglo XXI, Mexico, 1970.

10 That the residual sector of the economy of the underdeveloped countries is, in this phase, already *horizontally* disintegrated and vertically integrated with the developed sector, has been shown by Frank in case studies of Chile and Brazil. See Andre Gunder Frank, *Capitalism and Underdevelopment in Latin America*, Monthly Review Press, London and New York, 1968.

11 During this phase North America experienced the effects of primitive exploitation—disruption and disaccumulation—as did Latin America. But, in the next phase, North America underwent a rapid development of the forces of production, parallel to that of Western European industry, and which can be attributed to the influx of surplus and the importation of labour. A considerable part of the surplus which England absorbed from India and other colonies was invested in North America. See, for example, Amiya Kumar Bagchi, 'Some International Foundations of Capitalist Growth and Underdevelopment', *Economic and Political Weekly* (Bombay), 7, 31–3 (1972), pp. 1559–70.

12 See Business International Corporation, *Solving World-wide Sourcing Problems*, Business International Corporation Management Monographs No. 53, New York, 1971, pp. 1, 3, 4.

13 James W. Vaupel and Joan P. Curhan, *The Making of Multinational Enterprise*, Harvard University Graduate School of Business Administration, Boston, 1969; Raymond Vernon, *Sovereignty at Bay: The Multinational Spread of US Enterprises*, Basic Books, New York and London, 1971.

14 US Department of Commerce, *US Direct Investments Abroad—1966*, Part II: *Investment Position, Financial and Operating Data*, Group 1 (1971), Group 2 (1972), Group 3 (1973), National Technical Information Service, Springfield, Va., 1971; US Department of Commerce, *The Multinational Corporation, Studies on US Foreign Investment*, Vol. I (1972), Vol. II (1973), US Government Printing Office, Washington, 1972; US Department of Commerce, *Special Survey of US Multinational Companies 1970*, National Technical Information Service, Springfield, Va., 1972.

15 For example, Committee on Finance, *Implications of Multinational firms for World Trade and Investment and for US Trade and Labour*, Report to the Committee on Finance of the US Senate and its Subcommittee on International Trade, Russell B. Long, Chairman US Government Printing Office, Washington, 1973; Committee on Finance, *Multinational Corporations, A Compendium of Papers Submitted to the*

Subcommittee on International Trade of the Committee on Finance of the United States Senate, Russell B. Long, Chairman, US Government Printing Office, Washington, 1973; Committee on Finance, *The Multinational Corporation and the World Economy*, Russell B. Long, Chairman, US Government Printing Office, Washington, 1973.

16 United Nations (Department of Economic and Social Affairs), *Multinational Corporations in World Development*, UN Publication, E.73.II.A.11, New York, 1973.

17 *Ibid.*, p. 7.

18 *Ibid.*, p. 172.

19 Committee on Finance, *The Multinational Corporation and the World Economy*, p. 7.

20 United Nations, *Multinational Corporations in World Development*, p. 8.

21 Vernon, *Sovereignty at Bay*, p. 124.

22 United Nations, *Multinational Corporations in World Development*, p. 7.

23 John B. Rhodes, 'US Investment Abroad: Who's going where, how and why?', *Columbia Journal of World Business*, 7, 4 (1972), pp. 33–40.

24 United Nations, *Multinationa- Corporations in World Development*, p. 12.

25 *Ibid.*, p. 7.

26 *Ibid.*, p. 127.

27 Peter Hillmore, 'Megacorporations Unlimited', *New Statesman*, 17 November 1972, p. 720.

28 United States Senate, Subcommittee on Antitrust and Monopoly, *Economic Concentration, Hearings before the Subcommittee on Antitrust and Monopoly of the Committee on the Judiciary, United States Senate*, Part 8A, US Government Printing Office, Washington, 1969, p. 3.

29 United Nations, *Multinational Corporations in World Development*, p. 159.

30 The creation and operation of the multinational firms has been analysed by Hymer among others. See his article 'The Multinational Corporation and the Law of Uneven Development', in Jagdish N. Bhagwati ed., *Economics and World Order from the 1970s to 1990s*, Collier-Macmillan, London, 1972, pp. 113–40. Our following contributions should be seen as expansions of Hymer's analysis. Also, see Vernon, *Sovereignty at Bay; Annals of the American Academy of Political and Social Science*, Vol. 403; United Nations, Economic Commission for Latin America, *The Expansion of International Enterprises and their Influence on Development in Latin America, Economic Survey of Latin America 1970*, United Nations Publication, E.72.II.G.1., New York, 1972; Committee on Finance, *Implications of Multinational Firms for World Free Trade and for US Trade and Labour*; and United Nations, *Multinational Corporations in World Development*.

31 Labour productivity in modern industry differs among nations much less than the wage level. See Committee on Finance, *Implications of Multinational Firms for World Free Trade and for US Trade and Labour*, pp. 418, 634.

32 For details, see Constantine V. Vaitsos, 'Income Distribution, Welfare Considerations, and Transnational Enterprises', paper presented to the Bellagio Conference on The Multinational Enterprise and Economic Analysis, September 1972; Committee on Finance, *Implications of Multinational Firms for World Free Trade and for US Trade and Labour*, p. 517, 'The MNC's financial needs and IMM practices'.

33 Compare UNIDO, *United Nations Industrial Development Organisation Training Workshop in Industrial Free Zones as Incentives to Promote Export-Oriented Industries*, Shannon International Free Airport, Republic of Ireland, 5–16 March 1972 (ID/WG., 112/1–ID/WG., 112/37).

34 For the example of South Korea, see Peter Christian Darjes and Hans-Helmut Taake, 'Die Elektronikindustrie Sud-Koreas', *Internationales Asienforum*, 3, 1972, pp. 553–9 and 'The Latest on Korea's Export Processing Areas', *Business Asia*, 1972, pp. 324–5. This form of industrial location has become rapidly important in the last years, as the example of Masam Free Export Zone (South Korea) demonstrates. Although it first began functioning in mid-1971 by October 1972, 53 firms were already located and 17 more had been licensed. The products range from non-ferrous metals, packaging machines and electronic components to shoes, gloves, umbrellas, canned fish and frozen foods.

35 For example, in Columbia, unskilled labour is available for 0.30 to 0.36 US dollars per hour. The equivalent wage in the USA is 2.50 dollars. See UNIDO, *op.cit.*, ID/WG., 112/10, p. 2.

36 'Yields on all direct investment over the decade averaged 12.6% which is less than the 13.1% earned in 1970. Yields on investments in the developing countries were roughly twice those in developed countries. This was due to the structure of petroleum companies earnings which are consistently reported as higher in the producing (or developing) countries because of pricing agreements with these countries. Since 1969 yields on foreign manufacturing investments exceeded those earned in the United States.' US Department of Commerce, *The Multinational Corporation, Studies on US Foreign Investment*, p. 5. See also Peter G. Peterson, *The United States in the Changing World Economy, Statistical Background Material*, US Government Printing Office, Washington, 1971.

37 'Rather than treating the international economy as a summation of national units, it is more helpful I think to see it as a single, predominantly capitalist system, in which the geographical distribution of particular structural features of a capitalist system will be governed by market determined laws of location and only secondarily by the action of nation states. Competitive firms, particularly international firms, become the dominant units of the system. States, which in part reflect the interests of these firms, are subordinate, modifying elements . . . . My argument is that, increasingly, we can only fully understand these geographical differences in structural relations if we start from the laws governing the location of production and factor mobility in the international capitalist economy as a whole, modified but not determined by the organised power of states, firms, and labour.' Robin Murray, 'The Internationalisation of Capital and the Nation State', *New Left Review*, 67, May–June 1971, pp. 84–109.

38 This relationship is clarified in the case of Peru by Anibal Quijano, 'Imperialismo y Capitalismo de Estado', *Sociedad y Politica* (Lima), 1, 1 (1972), pp. 5–18.

39 See Murray, *op.cit.* The functions of the state are clearly discussed in Part I, 'The Structural Role of the State as an Economic Instrument of Capitalism'.

40 This development is stressed by Nicos Poulantzas, 'L'internationalisation des rapports capitalistes et l'état-nation', *Les Temps Modernes*, 319, 1973, pp. 1456–1500.

41 The *Declaration of London, IMF World Auto Company Councils, 23–25 March 1971*, Levinson, 1972, p. 126 deserves to be cited at length. 'Operating on the basis of centralised decisions made in complete disregard of national loyalties and social responsibilities, they [the international corporations] play a divide-and-rule game calculated to pit each national group of workers against the others to the mutual harm of all and to involve governments in demeaning competition for their favours. To intimidate workers and governments they use without inhibitions the threat to move investments and jobs elsewhere, unless they obtain submission to their dictates concerning wages, working conditions, legislation, regulations, taxation or governing subsidies . . . . In seeking to maximise profits, the global corporations follow a policy of "world-wide sourcing" which means buying human labour and raw materials in the cheapest markets and selling the products to consumers everywhere at prices reflecting the "price leadership" or outright collusion characteristic of oligopoly . . . . Through manipulation of transfer prices for goods and services among branches of the same company, they evade both taxation of their profits and national foreign exchange controls. By decisions concerning the international allocation of investments and production, they can frustrate national economic planning . . . . In all too many cases, they display an affinity for repressive regimes and dictatorships that deny workers the right to organise and to protect themselves through free collective bargaining and the right to strike. Everywhere, their policies take advantage of the lowest level of social responsibility permitted by the nations within whose borders they operate . . . . In every situation where a national affiliate of the IMF is locked in struggle with an international corporation to protect or advance the welfare and interests of its members, all other affiliates representing workers of the same corporation should make it clear that they regard an injury to one national group of workers as an injury

to all. The affiliates not directly involved should commit themselves to use all practicable means to aid those that are, and to do nothing which would lessen the possibility of a victory for the workers. Where financial assistance is required and requested it should be provided promptly and generously. Both to improve the conditions of the workers affected and to protect higher standards already achieved elsewhere from being undermined by the international corporations' relentless pursuit of "cheap labour" we pledge ourselves to support the efforts of the IMF directed to the upward harmonisation of wages and social benefits to the maximum degree possible and in the shortest time possible . . . .' In addition, see International Labour Organisation, 'The Relationship between Multinational Corporations and Social Policy', working paper MNC/D.1, Geneva, 1972; ICFTU, *World Economic Conference Reports*, No. 2: *The Multinational Challenge*, Brussells, 1973; Nijmegen Symposium 1973, *Multinational Corporations and Labour Unions*, selected papers edited by Kurt P. Tudyka Werkuitgave SUN, Nijmegen, 1973.

42 See Committee on Finance, *Multinational Corporations. A Compendium of Papers Submitted to the Subcommittee on International Trade.*

2 Underdevelopment and Dependence in Black Africa—Origins and Contemporary Forms*

SAMIR AMIN

Contemporary Black Africa can be divided into wide regions that are clearly different from one another. But it is more difficult to analyse these differences—and to study their nature, origin, and effects—than to see them.

The unity of Black Africa is, nonetheless, not without foundations. On the contrary, leaving aside the question of 'race'—in Africa, blacks are no more homogenous nor less mixed, since pre-historical times, than are the other 'races', whether white, yellow, or red—the common or kindred cultural background, and the striking similarities of social organisation, make a living unity of Black Africa. This physical reality, extensive and rich, did not wait for colonial conquest to borrow from, or give of itself to, the other wide regions of the Old World—the Mediterranean in particular, but also Europe and Asia. The image of an ancient, isolated and introverted Africa no longer belongs to this age: isolation—naturally associated with a so-called 'primitive' character—only corresponded to an ideological necessity born out of colonial racism. But these exchanges did not break the unity of Africa; on the contrary, they helped to assert and enrich the African personality. The colonial conquest of almost the whole of this continent strengthened this feeling of unity in Black Africa. Seen from London, Paris or Lisbon, Black Africa appeared to European observers as a homogenous entity, just as the North Americans regard Latin America as a continent which extends south of the Rio Grande.

Looked at from the opposite point of view, that is to say from inside, Black Africa, like Latin America, evidently appears as extremely variegated. It is true that the present states are the result of an artificial partition, but almost nowhere does this constitute the sole or even the essential basis of their diversity. We would be wrong again to think that this pattern, however recent, has not yet left its mark on Africa and is not likely—for better or for worse—to consolidate itself, at least as far as the foreseeable future is concerned. Of even more significance, perhaps, are some 100 or 200 micro-regions, varying in width, which readily cross the frontiers of the present states. They constitute yet another aspect of the reality; they do not derive their definition from their geographical position alone, but above all because of the homogenous nature of their social, cultural, economic and even political conditions.

Between these two extremes—African unity and micro-regional variety—the continent can be divided into a few wide macro-regions. I propose to identify three, and shall discuss the basis for such a distinction.

Traditional West Africa (Ghana, Nigeria, Sierra Leone, Gambia, Liberia, Guinea-Bissau, Togo, former French West Africa), Cameroun, Chad and the Sudan together constitute a first macro-region, which I wish to describe as *Africa of the colonial trade economy*. I shall give a precise definition to this term, which, unfortunately, is too often treated lightly. This integrated whole is clearly divisible into three sub-regions: (1) the coastal zone, which is easily

* From *Journal of Modern African Studies*, 10, 4 (1972), pp. 503–24.

accessible from the outside world, and which constitutes the 'rich' area; (2) the hinterland, which mostly serves as a pool of labour for the coast, and as a market for the industries which are being established there; and (3) the Sudan, whose particular characteristics will be examined later.

The traditional Congo River basin (Congo-Kinshasa, Congo-Brazzaville, Gabon and the Central African Republic) form a second macro-region, which I wish to define as *Africa of the concession-owning companies*. Here also it is necessary to explain how, over and above the difference in the policies and practices of the French and Belgian governments, genuine similarities in the mode of colonial exploitation characterise the whole of the region, and this justifies its demarcation.

The eastern and southern parts of the continent (Kenya, Uganda, Tanzania, Rwanda, Burundi, Malawi, Angola, Mozambique, Zimbabwe, Botswana, Lesotho, Swaziland and South Africa) constitute the third macro-region, which I wish to call *Africa of the labour reserves*. Here also, apart from the varied nature of each country, the region was developed on the basis of the policy of colonial imperialism, according to the principle of 'enclosure acts' which were applied to entire peoples.

Ethiopia, Somalia, Madagascar, Réunion and Mauritius, like the Cape Verde islands on the opposite side of the continent, do not form part of these three macro-regions, although here and there are to be found some aspects of each. However, they also display features of other systems which have played an important part in their actual development: the slavery-mercantilist system of the Cape Verde islands, Réunion, and Mauritius; the 'pseudo-feudal' system of Ethiopia and Madagascar. Obviously questions of frontiers between the regions remain: Katanga, for example, belonged to the area of the labour reserves, and Eritrea to that of the colonial trade.

Towards a Definition of Periods in African History

My proposed distinction is deliberately based on the effects of the *last* period in the history of Africa, that of colonisation. It will be necessary to study how the dialectic reveals itself between the major colonial policies and the structures inherited from the past. To do so we have to go back in time, and to distinguish four separate periods.

The pre-mercantilist period stretches from the earliest days until the seventeenth century. In the course of this long history, relations were forged between Black Africa and the rest of the Old World, particularly from both ends of the Sahara, between the savannah countries (from Dakar to the Red Sea) and the Mediterranean. Social formations emerged which cannot be understood if they are not placed, here as elsewhere, within the context of all the multitude of other social systems and their relationships with one another. During that period, Africa, by and large, does not appear as inferior, or weaker than the rest of the Old World. The unequal development within Africa was not any worse than that north of the Sahara, on both sides of the Mediterranean.

The mercantilist period stretches from the seventeenth century to 1800. It was characterised by the slave trade, and the first retrograde steps date back to this time. It was not only the coastal zone that was affected by this trade: there was a decline in productive forces throughout the continent. There were two distinct slave-trading areas: (1) the Atlantic trade (by far the most harmful because of the great numbers involved), which spread from the coast to the whole of the continent, from St. Louis in Senegal to Quelimane in Mozambique; and (2) the Oriental trade operating from Egypt, the Red Sea, and Zanzibar, towards the Sudan and East Africa. This second type of mercantilist activity was carried beyond 1800, because the industrial revolution which shook the foundations of society in Europe and North America did not reach the Turkish-Arab part of the world.

The next period lasted from 1800 to 1880–90, and was characterised by attempts—at least in certain regions within the influence of Atlantic mercantilism—to establish a new form of dependence with that part of the world where capitalism was firmly entrenched by industrialisation. These attempts, however, had very limited backing, as we shall see why later. The area of influence of Oriental mercantilism was not affected.

The fourth period, that of colonisation, completed the work of the previous period in Western Africa, took over from Oriental mercantilism in Eastern Africa, and developed with tenfold vigour the present forms of dependence of the continent according to the models of the three macro-regions mentioned above. The present throws light on the past. The completed forms of dependence —which only appeared when Africa was actually made the periphery of the world capitalist system in its imperialist stage, and was developed as such— enable us to understand, by comparison, the meaning of previous systems of social relations, and the way in which African social formations were linked with those of other regions of the Old World with which they had contact.

(1) The Pre-Mercantilist Period: up to the seventeenth century

During this time, Black Africa was not on the whole more backward than the rest of the world. The continent was characterised by complex social formations, sometimes accompanied by the development of the state, and almost invariably based on visible social differentiations which revealed the ancient nature of the process of disintegration of the primitive village community. The great confusion which arises in any discussion of traditional African society is due to a number of reasons, especially: (i) the scarcity of documents and remains of the past, leaving only the accounts of Arab travellers; (ii) the confusion between the concepts of 'mode of production' and 'social formation' which calls for clarification and a basic differentiation; (iii) the confusion between different periods of Africa history, particularly between the pre-mercantilist and actual mercantilist periods—and the justifiable concern of scholars to relate history in all its continuous detail, enhances this confusion; and last but not least, (iv) the ideological prejudices against Africa, clearly connected with colonial racism.

This is why I have formulated three sets of propositions, so that we can see our way clearly through this history, without claiming to recast its evolution. My intention is to emphasise the main differences between the Africa of this period—the only true 'traditional' Africa, neither isolated nor primitive—and that which followed.

The first thing to make clear is that *a society cannot be reduced to a mode of production*. This is an abstract concept which does not involve the notion of a fixed historical sequence with regard to the progress of civilisation, from the first differentiated communities up to the capitalist form of society. It is feasible to distinguish five types: (i) the primitive community mode of production, the only possible one to come first, for obvious reasons; (ii) the 'tributary' mode of production which involved the persistent parallel existence of a village community *and* a socio-political structure which exploited the former by exacting a tribute—this, the most common pre-capitalist mode, developed sometimes from earlier into evolved forms, when the village family community lost the right of ownership of land to feudal masters; (iii) the slave-based mode of production, which was less common but scattered; (iv) the small-scale trade mode of production, quite common but never likely to form the main structure of society; and lastly, (v) the capitalist mode of production.[1]

It is necessary to emphasise that social formations are *concrete* structures, organised and characterised by a *dominant* mode of production which forms the apex of a complex set of subordinate modes. Thus it is possible to have a small-scale trading mode linked to a dominant tributary ('early' or 'developed feudal'), and even based on a slave or a capitalist mode of production. Likewise, the mode based on slavery may not be of the dominant type, and this seems to be the rule when it is related to a dominant tributary mode of production (or even a capitalist mode, as in the United States until 1865); and only in exceptional cases does it become dominant itself, as in the classical societies of ancient times.

Modes of production, then, do not actually constitute historical categories, in the sense of occurring in a necessary sequence of time. On the other hand, social formations have a definite age, reckoned on the basis of the level of development of the productive forces. This is why it is absurd to draw any analogy between the same mode of production belonging to societies of different ages—for example, between African or Roman slavery and that of the nineteenth-century United States.[2]

Secondly, *social formations cannot be understood when taken out of their context*. Sometimes the relations between different societies are marginal, but often they are decisive. The problems connected with long-distance trade are thus very important. This is obviously not a mode of production, but a method of articulation between autonomous societies. This is the essential difference from internal trade, which is made up of exchanges between dealers in a particular society. Such exchanges are characteristic of the simple trading mode of production or that based on slavery (in this case a combination of both), which are elements of the society in question. But internal trade may also be an extension of long-distance trade, if the goods involved penetrate deeply within that particular society.

Long-distance trade brings into contact societies unknown to one another—ie. it involves the exchange of products for which each is unaware of the other s cost of production, 'rare' goods for which there are no substitutes in the importing country. As a result, the social groups engaged in that activity enjoy a monopoly position from which they derive their profits. Such a monopoly frequently explains the 'special' nature of these groups, often specialised foreign traders belonging to a particular caste or ethnic community, for example the Jews in Europe and the Dioula in West Africa. In this kind of trade, the subjective theory of value still had some significance—but it is meaningless when the cost of production of the goods is known to the respective trade partners, as in the capitalist system of exchange.

This long-distance trade could, in certain societies, become a decisive factor. This is the case when only a limited surplus is able to be extracted from the producers in a particular society by the dominant local classes. The reason for this may be the low development of the productive forces, and/or difficult ecological conditions, or the successful resistance by village communities to the extraction of this surplus. In such a case, long-distance trade makes possible, through its characteristic monopoly profit, the transfer (not, of course, the generation) of a fraction of the surplus of one society to another. For the receiving society, this transfer may be of vital importance, and may serve as the principal basis of the wealth and power of the ruling classes. Civilisation may then wholly depend on this trade, and any shift of trading centres can cause one region to fall into decadence, or create conditions for it to prosper, without bringing about either any regression or any noticeable progress in the level of its productive forces. This, in my opinion, is the explanation for the ups and downs in the history of the Old World and the Mediterranean, particularly with regard to the so-called Greek miracle, and the prosperity and decline of the Arab world.[3]

The third point is that *the African societies of the pre-mercantile period developed autonomously*, although they followed a parallel course to that of the Mediterranean world, both Eastern and European. The semi-arid zone which stretches diagonally across the Old World, from the Atlantic coast to Central Asia, has always separated the regions which were ecologically conducive to a high productivity in agriculture: monsoon Asia, tropical Africa and temperate Europe. This zone has seen the birth of some brilliant civilisations, almost all founded on long-distance trade, particularly Greece and the Arab Empire,[4] whose vicissitudes followed the course of this trade. On either side, autonomous societies—those of feudal Europe and, at least, some of those of tropical Africa, particularly in the Sudan-Sahel region immediately south of the Sahara—developed along parallel lines, precisely because of the long-distance trade which linked them all. Thus one can say that this part of Africa was already fully integrated, as much as Europe, into the history of the world.

This is why the trans-Sahara trade was so significant. It enabled the whole of the Old World—Mediterranean, Arab and European—to be supplied with gold from the main source of production in Upper Senegal and Ashanti, until the discovery of America. The importance of this flow can hardly be adequately stressed. For the societies of tropical Africa, this trade became the basis of their organisation. The mining of gold under the orders of the king provided the ruling classes of the countries concerned with the means to obtain across the Sahara, on the one hand, rare luxury goods (clothes, drugs, perfumes, dates and salt), and on the other, and in particular, the opportunity to establish and strengthen their social and political power by the acquisition of horses, copper, iron bars and weapons. This trade thus encouraged social differentiation, and the creation of states and empires, just as it promoted the improvement of instruments and the adaptation of techniques and products to suit local climatic conditions. In return, Africa supplied mainly gold, a few other rare products, notably gum and ivory, and some slaves.[5]

Some European historians, for obvious political reasons, have tried to confuse this trade between equal autonomous partners with the later devastating slave trade of the mercantilist period. The small number of black people in the southern areas of the Maghreb—a few hundred-thousand compared with about a hundred-million in America—shows the futility of this confusion. On the other hand, the stock of gold built up in Europe and in the East throughout these centuries, originating from tropical Africa, reminds us of the principal nature of this trade. After all, this is why the ideas which accompanied the traders were easily accepted—for example, the early adoption of Islam in the Senegal River areas. The important volume of this trade, its egalitarian nature, and the autonomous character of the African societies, are unambiguously described in the Arab literature of the period. Furthermore, one can understand the admiration expressed in the accounts of the Arab travellers if it is remembered that the development and structure of the societies of North and West Africa belonged to the same technological age, just as the place they occupied in the world system of the time was similar. The link between the royal monopoly of the mining of gold, and its marketing by Muslim traders, forms the basis of the structure of these societies. These traders were, as was very often the case, organised in a kind of caste system, and here belonged to a religious minority.

For centuries the Mediterranean societies and those of tropical Africa were united by a bond, for better or for worse. The vicissitudes of one area had quick repercussions on the other, just as wealth and glory reached them all simultaneously. Thus the gradual shifting of routes from west to east found a parallel shift in the civilisation and power of the nations both in North Africa and in the West African savannah lands—reflected, for example, in the successive might of the ancient empires of Ghana and Mali, the Hausa cities, Bornu, Kanem and Darfur. This also explains why there was a crisis in Africa when the centre of the newly-born European mercantile capitalism moved from the Mediterranean towards the Atlantic. This shift, studied by Fernand Braudel with his usual talent and care for detail, heralded the decline, in the sixteenth century, of the Italian towns which, since the thirteenth century, had opened the way for a decisive evolution in the future history of mankind.[6] Similarly we can say that this change was to cause the downfall of both the Arab world and the Sudan-Sahel regions of Black Africa. Soon afterwards the presence of Western Europe along the coasts of Africa was to become a reality. This shift of the centre of gravity of trade in Africa, from the savannah hinterland to the coast, was a direct consequence of the change of commercial emphasis in Europe from the Mediterranean to the Atlantic. But the new trade between Europe and Africa was not to play the same role as that of the preceding period; henceforth it was to take place under mercantile capitalism.

(2) The Mercantilist Period: the seventeenth and eighteenth centuries

As I have pointed out elsewhere, the mercantilist period saw the emergence of two poles of the capitalist mode of production: (i) the creation of a proletariat resulting from the decline of feudal relationships, and (ii) the accumulation of wealth in the form of money.[7] During the industrial revolution the two became united; money wealth turned into capital, and the capitalist mode of production reached its completed stage. During this long period of incubation covering three centuries the *American* periphery of the Western European mercantile centre played a decisive role in the accumulation of money wealth by the Western European bourgeoisie. Black Africa played a no less important role as the *periphery of the periphery*. Reduced to the function of supplying slave labour for the plantations of America, Africa lost its autonomy. It began to be shaped according to foreign requirements, those of mercantilism.

Let us finally recall that the plantations of America did not constitute autonomous societies, in spite of their slave-based form of organisation. As I have argued previously, this mode of production was here an element of a non-slave-based society, ie. it was not the dominant feature of that society. The latter was mercantilist, and the dominant characteristic of the plantation economy was the trade monopoly which, under its control and for its benefit, sold the products of these plantations on the European market, thus quickening the disintegration of feudal relations. The peripheral American society was thus an element in the world structure whose centre of gravity was in Western Europe.

The devastating effects of the mercantilist slave trade for Africa are now better known, thanks to the works of several historians free from race and colonial prejudices. I wish here to mention a recent and brilliant study of the Kingdom of Waalo by Boubacar Barry,[8] from which two main points emerge.

First, while the pre-mercantile trans-Sahara trade, in which the Waalo participated, had strengthened state centralisation and stimulated progress in that autonomous Senegalese kingdom, the Atlantic trade which replaced it (as soon as the French settled in 1859 in St. Louis), did not give rise to any productive forces; on the contrary, this caused a disintegration of the society and of the Waalo state. This explains why force had to be used by the French to cut off the trans-Sahara links, to subjugate that region of Africa, and to alter its external relations to suit the requirements of the French trading post of St. Louis. African societies obviously opposed this worsening of their situation, and Islam served as the basis for their resistance.

The traders of St. Louis paid with weapons for the slaves they bought from the king (*Brak*). This ruptured the former balance of power between (i) the *Brak* who maintained a permanent army of captives (*tyeddo*) under crown control; (ii) the council of elders (*seb ak baor*) which nominated him, and had a system of prerogatives super-imposed over the collective clan-ownership (*lamanat*) of lands in the village communities; and (iii) the village communities themselves, based on the *lamanat*. The customary dues paid by the traders of St. Louis encouraged a civil war which involved the *Brak*, the *tyeddo* and the *kangam* (leading notables), and a ransacking of communities to obtain slaves. The muslim priests (*marabouts*) tried to organise a resistance movement: their aim was to stop the slave trade, ie. the export of the labour force, but not to end internal slavery. Henceforth, Islam changed its character; from being a religion of a minority group of traders, it became a popular movement of resistance. The first war led by the *marabouts*, 1673–7, failed in its attempt to convert the people of the Fleuve region and to stop the slave trade. A century later, in 1776, the Toorodo revolution in Tukolor country overthrew the military aristocracy and ended the slave trade. But in the Waalo Kingdom, being too near to St. Louis, the attempt by Prophet Diile in 1830 failed in the face of French military intervention in support of the *Brak*.

Secondly, a study of the Waalo case is of special interest because the slave trade took place parallel to the trade in gum. However, the latter did not have the same impact on African society. The export of goods (instead of labour) does not necessarily have a devastating effect and may, on the contrary, lead to progress. This type of export was not characteristic of the mercantilist period for Africa as a whole, which almost exclusively supplied slaves. But here, rather exceptionally, it played an equally important role, because the slaves, like the Galam gold, mainly followed the road to Gambia. However, gum was supplied by the Waalo, and also in particular by the Trarza Moors. They could export this either via St. Louis to the French alone, or via Portendick which was open to competition between the English and the Dutch. To cut off the Portendick route, the French helped the Trarza to settle in the Fleuve region, and to cross it during the 'Gum War', in the first quarter of the eighteenth century. Such circumstances thus introduced a contradiction of secondary importance between the Waalo and the Trarza. It was this which explains the failure of the 'War of the *Marabouts*' in the seventeenth century, led simultaneously by those who were hostile to the slave trade, and by the Moors who put increasing pressure on the Waalo in order to monopolise the gum trade.[9]

The mercantilist slave trade had similar devastating effects on all the regions of Africa where it took place. Along the coast, from St. Louis to Quelimane, it affected almost the whole of the continent, except the north-eastern area of the Sudan, Ethiopia, Somalia, and East Africa. The similarity between the history of the Waalo and that of the Kongo Kingdom should be recalled.[10] The slave trade here also brought about the disintegration of the central authority, and led to anarchy which opened the way for the Yaga raids. Such examples abound. There were wars and anarchy almost everywhere on the continent, and the flight of peoples towards regions of shelter which were difficult to reach and also very often poor—such as those of the paleo-negritic peoples in the over-populated mountains of West Africa. It all ended with an alarming decrease in population. The processes of integration were stopped, as well as the construction of large communities, begun in the pre-mercantilist period. Instead there was an incredible fragmentation, isolation, and entanglement of peoples, and this, as we know, is the root cause of one of the most serious handicaps of contemporary Africa.

It is necessary to conclude this section with the question of the Oriental mercantilist period. I have certainly hesitated to define in this way the relations of the Near East (Egypt and southern Arabia) with Africa of the Nile and the eastern coast, from the Red Sea and the Indian Ocean as far as Mozambique. Neither the Ottoman Empire, nor Egypt under Mohammed Ali, and still less the southern Sultanates, were mercantilist societies similar to those of Europe from the renaissance to the industrial revolution. The disintegration of pre-capitalist relations—the necessary condition for the formation of a proletariat—was almost non-existent. This was the obstacle which Mohammed Ali attempted to overcome by setting up an entirely new state apparatus. I do not propose to study this here, except to bring out the main trends in the evolution of the Sudan, which Egypt was to conquer in the second half of the nineteenth century.[11] It was during the pre-mercantilist period that two Sultanates were established here, based on long-distance trade with Egypt and the East: the Sultanate of Darfur, still powerful at the time of the Egyptian conquest, and the Sultanate of Fung, between the two Niles, weakened through the wars waged by Ethiopia. Mohammed Ali's aim was very simple: to loot the Sudan of gold, slaves and ivory, and to export them in order to intensify the industrialisation of Egypt. This was a process of primitive accumulation similar to that of the European mercantilist period, and this is the reason for speaking of Oriental mercantilism. The industrial revolution had already occurred, and this was known to the Pasha; consequently the premercantilist period and that of the capitalist system were mixed up in an attempt to industrialise Egypt by raising finance through state taxation of the peasants, the monopoly of foreign trade and, whenever possible, the looting of the colonies.

Up to 1850 it was the Egyptian army itself that hunted for slaves and robbed the Sudan of local products. After that date, the soldiers handed the job to Sudanese nomads, particularly the Baqqara, who sold the slaves they seized to Turkish, Copt, Syrian and European merchants established under the aegis of the Khedive. These operations quickly entailed changes in the social system of the nomads concerned; their clan organisation was succeeded by 'nomad feudalism', founded on a territorial basis, and dominated by warrior nobles. In the zones of agriculture that had been thoroughly conquered, the Egyptian army destroyed the old chiefdoms and subjected the villagers to a tax in kind— livestock and grain—for the purpose of feeding the administration and the army of the conquerors. *Sheikhs* were created by the Egyptians and made responsible for the collection of taxes; they rapidly became rich by this means. Moreover, the best lands were taken from the communities and given to Egyptian *beys* and to some Sudanese *sheikhs*. Peasants were taken from their village and attached to these lands as half-slaves and half-serfs; the proceeds of their commercial farming went to swell the Egyptian treasury. Other peasants, hunted by the nomads and impoverished by the *sheikhs*, flocked into the market towns, established by the army at cross-roads, and on the borders of the slave-raiding areas. A craft industry grew up, distinct from agriculture, while on the land given to the *beys* and *sheikhs* Egyptian farming methods were introduced with higher productivity. By 1870 it was feasible to replace the tax in kind with a money tax, because of the increased marketed surplus. The Sudan was becoming unified, Islamised and Arabised.

The Mahdist revolt, 1881–98, was a rebellion of those oppressed by that system: the people of the village communities, the slave-peasants of the estates and the craftsmen, slaves and beggars of the market towns. The successful revolt drove out the Egyptian army, the *beys* and the *shiekhs*. But after the Prophet's death, Khalifa Abdullahi changed the power structure of the Sudan. The military leaders of the revolt, whose origins were in the people, and the Baqqara warrior chiefs who joined it, reorganised to their advantage a state similar to that of the Egyptians; they seized the estates and levied taxes on their own account. It is true that the export of slaves was prohibited, but this had largely lost its old importance at the beginning of the conquest, because that labour force was now used on the spot. But the new state intended to continue exploiting the masses to its advantage and, for that purpose, destroyed the popular elements surrounding the Prophet. His family was imprisoned and several of the people's military leaders were executed. Furthermore, the Mahdist state resumed the export of slaves, but this time for its own benefit. The Khalifa organised slave raiding among the neighbouring peoples of the Upper Nile, Darfur and Ethiopia, and he kept a large number of slaves to strengthen his army and his economy, but authorised Sudanese merchants to export some of them. The Khalifa's army, which had lost the popularity which made up its strength at the time of the revolt, did not resist the British colonial expedition at the end of the century.

The slave trade organised from Zanzibar in the nineteenth century certainly falls within a mercantilist framework. For centuries, Arab trade on the coast was carried out in a pre-mercantilist context, which brought these regions of Black Africa into contact with India, the Indian archipelago and even China. Here products were more important than slaves, as is shown by the very small black population of southern Arabia and the countries bordering the Indian Ocean. There would seem to be one exception, at the time when the Khalifa of Abbasside was organising sugar-cane plantations in Lower Iraq for which he imported black slaves. This short period ended with the Qarmat revolt.

From 1850 the slave trade suddenly became much more intense. There were in fact two new markets: the island of Réunion which was supplied in this way, although the slaves were disguised as 'contract labour' since the British had abolished the slave trade; and the island of Zanzibar itself. In 1840 the Sultan had transferred his capital from Oman, and gradually established a slave plantation economy producing the cloves for which European trade now offered a market. Zanzibar, hitherto a trading post, now became a plantation on a model very similar to that of the West Indies, Réunion or Mauritius—the Arab West Indies. Thus we once again see that integration into the world capitalist system was responsible for a devastating slave trade which had no resemblance to the long-distance trade of the pre-capitalist period.

(3) Integration into the Full Capitalist System: the nineteenth century

The slave trade disappeared with the end of mercantilism, that is to say essentially with the advent of the industrial revolution. Capitalism at the centre then took on its complete form; the function of mercantilism—the primitive accumulation of wealth—lost its importance, and the centre of gravity shifted from the merchant sector to the new industry. The old periphery of the plantation of America, and its African periphery of the slave trade, had now to give way to a new periphery whose function was to provide *products* which would tend to reduce the value of both constant and variable capital used at the centre: raw materials and agricultural produce. The advantageous terms under which these products were supplied to the centre are revealed by the theory of unequal exchange.[12]

However, central capital had only very limited means of achieving that goal until the end of the nineteenth century. It was only when monopolies appeared at the centre that large-scale exports of capital became possible, and when henceforth central capital had the means of organising directly in the periphery, by modern methods, the production which suited it under appropriate conditions. Until then the centre could only rely on the ability of local social systems to adjust 'spontaneously', 'by themselves', to any new requirements. The Americans could do this in their own country; the British imperialists could impose this in India, as could the Dutch in Indonesia. In certain Eastern countries, notably the Ottoman Empire and Egypt, the joint efforts of 'spontaneous internal adjustment' and external pressure produced some results. This is not the place to trace that history. Even in tropical Africa some new crops were produced, exclusively due to the internal adaptation of African societies. There are a number of studies which are highly informative on the mechanisms of these adjustments.

I wish again to refer to the exciting research work of Boubacar Barry. The project of establishing a colonial agricultural settlement in Waalo, making plantations for cotton, sugar cane and tobacco, was first formulated by the British Governor of St. Louis at the end of the eighteenth century; but it was put on the agenda again after the French Revolution, as a consequence of the slave revolt of Santo Domingo. When Waalo was 'bought' in 1819 by Governor Schmaltz, the experiment began. Barry analyses the causes of failure: the resistance of the village communities to their dispossession in favour of European planters, which had been agreed to by the aristocracy in return for extra 'customary' benefits; and the lack of manpower, since there was no reason why the peasants should leave their communities and become proletarians on the plantations. The *Brak* provided some warriors who to all intents and purposes were slaves—long-term recruits (*engagés à temps*). But the French settlement could only use 'tinkering' methods. It was not until the colonial conquest that ample resources enabled a proletariat to be created: by taxation, by pure and simple dispossession, and by forced labour—in short, by all the methods used in Africa after 1880, which were similar to those used earlier by the British in India, the Dutch in Indonesia, the French in Algeria, and the Egyptians in the Sudan.

The fact remains that the Waalo agricultural settlement ended in failure in 1831. But the attempt had accentuated the people's hatred of the aristocracy, and had prepared the way for their conversion to Islam: outside the official authority, Muslim communities organised themselves defensively around the *sérigne* to whom they paid tithes. When Faidherbe conquered the Waalo between 1855–9, with the intention of restarting the agricultural settlement, and at last procuring for French industry the cotton it needed, the vanquished aristocracy embraced Islam.[13] A new chapter opened, and we shall see later how the new production came to be organised in accordance with the requirements of the centre. Thus Islam changed its structure a second time since instead of being a resistance ideology, it was now to become a powerful means of integrating the new periphery and subordinating it to the design of the centre.

Other African societies made an effort to adjust themselves to this project, even before they were conquered. Walter Rodney points out that throughout the Benin coast the slaves who were still raided, but who could no longer be exploited, were put to work inside the society to produce, among other things, the exports which Europe demanded.[14] Cathérine Coquery-Vidrovitch has analysed in these terms the prodigious development of Dahomean oil-palm groves.[15] Onwuka Diké shows how another society, that of the Igbo, unable to have recourse to slaves, nevertheless adapted itself, again for the production of palm-oil for export.[16] Here again many more examples could be cited.

The constitution and subsequent destruction of Samori's empire reveals another aspect of the mechanism of integration. The collection of products for export, and the conveyance of imports received in exchange, strengthened the position of the Dioula Muslims, a minority inherited from the remote days of pre-mercantilism. The 'Dioula revolution' enabled them to establish a state which they controlled.[17] But this late episode occurred just at the beginning of the colonial period. The empire had scarcely been founded by Samori when it had to face the conquerors who destroyed it; they reorganised the channels of trade in the direction which suited them, and reduced the Dioula to the subordinate functions of colonial trade.

(4) Integration into the Full Capitalist System: colonisation

The partitioning of the continent which was completed by the end of the nineteenth century multiplied the means available to the colonialists to attain capital at the centre. We must remember that their target was the same everywhere: to obtain cheap exports. But to achieve this, capital at the centre—which had now reached the monopoly stage—could organise production on the spot, and there exploit both the cheap labour and the natural resources, by wasting or stealing them, ie. by paying a price which did not enable alternative activities to replace them when they were exhausted.[18] Moreover, through direct domination and brutal political coercion, incidental expenses could be limited by maintaining the local social classes as 'conveyor belts'. Hence the late development in Africa of the peripheral model of industrialisation by import substitution. It was not until independence that the local élites who took over from the colonial administration constituted the first element of a domestic market for 'luxury goods', according to inter-linkage relationships which I have discussed elsewhere.[19] Hence also the markedly bureaucratic nature of the 'privileged classes'.

However, although the target was the same everywhere, different variants of the system of colonial exploitation were developed. These did not depend, or only slightly, on the nationality of the coloniser. The contrast between French direct and British indirect rule, so frequent in the literature, is not very noticeable in Africa. It is true that a few differences are attributable to the nationality of the masters. British capital, being richer and more developed, and having additionally acquired the 'best pieces' of land, carried out an earlier and more thorough development than French capital.[20] Belgium, which had been forced to come to terms with the Great Powers, and had to accept the competition of foreign goods in the Congo, did not have the direct colonial monopolies which France used and abused to her advantage. Portugal similarly agreed to share her colonies with major Anglo-American capital.

In the region that I have called 'Africa of the labour reserves' capital at the centre needed to have a large proletariat immediately available. This was because there was great mineral wealth to be exploited (gold and diamonds in South Africa and copper in Northern Rhodesia), and an untypical settler agriculture in the tropical Africa of Southern Rhodesia, Kenya and German Tanganyika. In order to obtain this proletariat quickly, the colonisers dispossessed the African rural communities—sometimes by violence—and drove them deliberately back into small, poor regions, with no means of modernising and intensifying their farming. They forced the 'traditional' societies to be the supplier of temporary or permanent migrants on a vast scale, thus providing a cheap proletariat for the European mines and farms, and later for the manufacturing industries of South Africa, Rhodesia and Kenya.[21]

Henceforth we can no longer speak of a traditional society in this part of the continent, since the labour reserves had the function of supplying a migrant proletariat, a function which had nothing to do with 'tradition'. The African social systems of this region, distorted and impoverished, lost even the semblance of autonomy: the unhappy Africa of *apartheid* and the Bantustans was born, and was to supply the greatest return to central capital. The economists' ideological mythology of the 'laws of the labour market' under these circumstances, formulated by Arthur Lewis,[22] has been subjected to merciless criticism, and Giovanni Arrighi has restored the role of political violence to its true place.[23]

Until recently there was no known large-scale mineral wealth in West Africa likely to attract foreign capital, nor was there any settler colonialisation. On the other hand, the slave trade was very active on the coast, and caused the development of complex social structures which I have already analysed. The colonial powers were thus able to shape a system which made possible the large-scale production of tropical agricultural products for export under the terms necessary to interest central capital in them, ie. provided that the returns to local labour were so small that these products cost less than any possible substitutes produced in the centre itself.

The net result of these procedures, and the structures to which they gave rise, constituted what I have called 'Africa of the colonial trade economy' (*l'économie de traite*).[24] These processes were, as always, as much political as economic, and included the following: (i) the organisation of a dominant trade monopoly, that of the colonial import-export houses, and the pyramidal shape of the trade network they dominated, in which the Lebanese occupied the intermediate zones while the former African traders were crushed and had to occupy subordinate positions: (ii) the taxation of peasants in money which forced them to produce what the monopolists offered to buy; (iii) political support to the social strata and classes which were allowed to appropriate *de facto* some of the tribal lands, and to organise internal migrations from regions which were deliberately left in their poverty so as to be used as labour reserves in the plantation zones; (iv) political alliance with social groups which, in the theocratic framework of the Muslim brotherhoods, were interested in commercialising the tribute they levied on the peasants; and last but not least, (v) when the foregoing procedures proved ineffective, recourse pure and simple to administrative coercion: forced labour.

Under these circumstances, the traditional society was distorted to the point of being unrecognisable; it lost its autonomy, and its main function was to produce for the world market under conditions which, because they impoverished it, deprived the members of any prospects of radical modernisation. This 'traditional' society was not, therefore, in transition to 'modernity'; as a dependent society it was complete, peripheral, and hence at a dead end. It consequently retained certain 'traditional' appearances which constituted its only means of survival. The Africa of the colonial trade economy included all the subordination/domination relationships between this pseudo-traditional society, integrated into the world system, and the central capitalist economy which shaped and dominated it. Unfortunately the phrase 'colonial-type trade' has been used so frequently that its meaning has been reduced to a mere description: the exchange of agricultural products against imported manufactured goods.[25] Yet the concept is much richer: it describes analytically the exchange of agricultural commodities provided by a peripheral society shaped in this way, against the products of a central capitalist industry, imported or produced on the spot by European enterprises.

The results of this colonial-type trade have varied according to different regions of this part of Africa. To give honour where honour is due, it was British capital that initiated a perfectly consistent formulation of aims and procedures. At the beginning of colonisation, when Lever Brothers asked the Governor of the Gold Coast to grant concessions which would enable them to develop modern plantations, he refused because 'it was unnecessary'. It would be enough, the Governor explained, to help the traditional chiefs to appropriate the best lands so that these export products could be obtained without extra investment costs. Lever then approached the Belgians and obtained concessions in the Congo, as we shall see why later.

I have analysed elsewhere the conditions for the success of this colonial-type trade,[26] but these may be summarised as follows: (i) an 'optimum' degree of hierarchy in a 'traditional' society, which is exactly the case in those zones formed by the slave trade; (ii) an 'optimum' population density in the rural areas of 10–30 inhabitants per square kilometre; (iii) the possibility of starting the process of proletarianisation by calling upon immigrants foreign to the ethnic communities of the plantation zone; (iv) the choice of 'rich' crops, providing a sufficient surplus per hectare and per worker, at the very first stage of their development; and (v) the support of the political authority, making available to the privileged minority such resources—political and economic, especially agricultural credit—as would made possible the appropriation and development of the plantations.

The complete model of this colonial-type trade was achieved in the Gold Coast and German Togoland by the end of the nineteenth century, and was reproduced much later in French West and Equatorial Africa. This lateness reflected that of French capitalism, and was attributable to the attempts at quasi-settler colonialisation even under unfavourable conditions—for example, French planters in the Ivory Coast and in Equatorial Africa—and the corresponding maintenance of forced labour until the modern period, after World War Two.

This colonial economy took two main forms. Dominant in the Gulf of Guinea, where conditions enabled this kind of trade to develop, was the *kulak* class of indigenous planters of rural origin, who employed paid labour and secured virtually exclusive appropriation of the land. On the other hand, in the savannah zone from Senegal through Northern Nigeria to the Sudan, the Muslim brotherhoods permitted another type of colonial trade: the production and export of groundnuts and cotton in vast areas subject to a theocratic power—that of the Mourid brotherhoods of Senegal, the Emirates of Nigeria and the Ansar and Ashiqqa in the Sudan. They kept the form of a tribute-paying social system, but this was integrated into the international system, because the surplus appropriated in the form of tribute levied on the village communities was itself marketed. It was the Egyptian colonisation in the Sudan which created the most advanced conditions for the development of this type of organisation, which in that country tended towards a pure and simple latifundia system of large estates. The British merely gathered the fruits of this evolution. The new latifundia owners accepted the colonial administration after 1898, and grew cotton for the benefit of British industry. Powerful modern techniques were made available to them, notably large-scale irrigation in the Gezira.

There was a 'second transformation of Islam' in West Africa, after the colonial conquest opened the way to the same kind of evolution, although less definite and slower. We have already seen that Islam in this region underwent a first transformation: from being the religion of a minority caste of merchants in the pre-mercantilist period, integrated into an animist society (hence similar to Judaism in Eruope), it became the ideology of popular resistance to the slave trade in the mercantilist period. This second transformation made Islam— 'restored' by the aristocracy and the colonial authorities—the guiding ideology of peasant leaders for the organisation of the export production which the colonisers desired. The Mourid phenomenon of Senegal is probably the most striking example of this second transformation. The fact that the founders of the brotherhood, and some short-sighted colonial administrators, felt hostile to each other for some time, does not matter. Ultimately the brotherhood proved to be the most important vector for the expansion of the groundnut economy: and for the submission of the peasants to the goal of this economy: to produce a large amount, and to accept very low and stagnating wages despite progress in productivity.

To organise this colonial-type trade it was necessary to destroy the pre-colonial pattern, and to reorganise the flows in the direction required by the externally orientated nature of the economy. For there had been, before, regional complementarities with a broad, natural forest-savannah base, strengthened by the history of the relations between the West African societies. The domestic trade between herdsmen and crop farmers, and in kola and salt, as well as the outflow of exports and the dissemination of imports, constituted a dense and integrated network, dominated by African traders. The colonial trading houses had to gain control of these flows and to direct them all towards the coast; that was why the colonial system destroyed African domestic trade and then reduced African traders—when they were not eliminated—to the role of subordinate primary collectors. The destruction of the trade of Samori, like that of the Coloured people in St. Louis, Gorée and Freetown, like that of the Hausa and Ashanti of Salaga, and of the Igbo of the Niger Delta, bear witness to this other crippling socioeconomic effect of *l'économie de traite*.

Thus the colonial trade necessarily gave rise to a polarisation of dependent peripheral development at the regional level. The necessary corollary of the 'wealth' of the coast was the impoverishment of the hinterland. Predisposed by geography and history to a continental development, organised around the major inland river arteries (thus providing for transport, irrigation, electric power and so on), Africa was condemned to be only 'developed' narrowly along the coast. The exclusive allocation of resources to the latter zone, a planned policy of colonial trade, accentuated this regional imbalance. The mass emigration from the hinterland to the coast forms part of the logic of the system: it made cheap labour available to capital where capital required this, and only 'the ideology of universal harmony' can see in these migrations anything other than their impoverishment of the departure zones.[27] The culmination of the colonial trade system was a balkanisation, in which the 'recipient' micro-regions had no 'interest' in 'sharing' the crumbs of the colonial cake with their labour reserves.

Thus the bounties of the colonial trade were highly relative. However, it was impossible to implement this system in Central Africa, the third micro-region of the continent. Here, ecological conditions had to some extent protected the peoples who took refuge from the ravages of the slave trade in zones unlikely to be penetrated from the coast. The low density of population, and the lack of sufficient African hierarchies, made the colonial-trade model non-viable. Discouraged, the colonial authorities gave the country to any adventurers who would agree to try 'to get something out of it' without resources, since adventure does not attract capital. The misdeeds of the concessionary companies have been duly denounced; between 1890 and 1930 they ravaged French Equatorial Africa with no result except a trivial profit. As for the Congo, it will be remembered that Lever Brothers were welcomed by the Belgians, after the firm's unsuccessful attempt to establish itself in the Gold Coast. But it was only after World War One, when the solution was adopted of having industrial plantations established directly by the major capitalists, that a small-scale colonial-type trade infiltrated as an extension of the plantation zones belonging to foreign capital.[28] As for French Equatorial Africa, this area had to wait until the 1950s before seeing the first symptoms. Thus the negative impact of this period, still omnipresent, justifies the name which I have given to the region—'Africa of the concessionary companies'.

In all three cases, then, the colonial system organised the African societies so that they produced exports—on the best possible terms, from the point of view of the mother country—which only provided a very low and stagnating return to local labour. This goal having been achieved, we must conclude that there are no traditional societies in modern Africa, only dependent peripheral societies.

Notes

1 For further details, see my *L'Accumulation à l'échelle mondiale*, Paris, 1970, especially pp. 31, 165–8, and 341–72; also my article on 'La Politique coloniale française à l'égard de la bourgeoisie commerçante sénégalaise', in Claude Meillassoux ed., *The Development of Indigenous Trade and Markets in West Africa*, London, 1971, pp. 361–76.
2 This idea of the cumulative nature of technological progress, and the importance of the age of the social formation in assessing the significance of a mode of production to which it belongs, is stressed by H.S. Michelina, 'The Economic Formation: notes

on the problem of its definition', IDEP paper, Dakar, October 1971.

3 Cathérine Coquery-Vidrovitch, 'Recherches sur un mode de production africain', in *La Pensée* (Paris), April 1969, rightly emphasises the decisive role which long-distance trade played in the constitution of some African states. Cf. Ahmad El Kodsy, 'Nationalism and Class Struggles in the Arab World', in the *Monthly Review* (New York), July–August 1970; and also Antoine Pelletier and Jean-Jacques Goblot, *Matérialisme historique et histoire des civilisations*, Paris, 1969l who suggest this for Greece.

4 Except for Egypt and Mesopotamia, and hence the frequent mistake of speaking of 'Arab feudalism' criticised by El Kodsy, *op.cit.*

5 The role and the nature of this trade were highlighted for the first time by E.W. Bovill, *Caravans of the Old Sahara*, London, 1933, later revised as *The Golden Trade of the Moors*, London, 1958.

6 Fernand Braudel, *La Méditerranée et le monde méditerranéen à l'époque de Philippe II*, Paris, 1949.

7 See my *L'Accumulation à l'échelle mondial*, chapter 2, section 3.

8 Boubacar Barry, *Le Royaume du Waalo, 1659–1859*, Paris, 1971 (mimeo).

9 *Ibid.*

10 See Jan Vansina, *Introduction à l'éthnographie du Congo*, Brussels, 1967, and G. Ballandier, *La Vie quotidienne au royaume du Congo du XVI au XVIIIe siècle*, Paris, 1965.

11 See, inter alia, R. Hill, *Egypt in the Sudan, 1820–81*, London, 1959; P.M. Holt, *The Mahdist State in the Sudan, 1881–98*, Oxford, 1958, and J.S. Trimingham, *Islam in the Sudan*, Oxford, 1949.

12 For further details, see my *L'Accumulation à l'échelle mondiale*.

13 Boubacar Barry, *op.cit.*

14 Walter Rodney, 'African Slavery and other Forms of Social Oppression on the Upper Guinea Coast in the context of the Atlantic Slave Trade', in *The Journal of African History*, 3, 3 (1966).

15 Cathérine Coquery-Vidrovitch, 'De la traite des esclaves à l'exportation de l'huile de palme et des palmistes au Dahomey, XIXe siècle', in Meillassoux, *op.cit.*, pp. 107–23.

16 K. Onwuka Diké, *Trade and Politics in the Niger Delta, 1830–85*, Oxford, 1956.

17 See Yves Person, *Samori*, Dakar, 1970, 3 vols.

18 This problem of the looting of natural resources is beginning to be studied with the present-day awareness of 'environmental problems', although the term is ambiguous.

19 See my paper on 'Le Modèle théorique de l'accumulation dans le monde contemporain, centre et périphérie', IDEP, Dakar, 1971.

20 Thus the structures established in the Gold Coast in 1890, which have characterised Ghana up to the present day, made their appearance in the Ivory Coast only from 1950, after the abolition of forced labour. See R. Szereszewski, *Structural Changes in the Economy of Ghana, 1891–1911*, London, 1965; and Samir Amin, *Le Développement du capitalisme en Côte d'Ivoire*, Paris, 1967.

21 See Ralph Horwitz, *The Political Economy of South Africa*, London, 1967; Richard Gray, *The Two Nations*, Oxford, 1961; Serge Thion, *Le Pouvoir pâle*, Paris, 1969; and, above all, Giovanni Arrighi, *The Political Economy of Rhodesia*, The Hague, 1967.

22 Arthur Lewis, *Economic Development with Unlimited Supplies of Labour*, Manchester, 1954.

23 Arrighi, *op.cit.*

24 I have analysed this colonial trade in my *L'Afrique de l'Ouest bloquée*, Paris, 1971. See also Osende Afana, *L'Economie de l'ouest africain*, Paris, 1966; and André Van-haeverbeke, *Rémunération du travail et commerce extérieur*, Louvain, 1970.

25 As Suret Canale does in *L'Afrique noire, l'ète coloniale*, Paris, 1960.

26 See my *L'Accumulation à l'échelle mondiale*, pp. 347–8.

27 Elliot J. Berg, 'The Economics of the Migrant Labour System', in Hilda Kuper ed., *Urbanisation and Migration in West Africa*, Los Angeles, 1965, reflects better than anyone else this non-scientific ideology. The conventional assumption is that migrations 'redistribute' one factor of production (labour) which originally was unequally distributed. If that were so, migration would tend to equalise the rates of growth of

the economies of the various regions. But we can see that they are everywhere accompanied by a growing disparity between rates of growth: the acceleration of growth *per capita* in the immigration zones, and its reduction in the emigration zones.

28 Cathérine Coquery-Vidrovitch, *Le Congo française au temps des compagnies concessionaries, 1890–1930*, Paris, 1971 (mimeo); and R. Merlier, *Le Congo, de la colonisation belge à l'independance*, Paris, 1965.

3 Nigeria: The Neo-Colonial Political Economy*

GAVIN WILLIAMS

The development of the neo-colonial economy in Nigeria required the transfer of state authority into indigenous hands. Neither the colonial government, nor the colonial firms, secure in their dominant commercial position, initiated the transition from trading to manufacturing. The pricing policies of the Marketing Board delayed the development of industry by limiting the expansion of the market, and the development of indigenous capitalism by denying African traders the opportunity to profit from the post-war boom in commodity prices. The surpluses accumulated by the Marketing Board were sent to Britain, rather than invested in Nigeria.[1] Independence ended British control of public investment funds, of tariff and industrial policy, of fiscal policies and the allocation of foreign exchange. A Central Bank was established, able to regulate the money supply and currency exchange. State policy protected and subsidised industrial investment by protective tariffs, tariff rebates on imported machinery, tax holidays, and the provision of services and industrial estates.[2] The state controlled the allocation of profitable opportunities, which could be used to create protected niches for its clients, and enabled the Nigerian bourgeoisie to share in the spoils of the neo-colonial economy and accumulate capital.

Markets and sources of investment and technology have been diversified among different metropolitan countries, or, to put a different slant on the same thing, foreign exploitation has been multilateralised. The federal and the regional governments competed among themselves, and with other neo-colonial states, to attract foreign investment by a combination of subsidies and protection and by promising profit repatriation. Foreign investors responded in order to gain, extend or protect their access to the Nigerian market, and to oligopolistic niches within it, and to take advantage of the bounties offered by the states.[3] The dominant institution of neo-colonial capitalism is the multinational corporation (multinational in its operations more than its ownership and control, which remain firmly outside underdeveloped countries). The productive, distributive and financial activities of the corporation are vertically integrated. They are able to control and diversify their sources of inputs, investments and markets in such a way as to ensure their own profitability, security and expansion. They have invested in capital-intensive and technologically advanced industries in the import substituting sector, where state protection guarantees their markets.[4] These industries depend on foreign, or rather foreign-controlled, capital, supplies of intermediate goods and technical and managerial skills. These investments do generate backward and final demand, and sometimes forward linkages. But many of these linkages stimulate production in metropolitan rather than underdeveloped economies. These industries do generate a demand for the development of skills and learning, both for their own activities, and for the public administration which serves them. But these are the skills which the highly educated middle class have acquired in metropolitan and colonial universities, which make them employable in capitalist firms and state

* From *Nigeria: Economy and Society*, Rex Collings, London, 1976, pp. 28–54.

administration, and provide them with their economic privileges and political superiority over the poor. In this way they come to share with metropolitan capitalists a commitment to the development of capitalist production and the extension of state activity at the expense of peasant and petty commodity producers. The development of neo-colonial capitalism substituted imports of intermediate and producer goods for imports of consumer goods. This consolidates rather than undermines dependence on foreign suppliers, since production, as well as consumption, now depends on foreign imports.[5]

The development of capitalism depends on the domination of capitalist production over peasant and petty commodity production, enforced by the state rather than produced by market competition. The monopoly purchasing power of the Marketing Boards enabled the state to increase the rate of exploitation of peasant labour to finance the emergence of a Nigerian capitalist class, and to finance the development of industrial investment and the provision of urban services and amenities. Peasant and petty commodity producers provide inputs which capitalist firms cannot produce profitably. These include cheap food and consumer goods for the employees of capitalist firms and the state which services them, thereby reducing wage costs and inflating the salaries of managerial staff. Petty commodity production maintains the 'reserve army of labour', thus ensuring a flexible supply of labour to capitalist employers and limiting the bargaining strength of organised labour, thus again reducing wage costs. It provides opportunities for additional earnings to workers and gives them the hope of establishing themselves as independent men,[6] thus both subsidising and encouraging wage employment. Capitalist production depends for its market, firstly, on the incomes of export-crop farmers; secondly, on the incomes of workers and clerks employed by capitalist firms and the state; thirdly, on the incomes derived by the bourgeoisie from the exploitation of the producers and more recently from their appropriation of a share in the oil revenues; and fourthly, from the incomes of petty commodity producers, craftsmen and traders, and food-crop farmers generated by the spending of other classes.

At the same time, the development of capitalist production restricts the development of peasant and petty commodity production. The transfer by the state of resources from agriculture and the rural economy to itself and to capitalist production and the urban economy reduces the return on rural labour and investment, which impoverishes farmers and encourages the transfer of private resources, including skills, from the rural to the urban economy. Government loans and tax and tariff incentives subsidise capitalist firms at the expense of competition from petty commodity producers. Petty commodity production depends on imported materials, whose prices are determined by capitalist distributors and their clients, and on materials produced or even discarded by capitalist firms. Ease of entry into production and thus mutual competition among producers restricts opportunities for capital accumulation from petty commodity production. These restrictions can only be overcome when producers, and more particularly distributors, can gain privileged access to supplies or markets, which in turn depends on their gaining the patronage of agents of the state or of capitalist firms. Thus capitalist development is parasitical on peasant and petty commodity production. Control of state policy and relations of exchange enables capitalists to determine the conditions of production of peasant and petty commodity producers.[7]

Decolonisation altered the patterns of participation and influence in public affairs. Power was effectively devolved to the bourgeoisie who commanded the skills and resources necessary to determine public policy at the regional and national levels. The scale of the resources required to take advantage of the new opportunities for political participation was well beyond the reach of the petty traders and contractors who had previously been able to exercise some influence with the customary authorities at the local level. Allocation of resources at the local level was now determined by the interests of the ruling party at the regional, and ultimately the federal, level. Thus local influence depended on patronage relations with regional politicians, and the imposition of military rule has deprived people of even these limited opportunities for patronage.[8]

Decolonisation thus paved the way for capitalist development in Nigeria. But the development of capitalism consolidated rather than undermined foreign economic domination. It depended on the increasing exploitation of export-crop farmers, and restricted the development of peasant and petty commodity production.

Class Relations in the Neo-Colonial Political Economy

The transition from the colonial to the neo-colonial political economy both required and led to changes in class relations, and generated contradictions that could not be resolved within the framework of representative political institutions.

Expatriate domination of investment opportunities, thanks to their superior access to credit, supplies and the technology and managerial skills necessary to industrial production, inhibits the accumulation and reinvestment of capital by indigenous entrepreneurs who lack the resources necessary to compete with vertically integrated multinational corporations.[9] Consequently, indigenous entrepreneurs became 'compradores', ie., intermediaries between foreign interests and the indigenous polity and economy, and/or turned to the state as a source of both capital and contracts. Lucrative profits have accrued to those able to establish control of monopolistic niches in the distribution of commodities, rather than to those who have organised their production most efficiently. Consequently, politics and the favour of foreign companies, itself a product of political influence, became the primary sources of capital accumulation by Nigerians. Initially, this capital was accumulated from the surplus value appropriated from the peasants by the Marketing Boards. Tariff protection and monopolistic distributive arrangements for imported and factory-produced goods increased profits at the expense of consumers. Professionals, bureaucrats and merchants used state power to establish themselves as a bourgeoisie.[10]

Nigerian governments perpetuated the highly inegalitarian colonial administrative, salary and tax structure, with its complex of fringe benefits (car and child allowances, health facilities and housing subsidies available to the earners of high salaries). The state regulated expatriate quotas to encourage foreign companies to employ Nigerian managerial and professional staff. The lucrative salaries offered in the private sector and, by necessity, offered for professional and technical staff in the public sector, led administrators, followed by academics, to demand equivalent salaries for themselves.[11] The 1971 Adebo Commission[12] was instructed 'to examine areas in which rationalisation and harmonisation of wages, salaries and other remuneration and conditions of employment are desirable and feasible as between the public and private sectors of the economy'. In 1974, the Udoji Commission[13] in carrying out

47

similar instructions, repaid its bureaucratic sponsors handsomely. This provoked strikes by workers in the private sector, but more particularly by professional staff and technical students who felt that they had fallen behind in the process, and were only pacified by a guaranteed increase on previous salaries of 30 to 40 per cent, still below the 100 per cent increases to daily-paid workers earning $= 2$ (£1.40) per day at the bottom, and senior officials earning 28 times as much at the top.

The bourgeoisie sought to establish areas of economic activity in which they would be protected from foreign competition, or in which foreign companies would have to operate through them. Initially this was provided by the withdrawal of foreign companies from retail trading, by the exclusion of foreigners from land ownership, and by the established position of Nigerian entrepreneurs in such fields as produce and passenger transport. This did not resolve the conflict between indigenous businessmen and multinational corporations over the terms of their relationship. The initial focus of African aspirations has been to exclude Lebanese merchants from their position in the distributive trades and certain assembly industries. The 1972 Indigenisation Decree reserved large areas of economic activity for indigenous businessmen, including advertising and public relations, pools, assembly of radios, record-players, etc., blending and bottling of alcoholic drinks, block and brick making, bread making, clearing and forwarding, and retail trading. Multinational companies had only peripheral interests in these fields, in which Lebanese merchants were well represented. Local participation in equity shares and a minimum size are required for foreign firms operating in a wider range of activities, including beer brewing, tyre manufacture, construction, service and distribution of motor vehicles, manufacture of cement, paints, matches, metal containers and soaps, poultry farming, and the wholesale trade. Finance for indigenous participation in foreign industries or take-over of them has been provided by banks, now 40 per cent government-owned, and required to allocate at least 40 per cent of their loans to Nigerian businessmen, by the legally and illegally gained wealth of the state-sponsored bourgeoisie, and by employees of foreign companies who have been lent money by firms to buy their shares at favourable prices. Civil servants are reported to be among the main recipients of bank loans for share purchases. Thus managers and bureaucrats have assimilated themselves to Nigeria's capitalist class. Nigeria has expanded and consolidated its capitalist class. Geographically, its operations (if not always its personal origins) and the operations of the businesses which have been taken over are concentrated in Lagos and Kano, the major areas of industrial expansion. Increasing access to money and opportunities for the few will strengthen their ability to deny opportunities to the many. It may be, as a correspondent for West Africa[14] suggests, 'politically desirable that the transfer of ownership of foreign business should be spread both geographically and between social classes'; it is inconceivable that this should have been done. Multinational corporations have taken a leading role in sponsoring the acquisition of shares by Nigerians, and establishing on a firmer footing their alliance with Nigerian capitalism. This does not preclude future conflict over the relative share of foreign and indigenous capitalists in the profits of the neo-colonial economy.[15]

The ambiguous position of the bourgeoisie within the neo-colonial political economy is expressed in its ideological ambiguity.[16] Its nationalism is the outcome of its wish to appropriate resources back from the foreigner; its commitment to foreign investment is the outcome of its concrete dependence on the neo-colonial political economy. National unity and reconciliation express the ambition of the bourgeoisie to act as an hegemonic class, providing moral and political leadership at the national level and within the international political arena. Its tribalism is the outcome of its lack of control of the productive resources of the economy and hence of the competition among the bourgeoisie for favoured access to scarce resources, and the need to manipulate particularistic interests and sentiments among the poor to maintain the bourgeoisie's political domination. The bourgeoisie lacks the commitments of a religious, socialist or nationalist character of the rationalising, capital-accumulating, surplus-expropriating classes which directed the industrialisation of Britain, Russia, Germany and Japan. Perhaps it is this which lies behind the repeated call for a 'national ideology' which seeks to subordinate the energies of the people behind a single national goal. In fact, the Nigerian bourgeoisie do have an ideology, in the sense of a theoretical legitimation of the *status quo*. It is expressed in the concept of 'development', which is 'that which we are all in favour of', and given statistical respectability in figures measuring the growth of commodity production, particularly production by capitalist mining and manufacturing industries. The demand for Nigerianisation gives it a nationalist colouring. But this demand falls short of the demand for expropriation of foreign capitalists on whom the Nigerian bourgeoisie remains dependent. In this way, the ideology of 'national development' presents the bourgeoisie's image of itself as providing national leadership in the public interest, with its contradictions abolished and its immediate material interests preserved. What the bourgeoisie lacks, to use Mannheim's terminology,[17] is a Utopia, a set of ideas to inspire the transformation of the existing order and the liberation of human capacities.

The transition to a neo-colonial political economy changed the relationship between the surplus-producing and the surplus-appropriating classes. State monopoly Market Boards introduced a new form of exploitation of the surplus value of peasant labour, and increased the rate of exploitation, to a point where the continued production and marketing of agricultural crops came to be threatened. The price of export crops came to be determined by political decisions rather than through the impersonal operations of the market. Consequently, the exploitation of export-crop farmers, as a class, sharing a common destiny which is determined by the government's exercise of political decisions, has become clearly apparent to farmers. This has given rise to a specific peasant consciousness, at least among Yoruba cocoa farmers. Under conditions of falling crop prices, increasing taxes and inflation, it gave rise to the Agbekoya rebellion of 1968–9, which forced the government to reduce taxes and withdraw its officials from rural areas.[18]

Food-crop farmers and craftsmen and petty traders depend in large measure on the direct and multiplier effects of expenditure by cash-crop farmers for their incomes. Thus their own market situation is indirectly governed by the rate of exploitation of agricultural production, and by the terms of trade between export crops and manufactured goods. Even though oil has far surpassed agriculture's contribution to export and government revenues, agricultural incomes still provide the major source of expenditure on items produced with local skills and resources. The consolidation of the intermediary position of merchant traders has excluded craftsmen and petty traders from direct access to expatriate firms for credit and supplies. The Nigerian merchants who displaced expatriate trading firms, and more recently Levantine traders, tend to restrict the advance of credit to a limited network of dependents, and to take over many of the middleman activities of the petty traders themselves.

Craftsmen and petty traders find themselves competing in fields in which there are no effective formal and informal barriers to entry. Returns àre therefore low, and required to meet subsistence and conventional expenditures. Expansion of output is limited by the craftsman's own labour time, and by his ability to attract, organise and supervise apprentices. The more apprentices recruited, the greater the competition for clients in the future. Since craftsmen's prices are based on low marginal costs of labour and personal supervision, they cannot improve their relative position by organising their labour force on capitalist lines and meeting the increased costs of paying and supervising wage labour. Cooperative arrangements allow the sharing of certain costs and risks, but only permit a marginal extension of the limits to expansion.[19] Both craftsmen and petty traders know that higher profits are made by the merchants who sell them materials, or buy commodities from them, than they can make themselves. Tailors and petty cloth sellers thus aspire to become cloth merchants, mechanics plan to trade in motor parts, drivers to own their own taxis, yam sellers to trade in beans (requiring more working capital, and thus opportunities for profit). Access to these opportunities is controlled by the very merchants who exploit them. Thus craftsmen and petty traders, rather than combining to prevent their own exploitation, instead look to potential sponsors both for the supplies and credit necessary to carry out their immediate activities and for assistance in surmounting the barries to admission to the charmed circle of monopolistic advantage.[20] During the colonial period, merchants from an earlier era were sometimes able to take advantage of new opportunities. In other cases, produce buyers and traders started their careers as clerks to, or agents of, mercantile companies, thus overcoming the initial hurdles of credit, working capital and clientele. Since then, political influence, the favour of foreign companies, and lately influence with and marriage to army officers, have become the best-trodden paths to commercial success. Personal skills, the taking up of opportunities for innovation and the shrewd management of resources and personal relations, all determine an individual's chance of commercial success, thus encouraging and sustaining an ethic of competition.[21] But the situation of craftsmen and petty traders as a class is determined by the rate of exploitation of agricultural production on the one hand, and the expropriation of the resources and opportunities essential to their livelihood by manufacturers and merchants on the other. Relations with merchants and through them with the neo-colonial political economy as a whole are mediated through personal ties of clientage and patronage, and an ideology of entrepreneurial initiative, rather than through the impersonal ties of the market and an ideology of class conflict.

In more general terms, opportunities have been increased in capitalist enterprises and in state administration, to the advantage of those with education and formal qualifications, at the expense of the illiterate, and of people involved in craft and peasant production. This discriminates against women as a status group. They are less likely to be educated than men, and when they do acquire secondary and higher education, are more likely to be employed in lower status and worse-paid jobs than their male peers (as nurses, rather than doctors, secretaries rather than executives). In those activities in which women are most commonly engaged (craft production and petty trading), opportunities have been restricted by the requirements of capitalism. In these areas the proportion of men employed increases as the returns to employment increase, and the success of women is often dependent on the favour of influential men. While opportunities for access to education and formal employment qualifications have expanded dramatically, so has the size of the bourgeoisie and the number of its children at school or university. By virtue of the financial, political and cultural resources at its disposal, the bourgeoisie has been best placed to take advantage of publicly funded educational opportunities, thus putting these opportunities even further from the sons and daughters of the poor.

The expansion of industry and administration has dramatically increased the number of people in industrial and clerical employment. The major attraction of wage and salary employment is the opportunity which it may provide for income, experience and contacts, which can be used contemporaneously and subsequently in independent economic activity. This intensifies the wage- or salary-earner's determination to maintain and improve his real income, and thus his margin of savings, for both his immediate subsistence needs and family obligations, and his future trading or other opportunities depend on his maximising his income from employment.[22]

There are significant differences in the market situation of workers in different employment sectors. Wages are a relatively small proportion of total costs for capital-intensive foreign firms, usually operating in an oligopolistic market. Levantine and Nigerian firms tend to assemble consumer goods or process raw materials, or to be engaged in construction and transport, where they rely on cheap labour to maintain their position in more competitive markets. Trade union organisations tend to be promoted by the former, and severely repressed by the latter. Wage improvements in the latter firms tend to depend on a general increase in the wage level, which depends in turn on the industrial strength of workers in capital-intensive firms and government employment. During the colonial period, government was by far the most important employer of wage labour, and wage levels came to be determined by the decisions of a series of government commissions, concerned mainly to adjust wages upwards in line with trends in the cost of living. Industrial workers have been able to bargain for wage increases on a factory basis, but at the same time they have added their industrial strength to the periodic demands for overall wage increases in the face of inflation, and have insisted on the extension of public sector awards to the private sector. A few manual workers with scarce skills and some employees with relatively high levels of formal education are able to sell their skills in a favourable labour market, or look to promotion within their firm for advancement. But for most factory workers, collective bargaining, supported where necessary by militant action, is their only weapon in protecting their real wages and their security of employment.[23]

The social organisation of industrial production, the concentration of factories in a few centres, and of their labour force in certain suburbs, the common and intractable problems of urban life, and the common involvement of wage earners in a national system of wage determination in the form of periodic government commissions, combine to produce among industrial workers recognition of a common fate arising from a common class situation. Militancy has been greater in industrial centres, such as Ikeja (on the outskirts of Lagos) and Kano, than in cities like Ibadan and Zaria, where there are few opportunities for wage employment, and limited opportunities for strangers (who make up most of the wage-labour force). At least at the factory level, workers have the organisational resources with which to defend their own interests under their own leadership. The national system of wage determination has provided the issues, such as the demand for publication of the Morgan Commission award in 1964, the implementation of the Adebo Commission interim award in 1971 and the extension of the Udoji Commission awards to the private sector in 1975, on which they have been able to force a confrontation with the government and employers. The strike has provided them with the weapon for that confrontation, and has taken the form of a general strike, as in 1945 and in 1964, or waves of strikes in particular factories and industries as in 1950, 1955, 1960, 1971 and 1975, all coinciding with the preparation or publication of the reports of government commissions.[24]

Clerical and technical workers are concerned to increase the general level of wages. The system of regulating wage levels by periodic government awards has tied public to private and clerical to industrial wage levels. But clerical workers, and technical and professional staff, are often more concerned with the regrading of posts than with general wage levels. Clerical workers' militancy has usually focused on dissatisfaction with grading schemes, and demands for the implementation of various reports on grading in particular ministries; the dissatisfaction with regrading by the Udoji Commission was simply more general than earlier complaints.

Younger clerks seek advancement through further education, to the point where they are often accused of spending their working hours preparing for examinations. Since they have better opportunities for promotion than factory workers, they are more concerned to seek the favour of their seniors, which is usually alleged to be determined by kinship and ethnicity rather than merit. They also have greater security of tenure, and better prospects of a gratuity which can be invested on early retirement in commercial activities. Thus clerks, and professional and technical staff, may be militant in pressing wage demands, but they are more likely to be concerned with their relative grading than with raising wage levels as a whole.

What is the relation between the interests and actions of the workers and the self-employed? Economists of both left- and right-wing inclinations have argued that wage and salary earners constitute a 'labour aristocracy', whose strategic economic position and bargaining ability enable them to gain a disproportionate share both of the social product, which enables them to engage in 'discretionary consumption' at the expense of peasants, and of employment opportunities. Politically, they are alleged to be conservative, protecting their own privileges rather than advancing the interests of the poor and exploited classes in general.[25]

Industrial workers are interested in raising wage levels, which tends to push up urban price levels to the advantage of craftsmen and petty traders who produce primarily for urban markets. Workers' immediate demands are thus distinct from the demands of farmers, and of those craftsmen and petty traders primarily dependent on rural markets and the multiplier effects of farmers' income, who are more concerned with favourable crop prices. Further, the dependence of clerks on government revenues for their incomes made them ultimately dependent on the state's ability to sustain its financial commitments by exploiting farmers. Even since the expansion of oil revenues, clerks do compete with other possible beneficiaries for a share in overall government expenditure. Factory employment was initially financed by exploiting the rural producers through the Marketing Boards, and consumers through tariff protection and other devices for regulating markets. But, despite repeated assertions to the contrary, there is no empirical evidence that wage-earners' households enjoy significantly greater levels or better quality of consumption than do rural households. It certainly stretches the meaning of words to regard the wage-earner's occasional beer-drinking with friends or the celebration of family occasions as 'discretionary consumption', on a par with the conspicuous emulation of the metropolitan bourgeoisie by their Nigerian counterparts.[26]

The 'labour aristocracy' thesis argues firstly that marginal increments in workers' wages are gained at the expense of the peasantry. This assumes that if wage increases were not forced on employers, at least part of the resources thus made available would be used to improve rural amenities or relieve the tax burden on the peasantry, or be passed on to the consumer in the form of lower prices. Reduction of taxes on the peasantry has usually resulted only from militant agitation by the peasants themselves, as in the case of the Agbekoya rebellion, or the state's need to maintain output levels, rather than the concern of the ruling classes for their welfare. In the non-competitive markets typical of the products of capitalist firms in underdeveloped countries, there is no reason on the most orthodox neo-classical assumptions to expect that consumers will benefit from relative reductions in production costs. In any case, in the capital-intensive industries in which the alleged 'labour aristocracy' are employed, wages by definition make up a relatively small proportion of production costs, so that marginal changes in wages have little immediate effect on those costs.

It is further argued that 'development', whatever that means, depends on keeping down the incomes of the urban and rural poor in order to facilitate savings and investments by the state or by private capital.[27] This assumes that workers and farmers have a higher marginal propensity to consume, and specifically to consume imported goods or goods with a high import content, than do the expropriators of the surplus. The assumption that the rich save and invest and the poor do not (Engel's so-called 'Law') is inapplicable to peasants, whose incomes are not advanced by employers but dependent on their prior savings and investments.[28] Nor is it necessarily applicable to workers who seek to escape from wage slavery by saving up enough to establish their own business. When commercial profits depend on contacts and favours, the rich may be inclined to consumption rather than to savings and to investment in producer goods. And even investments in machinery are often oriented to gaining control of monopolistic distributive privileges, and depend for their profitability on the restriction of petty commodity production.

The interest in such theories is not in the validity of their assumptions but in their ideological import. The allegation that there is a conflict of interest between peasants and workers, made by the bourgeoisie, and especially by their professional ideologues, the economists, is a classic example of what Post[29] terms the 'displacement' of the 'primary contradiction' between the exploiters and the exploited on to a 'derived' contradiction between exploiting classes. But it is certainly not a contradiction which is widely recognised among the exploited classes themselves, tied to one another as they are through family, lineage and mutual support.

The consolidation of the bourgeoisie, especially in so far as it has advanced through the command of formal education, has accentuated the difference between the bourgeoisie and the poor and illiterate in terms of life style, patterns of interaction and patterns of residence. Interaction between rich and poor, even within the framework of kinship, is an interaction of unequals, and thus of patron and supplicant, where the patron, while meeting the appropriate conventions, is in command of the situation. The poor share an ambiguous attitude to the rich. On the one hand they are admired as exemplars of the success to which the poor aspire, to whom they look for assistance with employment, credit and other favours. On the other hand, they are berated for their selfishness in looking only to their own advantage and that of their immediate family, of monopolising educational and other opportunities, rather than helping others to better themselves. On the one hand inequality is regarded as part of the natural order of things and privilege as a proper reward for investment, skill and effort; on the other hand, egalitarian values are expressed in such phrases as 'our wives shop in the same market [as the wives of the rich]'.[30]

The social relations of production and distribution in which the urban petty bourgeoisie are involved preclude them from taking effective class action in their own interests. At times, they have followed populist leaders, to whom they have looked to favour them with a share of the resources appropriated by the bourgeoisie.[31] Alternatively, they have sought individual advancement in relations of clientage to better placed patrons. By contrast, the social relations of production, distribution and exchange in which the urban workers and cash-crop farmers are involved has produced significant class action on their part. In taking political action in support of their immediate class interests, both urban workers and peasant farmers have regarded themselves as fighting for their rights in general, and thus in opposing the unfairness of the existing order. In doing so, they provide a focus for the political consciousness of the urban petty bourgeoisie, and of food-crop farmers, who lack the resources to articulate and enforce their own demands of their own accord. Thus the proletariat have acted as a 'political élite', expressing the demands of the poor in general, and not as a 'labour aristocracy', maintaining their privileges at the expense of the poor.[32] On the other hand, we must recognise the limits to the political capacity, at least to date, even of urban workers and export-crop farmers. Workers have struck in defiance of government legislation, and cocoa farmers have expelled government agents from the countryside and forced down taxes. But workers have settled in the end for better wages, and cocoa farmers remain dependent on their rulers and the world market to determine the cocoa price. Neither of them have the resources to intervene politically in the routine process of resource allocation. Nor have they have resources, including education and leadership, necessary to take over society and organise it in their own interests. It was the military, not the workers and peasants, who ended the life of the First Republic. It is the military regime that seeks to consolidate the development of capitalist society in Nigeria.

Politics, the State and Capitalist Development

During the colonial period, merchants, traders and professionals sought political power as a condition of furthering their economic interests against their colonial masters. State power gave them access to a share in the profitable opportunities offered by the neo-colonial economy, and the finance necessary to establish themselves as a bourgeoisie. Success in business enterprise depended on the favour of the state and foreign capitalists. Thus the bourgeoisie were forced to compete amongst themselves for access to profitable opportunities.[33] This took the form of rivalry for control of the spoils of political office. Politics became a zero-sum game, in which opposition was ruthlessly suppressed, modified only by cartel agreements among the regional barons, aimed at securing their own fiefs from outside subversion and sharing out Federal revenues, which became increasingly important after independence and were to be decisive with the development of oil production.[34]

The unequal competition for resources at the federal level, in which the North was able to dominate its competitors, ensured the instability of the successive compromises which the bourgeoisie tried to patch up on successive occasions in order to save the game. No impersonal rules governing competition can be established to regulate it when the differences among regions and ethnic groups, and again within such groups, discriminate massively in favour of particular groups, and where access to office and its spoils is the object of politics. The ethics of business penetrated politics, the ethics of politics penetrated business; the ethics of the gangster penetrated both.[35]

In 1962 the crisis in Western Nigeria, and the public enquiries that followed it, established, for anyone in doubt, that the Whitehall and Westminster rules for regulating competition for state power and the allocation of state resources had broken down. Regional governments established monopolies of political power and state patronage. Competition at the federal level gave way to a ruthless cartel, determined to eliminate any opposition which could not be incorporated into the racket on its own terms. Crisis followed crisis: agreement could not be reached on census figures, the conduct of elections, the appointment of Vice-Chancellors and other public figures, and the siting of the iron and steel industry. The politicians had made it quite clear that their looting of public resources could not be challenged within the framework of electoral politics. Popular participation was limited to begging politicians to secure for individuals and communities a small slice of the national cake. Broader values of equality and legitimacy had no place in the politics of wheeling and dealing; they could only be sought through direct resistance to exploitation and oppression, as in the 1964 general strike, or in the Tiv and Yoruba resistance to their respective regional governments.[36]

Between 1962 and 1967 the Nigerian state failed to resolve the contradictions inherent in the neo-colonial political economy. The state opened the economy to foreign exploitation and subjected itself to the political tutelage of the Western powers.[37] It failed to regulate relations between foreign capitalists and the indigenous bourgeoisie in such a way as to accommodate nationalist aspirations for Nigerian control of economic opportunities. The state was an instrument of private and sectional interests. Unlike its colonial predecessor, it was unable to lay down the rules for, and arbitrate, competition for political office and its spoils. It failed to weld the bourgeoisie into a coherent unit,[38] able to institutionalise its rule over other classes. Successive threats of secession were made by offended Western, Northern and Eastern interests who threatened to withdraw their own fiefs from the general arena of exploitation. In the crisis of 1966–7 the state could not protect the lives and property of its own officers and citizens. This led the Igbo bourgeoisie, with the support of most of the Igbo people, to reject the legitimacy of the Nigerian state and the Nigerian nation, and follow the disastrous road to secession and defeat.[39] The state organised the exploitation by capitalists of peasant and petty commodity production. Farmers' living standards were reduced, opportunities for craftsmen and petty traders were restricted by politicians and their beneficiaries, urban living standards were threatened by price inflation, particularly in rents. Relations between capitalist and non-capitalist modes of production, and between the exploiting and exploited classes, could be maintained only by oppression. The state failed to retain the loyalty of the common man.

In 1966 the overthrow of the politicians' government forced the new military rulers to turn to civil servants for advice and direction. In 1966 and 1967 Federal permanent secretaries intervened decisively to maintain federal authority against successive Northern plans for secession, and Eastern plans for confederation.[40] State policy was to be directed by the statesmen,[41] committed in principle to the national interest, as institutionalised in the federal government. The dependence of the oil-producing states for their very existence on federal military power, and the defeat of Biafran claims to the oilfields, enabled the federal government to appropriate an increasing share of the oil revenues and control the allocation of the remainder to the states. The dramatic multiplication of oil revenues since the war provides the fiscal base for the direction by the federal state of the nation's affairs. The development of capitalist production in Nigeria requires the national regulation of the market and of production. It requires a state able to override particular capitalist interests, both domestic and foreign, in the interest of the overall development of a capitalist society. A strategy of developing capitalism under the overall direction of the federal state has the support of employers' organisations, multinational corporations and capitalist and socialist powers. It cannot succeed if the state surrenders itself to the dictation of any one of these interests. The development of capitalism is too serious a business to be left to the capitalists.[42]

The development of capitalism is more than a matter of just increasing manufactured output and establishing a capital goods sector.[43] Capitalist society requires the establishment of social and political institutions for reproducing and regulating the class relations necessary to capitalist production and domination. The institutional 'revolution', to use Allison Ayida's term, necessary for the maintenance and development of capitalism in Nigeria requires:

(1) The supremacy of the Federal state over both state governments and private and sectional interests, and the regulation of competition among them for the allocation of state patronage.

(2) Regulation and adjustment of the relation between Nigerian and foreign capitalists.

(3) Regulation and adjustment of the relations between public and private economic activity.

(4) Regulation and adjustment of relations between capitalist and non-capitalist modes of production, particularly between the need for surplus appropriation from, and for development of, peasant production.

(5) Regulation and adjustment of relations between the exploiting class and the exploited classes, especially the proletariat and export-crop farmers.

(6) The articulation of a 'national ideology' and the inculcation of commitments to the symbols of national authority.

Since 1966 a strategy has been taking shape which seeks to institutionalise state regulation of class relations, and take class issues outside the realm of politics. It aims to make good General Gowon's claim that the federal government 'operates a system which knows no loyalty other than loyalty to the nation and people'.[44] 'Development objectives' are to be above politics. As Allison Ayida explained to the 1971 National Conference on Reconstruction and Development:[45]

> Those who would like to involve the representatives of the people and members of the political class who are not in office, in the planning process, should recognise the limitations of representative institutions in the formulation and maintenance of plan objectives. It is the executive, made up of ministers, planners, administrators and other public officials, who are in a position to determine and maintain the objectives and targets of development policy. They should, however, ensure through regular intercourse and discussion with the spokesmen of the main economic groups in the society, that they are guided at all times in the discharge of their developmental responsibilities by the views

and expressed and reasonable wants of the people and society at large.

Although the government should take the initiative for formulating national development objectives and targets, it is the people who alone can provide the necessary support for the realisation of such goals. They should therefore be consulted at all stages and be made to feel a part of the planning and hence, the development process . . . .

In 1967 the four regions were replaced by twelve states, six from the former Northern Region and six from the three southern regions. This aimed to regulate political competition by ensuring to the bourgeoisie of each state an arena in which it was protected from outside competition, and by increasing the number of contenders so as to produce an equilibrium of diverse alliances at the centre rather than the domination of a single region and party. This would free the federal government from sectional domination, and help to relegate the struggle for patronage to the state level. Federal appropriation of the lion's share of the oil revenues and the right to allocate the remainder enabled it to act as arbitrator between state interests. It first took control of all off-shore royalties and rents, and then reduced the share of on-shore royalties and rents accruing to the state of origin to 45 per cent and then to 20 per cent. The federal state also benefited directly from the increasing share of profits taxes (70 per cent in 1971–2) in total oil revenues. As Philip Asiodu, then Permanent Secretary in the Federal Ministry of Mines and Power, told the annual National Management Conference in 1973:[46] 'The effect of all these is, in fact, to strengthen the principle of "national" management of the oil wealth or distribution of revenue on the basis of national wealth'.

Military support gave civil servants a wider degree of freedom from intervention in decision-making by private and sectional interests than was possible under the rule of politicians. And at a humbler level, since 1970, and despite arbitrary actions by some soldiers, individuals have been free to go about their business without being harassed by politicians and political thugs.[47]

On Independence Day (1 October) 1970 General Gowon outlined a nine-point programme which would pave the way for the establishment of a civilian government, and in words he used four years later, 'lay the foundation of a self-sustaining political system which can stand the test of time in such a manner that a national political crisis does not become a threat to the nation's continued existence as a single entity and which will ensure a smooth and orderly transition from one government to another'.[48] The programme[49] required:

(1) The reorganisation of the Armed Forces.
(2) The implementation of the National Development Plan.
(3) The eradication of corruption in our national life.
(4) The settlement of the question of the creation of [further] states.
(5) The preparation and adoption of a new constitution.
(6) The introduction of a new revenue allocation formula.
(7) Conducting a national population census.
(8) The organisation of genuinely national political parties.
(9) The organisation of elections and installation of popularly elected governments in the states and at the centre.

The *Second National Development Plan, 1970–74*[50] complemented these primarily political objectives with the promise to establish Nigeria as:

(1) A united strong and self-reliant nation;
(2) A great and dynamic economy;

(3) A just and egalitarian society;
(4) A land of bright and full opportunities for all citizens;
(5) A free and democratic society.

A just and egalitarian society puts a premium on reducing inequalities in inter-personal incomes and promoting balanced development among the various communities in the different geographical areas in the country. It organises its economic institutions in such a way that there is no oppression based on class, social status, ethnic group or state.

Although these pious declarations bore no resemblance to the expenditure and investment programmes listed in the Plan, they indicate a recognition of the necessity of a strategy for class and communal conciliation, which is outlined explicitly in the *Guidelines for the Third National Development Plan, 1975–80*.[51]

The first item in this strategy was the extension of indigenous control of economic opportunities. The 1972 Indigenisation Decree, implemented by 1974, reserved specific economic opportunities for Nigerians and required Nigerian participation in firms engaged in a wide range of other activities. Major expatriate companies, even when not affected by the terms of the decree, have issued shares to the Nigerian public, as the bourgeoisie styles itself. The government has taken a 40 per cent share in all commercial banks and 55 per cent shares in all oil companies. These measures are designed to enable it to regulate relations between foreign and indigenous capitalism within the neo-colonial economy.

Industries of 'strategic national importance' (oil, iron and steel) have been reserved to the state. Professor Aboyade has argued for the extension of the public sector as an instrument of 'decolonisation', of plan fulfilment, of financing long-term investment projects—and as a means of combating unemployment and bringing about distributive equity. Philip Asiodu has called for the strengthening of executive capacity and increasing operational autonomy for the public sector. Nigerian private capitalists have demanded curbs on the expansion of the state sector, particularly in such fields as distribution and insurance, and in taking over firms under the Indigenisation Decree. They demand that 'the government's role should be confined to drawing the rules of the economic game in the country and the provision of infrastructural facilities essential for productive economic operations'.[52] The *Guidelines* for the third plan note that the Indigenisation Decree makes it necessary to 'delimit areas for private and state participation'. Thus the federal government plans to delimit the respective arenas of economic activity open to foreign and domestic capitalists, and to federal and state governments, in order to regulate the relations among them.

The decline in the production of certain export crops, and the embarrassing failure of the Western state government to handle the farmers' Agbekoya rebellion in 1968–9, led the federal government to take over responsibility for fixing produce prices and taxes in January 1973. Henceforth, they declared, prices would be fixed in the light of 'trends in world prices and local production costs', 'with no trading surpluses in view', in order to provide 'adequate incentives to producers through the pursuit of a price policy which would substantially increase producers' income as an inducement to expansion'.[53] Prices would no longer be governed by the immediate revenue needs of individual states. The federal government is now in a position to regulate policy towards export-crop farmers and the rural economy in general in the light of broader requirements of capitalist development, viz. development of the rural market, discouragement of rural-urban migration, encouragement of agricultural output and the need to stem rural unrest.

The *Guidelines* place agriculture first, rather than among the also-rans as its predecessors did. But its diagnosis and remedies emphasise the importance of direct inputs by the state (credit, extension and marketing facilities), relative to the need for price incentives and rural feeder roads to stimulate peasant production. The burden of state marketing will be imposed on food crops in the cause of stable prices. The federal government plans to acquire large areas of land 'to be leased out on uniform terms to farmers as in the case of industrial estates', on which it 'will be much easier to provide extension services, agricultural inputs, etc.'.[54] The Nigerian Agricultural Bank's first loans went to the Co-operative Union of the North-Eastern State (₦ 3.7 million), and to twelve individual farmers, presumably one from each state, ₦ 900 000.[55] Neither North-East state co-operatives, with little experience in marketing let alone extension, nor private capitalist farmers in Nigeria, have shown any capacity to use investments on this scale, and the money will probably be diverted to more lucrative commercial purposes, along with a large part of the rest of the ₦ 24 million thus far allocated by the Bank and the ₦ 40 million allocated for 1975–6.[56]

Over the last two years, peasant farmers have benefited from a series of increases in the prices paid for export crops, which are three or four times as high as during the period of low prices in the 1960s.[57] But these increases follow the dramatic, if precarious, increases in world commodity prices in the 1970s, and except in the case of groundnuts, the production of which has been drastically curtailed by the Sahel drought, do little more than catch up with the rate of inflation, and do not restore the real price levels of the 1950s. For their part, food-crop farmers are reported to have been incensed by demands for increased wages from their labourers, following the Udoji award, as well as because of inadequate transport facilities, and farmers have attempted to prevent food from entering the towns.[58]

Before the development of oil production Nigeria's prosperity was built on peasant agriculture. Ventures into capitalist farming and state settlements have proved disastrous, and state marketing arrangements burdensome. Yet Nigeria plans to develop agriculture by encouraging capitalist and state farming and distribution. Defence expenditure rather than agriculture will cycle the oil revenues into the economy—and recycle a substantial share back into the economies of metropolitan arms suppliers.[59]

The *Guidelines* combine the rhetorical commitment of the *Second Plan* to 'equitable income distribution' with hard-headed proposals 'for the institutionalisation of the incomes review process'. Previous *ad hoc* commissions had been 'appointed under strong pressure exerted in the form of industrial unrest caused by widespread dissatisfaction with the level, structure and alignment of incomes in the country'. The *Guidelines* proposed an Income Analysis Agency which, apart from providing employment for economists, will keep government informed of wage and salary trends in both private and public sectors, and of movements in the cost of living, and would 'inform and educate the public on the realities of the relationship among prices, wages, standards of living and economic growth', and calculate 'growth dividends' as a basis for determining a 'national incomes policy'. Minimum wage levels are to be determined by minimum wage committees, established in each state, under the overall aegis of a National Wages Board, which would also encourage 'employers and workers in an industry to establish a joint industrial council'. Considerations of hardship and equity, the main concern of previous commissions on wages and salaries, would be relegated to the committees, and balanced by a concern for what the

Guidelines elegantly disguise as 'the inter-factoral distribution of national income'.

The implementation of these brave proposals requires restructuring of the patterns of wage determination and collective bargaining. In 1974 a Labour Decree was issued, with elaborate provision regarding wages, contracts of employment, recruitment, wage advances, and the rights of workers to join or not to join trade unions.[60] Since 1948 the Nigerian trade union movement has been divided into two or more factions, dependent on the financial sponsorship and ideological guidance of competing trade union internationals, and their cold war sponsors. Unity has been achieved only for the duration of campaigns for government wage reviews (1964, 1971 and 1975). The 1975 Apena Cemetery Declaration established a Nigerian Labour Council with two committees, one to examine Udoji and one to draft a constitution, and agreed to affiliate to, and presumably draw funds from, 'all international labour organisations', and to work towards the development of industrial unions.[61] Since trade union leadership is essentially an entrepreneurial activity, in which leaders compete for the custom of factory unions, and the sponsorship of metropolitan powers, the institutionalisation of class conflict through responsible trade unions will take more than a truce and a declaration of intent by labour leaders.[62]

Employers have long been anxious to break the link between government reviews of wages, usually based on cost of living criteria, and wage demands in the private sector. In 1971, and again in 1975, they attempted without success to prevent government wage awards, which followed periods of wage freeze in the public sector, being extended to the private sector, where they argued that wage increases had already taken account of the cost of living. The Adebo and Udoji Commissions were both invited to propose rationalisations of the wage and salary structure. Adebo followed its predecessors in emphasising hardship to low wage-earners. After Udoji, the government was forced by widespread unrest to concede a minimum increase of 30 per cent over pre-Udoji levels for all employees. While employers and government seek to separate the question of minimum wages and overall wage determination, and break the link between wage reviews in the public sector and wage demands in the private sector, the workers themselves have not been willing to allow them to do so.

The Nigerian state has contained the opposition of workers and peasants by its control of the means of violence and by buying them off with wage and price increases which tend to fuel rather than catch up with inflation. They have not been able to institutionalise procedures for regulating class conflict and determining income distribution. This in turn would require the establishment of constitutional arrangements supported by public sentiments which legitimated and effected bourgeois domination, guaranteed national unity and regulated competition among the bourgeoisie. The military state has been no more able to resolve this issue than the politicians who preceded it.

The federal government has taken over responsibility for higher education, exercised through the National Universities Commission, and has assumed shared jurisdiction over primary and secondary education. The National Youth Corps has posted young graduates to work in states away from home and sought to inculcate a commitment to national service—as well as guaranteeing a period of employment immediately after graduation. The state's declared aims are to rationalise and expand the provision of educational facilities at all levels, to meet the manpower needs of the economy, and to rectify the geographical imbalance in educational and thus employment opportunities. Its most ambitious undertaking is the commitment to implement universal and compulsory primary education in all states by September 1979. Whether this will fulfil its declared aim of evening up educational opportunities in different regions is uncertain. Initially, relatively advantaged states will find it easier to recruit the teachers on whom the success of the scheme depends. At best it may help the four most northern states to run faster in order to be able to stand still in relation to their southern rivals. There are ambitious plans for new universities, particularly in the North. This will not solve the problem of there being too few qualified applicants from certain states. At the state level, voluntary agencies, primarily mission schools, are being taken over in several states, in a bid to standardise the quality of schooling and inculcate national, rather than particularistic religious, sentiments. Neither of these moves prevents the rich from using private primary schools to ensure their offspring privileged access to state secondary schools and perpetuating class privilege.

As *New Nigerian* declared,[63] complaining about the predominantly Yoruba composition of the census staff, 'even the man on the farm knows that—contrary to what he has been told—the census is a political exercise. It is in fact the joker in the FMG's 9 point programme'. The census figures deflated the returns for the West and South-East to below the inflated 1963 returns, and dramatically inflated the returns of the northern states, to almost double the 1963 figure, and nearly four times the 1951–2 figure in several cases. The four predominantly Hausa-Fulani-Kanuri states, which dominated the old North and through it the federation, now claimed the 51 per cent controlling majority, which the six states making up the old North had previously held. While the southern states, and particularly the West, cried foul, and the federal government pleaded for restraint, and declared the figures provisional, and presumably negotiable, the *New Nigerian* declared that 'it would be incredible and disastrous to reject the 1973 census'.[64] Governor Audu Bako of Kano State added insult to injury by declaring that the idea of disbanding the Interim Common Services Agency, managing former Northern Region institutions, would be 'dividing the indivisible'.[65] Clearly, the twelve-state system had failed to exorcise the spectre of Northern domination, and, for a second time, the census had failed to provide an agreed basis for electoral competition.

The recognition of aspirations among minorities in the old regions for their own states did not end the demands for new states. In most states, groups who have felt themselves disadvantaged, threatened by competition from others, or merely out of power, have promoted campaigns for the further division of existing states to secure control of their own fiefs. State agitation and inter-state rivalries have been promoted by the new scheme for revenue allocation, and accentuated by the census figures. The federal government has increased the share of revenues which it distributes among the states rather than retains for itself or returns to the state of origin. Half of these revenues are divided into equal shares for each state; the other half are allocated according to population. Thus the census has strengthened the claims of northern states for an increased share of federal revenues, has justified the relative decline in the revenues of the West, and has encouraged agitation for the creation of more states.[66]

Nor was the spectre of corruption exorcised. Serious allegations of corruption were made against federal institutions, such as the Nigerian National Supply Company,[67] and against senior administrators and commissioners in the federal and state governments. The government's major concern was to take action against people who allege corruption 'against highly placed public officials with a view to discrediting the military régime'.[68] Detention of such people,

61

and later of workers and trade unionists, led to student disturbances and the closure of university campuses. Corruption is an integral part of parasitical capitalism. It cannot be abolished by moral persuasion or administrative regulation. The federal government failed to keep corruption at bay and allowed itself to be subverted by corrupt practices. But then it commands the most lucrative spoils of all.

In other words, the military government failed to establish the conditions necessary for the establishment of bourgeois rule through a constitutional government. It failed to eradicate corruption, arrive at agreed census figures or settle the question of new states. A counter-élite of businessmen, professionals and academics see themselves as the rightful rulers of Nigeria, by virtue of their education, experience and untested claims to popular support, and they regard the military increasingly as usurpers. But it is clear that they were simply preparing to resume the struggle for spoils and office once the military (themselves not unconcerned with spoils or office) had ceded political authority to them. As General Gowon declared, when he announced the indefinite postponement of the return to civilian rule on Independence Day 1974, four years after enunciating the nine-point plan, and two years before the vesting day for constitutional government:

> . . . there has already emerged such a high degree of sectional politick-
> ing, intemperate utterances and writings, all designed to whip up
> ill-feeling within the country to the benefit of a few . . . . We had
> thought that genuine demonstration of moderation and self-control
> in pursuing sectional ends in the overall interest of the country would
> have become the second nature of Nigerians.[69]

Nigeria has demonstrated its capacity to achieve a high rate of growth of manufactured output, and to establish certain producer goods industries. Neither the military government nor its political rivals has demonstrated the capacity to establish the social institutions necessary for a successful Nigerian 'capitalist revolution',[70] and the maintenance of a capitalist society.[71]

Notes

1 E.O. Akeredolu-Ale, 'The Competitive Threshold Hypothesis and Nigeria's Industrial-isation Process' (review of Kilby, *Industrialisation*), *Nigerian Journal of Economic and Social Studies* (hereafter *NJESS*), 14, 1972.

2 See John F. Weeks, 'Employment, Growth and Foreign Domination in Underdeveloped Countries', *Review of Radical Political Economics*, 4, 1972.

3 See P.C. Asiodu, 'Industrial Policy and Incentives in Nigeria', *NJESS*, 9, 1967, and compare P.C. Asiodu cited *Financial Times*, 4 August 1969: 'The Nigerian system, which is essentially pragmatic, has worked well in the past . . . . Excepting . . . [iron and steel] the whole field of industry remains open to private initiative. The usual tax and tariff incentives will be maintained'. Asiodu was then Permanent Secretary in the Federal Ministry of Mines and Power. He was compulsorily retired in 1975.

4 A striking recent example is the reintroduction of import licences for cars under 2000 cc capacity to protect the newly established Volkswagen and Peugeot assembly plants. Peugeot will presumably need this measure of protection to pay the cost of airlifting bodies and engines from Lyon to Kaduna, where Nigerian-made batteries, fittings, and furnishings will be added. *West Africa*, 3015, 7 April 1975, p. 409.

5 Williams, 'Social Stratification'. Cf. *Review of African Political Economy* (hereafter *RAPE*), 2, 1975 for an analysis of the activities of multinational corporations in other African countries.

6 See A.J. Peace, 'Industrial Conflict in Nigeria', in E. de Kadt and G. Williams eds., *Sociology and Development*, London, 1974.

7 The best theoretical analysis of petty commodity production is C. Gerry, 'Petty Producers and Capitalism', *RAPE*, 3, 1975; Cf. J.F. Weeks, 'Imbalance between the Centre and the Periphery and the "Employment" Crisis in Kenya', in Oxaal, *et.al.*, ed., *Beyond the Sociology of Development*.

8 Lloyd, 'Integration of New Economic Classes', 'Local Government in Yoruba Towns', D Phil thesis, University of Oxford, 1958; Post and Jenkins, *Price of Liberty*; G. Williams, 'Political Consciousness among the Ibadan Poor', in de Kadt and Williams, *Sociology and Development*.

9 See E.O. Akeredolu-Ale, *The Underdevelopment of Indigenous Entrepreneurship in Nigeria*, Ibadan, 1975, and Williams, 'Social Stratification', pp. 233–5.

10 Osoba, 'Ideological Trends'.

11 Cf. Nigeria, *Report of the Advisory Committee on Aids to African Businessmen*, Lagos, 1959; the memorandum of the Committee of Vice-Chancellors of Nigerian Universities; the demands of Nigerian academics for fringe benefits and a leading academic's description of their 'penury', *West Africa*, 7 May 1973; and the critique by Otoni Nduka, 'The Anatomy of Rationalisation', *Nigerian Opinion*, 7, I (1971), reprinted in P.C.W. Gutkind and Peter Waterman (eds.) *African Social Studies: a Radical Reader*, London, 1975.

12 Nigeria, *Second and Final Report of the Wages and Salaries Review Commission, 1970–71*, Chairman, S.O. Adebo, Lagos, 1971, esp. pp. 13–15, 24–31; *White Paper on the Second and Final Report of the Wages and Salaries Commission, 1970–71*, Lagos, 1971, esp. pp. 8–10.

13 Nigeria, *Government Views on the Report of the Public Service Commission*, Lagos, 1974, summarised in *West Africa*, 13, 20, 27 January 1975. Cf. 'Nigeria's Response to Udoji', *West Africa*, 3 March 1975.

14 11 February 1974, p. 143.

15 P. Collins, 'The Political Economy of Indigenisation', *The African Review*, 4, 1975.

16 Osoba, 'Ideological Trends'.

17 *Ideology and Utopia*, London, 1940.

18 Williams, 'Political Consciousness'.

19 See Koll, *Crafts and Co-operation*.

20 Williams, 'Political Consciousness'.

21 Cf. Peace, 'Lagos Factory Workers and Urban Belief Systems', University of Adelaide, 1974, 'Social Change at Agege', D Phil thesis, University of Sussex, 1973.

22 Peace, 'Lagos Factory Workers'.

23 See D. Remy, 'Economic Security and Industrial Unionism' on differences among workers. For a general overview of labour in Nigeria, and a comprehensive bibliography, see R. Cohen, *Labour and Politics in Nigeria*, London, 1974.

24 Cf. the accounts of events in Lagos, Kano and Zaria respectively in 1971 in Peace, 'Towards a Nigerian Working Class: the Lagos Proletariat as a Political Elite'; P. Lubeck, 'Unions, Workers and Consciousness in Kano'; and Remy, 'Economic Security' in R. Cohen and R. Sandbrook (eds.), *The Development of an African Working Class*, London, 1976. For a list of government commissions up to 1971 see Cohen, *Labour and Politics*, pp. 284–6, with note 13 above for 1975.

25 Cf. G. Arrighi and J. Saul, 'Socialism and Economic Development in Tropical Africa', *Journal of Modern African Studies* (hereafter *JMAS*), 6, 1968, and G. Arrighi, 'International Corporations, Labour Aristocracies and Economic Development in Tropical Africa', in R. Rhodes ed., *Imperialism and Underdevelopment*, New York, 1970, both reprinted in G. Arrighi and J. Saul, *The Political Economy of Tropical Africa*, New York, 1972; P. Kilby, *Industrialisation in an Open Economy, 1943–66*, Cambridge, 1969; Cf. Peter Waterman, 'The "Labour Aristocracy" in Africa', *Development and Change*, 6, 1975.

26 The evidence on rural-urban income differentials is critically reviewed by C.H. Allen, 'Unions, Incomes and Development', *Developmental Trends in Kenya* (Centre of African Studies, 1972), part reprinted in Gutkind and Waterman, *African Social*

Studies; and in a careful case study for Kaduna by K. Hinchliffe, 'Labour Aristocracy—a Northern Nigerian Case Study', *JMAS*, 12, 1974. The long debate as to whether trade unions have increased real wages in Nigeria is reviewed in Cohen, *Labour and Politics*, chapter 6.

27 Cf. W.A. Lewis. *Reflections on Nigeria's Economic Growth*, Paris, 1967; Helleiner, *Peasant Agriculture*, p. 140. See critique by S.M. Essang and S.O. Olayide, 'Economic Development or Income Distribution?: a False Dilemma', *Nigerian Journal of Sociology and Anthropology*, 1, 1974.

28 Available empirical evidence consistently indicates high average and marginal rates of savings for Nigerian farmers through a wide range of incomes. See R. Galetti, *et.al. Nigerian Cocoa Farmers*, London, 1956, pp. 471–5, 596–7; M. Upton, *Agriculture in South-Western Nigeria*, University of Reading, 1967, p. 42; G.E. Okurume, *The Food Crop Economy in Nigerian Agricultural Policy*, East Lansing and Ibadan, 1969, pp. 91–2. Cf. Berry 'Cocoa and Economic Development', Hill, *Rural Capitalism*.

29 *Arise ye Starvelings: The Jamaican Labour Rebellion of 1938* (forthcoming).

30 Williams, 'Political Consciousness', Peace, 'Urban Belief System', Cf. B.B. Lloyd, 'Education and Family Life in the Development of Class Identification among the Yoruba', and P.C. Lloyd, 'Class Consciousness among the Yoruba', in P.C. Lloyd ed., *The New Elites of Tropical Africa*, London, 1966.

31 Cf. Williams, review of Post, *The Price of Liberty*, in *African Affairs*, 283, 1974.

32 Peace, 'Towards a Nigerian Working Class', Cf. R. Jeffries, 'Labour Aristocracy? a Ghana Case Study', *RAPE*, 3, 1975.

33 See F. Fanon's superb analysis of 'The Pitfalls of National Consciousness', *The Wretched of the Earth*, London 1966; Williams, 'Social Stratification'.

34 Billy J. Judley, 'Federalism and the Balance of Political Power in Nigeria', *Journal of Commonwealth Political Studies*, 4, 1966; R.L. Sklar, 'Contradictions in the Nigerian Political System', *JMAS*, 3, 1965; K.W.J. Post and M. Vickers, *Structure and Conflict in Nigeria*, London, 1973, reviewed by Williams, *African Affairs*, 280, 1974.

35 This is not to suggest that this process is typically Nigerian, or African; US politics suggest perhaps that it is typically capitalist. And even today, it is not unlike the home life of our own dear politicians in the British Labour movement, as we know so well in North-East England.

36 Post and Vickers, *Structure and Conflict*; Post, *The Nigerian Federal Election of 1959*, London, 1963; Sklar, *Nigerian Political Parties*; J.P. Mackintosh, *Nigerian Government and Politics*, London, 1966; Williams, 'The Political Sociology of Western Nigeria', B Phil thesis, University of Oxford, 1967; Federation of Nigeria, *Report of the Commission of Enquiry into the Affairs of Certain Statutory Corporations in Western Nigeria*, Chairman, Mr Justice Coker, Lagos, 1962.

37 The most extensive analysis and indictment is S.O. Osoba, 'The Colonial Antecedents and Contemporary Development of Nigerian Foreign Policy', PhD thesis, Moscow State University, 1967.

38 A. Gramsci, *Selections from the Prison Notebooks*, London, 1971, *passim*.

39 A.M.H. Kirk-Greene ed., *Crisis and Conflict in Nigeria: a Documentary Sourcebook, 1966–70* (2 vols.), London, 1971; S.K. Panter-Brick ed., *Nigerian Politics and Military Rule*, London, 1970; R. Luckham, *The Nigerian Military*, Cambridge, 1971; R. First, *The Barrel of a Gun*, London, 1970; N.U. Akpan, *The Struggle for Secession, 1966–1970*, London, 1972; Billy J. Dudley, *Instability and Political Order*, Ibadan, 1973; C.C. Aguolu, *Nigerian Civil War, 1967–70*. An Annotated *Bibliography*, Boston, 1973.

40 First, *Barrel of a Gun*, pp. 320, 338, 354; A. Ayida, 'The Nigerian Revolution, 1966–76', Presidential address to Nigerian Economic Society, Ibadan, 1973, reported in *Africa Confidential*, 14, no. 13. Mr Ayida was then Permanent Secretary in the Ministry of Finance. In 1975 General Gowon appointed him Secretary to the Military Government.

41 The term is Philip Corrigan's. He applies it to the civil servant reformers of nineteenth-century England in 'Appeals to Society', BA dissertation, Department of Sociology, University of Durham, 1973.

42 Cf. H. Alavi, 'The Post-colonial State', *New Left Review*, 74, 1972; R. First, *Libya*,

Penguin, 1974. Cf. Corrigan, 'Appeals', and *Socialist Construction*, chapter 3; S. Graham, 'The Failure of Reform in Peru', BA dissertation, Department of Sociology, University of Durham, 1974.

43 The failure to recognise this seems to me to be the major fault in Bill Warren's 'Imperialism and Capitalist Industrialisation', *New Left Review*, 81, 1973, and to have been missed in the outcry at his heresies against the orthodoxies of the theory of underdevelopment, *New Left Review*, 84, 1974.

44 *Daily Times* (Lagos), 2 May 1973.

45 'Development Objectives', in A.A. Ayida and H.M.A. Onitiri eds., *Reconstruction and Development in Nigeria*, Ibadan, 1971.

46 *Daily Times*, 19, 20 March 1973; L. Rupley, 'Revenue Allocation Once Again', and 'The Next Revenue Allocation', *West Africa*, 1, 8 July 1974 and 6 January 1975.

47 Numerous people in Ibadan gave this reason to the author in 1970–71 for preferring a continuation of military rule to any prospect of the return of politicians.

48 Independence Day speech, 1974, in *West Africa*, 7 October 1974.

49 *Daily Times of Nigeria, The First Ten Years, Independent Nigeria*, Lagos, 1970, p. 4. Cf. A. Atta, 'The Development of Nigeria's Political Personality', *Quarterly Journal of Administration*, 6, 1971. Mr Atta was head of the civil service until his death in 1972.

50 Lagos, 1970. The plan is critically reviewed in *Quaterly Journal of Administration*, 5, 3 (1971).

51 Lagos 1973. The plan is outlined in *The Times* (London), 4 March 1975 (advertisement), and printed in *Africa*, 1975, and in more detail in *West Africa*, 7 April 1975.

52 Turi Muhammadu, 'Private Sector versus Public Sector', *New Nigerian* (Kanduna), 1 May 1973. Prof. Aboyade was the government's main adviser on economic policy. He was appointed Vice-Chancellor of the University of Ife in 1975. Chief Henry Fajemirokun and other spokesmen of the Chamber of Commerce have been the leading spokesmen for the private sector. For Asiodu's views, see *Daily Times*, 19, 20 March 1973. See also *Daily Times*, 19, 22 January 1973, 24 January, 4 February, 23 April 1974; *Sunday Times* (Lagos), 18, 25 November 1973; West *Africa*, 13 January 1975.

53 *Daily Times*, 13 January 1973; *Guidelines*, p. 11.

54 *Guidelines*, p. 14.

55 General Gowon, 1974 Budget speech, in *Daily Times*, 2 April 1974.

56 *West Africa*, 27 January 1975. See also issue of 7 April 1975.

57 1975 producer prices are cocoa ₦660, groundnuts ₦250, special palm oil ₦280, palm kernels ₦150, cotton ₦308 per ton. Cf. D. Olatunbosun and S.O. Olayide, 'Effects of the Marketing Boards on the Output and Income of Primary Producer', in Onitiri and Olatunbosun eds., *The Marketing Board System*.

58 *West Africa*, 31 March 1975.

59 Nigeria's current defence budget is ₦547 million of a total of ₦4 890 million. For a critique of Nigeria's rural development strategy, see Williams, 'Taking the Part of Peasants', P.C.W. Gutkind and I. Wallerstein eds., *The Political Economy of Contemporary Africa*, Los Angeles, 1976.

60 *Daily Times*, 11 June 1974; *New Nigerian*, 5, 12 July, 2, 9 August 1974.

61 *West Africa*, 24 February 1975.

62 On the history of Nigeria's trade union centres, see Cohen, *Labour and Politics*. For a critique of the Marxist NTUC and SWAFP, see Waterman, 'Communist Theory in the Nigerian Trade Union Movement', *Politics and Society*, 1973.

63 20 July 1973. See list of names of census officials, published in *New Nigerian* on 18 and again on 19 July. Of the 29, 19 are recognisably Yoruba.

64 Reported *West Africa*, 14 October 1974.

65 Reported, and criticised, *Daily Times*, 8 June 1974.

66 For census figures for 1952–3, 1963, 1973, see *West Africa*, 20 May 1974. Cf. Rupley, 'The Next Revenue Allocation'.

67 See *West Africa*, 18, 25 February 1975.

68 See *West Africa*, 5, 12, 19, 26 August, 2, 9, 16, 23 September 1974, 13 January 1975. Cf. letter by S. Egite Oyovbaire, 4 November 1974.

69 Reported *West Africa*, 4 October 1974.

70 Cf. B. Moore, jr. 'The American Civil War: the Last Capitalist Revolution', *Social Origins of Dictatorship and Democracy*, Boston, 1966, chapter 3.

71 Cf. speeches by Brig. Murtala Muhammed, *Daily Times*, 31 July, 1 August, 1975.

4 The Multinationals in Africa*

THE EDITORS OF THE REVIEW OF AFRICAN POLITICAL ECONOMY

It is all but impossible to summarise the impact of the multinational corporation (MNC) on Africa, for these firms play many parts: they are the expanded colonial trading companies; they are the vanguard of the most advanced technology, but also the purveyors of overpriced obsolete equipment; they are rapacious exploiters of raw materials and labour, but also the invaluable allies of petty-bourgeois élitist and in some cases 'progressive' governments; they are a source of capital, but also the major agents of profit repatriation and resource outflow. Which of these features is dominant depends on the specific circumstances of their operations.

This issue of the Review looks specifically at the operations of MNCs in four situations: in the Ivory Coast we see the French textile industry 'adjusting' to independence and maintaining its former position, courtesy of the new government; in Kenya we see the international soap giants destroying a local industry and displacing a functionally superior product by using a combination of market power and technological superiority; in Mauretania we see a mining giant controlling the exploitation of rich mineral resources so as to serve the interests of the West European producers who own the mining company; and finally in Tanzania we see a government which has taken nominal control of their MNC subsidiaries struggling to find an effective way of exercising this control.

Unfortunately, as case studies none of these articles provides an explicit view of the nature of international capitalist development, but without this it is difficult to assess the ultimate significance of the experiences described. While the MNC's hierarchical, supra-national and institutional character is undoubtedly important, and while its relations with nation-states are equally important, an understanding of these phenomena must be derived from an analysis of the forces underlying the international expansion of capital.

MNCs and the Accumulation of Capital

Capitalist development has always involved increasing concentration, and historically this has led to the creation of ever larger units, both of production and of management and control. The critical need for continued accumulation and expansion has forced firms to invest in new plant on an ever-increasing scale. This, combined with new technologies requiring increasingly larger 'production runs', has led to the familiar combination of bankruptcy, merger and expansion.

But even more important than the physical and technical aspects of these developments have been the financial implications, since the mobilisation of investment resources on the scale required is possible only for enormous organisations.

---

* From the *Review of African Political Economy*, 2, 1975, pp. 1–11.

These tendencies of course only reinforce the age-old search for opportunities for monopoly in the market, and this takes place through vertical integration and control of primary inputs, and/or through attempts to use product differentiation in order to protect the product market from substitutes.

It is clear therefore that the forces which underlie the processes described are not new, nor are international firms new (as, for example, the East India Company and the United Africa Company show). What is new is the scale and the prevalence of such operations, as well as the high degree of centralised control made possible by modern communications even when operations are highly scattered. Hence according to a UN study, the nine largest US oil multi-nationals had crude oil operations in 40 countries in 1938 and in 96 countries in 1967, while their subsidiaries in all petroleum-related activities increased in number during this period from 351 to 1 442. The MNCs are thus an integral part of the expansion of capital on a global scale, but for all its international dimensions, most of the capital involved still has a 'national' base both in terms of its origin and in terms of its control.

Not surprisingly the US has been responsible for the accumulation of the largest share of capital since the Second World War. US companies account for 60–65 per cent of all foreign direct investment—one third of which is in oil and one third of which is located in Europe. The book value of US companies in Europe was 25 billion dollars in 1970, which represented a six-fold increase from the 1957 level. During the same period the book value of European firms' assets in the US increased 250 per cent, amounting to 9.4 billion dollars by 1970.

Contrary to some expectations, most capital exports have been to the developed countries. Between 1961 and 1971, 460 US corporations established 11 061 operations abroad, and only 2 703 of these were in less-developed countries. In 1967 the UN estimated that 32 per cent of all foreign investment was in less-developed countries, but these patterns may well change in the light of the current crisis in the world economy. On one hand, the greater risks imposed by current instabilities may reduce the flow of investment funds. On the other hand, the increasingly fierce competition between the major capitalist centres will encourage each of these to invest in order to ensure material supplies from its particular sphere of influence, and this may well lead to regional increases in investment flows to the Third World.

MNCs and Underdeveloped Countries

Defenders of the MNCs' role point out that they provide scarce capital; provide equally scarce technology and know-how which provide commodities at lower prices for more people; in some cases provide access to export markets; and contribute through the taxes paid and the employment created to local development. Each of these claims, however, can be challenged.

First, although the MNCs provide capital, they do so to a much lesser extent than might be supposed from looking at figures of assets owned. Where such investment involves taking over existing facilities (admittedly more likely in developed country investment), there is no transfer of real resources or of capital goods, though in the short run there would be an easing of the import restraint. Where foreign enterprises start new ventures, it is common to raise much, if not most, of the capital required from the local economy, and this is a trend that is further encouraged by the proliferation of joint government-MNC ventures. Moreover, the benefits of the inflow which does take place are critically dependent on whether these resources are complementary to local resources—ie. their presence helps to mobilise previously idle resources or capacities—or whether they are competitive—ie. they destroy local productive activities and reduce local capital goods to scrap. Often the latter is true.

Finally, it is vital to remember that equity investment (ie. shareholding) is the worst possible form of 'assistance' for profitable ventures, since the claims on earnings (eg. dividend payments to shareholders) which it generates are essentially unlimited both in terms of their size and their duration. Heavy reliance on foreign equity thereby generates increasing claims on resources which must be offset by increasing foreign exchange inflows. *For MNCs operating in Latin America each dollar of net profit generated from 1960 to 1968 was based on investment that was 83 per cent financed from local sources, but only 21 per cent of this profit remained in the country.*

The problem of the outflow of resources is, furthermore, much greater than is suggested by looking at declared profit statements, since 'profits' can be shifted to any section of an integrated operation by pricing goods and services traded between different sections and branches in a certain way, through, for example, overpricing purchases and underpricing sales of a subsidiary which is supposed to make little or no profit. In addition, inflating the book values of assets allows what profit is earned to appear modest in proportion. For these reasons, therefore, the capital transfer functions of MNCs need careful scrutiny if an assessment of their net effect is to be made. Secondly, the MNCs do 'bring' modern technology to Third World countries, but there is again a question of the net effect. Certainly there are enormous potential benefits to be derived from international technology, and some countries, like Japan, have benefited greatly from assimilating and developing that technology. Unfortunately, the multinationals do not encourage the assimilation of technology in this sense, and one of the most striking features of Japan's assimilation has been precisely the fact that by and large they have not received the technology through the agency of MNCs. But simply introducing such technology, while impeding its assimilation, control and development, provides a very limited benefit at a considerable cost. More seriously it undercuts whatever local technological development exists or *might* develop otherwise. While the costs of this are not quantifiable, they may ultimately be extremely high in many countries.

Thirdly, it is true that MNCs are sometimes essential agents in gaining access to certain international markets, like those for oil or diamonds. While this may make them indispensable for a particular economy, it is hardly a 'benefit' of MNCs from a broader perspective, since it is their control of markets which makes their agency necessary in the first place. In addition, it is often the case that MNCs actively discourage exports in line with their global marketing strategies.

Finally, it is undeniable that MNCs do make major contributions to many public purses. This again can hardly be counted a net benefit without taking into account revenue lost through the outflow of funds or the other losses occasioned by their activities. In any event the generation of this revenue is not dependent on the MNCs as such, and would be equal or greater if the activities in question were financed through loan capital and managed individually.

Worse is the fact that the MNCs are often in a position to force Third World countries to forego large chunks of this potential revenue by demanding and obtaining extensive tax concessions. Their demands along these lines become more insistent and effective as the country in question becomes increasingly dependent on capital inflows to balance the effects of capital outflows generated by the stock of existing foreign capital.

In conclusion, there are undoubtedly some occasions when the activities of MNCs provide net long term benefits to an economy. By the same token there are undoubtedly even more where their effects are ultimately negative.

The MNCs in Africa

South Africa has long been a base for the operations of MNCs, and even today, with two-thirds of its direct investment still coming from abroad, it continues to represent the centre of gravity for MNC operations in Africa. Nevertheless, recent decades have witnessed a rapid increase in the penetration of MNCs of the economies of the entire continent, often with a predominance of the negative effects described above.

The MNCs' activities have taken on a special urgency recently as the extent of the vast mineral wealth of West Africa becomes more clear, and especially as the potential for oil appears greater than had been expected. The major oil companies are presently drilling in 15 African countries. It has been reported that in Angola Gulf Oil has given indirect support to the Cabinda secessionists in an obvious attempt to bring about a more manageable situation there.

It is American MNCs that are in the forefront of the recent drive to exploit Africa's mineral wealth (*African Development*, December 1974), especially with regard to copper in Zaire, bauxite in Guinea and Ghana, iron in Gabon, and copper-nickel in Botswana. This is true even though the American share in total foreign investment is only 15 per cent, compared to the 35 per cent of Britain and 25 per cent of France. Of course this apparent paradox reflects the accumulated total capital stocks resulting from the historical position of the major colonial powers. Indeed, the fact that the American share has grown to such relative size reflects its recent rapid growth. This growth is even more significant than the figure suggests because it is concentrated in the more advanced manufacturing and mining sectors. It represents an increasing challenge to these older-established interests, a challenge that was first mooted in the famous 'winds of change' speech by Harold Macmillan in 1960.

MNCs and the State

It has been the core of Marxist analysis of the state that under capitalism it represents the interests of the dominant capital. More recent analysts have suggested that the nation-state has become powerless in the face of the giant corporations, whose ability to move capital freely across national boundaries has made it all but impossible to control them.

However, this view has been sharply challenged by the actions of countries such as Libya, which have nationalised MNC subsidiaries outright, and by the oil-producing countries' initiatives in increasing the price of petroleum. But much more significantly it has been challenged by the major industrial states whose reaction to the increasing competition among themselves has clearly demonstrated their ability to act together with some of the MNCs to influence international markets and terms of trade in ways that reflect their interests.

Certainly, the capitalist state as such is not powerless, though some Third World states may be close to being so.

The issue becomes rather more complicated when one considers the extent to which the state itself comes to represent the interests of the MNCs. Certainly the state must make the country safe for capital, and hence for the MNCs, but this requires governments to balance the competing demands of rival capitals (principally domestic and international) and of those of other interests, principally those of the working class. This means, clearly, that the states' relations with MNCs will vary over time, but there is no question of either being independent of the other.

The MNCs, then, are not freely-floating, disembodied and denationalised bodies. They have national bases and they require the political, military and economic support provided by their base nation. It is no surprise that only insubstantial, fly-by-night operations actually do move their headquarters to the island tax-havens that are so well publicised. Indeed it seems possible, even probable, that with the United States' unchallenged dominance of the international economy giving way to a much fiercer rivalry, the free-wheeling of the multinationals may be much more firmly constrained in future by the national and/or regional interests that are in conflict.

Some of these points emerge clearly from a consideration of events in what was formerly Portuguese Africa. Here Portugal was actively providing the military and administrative resources required by the MNCs. The victory of the liberation struggles has certainly aroused great concern to ensure that the states which emerge will in fact take up this role in future. This concern reflects a recognition that some states are more easily dealt with than others. In southern Africa the search for 'reasonable' solutions and, what are euphemistically known as 'responsible' governments, is now directed by the great powers in conjunction with their allies, South Africa and Zaire.

Of course there are also differences among MNCs in their approach to local governments. These range from those which operate in a very hard-nosed 'businesslike' manner throwing diplomacy to the winds, and those which assiduously cultivate their local contacts and seek actively to make their interests synonymous with those of the ruling group in particular governments. The most clear-cut example of this latter type must surely be Lonrho, Africa's best known 'conglomerate'.

There are suggestions that Lonrho played a background role in the 1971 coup in the Sudan, and that their Chairman, Duncan Sandys, a former British Cabinet Minister, obtained for the 'new' government a £10 million loan, thus paving the way for Lonrho's advance in the Sudanese economy. Other examples of Lonrho's operations that are less speculative concern the very close personal relations which they have to various governments and leaders. The Company's first black African director, Udi Gecaga, is both Lonrho's managing director in East Africa and President Kenyatta's son-in-law, while the head of Lonrho's Ivory Coast operations is Houphouet-Boigny's son. In Zambia, too, relations with the government are so close that when a board of directors' revolt threatened 'Tiny' Rowland's position as managing director, the Zambian government intervened and offered £8 million to the company as long as Rowland remained in his post. This only shows the very keen appreciation which this company has of the need, from its point of view, to ensure a full representation of its interests in the councils of state.

Of course the interests of the MNCs do often largely overlap with at least the short-term interests of those in control of the state. It is they who are able to provide the hardware required by governments to give the appearance of promoting developments and more directly to consolidate their own political power. But these things are made available only so long as the states in question provide the right sort of climate for the MNCs, not least through inspiring the confidence of investors through tax concessions and a clear willingness and ability to ensure 'law and order'.

It has been noted that this two-way relationship between MNCs and the state is not particular to the less-developed countries. It is clear from the oil crisis to date that its explanation must be based on a recognition of the temporary coincidence of interests between the Middle Eastern states, the MNCs and the US economy. For the Arab countries higher prices, a bigger share of the proceeds and slower production rates was an unmistakable blessing; for the MNCs, and especially for the dominant American MNCs, restriction of supply for a product with an inelastic demand was the classic oligopolist's response, while for the American firms there was also a clear additional benefit derived from closing the embarrassing gap, both politically and economically increasingly untenable, between low world oil prices and high American domestic oil prices (that is, producer prices, not retail prices); finally, the oil crisis has had the effect of blunting the European and Japanese challenges to the American economy which had established the international monetary system in conjunction with American military adventures overseas, in a development which symbolised the demise of American economic hegemony. It is no coincidence that these events have been accompanied by the arrival in the White House of Nelson Rockefeller and by the arrival in the State Department of Henry Kissinger, his long time friend and advisor.

Of course such strategies are not without risks, and there is just a possibility that the oil states will take their independence 'too far' and will step out from under the tutelage of 'their' MNCs and begin to sell directly to individual states, as Libya has done already to ENI, the Italian state-owned oil corporation. Kissinger's recent threat of military intervention, should the oil states become 'unreasonable' and threaten the international economy, must be interpreted in this context.

Both the state and the MNCs are thus protagonists in a struggle in which the interests of different MNCs are far from coincident. Certainly the present 'crisis' has brought great advantages to the oil MNCs, at the expense of some other MNC groups, just as it has brought benefits to the American economy in relation to its competitors. For Africa this new conflict between the major powers can only mean more instability and more competition for its resources. This may improve opportunities for playing off one group against another, but it may also provoke tendencies towards more direct control of resource bases. After all, neo-colonialism is not a new phenomenon but has rather been the form of imperialism during periods when one power was sufficiently dominant economically to achieve its ends through 'indirect' means. Such a period seems presently to be coming to an end.

Challenging the Multinationals

The increasing penetration of Africa by the MNCs raises the question of how one can deal with their impact. It is sometimes suggested that this can be done satisfactorily through minor reforms in tax structures, in transfer pricing mechanisms or in programmes to employ local staff, and that it must be done in this way lest the corporations are alienated as potential investors. Unfortunately this last stricture is rather arbitrary in its effect and represents a threat which severely constrains the ability of governments to act effectively in these marginal ways.

Beyond such marginal action lies the strategy of nationalisation. Unfortunately nationalisation does not guarantee success, or even improvement. It is a sobering thought to see MNCs in some cases queueing up to be nationalised, and it is necessary to ask why this should be so. It is surely related to the extensive possibilities for MNCs to manipulate such joint ventures in order to derive even greater benefit than was previously the case. That this is possible is clear when it is realised that under such agreements: demands for protection and for concessions are more likely to be successful; that losses, however incurred, become arguments for greater protection and for public subsidy; that labour can be treated more brusquely; and that the public purse is committed to providing a large share of the operating capital. Hence, while such a strategy does raise the possibility of greater government control, it also harbours the danger of even cruder forms of exploitation.

Indeed, it is only if such nationalisation takes place in a situation where the oppressed hold political power, that it can achieve its purpose. It is undoubtedly true that the working class organisations which confront the MNC's challenge to their political and economic position can learn valuable lessons from looking at the problems raised by the attempts of countries like Tanzania to confront the challenge and to use it for their own purposes. It is all too easy for bureaucracies to slip into a fatal dependence on the MNCs, while covering this state of affairs under a pseudo-radical rhetoric equating 'socialism' with state participation. From this position then come righteous calls for sacrifice and discipline by the working class in the (so-called) national interest.

The increasing internationalisation of capital requires in the final analysis the increasing internationalisation of labour, for the ability to hold workers to ransom by the threat of re-locating production can be met only by international workers' solidarity. This means that trade union power in the industrial economies will be eroded to the extent that the MNCs do actually reduce the degree to which they are based in a particular political economy. Just as the emergence of a 'national' rather than a 'regional' economy in Britain led to the break-down of the 'tramping system' as a sensible response to local unemployment, and just as technical change and the assembly line have harboured an insistent demand for industrial unionism, so present developments call for another, and very difficult, step—namely, the development of international unionism.

This will surely be difficult, impaired by the existence of large international differentials and blocked at every step by the nationalist and racist ideologies always so ready to hand. Indeed, this kind of mystification is all too easily derived from critical analyses of MNCs which can readily come to buttress simple-minded forms of nationalism and xenophobia. On the other hand, to the extent that power continues to be exercised on a national plane, it is necessary to consider policy on this plane and to analyse the consequences of certain actions on that national economy.

In this case, as with most important questions of social development, there are no easy answers. Strategies to deal with MNCs must have both national and international dimensions, and questions regarding the correct weighting of the two cannot be answered except in relation to the historical realities of particular instances.

Bibliographical Note

Volume 1 of Marx's *Capital* (Lawrence and Wishart, chapter 23) is essential reading on the process of accumulation of capital. Particularly useful on the multinational and intercapitalist rivalry is C. Tugenhadt's *The Multinationals*, Penguin, 1973, and S. Hymer and R. Rowthorn, 'Multinational Corporations and International Oligopoly: the non-American challenge', in C.P. Kindleberger ed., *The International Corporation*, MIT, 1970. Chapter 9 of Michael Barratt Brown's *Economics of Imperialism*, Penguin, 1974, provides a good summary of the debate on the left about the 'large firm'. The United Nations Department of Economic and Social Affairs, *Multinational Corporations in World Development*, Praeger, 1974, is a thorough survey of the growth and dominance of the corporations and has a large statistical section, though much of the data only goes up to 1967.

On the impact of the MNCs on the Third World, see Ronald Müller, 'The Multinational Corporation and the Underdevelopment of the Third World' in Charles K. Wilber ed., *The Political Economy of Development and Under-development*, Random House, 1973, which is concise and informative, though deals with the MNCs and Latin America. On the oil MNCs and their relationship to American economic and political strategy see Ruth First, *Libya*, Penguin, 1974, chapter 10; also, Peter Odel, *Oil and World Power*, Penguin, 1974.

On foreign investment in South Africa, and the role of more recent American capital see Ruth First, Jonathan Steele and Christabel Gurney, *The South African Connection*, Penguin, 1973. And on Lonrho, Suzanne Cronje, 'The Lonrho Row', in *New Statesman*, 27 April 1973, has a great deal of useful information on the company's links with African governments.

Part Two
The Internal Structures of Dependency

Introduction and Select Bibliography

DENNIS L. COHEN

The second part of the collection is directed towards the structures within dependent areas in terms of social stratification and state institutions, which are engendered by, linked to and which facilitate the international structures of dependency discussed in Part One.

The analysis of social stratification in Africa has a long and chequered history as an area of academic controversy. Much of this scholarly dialogue is, in fact, an ideological polemic engaged in by Western scholars who reject Marxist class analysis because of its political implications. They have tended, instead, to use class concepts divorced of their analytical content and reduced to empirical constructs of only descriptive value, or have emphasised the importance of other stratifying factors, especially ethnicity, as being dominant in the sphere of social consciousness.

Rejecting these distortions, we prefer to frame our discussion of social stratification within a Marxist context, and to include articles which fit this framework. Such a usage sees classes as based upon the social relations of production in any society, but specifically, in the context of the capitalist societies being analysed here, upon the contradiction between those who own/control the means of production, on the one hand, and on the other hand that other class, consisting of those producers who are separated from their means of production and who, in order to engage in the labour necessary for their survival and reproduction, have no alternative but to sell their labour.

This standard pattern of capitalist social relations, culminating in the development of class consciousness and conflict as the gap between the two classes, the dominant bourgeoisie and the exploited proletariat, grows, is made more complex in the situation of dependency by at least two factors. First, uneven and combined development produced in the dependent areas by capitalist domination results in the coexistence of multiple modes of production within the same social formation, and of multiple class relations based upon these different modes. Non-capitalist classes, such as peasants and traditional rulers, survive and have important functions as they are linked to capitalist structures, whilst individuals can play multiple class roles, moving from one system to another, as when an urban bureaucrat accumulates surplus value from his salary which he invests in developing land which he controls through his feudal family relations. Secondly, dependency blocks the development of an indigenous bourgeoisie in the dependent areas, a role played by the external, international bourgeoisie, and gives much greater scope to the development of those intermediate strata of shopkeepers, self-employed artisans and craftsmen, professionals, civil servants, army officers, intellectual workers, etc., often lumped together under the heading of the petty bourgeoisie. The importance of the role of the petty bourgeoisie in political and ideological domination, rather than its relations to production, is stressed by many scholars.

Another important focus of analysis in this area is on the political consciousness of the dominated classes, the peasantry and the proletariat. The unorthodox views of Fanon have been influential with many who have confidence in the revolutionary potential of the peasants and distrust the conservative role of the so-called 'labour aristocracy'. Both these views are critically discussed here, and bring us to a discussion of the role of the state, which pulls together the various strands of class analysis and sharpens the political context of these intellectual controversies.

The first selection, 'Class and the Analysis of African Politics: Problems and Prospects', by D.L. Cohen, surveys the controversy over the applicability of Marxist class analysis to Africa, and advances a framework for such an analysis. Rejecting the concepts of African classlessness and cultural pluralism, as well as the eclectic formulation of transitional classes, Cohen seeks to identify bourgeois, proletarian and peasant classes, to discuss their particular characteristics in the African context, and to speculate on their role in the processes of political change.

The following selections expand on various areas of class analysis touched on by Cohen. The first two deal with particular classes—peasants and proletarians—and the latter two with class conflicts in particular social formations —South Africa and Nigeria.

The brief article by John Saul and Roger Woods, 'African Peasantries', performs a useful service in de-mystifying Fanonist views of the peasantry and essaying an analysis of rural differentiation. By defining peasants as those who have some family rights to control of the means of production, and who also use these means to produce some output for the market, they are able to differentiate peasants from the rural proletariat, who have been wholly separated from the means of production and can only sell their labour; subsistence farmers who are not tied to the capitalist market; and rural capitalists who buy and sell their means of production. They also discuss differentiation within the peasantry between wealthier peasants (often known as kulaks and considered a petty bourgeois group) and poorer peasants. Finally, they relate these class strata to varying political interests and activities, pointing towards the need for detailed case studies to analyse the actual political potential of different groups in different places. Such a conclusion is the beginning of a scientific analysis of rural politics, and a useful corrective to the messianic tendencies of Fanon's views.

The 'labour aristocracy' concept has a long history in Marxist analysis and has been extensively used in discussion of the African proletariat by Arrighi and Saul, Fitch and Oppenheimer, and others. It has been used to deny the utility of class analysis in Africa; to justify policies holding down the wage levels of African workers and controlling their organised expressions of greivance; and to attribute political conservatism to African workers. Peter Waterman's 'The "Labour Aristocracy" in Africa: Introduction to an Unfinished Controversy', summarises the debate on this issue and concludes that the economically privileged position of African workers has been exaggerated; that the elitist psychology often attributed to them has little basis in empirical evidence; and that the political consciousness and activities of this class have been much more radical than is often claimed.

Waterman, like Saul and Woods in their discussion of peasants, is highly conscious of differentiation between categories of workers, especially between the small industrial proletariat, who have tended to be in the vanguard of radical political movements in Africa, and the larger category of skilled, clerical

76

and managerial employees, whose education, incomes and life-style set them off from the former. Waterman also discusses the political consequences of these differences. Both these articles are directed at the important task of producing an original analysis of the particular kinds of class formations found in a dependent, capitalist mode of production.

Sam Mhlongo's 'An Analysis of the Classes in South Africa', represents an attempt to apply class analysis to the understanding of a concrete social formation—the Republic of South Africa. As such, he is forced to deal with some of the anomalous problems of cultural pluralism and intensifying capitalist relations both specific to South Africa and broadly characteristic of Africa as a whole.

A controversial feature of his article is the analysis of separate class fractions along racial lines, ie. the Afrikaner bourgeoisie, the Indian urban petty bourgeoisie, the African urban petty bourgeoisie, white urban workers, etc. Such an analysis is seen as essential in the South African situation, where race not only structures cultural consciousness but also defines relations of production. Mhlongo does not make the mistake, however, of elevating these racial divisions into determinant categories of social action, seeing them instead as an overlay which increases the complexity, but does not obviate the significance, of the basic class divisions in society.

For example, the specific historical conditions in which the white working class was formed are seen as explaining its alliance with capital against African workers, which produced, in turn, the evolution of its production relations in a way that further separated it from its original class cohorts. At the same time, the restriction of the black petty bourgeoisie to a miniscule role explains its willingness to cooperate with black workers in broad movements for democratic, and, in the South African context, revolutionary change.

Secondly, Mhlongo rejects a two-step theory of revolution in South Africa, ie. national democratic first, proletarian socialist second, in favour of a proletarian-led, socialist revolution as the immediate goal of the class struggle. This conclusion is based upon his rejection of the significance of the South African peasantry and African petty bourgeoisie as important political actors, as well as his view of the cohesiveness and unyielding style of rule of the white ruling class. Some of these judgments may be questionable—by those, for example, who believe that the Homelands policy represents a viable strategy to create a black bourgeoisie which can act as a reliable, junior partner to Pretoria. Mhlongo, nevertheless, has provided a useful framework for the continuation of this debate.

Finally, Terisa Turner's 'Commercial Capitalism in Nigeria: The Pattern of Competition' examines the class relations of neo-colonialism in the more typical setting of Nigeria. The analysis here of the relations between foreign capital, indigenous compradors and the Nigerian state pursues some of the points made in Part One by Gavin Williams.

Ms. Turner concentrates on this 'triangular relationship' of economic exchange and political influence, showing how the pattern of cooperation and conflict produces both a hierarchy of benefit and a mutuality of interest between the members of the triad. Elsewhere, she has clothed this argument with greater specificity in explaining the nature of Nigerian political regimes and *coups*.

The high level of controversy in the area of class and state analysis found here and in the earlier sections indicates that this is a fertile field for further development, and that increased sophistication of our conceptual framework for understanding the internal structures of dependency is urgently needed.

Select Bibliography

1 Class theory and the bourgeoisie

E.O. Akeredolu-Ali, 'Private Investment and the Under-development of Indigenous Entrepreneurship in Nigeria', in G. Williams ed., *Nigeria: Economy and Society*, Rex Collings, London, 1972.

Samir Amin, 'Class Struggle in Africa', *Revolution*, 1, 9 (1964).

D.R. Aronson, 'Ijebu Yoruba Urban-Rural Relationships and Class Formation', *Canadian Journal of African Studies*, 5, 3 (1971).

Björn Beckmann, *Organising the Farmers: Cocoa Politics and National Development in Ghana*, Scandinavian Institute of African Studies, Uppsala, 1976.

Charles Bettelheim, *Class Struggles in the USSR: First Period, 1917–1923*, Monthly Review Press, New York and London, 1976.

L. Bondestam, 'People and Capitalism in the North-Eastern Lowlands of Ethiopia', *Journal of Modern African Studies*, 11, 3 (1973).

Amilcar Cabral, *Revolution in Guinea*, Monthly Review Press, New York and London, 1969, esp. chapter 5.

Bonnie Campbell, 'Social Change and Class Formation in a French West African State', *Canadian Journal of African Studies*, 8, 2 (1974).

Robin Cohen, 'Class in Africa: Analytical Problems and Perspectives', in R. Miliband and J. Saville eds., *The Socialist Register 1972*, Merlin Press, London, 1972.

S. Chodak, 'Social Stratification in Sub-Saharan Africa', *Canadian Journal of African Studies*, 7, 3 (1973).

Kren Eriksen, 'Zambia: Class Formation and Detente', *Review of African Political Economy*, 9, May–August 1977.

Frantz Fanon, *The Wretched of the Earth*, Penguin, 1967, esp. chapter 3.

Peter Flynn, 'Class, Clientelism, and Coercion: Some Mechanisms of Internal Dependency and Control', *Journal of Commonwealth and Comparative Political Studies*, 12, 2 (1974).

Terence K. Hopkins, 'Notes on Class Analysis and the World System', *Review*, I, 1, Summer 1977.

R.H. Jackson, 'Political Stratification in Tropical Africa', *Canadian Journal of African Studies*, 7, 3 (1973).

Paul Kennedy, 'Indigenous Capitalism in Ghana', *Review of African Political Economy*, 8, January–April 1977.

———, 'African Businessmen and Foreign Capital', *African Affairs*, 76, 303 (1977).

———, 'Dependency Theory and the Role of Third World Businessmen: the case of Ghana', *West African Journal of Sociology and Political Science*, 2, 1–2 (1976–7).

G.N. Kitching, 'The Concept of Class and the Study of Africa', *The African Review*, 2, 3 (1972).

Bernard Magubane, 'The Evolution of the Class Structure in Africa', P.C.W. Gutkind and I. Wallerstein eds., *The Political Economy of Contemporary Africa*, Sage Publications, Beverly Hills, 1977.

Mahmood Mamdani, 'Class Struggles in Uganda', *Review of African Political Economy*, 4, 1975.

———, *Politics and Class Formation in Uganda*, Monthly Review Press, New York and London, 1976.

J. Markakis, 'Social Formation and Political Adaptation in Ethiopia', *Journal of Modern African Studies*, 11, 3 (1973).
————, and Nega Ayele, *Class and Revolution in Ethiopia*, Spokesman Books, Nottingham, 1978.
Kwame Nkrumah, *Class Struggle in Africa*, Panaf Books, London, 1970.
J.K. Nyerere, 'Ujamaa—the Basis of African Socialism', in *Essays in African Socialism*, Tanzania Publishing House, Dar es Salaam, 1967.
G.N. Nzongola, 'The Bourgeoisie and Revolution in the Congo', *Journal of Modern African Studies*, 8, 4 (1970).
D.C. O'Brien, 'Co-operators and Bureaucrats: Class Formation in a Senegalese Peasant Society', *Africa*, 61, 4 (1971).
Nicos Poulantzas, *Political Power and Social Classes*, New Left Books, London, 1973.
Joel Samoff, 'Education in Tanzania: Class Formation and Reproduction', *Journal of Modern African Studies*, 17, 1, March 1979.
I.G. Shivji, 'The Silent Class Struggle', and 'The Class Struggle Continues', Tanzania Publishing House, Dar es Salaam, 1973.
————, *Class Struggles in Tanzania*, Monthly Review Press, New York and London, 1976.
Nicola Swainson, 'The Rise of a National Bourgeoisie in Kenya', *Review of African Political Economy*, 8, January–April 1977.
I. Wallerstein, 'Class and Class Conflict in Contemporary Africa', *Canadian Journal of African Studies*, 7, 3 (1973).
————, 'Class and Class Conflict in Africa', *Monthly Review*, 26, 9 (1975).
Gavin Williams, 'The Social Stratification of a Neo-Colonial Economy; Western Nigeria', in Christopher Allen and R.W. Johnson eds., *African Perspectives: papers in the history, politics and economics of Africa presented to Thomas Hodgkin*, Cambridge University Press, 1970.
Jack Woddis, *New Theories of Revolution*, Lawrence and Wishart, London, 1972.

2 The peasants

Adrian Adams, 'The Senegal River Valley: What Kind of Change?', *Review of African Political Economy*, 10, September–December 1977.
Hamza Alavi, 'Peasants and Revolution', in R. Miliband and J. Saville eds., *The Socialist Register 1965*, Merlin Press, London, 1965.
G. Arrighi, 'Labour Supplies in Historical Perspective: a Study of the Proletarianization of the African Peasantry in Rhodesia', in G. Arrighi and J.S. Saul eds., *Essays in the Political Economy of Africa* Monthly Review Press, New York and London, 1973.
A. Awiti, 'Economic Differentiation in Ismani, Iringa Region', *The African Review*, 3, 2 (1973).
C. Beer and G. Williams, 'The Politics of the Ibadan Peasantry', *The African Review*, 5, 3 (1975).
Henry Bernstein, 'Notes on Capital and Peasantry', *Review of African Political Economy*, 10, September–December 1977.
Colin Bundy, 'The Emergence and Decline of a South African Peasantry', *African Affairs*, 71, 285 (1972).
S. Chodak, 'The Birth of an African Peasantry', *Canadian Journal of African Studies*, 5, 3 (1971).
L. Cliffe, 'Rural class formation in East Africa', *Journal of Peasant Studies*, 4, 2 (1977).
————, 'Rural Political Economy of Africa', in P.C.W. Gutkind and I. Wallerstein

eds., *The Political Economy of Contemporary Africa*, Sage Publications, Beverly Hills, 1977.

Cathérine Coquery-Vidrovitch, 'The Political Economy of the African Peasantry and Modes of Production', in P.C.W. Gutkind and I. Wallerstein eds., *The Political Economy of Contemporary Africa*, Sage Publications, Beverly Hills, 1976.

A. Coulson, 'Peasants and Bureaucrats', *Review of African Political Economy*, 3, May–October 1975.

——, 'Agricultural Policies in Mainland Tanzania', *Review of African Political Economy*, 10, September–December 1977.

Lloyd Fallers, 'Are African Cultivators to be called Peasants?', *Current Anthropology*, 11, 1961.

Caroline Hutton and Robin Cohen, 'African Peasants and Resistance to Change: a reconsideration of sociological approaches', in Ivar Oxaal, Tony Barnett and David Booth eds., *Beyond the Sociology of Development: Economy and Society in Latin America and Africa*, Routledge and Kegan Paul, London and Boston, 1975.

Allen Isaacman, 'Social Banditry in Zimbabwe (Rhodesia) and Mozambique, 1894–1907: An Expression of Early Peasant Protest', *Journal of Southern African Studies*, 4, 1 (1977).

Christopher Leo, 'The Failure of the "Progressive Farmer" in Kenya's Million-Acre Development Scheme', *Journal of Modern African Studies*, 16, 4, December 1978.

Colin Leys, 'Politics in Kenya: the Development of Peasant Society', *British Journal of Political Science*, 1, 1972.

Michael F. Lofchie, 'Agrarian Crisis and Economic Liberalisation in Tanzania', *Journal of Modern African Studies*, 16, 3, September 1978.

Maud Shimwaayi Muntemba, 'The Underdevelopment of Rural Zambia: Kabwe District, 1960–1970', *Journal of Southern African Studies*, 5, (1978).

J.V. Mwapachu, 'Operation Planned Villages in Rural Tanzania: A Revolutionary Strategy for Development', *The African Review*, 6, 1 (1976).

K.W.J. Post, '"Peasantization" and Rural Political Movements in Western Africa', *Archives Europeènnes d'Sociologie*, 13, 1972.

Terence Ranger, 'Reflections on Peasant Research in Central and Southern Africa', *Journal of Southern African Affairs*, 5, 1 (1978).

Robert Redfield, *Peasant Society and Culture*, University of Chicago Press, 1956.

J.S. Saul, 'Peasants and Revolution', *Review of African Political Economy*, 1, 1974.

I.G. Shivji, 'Peasants and Class Alliances', *Review of African Political Economy*, 3, May–October 1975.

H.U.E. Thoden Van Velzen, 'Staff, Kulacks and Peasants', in L. Cliffe and J.S. Saul eds., *Socialism in Tanzania*, 2, East African Publishing House, Dar es Salaam, 1973.

Gavin Williams, 'Taking the Part of Peasants: Rural Development in Nigeria and Tanzania', in P.C.W. Gutkind and I. Wallerstein eds., *The Political Economy of Contemporary Africa*, Sage Publication, Beverly Hills, 1977.

Eric Wolf, *Peasants*, Prentice-Hall, Englewood Cliffs, N.J., 1966.

3 The proletariat

G. Arrighi, 'International Corporations, Labour Aristocracies, and Economic Development in Tropical Africa', in G. Arrighi and J.S. Saul eds., *Essays in the Political Economy of Africa*, Monthly Review Press, New York and London, 1973.

R.H. Baguma, 'Inefficiency, Irresponsiveness and Irresponsibility in the Public Services: Is Mwongozo to Blame?', *The African Review*, 5, 2 (1975).

Robin Cohen, *Labour and Politics in Nigeria*, Heinemann, London, 1974.

———, 'From Peasants to Workers in Africa', P.C.W. Gutkind and I. Wallerstein eds., *The Political Economy of Contemporary Africa*, Sage Publications, Beverly Hills, 1977.

Robert Davies, 'The White Working-Class in South Africa', *New Left Review*, 82, November–December 1973.

Bob Fitch, and Mary Oppenheimer, *Ghana: End of an Illusion*, Monthly Review Press, New York, 1966, chapter 7.

Robert J. Gordon, *Mines, Masters and Migrants: Life in a Namibian Compound*, Ravan Press, Johannesburg, 1977.

P.C.W. Gutkind, 'The Emergent African Urban Proletariat', Occasional Paper No. 8, Centre for Developing Areas Studies, McGill University, 1974.

Peter Harris, 'Industrial Workers in Rhodesia, 1946–1972', *Journal of Southern African Studies*, I, 2 (1975).

Keith Hart, 'Informal Income Opportunities and Urban Employment in Ghana', *Journal of Modern African Studies*, 11, 1 (1973).

———, 'The Politics of Unemployment in Ghana', *African Affairs*, 75, 301 (1976).

Hemson, David, 'Dock Workers, Labour Circulation and Class Struggles in Durban, 1940–1959', *Journal of Southern African Studies*, 4, 1 (1977).

K. Hinchcliffe, 'Labour Aristocracy—A Northern Nigerian Case Study', *Journal of Modern African Studies*, 12, 1 (1974).

Institute for Industrial Education, *The Durban Strikes, 1973*, Ravan Press, Johannesburg and Durban, 1974.

Richard Jeffries, *Class, Power and Ideology in Ghana: The Railwaymen of Sekondi*, Cambridge University Press, 1978.

———, 'The Labour Aristocracy? A Ghana Case Study', *Review of African Political Economy*, 3, May–October 1975.

Clements Kadalie, *My Life and the ICU*, Case, London, 1970.

Kirstin Leitner, 'The Situation of Agricultural Workers in Kenya', *Review of African Political Economy*, 6, May–August 1976.

Paul Lubeck, 'Labour in Kano since the Oil Boom', *Review of African Political Economy*, 13, May–August 1978.

H. Mapolu, 'The Organisation and Participation of Workers in Tanzania', *The African Review*, 2, 3 (1972).

P. Mihyo, 'The Struggle for Workers' Control in Tanzania', *Review of African Political Economy*, 4, September–December 1975.

Richard Moorsom, 'Underdevelopment, Contract Labour and Worker Consciousness in Namibia, 1915–1972', *Journal of Southern African Studies*, 4, 1 (1977).

P. Msekwa, 'Workers' Participation in Management in Tanzania: A Background', *The African Review*, 5, 2 (1975).

J.V. Mwapachu, 'Industrial Labour Protest in Tanzania: An Analysis of Influential Variables', *The African Review*, 3, 3, 1973.

Adrian Peace, 'Industrial Protest in Nigeria', in Emmanuel de Kadt and Gavin Williams eds., *Sociology and Development*, Tavistock Publications, London, 1974.

Margaret Peil, *The Ghanaian Factory Worker: Industrial Man in Africa*, Cambridge University Press, 1972.

Charles Perrings, 'Consciousness, Conflict, and Proletarianization: An Assessment of the 1935 Mineworkers' Strike on the Northern Rhodesian Copperbelt', *Journal of Southern African Studies*, 4, 1, October 1977.

Adam Przrworski, 'Proletariat into a Class: The Process of Class Formation from Karl Kautsky's *The Class Struggle* to Recent Controversies', *Politics and Society*, 7, 4, 1977.

Richard Sandbrook, *Proletarians and African Capitalism*, Oxford University Press, London, 1976.

——, 'The Political Potential of African Urban Workers', *Canadian Journal of African Studies*, 11, 3 (1977).

—— and Robin Cohen eds., *The Development of an African Working Class*, Longman, London, 1975.

—— and Jack Arn, 'The Labouring Poor and Urban Class Formation: The Case of Greater Accra', Occasional Monograph Series No. 12, Centre for Developing Areas Studies, McGill University, 1977.

Jim Silver, 'Class Struggle in Ghana's Mining Industry', *Review of African Political Economy*, 13, May–August 1978.

Sharon Stichter, 'Workers, Trade Unions and the Mau Mau Rebellion', *Canadian Journal of African Studies*, 9, 2 (1975).

Charles Van Onselen, *Chibaro: African Mine Labour in Southern Rhodesia, 1900–1933*, Pluto Press, London, 1976.

Peter Waterman, 'Communist Theory in the Nigerian Trade-Union Movement', *Politics and Society*, 3, 3, Spring 1973.

——, 'Conservatism among Nigerian Workers', in G. Williams ed., *Nigeria: Economy and Society*, Rex Collings, London, 1976.

——, 'Consciousness, Organisation and Action amongst Lagos Portworkers', *Review of African Political Economy*, 13, May–August 1978.

Francis Wilson, *Migrant Labour in South Africa*, South African Council of Churches and Spro-Cas, Johannesburg, 1972.

——, *Labour in the South African Gold Mines, 1911–1969*, Cambridge University Press, 1972.

Harold Wolpe, 'The White Working Class in South Africa', *Economy and Society*, 5, 2 (1976).

4 Class in South Africa

Heribert Adam, *Modernizing Racial Domination: The Dynamics of South African Politics*, University of California Press, Berkeley, Los Angeles and London, 1971.

Manfred Bienefeld and Duncan Innes, 'Capital Accumulation and South Africa', *Review of African Political Economy*, 7, September–December 1976.

Belinda Bozzoli, 'Capital and the State in South Africa', *Review of African Political Economy*, 11, January–April 1978.

Robert Davies, 'Mining Capital, the State and Unskilled White Workers in South Africa', *Journal of Southern African Studies*, 3, 1 (1976).

——, David Kaplan, Mike Morris, Dan O'Meara, 'Class Struggle and the Periodisation of the State in South Africa', *Review of African Political Economy*, 7, September–December 1976.

Philip Ehrensaft, 'Polarized Accumulation and the Theory of Economic Dependence: The Implications of South African Semi-Industrial Capitalism', in P.C.W. Gutkind and I. Wallerstein eds., *The Political Economy of Contemporary Africa*, Sage Publications, Beverly Hills, 1977.

Ruth First, Jonathan Steele and Christabel Gurney, *The South African Connection: Western Investment in Apartheid*, Penguin, 1973.

Duncan Innes and Dan O'Meara, 'Class Formation and Ideology: The Transkei Region', *Review of African Political Economy*, 7, September–December 1976.

Innes and Plaut, 'Class Struggle and the State', *Review of African Political Economy*, 11, January–April 1978.

Frederick A. Johnstone, *Class, Race and Gold: A Study of Class Relations and Racial Discrimination in South Africa*, Routledge and Kegan Paul, London and Boston, 1976.

B.S. Kantor and H.F. Kenny, 'The Poverty of Neo-Marxism: the case of South Africa', *Journal of Southern African Studies*, 3, 1, October 1976.

D.E. Kaplan, 'The Politics of Industrial Protection in South Africa, 1910–1939', *Journal of Southern African Studies*, 3, 1, October 1976.

Leo Kuper, *An African Bourgeoisie: Race, Class and Politics in South Africa*, Yale University Press, New Haven and London, 1965.

——, *Race, Class and Power: Ideology and Revolutionary Change in Plural Societies*, Duckworth, London, 1974.

Martin Legassick, 'South Africa: Capital accumulation and violence', *Economy and Society*, 3, 3 (1974).

——, 'Legislation, Ideology and Economy in Post-1948 South Africa', *Journal of Southern African Studies*, 1, 1 (1974).

—— and Harold Wolpe, 'The Bantustans and Capital Accumulation', *Review of African Political Economy*, 7, September–December 1976.

Philip Mayer, 'Class, Status, and Ethnicity as Perceived by Johannesburg Africans', in Leonard Thompson and Jeffrey Butler eds., *Change in Contemporary South Africa*, University of California Press, Berkeley and Los Angeles, 1975.

Thomas E. Nyquist, *Toward a Theory of the African Upper Stratum in South Africa*, Center for International Studies, University of Ohio, Athens, Ohio, 1972.

Edward Roux, *Time Longer than Rope*, University of Wisconsin Press, Madison and London, 1964.

H.J. and R.E. Simons, *Class and Colour in South Africa*, Penguin, 1969.

Stanley Trapido, 'Landlord and Tenant in a Colonial Economy: The Transvaal 1880–1910', *Journal of Southern African Studies*, 5, 1 (1978).

Pierre Van den Berghe, *South Africa: A Study in Conflict*, University of California Press, Berkeley and Los Angeles, 1965.

E. Webster ed., *Essays in Southern African Labour History*, Ravan Press, Johannesburg, 1978.

Brian Willan, 'Sol Plaatje, De Beers and an Old Tram Shed: Class Relations and Social Control in a South African Town, 1918–1919', *Journal of Southern African Studies*, 4, 2 (1978).

Harold Wolpe, 'The changing class structure of South Africa', in P. Zaremblea ed., *Research in Political Economy*, Jai Press, Greenwich, Conn., 1977.

——, 'A Comment on "The Poverty of Neo-Marxism"', *Journal of Southern African Studies*, 4, 2 (1978).

5 The State

Hamza Alavi, 'The State in Post-Colonial Societies—Pakistan and Bangla Desh', *New Left Review*, 74, July–August 1972.

Paul Collins, Terisa Turner, and Gavin Williams, 'Capitalism and the Coup', in G. Williams ed., *Nigeria: Economy and Society*, Rex Collings, London, 1976.

Steven Langdon, 'The State and Capitalism in Kenya', *Review of African Political Economy*, 8, January–April 1977.

Colin Leys, 'The "Overdeveloped" Post-Colonial State: A re-evaluation', *Review of African Political Economy*, 5, January–April 1976.

Judith Marshall, 'The State of Ambivalence: Right and Left Options in Ghana', *Review of African Political Economy*, 5, January–April 1976.

Claude Meillassoux, 'A Class Analysis of the Bureaucratic Process in Mali', *The Journal of Development Studies*, 6, 2 (1970).

Ralph Miliband, *The State in Capitalist Society*, Weidenfeld and Nicholson, London, 1969.

————, 'Poulantzas and the Capitalist State', *New Left Review*, 82, November–December 1972.

Roger Murray, 'Second Thoughts on Ghana', *New Left Review*, 42, March–April 1967.

————, 'Internationalization of Capital and the Nation State', *New Left Review*, 67, May–June 1971.

James Petras and Robert Rhodes, 'The Reconsolidation of Hegemony', *New Left Review*, 97, May–June 1976.

Nicos Poulantzas, 'The Capitalist State: A Reply to Miliband and Laclau', *New Left Review*, 95, January–February 1976.

John S. Saul, 'African Socialism in One Country', in G. Arrighi and J.S. Saul eds., *Essays in the Political Economy of Africa*, Monthly Review Press, New York and London, 1973.

————, 'The State in Post-Colonial Societies: Tanzania', in R. Miliband and J. Saville eds., *The Socialist Register 1974*, Merlin Press, London, 1974.

————, 'The Unsteady State: Uganda, Obote and General Amin', *Review of African Political Economy*, 5, January–April 1976.

Terisa Turner, 'Multinational Corporations and the Instability of the Nigerian State', *Review of African Political Economy*, 5, January–April 1976.

————, 'Commercial Capitalism and the 1975 Coup', in Keith Panter-Brick ed., *Soldiers and Oil: The Political Transformation of Nigeria*, Frank Cass, London, pp. 166–97.

Michaela Von Freyhold, 'The Post-Colonial State and its Tanzanian Version', *Review of African Political Economy*, 8, January–April 1977.

I. Wallerstein, 'The State and Social Transformation: Will and Possibility', *Politics and Society*, 1, 3 (1971).

————, 'The Range of Choice: Constraints and the Policies of Governments of Contemporary Independent African States', in M. Lofchie ed., *The State of the Nations*, University of California Press, Berkeley, 1971.

Isobel Winter, 'The Post-Colonial State and the Forces and Relations of Production', *Review of African Political Economy*, 9, May–August 1977.

5 Class and the Analysis of African Politics: Problems and Prospects

DENNIS L. COHEN

This essay is an attempt to analyse the relevance and utility of the application of Marxism to the study of politics in Africa. It does this through an examination of the history of class analysis in the work of students of African politics. The conclusion drawn from this enquiry is that class analysis has come increasingly into the mainstream of African studies, and that this analysis has continuously moved away from an a-political, non-Marxist concern with class as a descriptive category, toward the use of various Marxist versions of the concept.

I shall try to synthesise recent work employing class analysis, both theoretically and in the form of case studies, into a set of concepts capable of being more widely and effectively used. I am not putting forward a comprehensive model of class analysis, only making a modest effort at increasing the clarity and orderliness of this rapidly changing field.

I

Professional academic study of politics in Africa is a recent undertaking.[1] Political science as an academic specialisation has itself a relatively short history[2] and a considerable bias towards the study of the politics of Europe and its diaspora.[3] The incursion into Africa of the political scientist was retarded by:

(1) the ethnocentric (or, to be more charitable, parochial) attitudes of the bulk of American and European practitioners;

(2) the restriction, for a long period, of African studies to the field of anthropology, both as a means of justifying colonialism and as an emanation of the colonial ideology;[4]

(3) the inadequacy of the theoretical framework current in political science which, until the second half of the twentieth century, was unable to see either past African political development or the bulk of contemporary African political processes because of the narrow scope of its institutional gaze,[5] and treated those processes it could recognise, ie. those which involved colonial structures, as the excrescences of European ruling states;[6]

(4) the elimination of indigenous African educational institutions and simultaneous tardy development of Westernised educational institutions in Africa, resulting in a paucity of African scholars capable of analysing the politics of their own societies.

This situation gradually began to change around the midpoint of this century. Change resulted both from pressures internal to the academic community, as scholarly development itself made available new ideas, and from external pressures, as the new political environment of decolonisation and global conflict created a demand for more information about, and explanation of, what was happening in Africa.[7]

The first studies emerging from this new academic concern were shaped by the theories of politics then dominant in American and British departments of political studies. These theories were either descriptive/historical/institutional in nature, or, increasingly in the late 1950s and 1960s, reflected the spread of Parsonian sociology throughout the social sciences in America.[8] Rather than having a class perspective, such studies tended either to ignore issues of systematic inequality and social stratification, or to subordinate them to an interest in ethnic stratification, especially in the arcane form of 'tribalism'.[9]

Furthermore, we need to keep in mind the degree to which, at this time, Marxist intellectual perspectives had been largely excluded from the Western academic world, especially in the United States. Both through direct political control and indirect pressures,[10] the sources of Marxist scholarship which had existed before 1945 had been, in the main, driven to cover by 1950. It should also be remembered that the Marxist perspective had never flourished in the English-speaking world, where it contradicted the dominant ideology of the most successful exponents of capitalism.

The 1960s was the decade of modernisation theory, with Africa as one of the areas of the Third World in which this theory could be tested. By the latter part of the decade, however, the failure of the modernisation theorists to predict, or even describe, the course of political change began to cast into some doubt its status as an intellectual framework. In Asia, where the strength of Marxist political movements has always confronted modernisation theory with a viable alternative model, the success of the Vietnamese liberation struggle forced Western scholars to re-examine their assumptions. In Latin America, a tradition of indigenous scholarship produced the theoretical innovations of dependency theory.[11] In terms of African studies, too, ideas percolating from other area studies, the beginnings of indigenous scholarship, renewed interest in the Marxist scholarly tradition in the West, and the decline in optimism about the course of political and economic development in Africa, began to produce changing perspectives.

Studies reflecting these changes include those of Arrighi and Saul, Cohen, Kitching and Williams.[12] In them, a new consensus began to emerge by the early 1970s which had the following main elements.

(1) Modernisation theory had reflected a pro-Western political bias. Its interest in promoting political stability and economic interdependency was too closely guided by Western structural assumptions in its model-building to to able to deal with the different conditions of non-Western reality, and had proven of little use in field work to those seeking to translate its principles from grand theory to empirical testing; consequently, major new theoretical work was required.

(2) Economic inequality was increasing in Africa and becoming more systematic, while political experiments aimed at preventing this outcome were being rejected in favour of conservative bureaucratic/military regimes.

(3) The concept of social classes had increasing relevance in Africa as economic change progressed, and, as classes 'emerged' in an economic sense, they would begin to produce political consequences.

(4) A kind of half-way point had been reached in Africa with modern class forces produced by development combining with the ethnic loyalties of traditional stratification, while a modern elite based on education was poised on the brink of 'embourgeoisement' and workers were being 'proletarianized'.[13]

This period was characterised by an eclectic approach to analysis, with scholars borrowing concepts from the residue of modernisation theory and their limited exposure to Marxism. A new willingness to question received opinion represented a major advance over the optimistic complacency of the previous decade. As the 1970s unfolded, however, the situation evolved further.

(1) As scholars working in this field acquired greater sophistication in Marxist theory, and as scholars with such skills entered the field, the eclectic approach began to give way to a more systematic, intensive and innovative application of Marxist theory. It became clear that there were ways of dealing with such problems as dependency, prolonged coexistence of advanced and backward sectors in one economy, and blocked class consciousness, while remaining committed to the centrality of class struggle as the motor of historical change.

(2) The concrete political changes which had seen the shunting aside of leading exponents of African Socialism like Nkrumah in the 1960s, entered a new phase in the mid-1970s. The success of armed anti-colonial liberation movements in the Portuguese colonies, the renewal of intense political conflict in South Africa after a decade-long hiatus, and an increase in major power political conflict in areas like Angola, Zaire and the Horn of Africa, combined to bring about fresh interest in radical analysis and solutions for African political problems.

(3) Important developments in the international community of Marxist scholarship were also involved. As the Cold War gave way to a multipolar world the 'socialist camp' was increasingly divided into various Soviet, Chinese, Euro-communist and national roads to socialism. The clear confrontation of the period 1917–60 had enforced a degree of unity in the form of ideological conformity in the socialist world, with dissident 'Trotskyites' cast into limbo without a material base. In the new environment of the post-1960 world, a 'thousand flowers' have indeed flourished, in places as widely separated as the streets of 1968 Paris, the guerrilla *focos* of Cuba, the offices and classrooms of Prague and the jungles of Cambodia. The consequence of this political disunity has been, on the intellectual level, a rich ferment of ideas, some of which have filtered into African studies.[14]

The most important theoretical statements of this 'neo-Marxist' scholarship[15] are found in the work of Samir Amin,[16] Geoffrey Kay,[17] and Immanuel Wallerstein.[18] Particularly influential in establishing the claims of a Marxist perspective throughout the field of African studies have been the high quality case studies that have been produced in this period applying Marxist concepts, to a greater or lesser degree, to various specific areas.[19]

This 'neo-Marxist' approach is far from achieving the status of a new orthodoxy, since it coexists with exponents of the older modernisation school, who still control the commanding heights of institutional and financial authority in African studies. Nor can it be considered a cohesive school of thought since it includes scholars of widely divergent theoretical positions and significant conflicts on the level of application. We should also remember that some earlier studies of African politics were informed by the kind of concerns motivating the 'neo-Marxists'.[20] Nevertheless, the congruence of interest, method and theoretical perspective of the studies just mentioned is sufficient to draw together the common ideas they share, highlight and clarify the problems that remain, and point in the direction of further theoretical development.

II

Before undertaking the task outlined above it is necessary to resolve the major question that concerned those interested in class analysis in Africa ten years ago, ie, is Marxism relevant to Africa?

First, it is necessary to give a brief outline of what we mean by Marxist class analysis. Such an historical materialist method of analysis should include the following main elements.

(1) In every society the most important human activities are those by which men and women produce and distribute the goods necessary for their survival and reproduction. The forces used to bring about such productive activities, the level of production and the social relations of production are the key elements determining the nature of society. Societies change as one set of productive relations makes possible increased levels of production, which in turn make possible new productive relations upon which the process begins a new cycle. This change is not a steady progress along a straight line, but consists of a series of disjointed forward and backward movements, produced by resolution of contradictions between the material conditions of nature, the forces and relations of production and human needs. Each resolution contains new contradictions, hence the seeds of new change. The concept of transition is meaningless here, as every era is a transitional one.[21]

(2) Depending upon the level of productive forces, the ways in which the social product is appropriated, and the relations of production and appropriation found in any given society, there are engendered certain social classes, characterised by possessing common and opposed relations to production, ie. some appropriate that which is produced by others. These classes tend toward a bipolar model as each stage of social change works out its history, but in any epoch they are also internally differentiated into various fractions, strata and categories.[22] Furthermore, different sets of productive forces and relations (ie. modes of production) can be combined together in the same social formation, resulting in their different sets of classes also being combined together.

(3) Classes are in conflict because they have different and opposed interests in this changing process of production and appropriation, and this class struggle is the human arena within which are played out the basic contradictions arising from the nature of production. The pace and manner of this conflict exercises, in turn, an influence upon the pace and manner of all social change. This concept of determination, quite different from the vulgar economic determinism associated with Marxism by many of its critics, is illustrated by the following passage from Engels:

> According to the materialist conception of history the determining element in history is *ultimately* the production and reproduction in real life. More than this neither Marx nor I have ever asserted. If therefore somebody twists this into the statement that the economic element is the *only* determining one, he transforms it into a meaningless, abstract and absurd phrase. The economic situation is the basis, but the various elements of the superstructure—political forms of the class struggle and its consequences, constitutions established by the victorious class after a successful battle, etc.—forms of law—and then even the reflexes of all these actual struggles in the brains of the combatants: political, legal, philosophical theories, religious ideas and their further development into systems of dogma—also exercise their influence upon the course of the historical struggles and in many cases are preponderant in determining their form.[23]

(4) The relations between classes are relations of domination and exploitation, as the stronger class uses its control over production relations to exploit the

weaker class. The dominant class may consist of various fractions, strata and categories, with conflicting interests, allied together to further their more important common interest vis-a-vis the dominated class. Within such an alliance (ie. power bloc) hegemony is exercised by the strongest section of the ruling class.[24] The instrument of domination is the state, through which the ruling class manages its common interests, against both the dominated class and, in some aspects, weaker elements of the ruling class.[25]

(5) The ruling class has an ideology, ie. a set of myths, ideas, values, principles and attitudes, which it uses to justify, explain and reinforce its rule. The more the dominated class subscribes to this ideology the more efficiently can its exploitation be carried out.[26] The realm of ideas not only has this conservative function, but is also the source for the formation of counter-ideas, through which the dominated can become conscious of the illegitimacy of their domination, and of their common interest in producing a revolution, ie. a basic change in the nature of production relations which brings a new class into a position of dominance.

> From the conception of history we have sketched we obtain these further conclusions: in the development of productive forces there comes a stage at which productive forces and means of intercourse are called into existence, which, under the existing relationships, only cause mischief, and which are no longer productive but destructive forces . . . ; and connected with this a class is called forth, which has to bear all the burdens of society without enjoying its advantages, which, ousted from society, is forced into the most decided antagonism to all other classes; a class which forms a majority of all members of society, and from which emanates the consciousness of the necessity of a fundamental revolution, the communist consciousness, which may, of course, arise among the other classes too through the contemplation of the situation of this class.[27]

(6) The present era is characterised by the central position of the capitalist mode of production, within which the goods produced have become commodities, produced for exchange not use, while labour, land and capital goods are also exchanged on markets, and controlled through relations of ownership. Older modes of production have been reduced to minimal importance. The next change towards which capitalist society is headed is a socialist society, in which the workers whose labour produce commodities will regain control over them through overthrowing the domination of the capitalist class of property owners. Such a revolution of the proletariat will create a socialist society which will then evolve toward a communist society which will represent the resolution of the final contradictions in productive relations by bringing about an abundant level of production combined with equality in relations of production and appropriation. In Marx's words:

> In a higher phase of communist society, after the enslaving subordination of the individual to the division of labour, and therewith also the antithesis between mental and physical labour, has vanished; after labour has become not only a means of life but also life's prime want; after the productive forces have also increased with the all-round development of the individual, and all the springs of cooperative wealth spring more abundantly,—only then can the narrow horizon of bourgeois wants be crossed in its entirety and society inscribe on its banners 'From each according to his ability, to each according to his needs!'[28]

This will be the culmination of the historical process and see the end of the class struggle, the 'withering away' of the state, and presumably of our interest in politics.[29]

Taking the above as our simplified outline of the historical materialist model, to what extent can it help us understand contemporary African politics? Since our main concern is on the political level, we shall concentrate on the features of the model most directly relevant to politics, ie. class conflict and the state, while not forgetting that these are inseparable parts of the model as a whole, and cannot be understood in isolation from their economic base.

We shall discuss in turn five objections to the use of Marxist analysis frequently found in the literature.

First, it is argued that African economies are not primarily capitalist economies. Instead, they are seen as still largely agricultural, subsistence-oriented economies, within which capitalist structures are confined to a small, modern enclave. As such, Marx's focus on capitalist exploitation and socialist revolution is seen as irrelevant to the problems of Africa, which is seen as having its own unique mode of production, to which the Eurocentric theories of Marx are not appropriate.[30]

It should be noted immediately that this objection is not really aimed at the relevance of historical materialist theory to Africa, but at its specific propositions relating to capitalism. Even the charges of European bias do not justify rejection of the model because, unless one regards Marxism as a form of biblical exegesis of original texts, there is no reason why Marxist methods, concepts and theories cannot be adapted to the analysis of phenomena to which early Marxists were only marginally exposed.[31]

Such an agonising reappraisal is unnecessary, however, if we reject the original objection, which maintains that there is only limited capitalist penetration of Africa. The dual economy thesis, once popular with Africanists, [32] has now been discredited. Instead, the following points have become well-established.

(1) Traditional, ie. pre-colonial, African economies contained a wide variety of pre-capitalist modes of production. These ranged from communal hunting, pastoral and agricultural modes with varying levels of surplus productions and exchange, allowing little scope for surplus accumulation (despite the presence of inequalities of appropriation), and varying scales of social and political organisation, on the one hand, to some social formations with features resembling feudal, slave and Asiatic modes of production, on the other hand.[33]

(2) In parts of Africa pre-colonial trading relations with European capitalist states called into being capitalist structures, including expanded commodity production; the formation of classes of merchants, peasants and workers linked to external capitalist markets while still exhibiting some pre-capitalist features; more intense forms of domestic slavery as well as the slave trade; and rapid increases in the scale of states and their structural differentiation.[34]

(3) Colonialism both accelerated and modified the course of capitalist penetration, providing the organisational and technological basis for the rapid spread of capitalism and sharp increases in the level of production, while tying this development more closely to a dependent relation to European capitalism. This modern imperialism, in the form of plantations and mines using forced and cheap labour, peasant production providing cheap raw materials and foodstuffs for European processing and consumption, and sheltered markets for the sale of European-produced commodities, transformed the bulk of the

African economy, within half a century, into a substantially capitalist mode of production.[35]

(4) Post-colonial development in the new states of Africa has further deepened the development of capitalist relations: encouraging the decomposition of communal production and the rise of a free market in land;[36] proletarianising the peasantry into a source of cheap labour for capitalist employers;[37] stimulating increased foreign investment, often in partnership with the indigenous state;[38] and subsidising a rising indigenous capitalist class.[39] The form of these changes, often appearing disguised with great inventiveness by the cosmetic ideology of African Socialism, as well as their rate, differs from area to area, but the dominance of the capitalist mode of production is indisputable.

Secondly, it is argued in some quarters that the nature of 'traditional' African values, especially the function of the extended family as a redistributive mechanism, will, despite the structural economic changes discussed above, soften the virulence of exploitation and domination as they are known in capitalist systems elsewhere, and maintain the cooperativeness, egalitarianism and humaneness of African societies. This is the premise that has inspired the advocates of African Socialism.[40] In it they see a force which will save Africa from the class conflicts and violent revolutions foreseen by Marx.

There can be no denying the fact that African Socialism has been the most powerful ideology in contemporary Africa. The reason for its success lies in its role as an effective ideology for the dominant class. It legitimates dependency through combining rhetorical challenge with practical acquiescence, private appropriation of wealth by local elements of the ruling class through the state, their monopoly of state power through the single-party regime, and their claim to cultural leadership through bridging African and European cultures. The effectiveness of this ideology, however, need not lead us to accept its validity as a tool of social analysis, when this validity is so clearly contrary to material reality.

In the first place, it seems unlikely that the rosy picture of traditional society painted by the advocates of African Socialism bears much resemblance to reality, as recorded, remembered or reasonably extrapolated from the present.[41] We have already discussed the evidence of pre-colonial class formation, with its consequences in terms of inequality, oppression and conflict. We need not accept a Hobbesian version of 'the war of all against all', nor the crude racism of the colonialists' view of the 'savagery' of African society, in order to reject an equally stereotyped Arcadian view of traditional society. Real societies have always existed in response to the harshness of their environments and the opportunities created by the level to which their modes of production have developed, whether in Europe, Africa, Asia or America. The myriad forms of adaptation created by various societies have been characterised by a mixture of fear, greed, generosity and grace, but always shaped by the need to survive. African societies, before colonial conquest, did survive and did develop. To pretend that they did so without paying the same human price that others have had to pay is to deny them their history just as conclusively as did colonial historiography.

Even if we were to accept the gloss on pre-colonial African development provided by the apologists for African Socialism, this does not establish their case in terms of contemporary African society. Here, President Nyerere of Tanzania reveals his greater realism in comparison to many other African Socialists, in admitting that capitalist values and attitudes were firmly implanted in Africa during the colonial period, and represent a real danger that cannot be avoided through the force of tradition alone. The strategy formulated by him, and others, to maintain traditional values through cultural revival, educational programmes and innovative socialising techniques, has proven, however, to be less than massively successful.[42] Tanzania's neighbour, Mozambique, has adopted a different strategy, based on more clearly Marxist assumptions, which is more sceptical about the role of tradition.[43]

The debate on this point will continue, but the increasing hostility with which opposition political movements in Africa attack the corruption, oppression and conspicuous consumption of the indigenous 'big men'[44] would seem to be a forceful indictment of the African bourgeoisie. The security of 'trans-class man'[45] in Africa seems threatened by those no longer willing to accept the doctrine of deference.

Third, the argument is frequently advanced that the state in Africa is being used, or at least may be used, by a 'modernising elite' not with the objective of managing the interests of the ruling class and organising the exploitation of the people, but rather with the aim of developing society in the interests of the masses and preventing the path of historical change outlined by Marx from proceeding through its many horrors to its ultimate conclusion.[46]

The state is seen, in this view, as responsive to popular needs, guided by the disinterested expertise of an educated, patriotic elite. It confronts problems which are technical and economic, or caused wholly by external forces of malevolence, which can be overcome through national unity, economic growth and education.

This perspective is a powerful, widely accepted one, not only in relation to Africa but also with respect to the rest of the Third World. It can, perhaps, be best confronted from a historical viewpoint. Why should we be led to believe that the current crop of Third World elites is any less self-interested than were their predecessors in the industrialised world? Has the spread of education brought about more humane societies there? Has economic growth been translated into greater equality, or even into more secure, fulfilling lives for the masses there? Has national unity been in the interest of all the people there?

A more empirical approach would be to view what has been occurring in specific cases where this kind of leadership has guided the development of African states. Few of the charismatic leaders of Africa have survived more than a decade in office without falling victim to military *coups* which expose the hollowness of their claims, as in Ghana[47] and Mali,[48] or survive with gravely diminished stature, as in Kenya,[49] Tanzania[50] and Zambia.[51] Claims of success are still made on behalf of some—eg. the Ivory Coast[52] and Tanzania—but with little conviction. The expectation of a sudden *coup*,[53] revelations of corruption,[54] and economic debacle[55] lurk menacingly behind the back of each. The causes of this instability, stagnation and continued dependence are sited by some in the nature of the global economy, by others in the resurgence of tribal animosities, and by still others in the personal failings of the rulers themselves, but few would continue to maintain the optimism that was once widespread.

Fourth, and connected to the viewpoint challenged immediately above, is the contention that the ruling class in Africa is not a class but an elite group. Specifically, the following points are made:

(1) the holders of political power in Africa do not combine that power with extensive property ownership, and therefore lack the common relation to production specified by the Marxist model;

(2) membership in this power elite is characterised by intense social mobility, uncharacteristic of class relations, so that the powerful have risen from the ranks of the oppressed and exploited, with whom they can be expected to identify;

(3) education is the key to power in modern Africa, so that the powerful are nearer to a meritocracy of experts than an oligarchy of exploiters.[56]

Even those who are less optimistic about the selflessness of this group, seeing instead the likelihood of its transforming itself into a bourgeoisie of property (embourgeoisement), remain fascinated with the significance of power rather than property relations in defining this class, contending that it is, therefore, less of a 'pure' bourgeois class.[57]

This proposition is the product of both a misunderstanding of theory and a misapprenhension of the facts. The argument is frequently carried out in terms of the occupants of political office. If it can be shown that these are not men of wealth, have risen from poor beginnings and have advanced education as their most salient social characteristic, the argument is taken as won.

Unfortunately, for the proponents of this view, the Marxist model is not meant to apply to the holders of office but to the holders of power, and the two categories need not be identical. The ruling class may well co-opt individuals from other classes to exercise power on its behalf, thereby strengthening its power through disguise. If this were not the case, we would find it hard to understand the defeat, in American politics, of super-capitalist Nelson Rockefeller by petty bourgeois Richard Nixon! The analysis of power is based not on the question by whom is power exercised, but for whom is it exercised.[58]

Leaving aside this theoretical confusion, however, it can be convincingly demonstrated that the holders of power in Africa are, to a large extent, part of the ruling class itself. They come not from the peasantry or the proletariat, ie. the oppressed masses of the nation, but from a petty bourgeoisie of above-average wealth, owners of capital or the servants of capital.[59] They use office to increase their wealth, often through the grossest forms of primitive accumulation.[60] Their education is itself a commodity purchased on a market to which entry is narrowly restricted.[61] What social mobility there is into this group is rapidly declining. We shall return below to a discussion of the nature of the petty bourgeoisie in Africa, but we can leave the issue now assured that it is a class.

Finally, we come to the issue of the relationship between class, consciousness and political activity. Here, the argument advanced against Marxism is that it provides no way of understanding the major source of political conflict in Africa, ie. tribalism, often more euphemistically referred to as ethnicity. It is argued by many that the vitality of the ethnic community and the intensity of its grip on African culture is uniquely strong and persistent. If classes are admitted to exist at all they are still held, in this perspective, to be insignificant agents in affecting consciousness and hence behaviour.

> The Marxist concept of the integrative process assumes a high degree
> of a preexistent ethnic and cultural integration. This is an assumption
> which cannot be made in analysing integration in, say, African
> countries. In fact, tribes and races are more total identities than are
> economic classes.[62]

Such a viewpoint, on the theoretical level, rejects the most fundamental principles of historical materialism, those relating to social determination, ie. the relation between material reality, consciousness and behaviour. As Marx put it, 'It is not the consciousness of men that determines their being, but on the contrary, their social being that determines their consciousness'.[63]

Rather than pursuing the issue on the level of theory, however, we should be able to answer this charge on a more concrete level. Marxist analysis has not neglected the problem of ethnic loyalty, as in the substantial body of literature devoted to the 'national question'.[64] The line pursued has been that ethnicity (ie. nationality) is a significant element in human consciousness, and that it must be analysed and dealt with by those involved in political action.

It is seen, however, not as an alternative to the class struggle, but as a force shaped by the class struggle. In early capitalism, nationalism is used by the bourgeoisie to help create a capitalist system; in this phase it can have the progressive role of uniting the people against foreign oppression. But once this goal has been achieved it passes to a second phase, in which nationalism is used to manipulate and divide the working classes. Depending upon the role played by nationalism within the concrete reality of a particular class struggle, it may be necessary, at times, to evince a temporary commitment to 'national consciousness', or to work for its submersion within a greater class consciousness.[65]

At all times, however, the class relation must be seen as historically more important than the ethnic relation, whatever the ideological appearance of the moment. Such a perspective is only now entering the literature on Africa, and still remains to be reconciled with the problem, discussed below, of whether independent national development is possible in the modern epoch of global capitalism. This last issue constitutes a better point of departure for analysis of the 'national question' than do hair-splitting controversies over the definition of nations, peoples and ethnic groups.

In conclusion, we can see that the Marxist framework, correctly understood, is adaptable enough to be applied in the African context. The objections to its use can be seen to rest on a misunderstanding of its concepts, deliberate or otherwise, and a poor grasp of empirical reality.

In the final section of this essay, I wish to turn to a more detailed discussion of various class concepts which need to be developed and systematised to improve their use in examining African politics.

III

Bourgeoisie

We should begin our examination of African class relations with the dominant class. Accepting the argument advanced above that the dominant mode of production in the social formations of Africa is capitalist, the dominant class must be the bourgeoisie. What are the specific characteristics of the bourgeoisie in Africa?

Its most important general characteristics result from the dependent status of Africa in relation to the global capitalist system.[66] Production is geared to the needs of international capital through international markets for the exports and imports that are the key elements in African economies; through the investment decisions of international capital, which constitute the motor of economic growth in dependent economies; and through the provision of technology and managerial skills by international capitalist institutions. External to Africa, sited in Western Europe and North America, primarily, the controllers of international capitalism can be seen as an *international bourgeoisie*, which constitutes the hegemonic fraction of the bourgeoisie in Africa.

The dominant role of the international bourgeoisie is, then, the first main characteristic of the bourgeoisie in Africa. It consists of those who share in the appropriation of surplus value through their ownership and control of international capital, ie. capital capable of acting in the global sphere.

Its domination and exploitation of African producers is organised through a variety of institutional arrangements: in the economic sphere, multinational corporations, international banking houses and international markets; in the political sphere, the national (eg. United States government, Ghana government) and international (eg. World Bank, International Monetary Fund) state structures of the capitalist world; in the cultural sphere various international media, educational and cultural organisations.

While secondary divisions exist within the international bourgeoisie, including national divisions (eg. between American and Japanese capital), and structural divisions (eg. between merchant, finance and industrial capital), the modern epoch has seen decreasing conflict between these strata and increasing class cohesion.

Analysis of the international bourgeoisie generally focuses on its foreign-ness to Africa as its most important characteristic, though this may be misleading. Those who see international exploitation of one state and people by foreign states and peoples, emphasise this class's foreign position and orientation as the source of dependency and underdevelopment.[67] Others see the internationalisation of capital, in the form particularly of the multinational corporation, as the key feature of the present epoch. They argue that the international bourgeoisie is best characterised, not by its national composition, but by its response to investment opportunities, and that localising it would not change its behaviour.[68]

Since the only real candidates for such status in the African world, as yet, would be certain South African white-controlled institutions, such as the Anglo-American Corporation, it is difficult to test this hypothesis, as these are not widely accepted as indigenous institutions. Perhaps Nigeria may soon provide a more conclusive test.

Within Africa, we find various social classes which are of a bourgeois type, ie. controlling the means of production and accumulating surpluses from the labour of others. This indigenous bourgeoisie has been classified by various analysts in different ways. One important tendency has been to emphasise the subordination of this class to the international bourgeoisie, referring to it as a *comprador* class, which serves the interests of international capital and can only survive in this inferior role.[69]

A contrary perspective has been to see the indigenous bourgeoisie as a prospective *national bourgeoisie*, struggling to free itself from foreign control and develop the productive forces of its own society in a more autonomous, and, of course, more profitable, manner. Although the role of such a national bourgeoisie has been seen as significant in much of the Third World, the concept has usually been applied more hesitantly in Africa.

> The so-called 'national bourgeoisies' in Africa, in this sense, are neither national nor bourgeois. They lack both the historical maturity of their metropolitan counterpart and the latter's objective economic base. The natural process of the development of the authentic national bourgeoisies and the national capitalisms in Africa was irreversibly arrested by these countries coming into contact with advanced capitalism.[70]

It is generally argued that most African states are too small, have too narrow resource bases, lack adequate capital and technical expertise, and have no tradition of capitalist behaviour, making independent capitalist development of the kind favoured by a national bourgeoisie impossible. Socialist strategies have been defended by some on this basis alone.[71]

This has not prevented African states from continuing to pursue capitalist development strategies, indicating that some national bourgeois impulse is likely to be at work within their ruling classes. Some scholars have reported a degree of success for such policies, although their findings should be treated with some scepticism.[72]

A further argument against the importance of a national bourgeoisie in Africa is that which emphasises its strangulation by the metropolitan bourgeoisie. It can be argued that where the national bourgeoisie has deep roots in pre-colonial merchant and petty producing classes, these have been extinguished by colonialism.[73] Where material conditions of size and natural wealth are much more favourable for development than in many industrialised states, as in Nigeria, Ethiopia and Zaire, subordination to global imperialism has blocked their development. In this view the indigenous bourgeoisie of Africa is forced into a comprador role rather than developing into a truly national bourgeoisie primarily because of external restraints, not internal material conditions. External restraint may be articulated through a process of balkanisation which has often produced debilitating internal conditions, but it is the factor of external domination that is the determining one. The insignificance of the national bourgeoisie and comprador character of the indigenous bourgeoisie is, therefore, the second main characteristic of the bourgeoisie in Africa.

One attempt to rescue the indigenous bourgeoisie from the etiolated state in which it is generally viewed in Africa is in the use of the concept of the *bureaucratic bourgeoisie* found in recent literature.[74] The proponents of this concept contend that, because of the very weaknesses of the indigenous bourgeoisie discussed above, they are unable to follow the classic pattern of development through private ownership of capital. Instead, a new path is followed in which the state becomes the mechanism through which the bourgeoisie controls capital and labour and by means of which it appropriates and accumulates surplus. This focuses us on the third major characteristic of the bourgeoisie in Africa, ie. it has been able to flourish only through a close attachment to the state, which it requires not only to exercise its global function in the class struggle, but also to establish its own control over the means of production.

This is a very appealing concept that appears to explain a great deal. Borrowed from the analysis of so-called socialist or state capitalist stystems in the industrialised world, it succeeds a number of similar attempts to construct a concept capable of illuminating the relationships between the state, private wealth and power, found in many areas, which do not fit the classical capitalist pattern.[75]

However, it is necessary to point out several problems with this concept. First of all, while the contention that it is the real social relations of production and not their juridical reflection that determines the nature of classes is a convincing one, those who use this principle to establish the validity of the concept of the bureaucratic bourgeoisie have not fully come to grips with the distinction between private and public property.

While it is true that ownership is only a form of control, and that control is the key relation, it is also true that each form of control has its own consequences, and that ownership has proven to be a particularly strong and stable form of control. Control of production by a bureaucracy through the state is certainly something far less than socialism, but it may also be something more than capitalism. The consequences of this form of control for the way in which surpluses are held and used can be quite important, although they may be extracted in very similar fashions. In the African context, for example, the bureaucratic form of control may mean a greater disposition to use capital in the national rather than the international sphere. In other words, a bureaucratic bourgeoisie like the one described by Shivji in Tanzania may, contrary to his view, be more of a national bourgoisie than, for example, the comprador land-owning bourgeoisies of Latin America.

This contention assumes, however, that the group referred to as a bureaucratic bourgeoisie is really unable to transform the surpluses it appropriates into the form of private property, and is restricted to control through the state, as in the Soviet Union. The second main problem with the concept of the bureaucratic bourgeoisie is, however, that it is too often applied to social formations in which private ownership of the means of production is still significant. To use the concept of the bureaucratic bourgeoisie in such cases, which are characteristic of Africa, where individuals use power to accumulate private wealth which is then reproduced in the private sphere of production, is certainly a mis-use of the concept, but a trap which is easily fallen into.[76]

This discussion leads us to a consideration of that element of the dominant class, defined by a heterogeneous range of production relations, which can be called the *petty bourgeoisie*. Marx himself lumped a variety of different categories into this class, from petty producers (the famous shoemakers), and owners of petty capital (the shopkeepers), to the servants of capital who do not necessarily possess any themselves (professionals, managers, administrators, army officers, etc.). He also characterised this as an unstable class, in the process of polarisation with most of its members being plunged down into the ranks of the proletariat.[77]

Nevertheless, in the context of contemporary Africa, the petty bourgeoisie has become the most important focus for class analysis of politics. It is often seen as the strongest indigenous class, and as the class that provides the leader-ship for nationalist movements, inheriting political power at the time of decolonisation. Its orientation as either nationalist or comprador is hotly debated. It is generally agreed that its main interest is to advance up the class hierarchy into positions of greater wealth and power, ie. to transform itself into a genuine bourgeoisie. Scholars have contended that the petty bourgeoisie has tried to do this but failed in Ghana, succeeded in Nigeria and Kenya, and succeeded, but through becoming a bureaucratic bourgeoisie, in Tanzania. The significance of this class has led to more attention being paid to its various internal divisions into different fractions, eg. a commercial petty bourgeoisie of small traders, shopkeepers, lorry and taxi owners, etc.; a rural petty bourgeoisie defined in similar terms to the *kulak* peasant class discussed below; and a bureaucratic petty bourgeoisie of civil servants, teachers, etc.[78]

Some have held out the possibility that this class may orient itself downwards rather than upwards, linking its fortunes to those of peasants and workers in opposition to the international bourgeoisie.[79] This possibility of 'committing class suicide' stems from Maoist theory, although its proponents often neglect the subordinate role Mao designated for the revolutionary petty bourgeoisie in the 3-class alliance of revolutionary forces.[80] Too often, the idea of petty bourgeois class suicide has appealed to those petty bourgeois intellectuals with a stronger commitment to Marxism as a vision of social change than as a mode of social analysis.[81]

The dominant internal political role heretofore played by the petty bourgeoisie in Africa, which constitutes the fourth main characteristic of the bourgeoisie in Africa, cannot be denied. Nor can the fact that this class has rarely confronted international capitalism directly, but has, instead, compromised and collaborated with it, accepting a subordinate role in the world economy in classic comprador fashion. Its opposition to this subordination has been largely rhetorical. In certain areas, such as Algeria and the former Portuguese colonies of Guinea-Bissau, Angola and Mozambique, the intransigence of the metropole has forced a more revolutionary path upon petty bourgeois-led guerrilla movements, but not enough time has transpired since their accession to state power to test whether this revolutionary orientation is more than skin deep.[82] The settler-ruled colonies of Zimbabwe, Namibia and South Africa are now engaged in a similar process, although there, especially in South Africa, the greater development of the class struggle may produce a more conclusive answer.

Finally, a few words about one of those pre-capitalist social classes mentioned earlier. It seems reasonable to place within the ranks of the dominant class those surviving holders of traditional authority who continue to be significant in many parts of Africa. This group encompasses, of course, many different relations to production within the catch-all concept of tradition. In some areas, like Swaziland, this group continues to control the state, although this power does not seem likely to last much longer, as the recent Ethiopian case illustrates. In many more places traditional authority holders, while having lost their political power, retain a significant control over production through powers of land allocation. In the immediate past these powers, including taxation and labour control, strengthened by colonialism through so-called 'indirect rule' structures, were much more important. Finally, in many other cases, while political and economic power may be lost, some ideological power remains as their former subjects only gradually change their attitudes.

The most important point about the traditional rulers, from the class perspective, is that they seem to represent a class being decomposed by the pressures of capitalism. Where economic power has been maintained it has been done by the traditional relations of production being transformed into, or linked with, capitalist relations. Chiefs become landlords charging economic rents rather than accepting tribute in kind. They tax the labour of migrant workers through fees paid by recruiting agencies. They use as their personal wealth the mineral royalties paid for rights to use what was once communal land. Those who have been able to use these techniques successfully have joined the bourgeoisie; those with less luck or more scruples find themselves pushed down into a petty bourgeoisie of salaried office-holding, or are dispensed with entirely and join the ranks of the oppressed.[83] As their role now seems to be based less on their relations to production, and more on their political and ideological relations, they can be understood best as a social category, like intellectuals, with interests associated to the bourgeoisie, rather than as a fraction of the bourgeoisie.

To summarise, then, it has been argued that dependency has produced four main characteristics of the bourgeoisie in Africa:

(1) the hegemonic role of the international bourgeoisie;
(2) the inability of indigenous bourgeois groups to constitute a national bourgeoisie by taking a hegemonic role and building a national economy;
(3) the dominant role of the petty bourgeoisie within the political practices of dependent social formations; and
(4) the critical role of the state in both political and economic spheres.

Proletariat

Having discussed the dominant classes in society, we can now turn to the oppressed. Recognising that Marxism views the proletariat as the key to revolution, its opponents offer a number of objections on this score in relation to Africa:

(1) workers in Africa do not constitute a permanent, urbanised, proletarianised class, but an amorphous collection of migrant workers (often 'target' workers) with rights to land in rural areas, hence not fully separated from their means of production and reduced to a level on which they 'have nothing to lose';

(2) urban workers, far from being exploited, are, in Africa, a highly-paid 'labour aristocracy', attuned to political conservatism by being better off than the 'wretched of the earth' in the rural areas;

(3) the inculcation of revolutionary consciousness in the African worker is a hopeless task, given his commitment to ethnic consciousness, constantly refreshed by the maintenance of his rural roots, and exacerbated by the heightened inter-ethnic contact and conflict found in urban areas.

'True proletarians', with only their labour to exchange for necessary income and security, are only just emerging in Africa, is the conclusion of these arguments.[84]

The last of these points has been considered in its more general form in the second section of this paper. The first, or 'man of two worlds', argument, is an important one. First of all, there is considerable evidence to suggest that the African urban work force is much more stable and committed to paid employment than is commonly supposed.[85]

In many places, rights in rural land have been lost by land alienation or overpopulation. Often several generations of a family have grown up and worked in the city. In one of the most industrialised areas, South Africa, the full proletarianisation of industrial workers has been artifically blocked by racist legislation at the same time as the area of recruitment of migrant workers has been spread into neighbouring countries to cheapen the costs of labour. It has been shown in this case, however, that far from being a force retarding capitalist development, this strategy has been used to lock the pre-capitalist mode of production into a debilitating symbiosis with capitalism. The mass of workers may not be fully proletarianised, retaining residual formal rights to land, but their dominant relation to production is their capacity to sell labour, which alone creates the conditions for the survival and reproduction of their families. The pre-capitalist mode is maintained in an attenuated form, fattening the surpluses accruing to the bourgeoisie.[86]

The second criticism listed above, generally styled the 'labour aristocracy' thesis, has been effectively used to cast doubt on the efficacy of the proletariat as a revolutionary class in Africa.[87] Increasing evidence has been produced, however, which discredits the way in which the thesis has been used. It is generally based on a comparison of rural and urban incomes which is meaningless as evidence of class differences. Instead, real living standards of urban workers are not, on average, significantly higher than those of the rural masses. The tendency has been to compare average urban incomes, inflated by including incomes of the petty bourgeois salariat, with average rural incomes deflated by including those of the rural proletariat. Furthermore, higher costs of living in urban areas, transfers of income from urban workers to rural families, and the greater insecurity of the worker compared to the peasant, have all been ignored.[88]

New interest has also been shown in the participation by proletarian elements in political movements, and their militancy, despite state control and petty bourgeois trade union leadership, has been highlighted.[89] Undoubtedly, a stratum of better-off labour aristocrats does exist in Africa, as in all capitalist societies,[90] but to include all the proletariat in this category would be a mistake.[91]

Many observers have sharply differentiated between the urban and rural strata of the proletariat, claiming that the greater size, isolation cultural backwardness and political weakness of the latter militates against their role as part of a revolutionary class. While there is some truth to these arguments, the greater exploitation and suffering of the rural proletariat should also be remembered.[92] Most of the points made by Fanon about the revolutionary role of the peasantry in Africa may, in fact, pertain more closely to the rural proletariat.

African workers can, therefore, be seen as a proletariat, albeit with their own unique characteristics, varying from one social formation to another.

The labour aristocracy concept can be used to stratify the proletariat into a high-paid aristocracy of skilled, white-collar and/or multinational corporation-employed workers on the one hand, deemed to be conservative in political orientation, and a mass of low paid, exploited workers, urban and rural, on the other hand, the revolutionary class described by Marx. The size of this class, its history, its degree of organisation and ideological awareness, all become relevant questions, with answers dependent upon the examination of specific social formations. Is there a *lumpenproletariat* in Africa's cities and rural areas, and is it as politically useless as Marx believed, or is it, as Fanon argues, a revolutionary class?[93] Fortunately, increasing attention is now being paid to these kinds of questions.

Peasantry
Mention of the rural proletariat leads us to a discussion of the peasantry in Africa. The literature on the question of rural economic relations is extensive. Various scholars have discussed African rural society in terms of models of communalism, feudalism and capitalism. Many have concluded that the continued significance of subsistence production, the maintenance of various systems of control over land by kinship groups rather than individuals, and the cultural isolation of rural communities, combine to frustrate the applicability of Marxist analysis in this sphere.[94]

Increasingly, however, detailed case studies have challenged such conclusions. It has been amply illustrated by now that, while capitalist relations may not have fully transformed rural societies, leaving some isolated areas of primarily subsistence production and various quasicapitalist relations in terms of land control and labour provision, most rural dwellers have been substantially linked to capitalist markets as peasant producers of commodities and/or as migrant workers and their dependents (both relations often being combined within the same family). Their participation in the capitalist mode of production can thus be seen as their primary relation to production. The mass of rural producers have not been fully proletarianised as yet, nor are they subsistence farmers, but they can be correctly characterised as peasant producers.

As such, their primary relation to production is as producers of commodities for the international market (and, to a lesser extent, for their own urban markets), as well as being involved in the production of some of their own use values. They utilise a combination of family and hired labour, on land held through a range of juridical forms from freehold tenure to usufruct rights, using tools, fertilisers, etc., largely purchased on the market. A continuum of rural producer relations can be seen, differentiated on the basis of these characteristics into various strata.[95]

At one pole we find land-owning capitalists who are so fully integrated into capitalism by their ownership of land, exclusive use of hired labour and production of commodities for exchange rather than use, that they are not peasants at all. Such extreme development, however, is not yet characteristic of Africa, outside of settler-occupied areas and foreign-owned plantations, though it can be seen developing in areas like Kenya, the Ivory Coast and northern Ghana.

The wealthiest peasants, and an increasingly politically significant class, are the *kulaks*, a kind of agricultural petty bourgeoisie who still provide some of their own labour and consume some of their own produce, as well as holding land through non-capitalist, often kinship-based, tenure systems, but who are accumulating surpluses with which, over time, they are able to change their relations of production, economically and politically, into more fully capitalist ones. The political role of the kulaks has been given some attention in recent work on Uganda and Tanzania.[96]

It is possible to create artificial benchmarks between rich, middle and poor peasants, decreasingly productive and prosperous, and more bound to non-capitalist tenure relations, and to the need to provide their own labour and consume their own production. At the other end of this continuum we find peasant families which survive only because some family members supplement the family income by selling their labour elsewhere, as migrant workers in the towns or as farm labourers on the land of foreign plantations, settlers and wealthier peasants. Families which are surviving as subsistence producers have been reduced to minimal numbers almost everywhere.

The political orientation of the peasantry, given its great size in most African societies, has been rightly viewed as of critical importance. The debate on these orientations is now, as it was in late nineteenth-century Europe and China in the 1920s, between those who believe in its revolutionary capacity, on the one hand, and those who see it as an essentially conservative force on the other.[97]

The former have been particularly concerned to make their case in relation to Africa, as the small size of the African proletariat seems to leave little alternative to the peasants as a revolutionary class. Some of the examples used to establish their argument would seem, however, to be of still dubious revolutionary content, or to have seriously underestimated the role of urban workers and confused peasants with a land-hungry rural proletariat. It should also be noted that, while not endorsing the universal determinism of a stage-by-stage advance to socialism adhered to by some,[98] Marxism cannot be understood as guaranteeing that the revolution is just around the corner.

In conclusion, we must mention several of the remaining lacunae in this analysis, which should constitute an agenda for further exploration. These problem areas are only meaningful once we have accepted the relevance of Marxist analysis to African politics, including its acceptance of the need to struggle for revolutionary change.

We do not mean to suggest by this, however, that we have forgotten our earlier contention concerning the nature of this essay. We have attempted to present a survey of a wide range of work applying Marxist analysis to African politics, from varying perspectives and with different results. We are not dealing with a cohesive school of thought, nor advancing a systematic model. Nor do we wish to suggest that such theorising can be a substitute for the concrete analysis of specific social formations. We hope only that a common tendency in the field will be made somewhat clearer and more comprehensible.

The first of these unresolved issues is the problem of who is the immediate enemy. Some have tended to see foreign exploitation as the main enemy and have advanced national unity, albeit leaving out certain comprador elements, as a weapon against the metropolitan bourgeoisie. Others have emphasised the primacy of the internal class struggle. The first group hope to achieve a kind of self-reliant development free of the clutches of international capitalism. The second group look to the internalisation of labour and international struggle as necessary prerequisites for meaningful local advances.

The second, related issue is that of the mechanism and pace of change. Some argue that a capitalist revolution is required in Africa in order to create the pre-conditions for further change toward a better society. Others contend that socialist revolutions, or at least revolutions which open the path to socialist transformation, should be the immediate goal of the struggle. Finally, there are those who have suggested a middle road, 'the non-capitalist path to development', not fully capitalist but not yet socialist, in which the pre-conditions for socialist development can evolve in a guided manner.[99]

These different strategies have different implications for class struggle. If the first is accepted, then the development of a national bourgeoisie and its exploitation of the masses is seen as inevitable and progressive. In the socialist scenario the seizure of power by the oppressed, usually led by the proletariat, but with varying roles for alliances with peasants and the petty bourgeoisie, is the desired goal. In the last option, however, the weakness of the proletariat is accepted and the important role of the 'progressive petty bourgeoisie' is stressed.

Finally, there is the question of the relation between the global and the local communities. Are national revolution, national development and national socialism realistic goals, or is the global system created by international capitalism so integrated and pervasive that the system as a whole must change before further progress can be made in any particular part of the system?

This question has a long history in socialist polemics.[100] It has recently been joined in the African context. Its further consideration, and the development of new theory to cope with the problem, is, in the sphere of ideology, the next important step in the struggle.

Notes

1 See Gwendolen M. Carter, 'African Studies in the United States, 1955–1975', *Issue*, VI, 2/3, Summer/Fall (1976); and Thomas Hodgkin, 'Where the Paths Began', in C. Fyfe ed., *African Studies since 1945: a Tribute to Basil Davidson*, Longman Group, London, 1976.

2 Bernard Crick, *The American Science of Politics*, Routledge and Kegan Paul, London, 1959.

3 A point made, for example, by Donal Cruise O'Brien, 'Modernisation, Order, and the Erosion of a Democratic Ideal: American Political Science, 1960–70', *Journal of Development Studies*, 8, 4 (1972), pp. 351–78; and Jonathan A. Sanford, 'Political Development and Economic Change: A Radical Interpretation of Almond and Powell's Developmental Approach', *Journal of International and Comparative Studies*, 4, 2 (1971), pp. 1–36.

4 See David Goddard, 'Limits of British Anthropology', *New Left Review*, 58, November–December 1969, pp. 79–89; and Archie Mafeje, 'The Problem of Anthropology in Historical Perspective: An Inquiry into the Growth of the Social Sciences',

Canadian Journal of African Studies, 10, 2, pp. 307–34.

5 The widening of this focus is often dated from the publication, in 1940, of *African Political Systems*, edited by M. Fortes and E.E. Evans-Pritchard (Oxford University Press, London); but that the process was a slowly accelerating one can be seen by comparison with John Middleston and David Tait eds., *Tribes Without Rulers*, Routledge and Kegan Paul, London, 1958, and David Apter, *The Politics of Modernisation*, Chicago University Press, Chicago and London, 1965.

6 Allen Isaacman and Jennifer Davis, 'United States Policy Toward Mozambique Since 1945', *Africa Today*, 25, 1 (1978), pp. 29–55.

7 Carter, *op.cit.*

8 Particularly important in translating Parsonian sociology into political science were the works of David Easton, Marion J. Levy Jr. and Gabriel Almond. For example, see David Easton, *The Political System*, Alfred A. Knopf, New York, 1953; M.J. Levy Jr., *Modernisation and the Structure of Society: A Setting for International Affairs*, Princeton University Press, 1966; and Gabriel Almond and James S. Coleman eds. *The Politics of the Developing Areas*, Princeton University Press, 1960.

9 For an incisive critique of this perspective see Archie Mafeje, 'The Ideology of "Tribalism"', *The Journal of Modern African Studies*, 9, 2 (1971), pp. 253–62.

10 For an example of the subtlety of such indirect pressures see the exchange of letters in the pages of the *New York Review of Books* during 1977–8 between various luminaries of the American academic firmament concerning the appointments process at Harvard during the McCarthy period. That this purge was not wholly successful can be seen in the survival of a scholar like Paul Baran, whose *The Political Economy of Growth*, Prometheus Books, New York, 1957, and (with Paul Sweezy), *Monopoly Capital*, Monthly Review Press, New York, 1966, have profoundly influenced modern dependency theory.

11 See the seminal essay by Andre Gunder Frank, 'The Development of Underdevelopment', *Monthly Review*, September 1966, as well as such later works as *Capitalism and Underdevelopment in Latin America*, Monthly Review Press, New York and London, 1967; *Latin America: Underdevelopment or Revolution?*, Monthly Review Press, New York and London, 1969; and *Lumpen-Bourgeoisie and Lumpen-Development: Dependency, Class and Politics in Latin America*, Monthly Review Press, New York and London, 1972. See also Celso Furtado, *Development and Underdevelopment*, University of California Press, Berkeley, 1964; T. Dos Santos, 'The Crisis of Development Theory and the Problem of Dependence in Latin America', in Henry Bernstein ed. *Development and Underdevelopment: The Third World Today*, Penguin, 1973, pp. 57–80; and F.H. Cardoso, 'Dependent Capitalist Development in Latin America', *New Left Review*, 74, July–August 1972, pp. 83–95.

12 Giovanni Arrighi and John S. Saul, *Essays in the Political Economy of Africa*, Monthly Review Press, New York and London, 1973; Robin Cohen, 'Class in Africa: Analytical Problems and Perspectives', in R. Miliband and J. Saville eds., *The Socialist Register 1972*, The Merlin Press, London, 1972, pp. 231–55; Gavin N. Kitching, 'The Concept of Class and the Study of Africa', *The African Review*, 2, 3 (1972); and Gavin Williams, 'The Social Stratification of a Neo-Colonial Economy: Western Nigeria', in Christopher Allen and R.W. Johnson eds. *African Perspectives: Papers in the History, Politics and Economics of Africa Presented to Thomas Hodgkin*, Cambridge University Press, 1970, pp. 225–50.

13 'We have argued that class and class consciousness have a partial manifestation which may be activated in certain situations and in certain measure', Cohen, *op.cit.*, p. 252.

14 For example, the work of Nicos Poulantzas and, through him, Antonio Gramsci, had had a profound influence on scholars like Leys and Saul in East African studies, and Wolpe, Legassick, Kaplan and Davies in Southern African studies, introducing such concepts as 'the relative autonomy of the state', 'the power block', and 'hegemony'. See Nicos Poulantzas, *Political Power and Social Classes*, New Left Books, London, 1973, and *Classes in Contemporary Capitalism*, New Left Books, London, 1975.

15 For the use of this term see Aidan Foster-Carter, 'Neo-Marxist Approaches to Development and Under-development', in Emmanuel de Kadt and Gavin Williams eds., *Sociology and Development*, Tavistock Publications, London, 1974, pp. 67–105.

16 Amin's essay 'Class Struggle in Africa', *Revolution*, 1, 9 (1964), reprinted by the African Research Group, Cambridge, Mass., is an early precursor of the post-1970 trend. Its more mature development can be seen in his *Accumulation on a World Scale*, Monthly Review Press, New York and London, 1974; *Un-Equal Development: An Essay in the Social Formations of Peripheral Capitalism*, Monthly Review Press, New York and London, 1976; and 'Universality of Cultural Spheres', *Monthly Review*, 28, 9 (1977), pp. 25–44. Directly relevant to Africa are his *Neo-Colonialism in West Africa*, Penguin, 1973; 'Under-development and Dependence in Black Africa—Origins and Contemporary Forms', *Journal of Modern African Studies*, 10, 4 (1972), pp. 508–20; and 'The Future of Africa', *Journal of Southern African Affairs*, 2, 3 (1977), pp. 355–70.

17 Geoffrey Kay, *Development and Underdevelopment: A Marxist Anlysis*, Macmillan, London, 1975.

18 The most comprehensive presentation of Wallerstein's views on the modern world economy can be found in his *The Modern World-System: Capitalist Agriculture and the Origins of the European World-Economy in the Sixteenth Century*, The Academic Press, New York and London, 1974. Recent applications of his approach to Africa include: 'Class and status in contemporary Africa', pp. 277–83 in Peter Gutkind and Peter Waterman eds., *African Social Studies: A Radical Reader*, Monthly Review Press, New York and London, 1973; 'Class Formation in the Capitalist World-Economy', *Politics and Society*, 5, 3 (1975), pp. 367–76; and 'The Three Stages of African Development in the World-Economy', in Peter C.W. Gutkind and Immanuel Wallerstein eds., *The Political Economy of Contemporary Africa*, Sage Publications, Beverly Hills, 1976, pp. 30–57.

19 To illustrate the kind of work meant, reference can be made to, *inter alia*: Björn Beckmann, *Organising the Farmers Cocoa Politics and National Development in Ghana*, Scandinavian Institute of African Studies, Uppsala, 1976; Henry Bernstein, 'Notes on Capital and Peasantry', *Review of African Political Economy*, 10, September–December, 1977, pp. 60–73; Bonnie Campbell, 'Social Change and Class Formation in a French West African State', *Canadian Journal of African Studies*, 8, 2 (1974), pp. 285–306, and 'Neo-Colonialism, Economic Dependence and Political Change: Cotton Textile Production in the Ivory Coast', *Review of African Political Economy*, 2, 1975, pp. 36–53; Robert Davies, David Kaplan, Mike Morris and Dan O'Meara, 'Class Struggle and the Periodisation of the State in South Africa', *Review of African Political Economy*, 7, September–December 1976, pp. 4–30; Gavin Kitching, 'Modes of Production and Kenyan Dependency', *Review of African Political Economy*, 8, January–April 1977, pp. 56–74; Olivier LeBrun and Chris Gerry, 'Petty Producers and Capitalism', *Review of African Political Economy*, 3, May–October 1975, pp. 20–2; Martin Legassick, 'South Africa: Capital accumulation and violence', *Economy and Capitalism*, *Review of African Political Economy*, 3, May–October 1975, pp. 20–Post-1948 South Africa', *Journal of Southern African Studies*, 1, 1 (1974), pp. 5–35; Colin Leys, *Underdevelopment in Kenya: The Political Economy of Neo-Colonialism*, Heinemann, London, 1975; Mahmood Mamdani, *Politics and Class Formation in Uganda*, Monthly Review Press, New York and London, 1976; John Markakis and Nega Ayele, *Class and Revolution in Ethiopia*, Spokesmen, Nottingham, 1978; Claude Meillassoux, 'A Class Analysis of the Bureaucratic Process in Mali', *The Journal of Development Studies*, 6, 2 (1970), pp. 97–110; Robin Palmer and Neil Parsons eds., *The Roots of Rural Poverty in Central and Southern Africa*, Heinemann, London, 1977; John Saul, 'African Peasants and Revolution', *Review of African Political Economy*, 1, 1974, pp. 41–68, 'The State in Post-Colonial Societies: Tanzania', in Ralph Miliband and John Saville eds., *The Socialist Register 1974*, The Merlin Press, London, 1974, pp. 349–72, and 'The Unsteady State: Uganda, Obote and General Amin', *Review of African Political Economy*, 5, January–April (1976), pp. 49–62; Issa G. Shivji, *Class Struggles in Tanzania*, Monthly Review Press, New

York and London, 1976; Terisa Turner, 'Multinational Corporations and the In-stability of the Nigerian State', *Review of African Political Economy*, 5, January–April 1976, pp. 63–79; Gavin Williams, *Nigeria: Economy and Society*, 1, 4 (1972), pp. 425–56, and H. Wolpe, 'The "white working class" in South Africa', *Economy and Society*, 5, 2 (1976), pp. 197–240.

20 For an exchange illustrating the continued distance between anti-Marxist and neo-Marxist perspectives, as well as the tension between 'orthodox' and neo-Marxist scholars, see B.S. Kantor and H.F. Kenny, 'The Poverty of Neo-Marxism; the case of South Africa', *Journal of Southern African Studies*, 3, 1 (1976), pp. 20–40, answered by Harold Wolpe, 'A Comment on "The Poverty of Neo-Marxism"', *Journal of Southern African Studies*, 4, 2 (1978), pp. 240–56.

21 See Karl Marx, *A Contribution to the Critique of Political Economy*, Progress Publishers, Moscow, 1970, pp. 20–2, for a succinct statement of the historical materialist conception of change.

22 See Poulantzas, *Political Power and Social Classes*, pp. 77–85, for a discussion of these concepts based on their relation to a combination of modes of production within a single social formation. Social categories are defined as non-economically defined groups with interests associated to those of a class; fractions as elements in a class capable of competing for hegemony; and strata as elements in a class that is differentiated but lacks the capacity to compete for hegemony.

23 Friedrich Engels, letter to Joseph Bloch (1890), reprinted in Howard Selsam, David Goldsworthy and Harry Martell eds., *Dynamics of Social Change: A Reader in Marxist Social Science*, International Publishers, New York, 1970, pp. 76–7.

24 For a discussion of the concepts of hegemony and power bloc see Poulantzas, *op.cit.*, pp. 137–41. Simply, the former refers to the domination of the ruling class over society, as well as to the domination of the strongest fraction of the ruling class over its allies, and the latter refers to the alliance of groups within the ruling class.

25 ' ... the State is the form in which the individuals of a ruling class assert their common interests', Karl Marx and Friedrich Engels, *The German Ideology*, 1846, quoted in T.B. Bottomore and Maximilien Rubel eds., *Karl Marx: Selected Writings in Sociology and Social Philosophy*, Penguin, 1963, p. 228.

26 For a discussion of this oppressive role of ideology see Poulantzas, *op.cit.*, pp. 195–221.

27 Marx and Engels, *The German Ideology*, quoted in Selsam, *et.al.*, *op.cit.*, pp. 328–9.

28 Marx, Karl, *Critique of the Gotha Program*, 1875, reprinted in Lewis S. Feuer ed., *Basic Writings on Politics and Philosophy: Karl Marx and Friedrich Engels*, Anchor Books, New York, 1959, p. 119.

29 For a discussion of the political processes involved in this final transition see V.I. Lenin, *The State and Revolution*, Foreign Languages Publishing House, Moscow, 1917, esp. pp. 147–56.

30 For examples of this argument see Elliot J. Berg, 'The Character and Prospects of African Economies', in Walter Goldschmidt ed., *The United States and Africa*. Praeger, New York and London, 1963, pp. 115–55. Berg claims that 'In most African countries, between 80 and 90 per cent of the population is found in rural areas engaged in agriculture .... Within the agricultural sector, subsistence farming remains the pre-dominant activity' (p. 123).

31 Charges of Marx's supposed ethnocentricism, or even racism, have generated some heated discussion. See, for example, the exchange between Okello Oculi, 'Marx's Attitude to Colonialism', and Kwesi Botchwey, 'A Short Rejoinder', in *The African Review*, 4, 3 (1974), pp. 381–400.

32 For a statement of the dual economy thesis see Ann Seidman, *Comparative Development Strategies in East Africa*, East African Publishing House, Nairobi, 1972, pp. 13–32.

33 On pre-capitalist modes of production see: David Beach, 'The Shona Economy: Branches of Production', in Palmer and Parsons, *op.cit.*, pp. 37–65; Catherine Coquery-Vidrovitch, 'Research on an African mode of production', in Gutkind and Waterman, *op.cit.*, pp. 71–92; Jack Goody, *Technology, Tradition and the State in*

Africa, Oxford University Press, London, 1971; Barry Hindess and Paul Q. Hirst, *Pre-Capitalist Modes of Production*, Routledge and Kegan Paul, London and Boston, 1975; E.J. Hobsbawm ed., *Karl Marx: Pre-Capitalist Economic Formations*, Lawrence and Wishart, London, 1964; Mamdani, *op.cit.*, pp. 17–39; Jacques J. Maqeut, *The Premise of Inequality in Ruanda*, Oxford University Press, London, 1961; Claude Meillassoux, *op.cit.*, pp. 99–101; Suzanne Miers and Igor Kopytoff eds., *Slavery in Africa*, University of Wisconsin Press, Madison, 1977, and Emmanuel Terray, *Marxism and 'Primitive' Societies*, Monthly Review Press, New York and London, 1972.

34 This period is referred to by Wallterstein as Phase I in the integration of Africa into the world economy. See his 'The Three Stages of African Involvement in the World Economy', *op.cit.*, pp. 32–9. It is also similar to Samir Amin's concept of the 'mercantilist' period in 'Under-development and Dependence in Black Africa', *op.cit.* For further studies of this period, illustrative of our argument, see: E.A. Alpers, 'Re-thinking African Economic History', *Kenya Historical Review*, 1, 2 (1973), pp. 163–87; Colin Bundy, 'The Emergence and Decline of a South African Peasantry', *African Affairs*, 71, 285 (1972), pp. 369–88; Gervase Clarence-Smith, 'Underdevelopment and Class Formation in Ovamboland, 1844–1884', Palmer and Parsons, *op.cit.*, pp. 96–112; Philip Ehrensatt, 'The political economy of informal empire in pre-colonial Nigeria, 1807–1884', *Canadian Journal of African Studies*, V1, 3 (1972), pp. 451–90: S. Miers and I. Kopytoff eds., *op.cit.*; Neil Parsons, 'The Economic History of Khama's Country in Botswana, 1844–1930', Palmer and Parsons, *op.cit.*, pp. 144–70; Walter Rodney, *How Europe Underdeveloped Africa*, ch. 4, Tanzania Publishing House, Dar es Salaam, 1972; and Fole Soremekun, 'Trade and Dependency in Central Angola: The Ovimbundu in the Nineteenth Century', Palmer and Parsons, *op.cit.*, pp. 82–95.

35 For a discussion of the colonial period *per se* see E.A. Brett, *Colonialism and Underdevelopment in East Africa*, NOK Publishers, New York, 1973; G.B. Kay, *The Political Economy of Colonialism in Ghana*, Cambridge University Press, London, 1972; Leys, *op.cit.*; Mamdani, *op.cit.*; Palmer and Parsons, *op.cit.*; Shivji, *op.cit.*; Jean Suret-Canale, *French Colonialism in Tropical Africa, 1900–1945*, London C. Hurst & Co., 1971; and Richard D. Wolff, *The Economics of Colonialism: Britain and Kenya, 1870–1930*, Yale University Press, New York and London, 1974.

36 In Kenya, where, in the late colonial period, freehold tenure was made available for the indigenous people, having previously been reserved for white settlers and plantation owners, the process was sharply accelerated after independence. Leys, *op.cit.*, p. 72, 'the drive towards complete individual freehold tenure ... flowed logically from the critical decision to accept the general structure of the colonial economy. That structure rested on individual property. The main capital asset of the Africans in Kenya was land. For it to be held ultimately on the basis of some other principle was simply inconsistent with the effective incorporation of the African economy into the wider capitalist structure'. While correct in principle, that this passage illustrates an overly economistic view can be seen by comparison to South Africa, where opposite policies produced by a different conjunction of class forces, resulted in a white monopoly over freehold tenure, but still linked Africans, in a different way, to the needs of the capitalist economy.

37 Discussion of the process of peasant proletarianisation in Africa was initiated by Giovanni Arrighi, 'Labour Supplies in Historical Perspective: A Study of the Proletarianization of the African Peasantry in Rhodesia', *The Journal of Development Studies*, 3 (1970).

38 See, for example, Terisa Turner, *op.cit.*, and M. Burdette, 'Nationalization in Zambia: a Critique of Bargaining Theory', *Canadian Journal of African Studies*, 11, 3 (1979), pp. 471–96.

39 While most observers stress the dependency on metropolitan capital of indigenous capitalists, there is still a good deal of material discussing the rise and significance of this class. *Eg.*, Paul Kennedy, 'The Indigenous Capitalism in Ghana', Nicola Swainson, 'The Rise of a National Bourgeoisie in Kenya', and Steven Langdon, 'The

State and Capitalism in Kenya', all in the *Review of African Political Economy*, 8, (1977).

40 See, for example, President J.K. Nyerere of Tanzania, 'Ujamaa—the Basis of African Socialism' originally published as a TANU pamphlet in 1962 but reprinted frequently, as in Julius K. Nyerere, *Ujamaa: Essays in Socialism*, Oxford University Press, London and Dar es Salaam, 1968, and the Republic of Kenya, *Sessional Paper No. 10: African Socialism and its Application to Planning in Kenya*, Government Printer, Nairobi, 1965, for the minimalist and maximalist statement of this position. Nyerere argues that traditional values *can* prevent class formation in Africa, if supported by socialist structures. The Kenyan planners appear to believe that it *will* achieve this goal necessarily, despite the policies of the Kenyan Government.

41 President Nyerere's view of traditional Tanzanian society has been directly challenged by his countryman, S.S. Mushi, in 'Ujamaa: Modernisation by Traditionalisation', *Taamuli*, 1, 2 (1971). Mushi sees much more scope for private appropriation in traditional society than does Nyerere. Other critiques of African Socialism's structures on tradition include J. Mohan, 'Varieties of African Socialism', *The Socialist Register 1966*, Monthly Review Press, New York, 1966, pp. 220–66; and Ehud Sprinzak, 'African Traditional Socialism', *Journal of Modern African Studies*, 2, 4 (1973), pp. 629–47.

42 Critiques of African educational strategies, which conclude that they are effective in transferring to students the attitudes and values required by these countries' capitalist economies, not those formally inculcated in educational programmes, include Joel D. Barkan, *An African Dilemma: University Students and Politics in Ghana, Tanzania and Uganda*, Oxford University Press, Nairobi, 1975; David Court, 'The Education System as a Response to Inequality in Tanzania and Kenya', *Journal of Modern African Studies*, 14, 4 (1976), pp. 661–90; Philip Foster, *Education and Social Change in Ghana*, Routledge & Kegan Paul, London, 1965; and Kenneth Prewitt ed., *Education and Political Values: an East African case study*, East African Publishing House, Nairobi, 1971.

43 Delegation from Maputo to the Conference of African Ministers of Education held in Lagos, 27 January to 9 February, 1976, 'Education Policy in the People's Republic of Mozambique', *Journal of Modern African Studies*, 14, 2 (1976), pp. 331–9.

44 For a discussion on the pattern of superordination-subordination at least one observer has found typical of African authority patterns, see Robert Price, 'Politics and Culture in Contemporary Ghana: The Big-Man Small-Boy Syndrome', *Journal of African Studies*, 1, 2 (1974), pp. 173–204.

45 The proposition that, in Africa, authority is wielded with *noblesse oblige* and responded to with deference is defended by Ali A. Mazrui, 'Political Superannuation and the Trans-Class Man in Africa', *International Journal of Comparative Sociology*, 9, 2 (1968), pp. 81–96.

46 For the concept of the 'modernising elite' see Apter, *op.cit.*, pp. 138–44. Such trust is more often placed, by academics of the West in a military elite, *eg.*, Morris Janowitz, *The Military in the Political Development of New Nations*, University of Chicago Press, Chicago and London, 1964; or a bureaucratic elite, *eg.*, Joseph LaPolambara ed., *Bureaucracy and Political Development*, Princeton University Press, Princeton, New Jersey, 1963; than in politicians embarrassed by popular responsibilities.

47 Beckman, *op.cit.*, and Bob Fitch and Mary Oppenheimer, *Ghana: End of an Illusion*, Monthly Review Press, New York and London, 1966.

48 Martin, Guy, 'Socialism, Economic Development and Planning in Mali, 1960–1968', *Canadian Journal of African Studies*, 10, 1 (1976); and Meillassoux, *op.cit.*

49 Contrast the positive attitude toward the regime expressed by Henry Bienen, *Kenya: The Politics of Participation and Control*, Princeton University Press, Princeton, New Jersey, 1974; with that of Leys, *Underdevelopment in Kenya*, *op.cit.*

50 Contrast the adulation showered on the regime by Cranford Pratt, *The critical phase in Tanzania: 1945–1968*, Cambridge University Press, London, 1976; with the scorn of Shivji, *op.cit.*

51 Contrast Richard Hall, *The High Price of Principles: Kaunda and the White South*,

107

Penguin Book, Harmondsworth, 1969; with Kren Eriksen, 'Zambia: Class Formation and Detente', *Review of African Political Economy*, 9 (1968), pp. 4–26.

52 Contrast Elliot J. Berg, 'Structural Transformation versus Gradualism: Recent Economic Developments in Ghana and the Ivory Coast', pp. 187–230, in Philip Foster and Aristide R. Zolberg eds., *Ghana and the Ivory Coast: Perspectives on Modernisation*, University of Chicago Press, Chicago and London, 1971; with Samir Amin, *Neo-Colonialism in West Africa*, *op.cit.*

53 Hutchful, Eboe, 'The Political Economy of Military Intervention in Ghana', paper presented to the Annual Conference of the Canadian Association of African Studies, 1977, and Judith Marshall, 'The State of Ambivalence: Right and Left Options in Ghana', *Review of African Political Economy*, 5 (1976), pp. 49–62.

54 Adelman, Kenneth Lee, 'The Church-State Conflict in Zaire: 1969–1974', *African Studies Review*, 18, 1 (1975), pp. 102–16.

55 Eripsen, *op.cit.*, and Lofchie, Michael F. 'Agrarian Crisis and Economic Liberalism in Tanzania', *Journal of Modern African Studies*, 11, 3 (1978), pp. 451–75, discuss two recent examples.

56 See, for example, Peter Lloyd ed., *The New Elites of Tropical Africa*, Oxford University Press, London, 1967; and *Africa in Social Change*, Penguin Books, Harmondsworth, 2nd ed., 1967.

57 Such reasoning lies behind the use of terms such as 'political class' (Cohen, *op.cit.*, p. 248), and 'ruling class', (Kitching, *op.cit.*, p. 348).

58 Poulantzas, *op.cit.*, pp. 115–7.

59 To take three widely separated examples of supporting evidence for this proposition: Dennis Austin, *Politics in Ghana, 1946–1960*, Oxford University Press, London, 1964, pp. 195, 197–8, 253, 321–3; Dennis L. Cohen and Jack Parson, 'The Uganda Peoples' Congress Branch and Constituency Elections of 1970', *The Journal of Commonwealth Political Studies*, 11, 1 (1973), pp. 203–5; and John D. Holm, 'Rural development in Botswana: three basic trends', *Rural Africana*, 18 (1972).

60 See Shivji, *op.cit.*, for a discussion of 'legitimate' methods of accumulation; and Victor T. LeVine, *Political Corruption: The Ghana Case*, Hoover Institution, Stanford, Calif., 1975, for 'illegitimate' forms.

61 See note 42.

62 Mazrui, Ali, A., 'Pluralism and National Integration', p. 339 in Leo Kuper and M.G. Smith eds., *Pluralism in Africa*, University of California Press, Berkeley and Los Angeles, Calif., 1969. For another example of this kind of argument see R.H. Jackson, 'Political Stratification in Tropical Africa', *Canadian Journal of African Studies*, 7, 3 (1973), pp. 381–400.

63 Marx, Karl, *A Contribution to the Critique of Political Economy*, *loc.cit.*

64 See, for example, V.I. Lenin, 'The Right of Nations to Self-Determination', Selsam, *et.al.*, *op.cit.*, pp. 375–9; Joseph Stalin, *Marxism and the National Question*, Mass Publications, Calcutta, 1976; and James Blaut, 'Are Puerto Ricans a National Minority?', *Monthly Review*, 29, 1, May (1977).

65 See, for example, the analysis of South African society as consisting of two nations, resulting in a two-stage strategy of revolution, first national, then socialist, in Ben Molapo, 'On the National Question', *The African Communist*, 66 (1976), pp. 82–93; and Toussaint, 'Class and Nation in the S. African Revolution', *The African Communist*, 72 (1978), pp. 19–31.

66 An example of the many issues of controversy surrounding the analysis of relations of production in the dependent mode of production is the criticism of theorists like Amin, Kay and Emmanuel, who, it is claimed, concentrate too much on unequal relations of trade and the role of merchant capital in dependency rather than on unequal relations of production and the internalisation of capital and labour. See Bernstein, 'Underdevelopment and the Law of Value, a critique of Kay', *Review of African Political Economy*, 6 (1976), pp. 51–64.

67 Shivji's (*op.cit.*, p. 45) use of the concept 'metropolitan bourgeoisie' is representative of this tendency, as is the centre-periphery or core-periphery imagery of dependency theory.

68 This argument is advanced by, for example, Manfred Bienefeld and Duncan Innes, 'Capital Accumulation and South Africa', *Review of African Political Economy*, 7 (1976), pp. 31–55; and Stephen Hymer, 'International Politics and International Economies: A Radical Approach, *Monthly Review*, 29, 10 (1978), pp. 15–36.

69 This position has had its greatest impact on African studies through the work of Frantz Fanon, especially *The Wretched of the Earth*, Macgibbon & Kee, London, 1965.

70 Shivji, *op.cit.*, p. 20.

71 See R.H. Green, 'Political Independence and the National Economy: An Essay in the Political Economy of Decolonisation', Allen and Johnson, *op.cit.*, pp. 273–324, for an example of this perspective.

72 See note 39 above. For an argument which sees the national bourgeoisie as a class of increasing significance in Africa, see Jack Woddis, *New Theories of Revolution*, Lawrence and Wishart, London, 1972, pp. 84–100.

73 Mamdani, *op.cit.*, pp. 28–35, discusses this process in Uganda. Also see Rhoda Howard, *Colonialism and Underdevelopment in Ghana*, Croom Helm, London, 1978.

74 See the work of Shivji, *op.cit.*, and Mamdani, *op.cit.*, as well as the excellent critique of the use of the concept by Colin Leys, 'The "Over-developed" Post-Colonial State: A Re-evaluation', *Review of African Political Economy*, 5 (1976), pp. 39–48.

75 Examples include the concept of 'ruling class' and 'political class' used by Kitching and Cohen respectively (see note 12), as well as 'organisational bourgeoisie', used by I.L. Markovitz, *Power and Class in Africa*, Prentice-Hall, Englewood Cliffs, New Jersey, 1977; and the 'Nizers' (Africanizers), used by Michaela von Freyhold, 'The Post-Colonial State and its Tanzanian Version', *Review of African Political Economy*, 8 (1977), pp. 75–89.

76 Mamdani's concept of the 'petty bureaucratic bourgeoisie', referring to groups such as civil servants and teachers employed by the colonial state would seem to be such a mis-use. It seeks to elevate into a class fraction what is only a social category.

77 Marx, Karl and Friedrich Engels, *The Communist Manifesto*, Monthly Review Press, New York and London, 1968, pp. 45–47. The concept has only come into use in studies of Africa recently, but the class referred to has been discussed previously under more ambiguous labels, such as Cohen's 'intendant class' (R. Cohen, *op.cit.*, pp. 249–50) and Kitching's 'middle class' 'Kitching, *op.cit.*, p. 349).

78 See, on Ghana, Marshal, *op.cit.*, on Nigeria, Williams, *op.cit.*; on Tanzania, Shivji, *op.cit.* The fullest example of analysing the relation between petty bourgeois class fractions and political movements can be found in Mamdani, *op.cit.*

79 Cabral, Amilcar, *Revolution in Guinea*, Monthly Review Press, New York and London, 1969.

80 See Stuart R. Schram, *The Political Thought of Mao Tse-tung*, Praeger, New York and London, 1963, pp. 202–64; and Paul M. Sweezy, 'Theory and Practice in the Mao Period', *Monthly Review*, 28, 9 (1977), pp. 1–12.

81 See Shivji, *op.cit.*, pp. 22–4 and 116–20, for evidence of this tendency in the emphasis given to proletarian ideology, not a proletarian class, as the key to revolutionary success.

82 For an optimistic perspective on the course of the revolution in Mozambique see Allen Isaacman, *A Luta Continua: Creating a New Society in Mozambique*, State University of New York, Binghampton, New York, 1978.

83 For a discussion of this tendency see Beckmann, *op.cit.*, and Meillassoux, *op.cit.* Woddis, *op.cit.*, pp. 74–9, gives a brief account of the reactionary role of African chiefs.

84 'Most wage earners are not solely dependent upon the demand for labour but maintain a hedge against unemployment and insecurity by retaining strong kinship links with both urban and rural relatives and their rights to land in the countryside', Jackson, *op.cit.*, p. 387. Once again, there has been an attempt to avoid these problems in some of the neo-Marxist literature through the use of more ambiguous terms. See, for example, R. Cohen, *op.cit.*, 'working class'; Kitching, *op.cit.*, 'urban manual workers', and Williams, 'the social stratification of a neo-colonial economy ...', *op.cit.* The tension between narrow and broad definitions of the proletariat, the

former based strictly on economic relations and focused on industrial, manual workers, and the latter including, *inter alia*, wider political and ideological relations and white collar, salaried and intellectual workers, is long-standing in Marxist literature. See the discussion in Adam Przeworski, 'Proletariat into a Class: The Process of Class Formation from Karl Kautsky's *The Class Struggle* to Recent Controversies', *Politics and Society*, 7, 4 (1977), pp. 343–401.

85 See the essays collected in Richard Sandbrook and Robin Cohen eds., *The Development of an African Working Class*, Longman, London, 1975; and Margaret Peil, *The Ghanaian Factory Worker: Industrial Man in Africa*, Cambridge University Press, London, 1972.

86 Martin Legassick and Harold Wolpe, 'The Bantustans and Capital Accumulation in South Africa', *Review of African Political Economy*, 7 (1976), pp. 87–107.

87 See, for example, Giovanni Arrighi, 'International Corporations, Labor Aristocracies, and Economic Development in Tropical Africa', Robert I. Rhodes ed., *Imperialism and Underdevelopment: A Reader*, Monthly Review Press, New York and London, 1970.

88 Hinchcliffe, K., 'Labour Aristocracy—A Northern Nigerian Case Study', *Journal of Modern African Studies*, 12, 1 (1974), pp. 57–68; Peter Waterman, 'The "Labour Aristocracy" in Africa: Introduction to an Unfinished Controversy', *South African Labour Bulletin*, 2, 5 (1975), and Woddis, *op.cit.*, pp. 101–14.

89 On workers' political militancy in the colonial period see Frank Furedi, 'The African Crowd in Nairobi: Popular Movements and Elite Politics', *Journal of African History*, 14, 2 (1973), pp. 275–90; and for the post-colonial period P. Mihyo, 'The Struggle for Workers' Control in Tanzania', *Review of African Political Economy*, 4 (1975), pp. 62–85. See also Woddis, *op.cit.*, pp. 114–15; and Jim Silver, 'Class Struggles in Ghana's Mining Industry', *Review of African Political Economy*, 12, May–August 1978, pp. 67–86.

90 'That the condition (of the English trade unions) has remarkably improved since 1848 there can be no doubt, and the best proof of this is the fact that for more than fifteen years not only have their employers been with them, but they with their employers, upon exceedingly good terms. They form an aristocracy among the working-class; they have succeeded in enforcing for themselves a relatively comfortable position, and they accept it as final'. Friedrich Engels, *The Condition of the Working Class in England*, Foreign Languages Publishing House, Moscow, 1962, Preface.

91 Similar conclusions are drawn by Adrian Peace, 'The Lagos Proletariat: Labour Aristocrats or Populist Militants', Sandbrook and Cohen, *op.cit.*, pp. 281–302; and Waterman, *op.cit.*

92 Leitner, Kirstin, 'The Situation of Agricultural Workers in Kenya', *Review of African Political Economy*, 6 (1976), pp. 34–50, recounts a striking example.

93 See Fanon, *op.cit.*, as well as Peter Worsley, 'Frantz Fanon and the "Lumpenproletariat"', R. Miliband and J. Saville eds., *The Socialist Register 1972, op.cit.*; and Charles van Onselen, 'South Africa's Lumpenproletarian Army: "Umkosi wa Ntaba" —the "Regiment of the Hills", 1890–1920', University of London, Institute of Commonwealth Studies, *Societies of Southern Africa in the 19th and 20th Centuries*, 7, Collected Seminar Papers No. 21, 1977; see also Woddis, *op.cit.*, pp. 79–84.

94 Examples include Simon Chodak, 'The Birth of an African Peasantry', *Canadian Journal of African Studies*, 5, 3 (1971), pp. 327–48; and R.H. Jackson, *op.cit.*, pp. 391–3.

95 See Beckman, *op.cit.*; Lionel Cliffe, 'Rural Political Economy of Africa', Gutkind and Wallerstein, *op.cit.*, pp. 112–31; Catherine Coquery-Vidrovitch, 'The Political Economy of the African Peasantry and Modes of Production', *Ibid.*, pp. 90–111; Colin Leys, 'Politics in Kenya: the Development of a Peasant Society', *British Journal of Political Science*, 1, 3 (1972), pp. 307–77; and Palmer and Parsons, *op.cit.* For a wealth of data illustrative of this point in a country which is usually thought of as one of the least developed in Africa, see Republic of Botswana, *The Rural Income Distribution Survey in Botswana, 1974/75*, Government Printer, Gaborne, 1976; Colin

Leys, *Underdevelopment in Kenya, op.cit.*, pp. 183–92, provides one of the best discussions of rural stratification along these lines.

96 On Uganda see Mamdani, *op.cit.*, pp. 151–6, 195–200, 230–6; on Tanzania see A. Awiti, 'Economic Differentation in Ismani, Iringa Region', *The African Review*, 3, 2 (1973); and H.U.E. Thoden van Velsen, 'Staff, Kulacks and Peasants', Lionel Cliffe and J.S. Saul eds., *Socialism in Tanzania*, 2, Dar es Salaam: East African Publishing House, 1973; pp. 153–80.

97 'Incensed as were the peasants under terrible pressure, it was still difficult to arouse them to revolt. Being spread over large areas, it was highly difficult for them to come to a common understanding; the old habit of submission inherited from generation to generation, the lack of practice in the use of arms in many regions, the unequal degree of exploitation depending on the personality of the master, all combined to keep the peasant quiet', Friedrich Engels, *The Peasant Wars in Germany*, quoted in Selsam, *et.al., op.cit.*, p. 227. For a more positive view of peasant political activity in Africa see K.W.J. Post, '"Peasantisation" and Rural Political Movements in Western Africa', *Archives Europeenes d'Sociologie*, 13 (1972).

98 Shivji, *op.cit.*, pp. 14–18, deals with this issue effectively.

99 On the non-capitalist path to development see Beckmann, *op.cit.*; I. Potehkin, 'On African Socialism: A Soviet View'; William H. Friedland and Carl G. Rosberg, Jr., *African Socialism*, Stanford University Press, Stanford, Calif., 1964; and E.A. Tarabrin ed., *Neocolonialism and Africa in the 1970's*, Progress Publishers, Moscow, 1975; Magdoff, Harry, 'Is There a Non-Capitalist Road?', *Monthly Review*, 37, 7 (1978); and Marina Ottaway, 'Soviet Marxism and African Socialism', *Journal of Modern African Studies*, 16, 3 (1978), pp. 477–86; and *Developing Countries on the Non-Capitalist Road*. Proceedings of the Third International Conference of Africanist Marxists of the Socialist Countries, Vienna, September 5–12, 1971, Bulgarian Academy of Sciences, Sofia, 1974.

100 The time would seem to have arrived for a re-examination and re-appraisal of Trotsky's views on 'permanent revolution'. See Leon Trotsky, *The Permanent Revolution*, Pathfinder Press, New York, 1970.

6 African Peasantries*

JOHN S. SAUL and ROGER WOODS

The terms 'peasant' and 'peasantry', in addition to their popular and political usages, have been used in the social sciences for the description and analysis of types of rural society with reference to a wide range of geographical settings and historical periods; unfortunately, despite considerable usage, there has been no consistent definition of the term. This conceptual inconsistency has had the consequence that analyses of 'peasant society' are by no means readily comparable in either their scope or their theoretical underpinnings. There have been, it is true, some recent attempts at a more systematic categorisation in which peasants have been differentiated from 'primitive agriculturalists' on the one hand and from 'farmers' or 'agricultural entrepreneurs' on the other.[1] Yet what appears to be a successful way of specifically differentiating 'peasants' from other agriculturalists and non-agriculturalists in any particular area often presents difficulties when applied to another. Thus the variety of peasant types and the variety of approaches to them by social scientists promises to provide sufficient fuel for a virtually endless debate on the appropriate dimensions of the concept. There is a danger, however, that the definitional exercise will obscure the real point at issue. For the value of any concept lies in its ability to illuminate and explain empirical data when used in a theoretical argument. Thus the proper questions to ask before trying to define the 'peasant' in an African context are: what are we trying to explain, and will a concept defined in a particular way do justice to the empirical data and be logically appropriate to the argument?

Our interest lies in identifying and explaining the patterns of change and development in contemporary Africa, and we are therefore concerned to use terms such as 'peasantry' and 'peasant' as effective concepts within an analytical framework which usefully structures such an explanation. A precise identification of the phases of social evolution and world economic history during which the peasant may become an important actor on the African stage, and his role a crucial one in the understanding of the process of historical change, thus becomes of central importance in pinpointing this category. Moreover, as we shall in fact see, the changing African social structure has thrown up, during certain periods, strata which may be usefully so identified in structural terms.

It should also be stressed, however, that any definition must not aggregate together uncritically all peasants under a monolithic category, for the peasantry may also be differentiated internally in terms of certain structurally significant variables. This becomes all the more important an emphasis in the light of our focus upon the changing context within which the peasantry operates, for the category will of necessity remain fluid at the margins as various segments of society pass in and out of the relevant range of social involvements which it epitomises, and will do so at different rates. Not surprisingly, under certain circumstances different segments of the peasantry can come to play diverse historical roles with important consequences for the pattern of historical development. In brief, there can be among the peasants *different peasantries*—

---

* Source: *Peasants and Peasant Societies* edited by T. Shanin, pp. 103–13 Penguin Books, 1971.

differentiated according to their structural position at a specified moment of time.

This much having been said, we must still specify some criteria for differentiating peasants from other rural people. Our emphasis here is twofold and highlights economic characteristics. Firstly, our concern with the structural position of the peasantry suggests that it must be seen as being a certain stratum within some wider political and economic system. A second dimension centres on the importance to the peasantry of the family economy.[2] Thus peasants are *those whose ultimate security and subsistence lies in their having certain rights in land and in the labour of family members on the land, but who are involved, through rights and obligations, in a wider economic system which includes the participation of non-peasants*.[3] The fact that for peasants ultimate security and subsistence rests upon maintaining rights in land and rights in family labour will be seen to be an important determinant shaping and restricting their social action. It is also the characteristic which peasants share with 'primitive agriculturalists', though not with capitalist farmers. For while the capitalist farmer may *appear* to depend upon his land and even upon family labour in some cases, he is not *forced* to rely solely upon these in the last instance; he has alternative potential sources of security and investment. What the peasant does share, in general terms, with the capitalist farmer (though not with the primitive agriculturalist) is his integration into a complex social structure characterised by stratification and economic differentiation. In fact, it is precisely the characterisation of the peasantry in terms of its position relative to other groups in the wider social system which has particularly important explanatory value in the analysis of development.

The work of elaborating upon such criteria can only be begun here, but it is certainly possible to carry the discussion beyond the point reached by Fallers, for example, in his article entitled 'Are African Cultivators to be Called Peasants?'[4] Confining himself to the discussion of 'traditional' social systems, rather abstractly conceived and working partly in the anthropological tradition of Kroeber and Redfield, he defined peasant society as being a society 'whose primary constituent units are semi-autonomous local communities with semi-autonomous cultures'. This semi-autonomy he broke down further into economic, political and 'cultural' dimensions. He demonstrated the involvement of many Africans in the trade and exchange of agricultural produce and even the existence, albeit more limited in scope, of political states which in some areas allowed for the emergence of many political attributes of a peasantry. But crucial to his argument was the nonexistence, as he saw it, of any juxtaposition between high and low cultures even in those African societies which had, in effect, economic and political proto-peasantries. Fallers concludes, in fact, with the suggestion 'that one of the reasons why Christianity, Islam and their accompanying high cultures have been so readily accepted in many parts of Africa is that many African societies were structurally 'ready' to receive peasant cultures'!

Yet such a conclusion graphically demonstrates the dangers of looking for cultural aspects of peasant societies within the framework of an abstract and a historical approach.[5] For the history of colonial Africa shows, on the contrary, not any structural readiness to accept, and consequent acceptance of a 'high culture', but rather a clash between different types of social systems in which the resulting system, independent of its cultural content, was the product of the interaction of the two systems. Moreover, despite the existence of some prefigurings of a peasant class in earlier periods, it is more fruitful to view both the creation of an African peasantry, as well as the creation of the present differentiation among African peasantries, as being primarily the result of the interaction between an international capitalist economic system and traditional socio-economic systems, within the context of territorially defined colonial political systems.

Sub-Saharan Africa viewed in continental perspective is still predominantly rural in its population, but the ubiquitous reach of colonialism has ensured that no significant numbers of the primitive agriculturalists who previously comprised the vast majority of the population have remained outside the framework of a wider economic system. Under our usage, most of this rural population has thus been transformed into a peasantry. Of course, in certain areas, not only have non-African immigrants established themselves as capitalist farmers, but a significant number of African cultivators have moved out of the peasant category and must also be called capitalist farmers. In addition, as the logic of capitalist development has worked itself out in Africa, other peasants have lost their land rights and have been *proletarianised* either in the rural or industrial sectors of the economy. In other words, the further development of capitalism has begun to phase out the very peasantry it first defined and created. Moreover, in most of the continent it is a capitalist route to development that is favoured and in so far as capitalism does have the inherent strength to fully transform African societies, the existence of a peasantry could be viewed all the more as a transitional phenomenon. The possibility of a realisation of this kind of transformation is of course most problematic and, in any event, remains a very long-term proposition. The identification of a continental bias toward the further encouragement of this possibility may therefore help to explain the fluidity at the margins of the peasant category referred to earlier; it does not relieve one of the necessity of analysing the contemporary characteristics of that peasantry itself or of suggesting its likely response to the social structures which are emerging and serving to reshape it.

The colonial situation was everywhere one in which the local populations were both exposed to new goods and services and, in many cases, subjected to specific government-enforced economic or labour demands, with the result that new needs were generated which could only be met by participation in the cash-based market economy. Two ways of participating were open to them: sale of their labour or sale of their agricultural produce. Within this broad process four variables have been of particular importance in defining the nature of the 'participation' in the overall system by primitive agriculturalists through which they acquired, in effect, their peasant characteristics.[6] These variables are:

(1) the presence, or otherwise, of centres of labour demand, such as mines, plantations, industries, and the like;

(2) the presence, or otherwise, of a suitable local environment for the production of agricultural crops for sale, combined with the degree of availability of marketing opportunities for these crops;

(3) The presence, or otherwise, of an immigrant settler group of capitalist farmers who would be competitors with African producers; and

(4) at a later stage, the presence, or otherwise, of an indigenous elite (basing themselves upon educational attainment and, in some cases, upon political skills) which under certain circumstances (notably the absence of an immigrant settler group) could take over formal political power from the colonial regime. This new stratum might be complemented and reinforced in its exercise of

authority by a newly emergent, indigenous 'national bourgeoisie', to be found in trade and in agriculture itself.

Equally important, it must be remembered that these variables have operated upon a pre-colonial Africa that was itself characterised by a large number of ethnic and political groups at different levels of political and economic organisation. By taking full cognisance of such a wide variety of factors, it may be easier to get a clear idea of the full range of permutations and actual consequences possible within the overall process of 'peasantisation'.

It is perhaps worth extending briefly the discussion about the importance of environmental potential, a factor which helps to define both the character of the traditional agroeconomic systems as well as their subsequent responses. For the extent to which labour-exporting peasantries developed was not only a function of the labour demand/economic need dimension introduced by an absence of readily available cash crops. It also reflected in some instances the degree to which adult men were under-employed in the traditional agricultural system and hence the extent to which they could be absent without threatening the security of minimal subsistence production. Similarly, the extent to which a peasantry could respond to cash-cropping also depended on the adaptability of the traditional agricultural system to the incorporation of new crops or the expanded production of established crops *without threatening the security of minimal subsistence production*. Of course, these complexities further contribute to the process whereby a number of 'African peasantries' are tending to be created, rather than a single monolithic stratum. But the reiteration of the italicised phrase is equally significant, for we are reminded of the second of the general characteristics of the peasantry mentioned earlier. In so far as particular African cultivators can continue to be identified as peasants, one will observe such a calculation to be central to the defining of their existence and to the grounding of their activities.

A distinctive African peasantry exists, therefore, though it may find itself involved in broader national systems which can have a range of possible characteristics—societies in which the dominant elements will be a variable combination of international corporations, immigrant settlers and immigrant trading groups, indigenous elites and indigenous national bourgeoisies. Secondly, in each territory we can distinguish a number of peasantries who are differentiated according to locality—some localities being labour exporting, some food-crop exporting, some cash-crop exporting and some with varying proportions of each. In addition, these differentiations will often coincide with, and be reinforced by, localised cultural identifications, often of an ethnic or tribal nature. Of course, the pattern will not be a static one, but rather one changing over time as the system develops. Thirdly, the dynamic of capitalist development tends to introduce a further element which cuts across the differentiation of peasants by locality with a differentiation based on the degree of involvement in the cash economy. This involves, as we have seen, the possible movements toward proletarianisation of migrant labourers on the one hand and toward capitalist agriculture on the other, and these two can chip away at the peasantry, pulling it in different directions.

It will be apparent that these complexities make any attempt to identify the historical role which the African peasantry is likely to define for itself a most treacherous one. For even were 'peasants', under certain circumstances, to become conscious of their common interests and act politically on the basis of that awareness, the likely results are not readily predictable. Upon occasion, for example, one might find that the bulk of the peasantry in a given territory was available for an attempt to press its demands upon the other classes and interests in the society—where abuses by an alien authority or a highly compromised indigenous urban elite become so unbearable as to override consciousness of other fissures. More often, perhaps, localisms of various sorts (eg. tribal consciousness) will prevail, to the point where even those aspects of the peasantry's economic and social grievances which might be generalised on to a territorial scale become obscured.[8] Similarly, where it is nascent horizontal dimensions which define a variety of peasantries, these may become the overriding determinant of peasant intervention in the historical process. Thus wealthy peasantries may move merely to open their own paths to capitalist farming (thereby altering the options for other peasants, some of whose passage to the agrarian proletariat may be correspondingly accelerated).[7] Or the 'lower' peasantries may awaken to the burden of their condition and the quality of their likely fate before the latter is in fact sealed, and act on that awareness. For the latter, the means of their gaining consciousness, much less power, are particularly circumscribed, and as yet this is perhaps the most speculative of the alternatives which we have thrown up.

But in any case, such a discussion cannot be taken far in the abstract. Continental trends may be fruitfully discussed, of course, but cumulative insight into the peasant's role is more likely to be gained by bringing together an analysis of the nature of a particular national social system (situated within the context of the world economy) with a characterisation of the internal dynamics of its peasantry. And this can be done satisfactorily only through case studies of actual historical experiences. We will therefore conclude with some brief reference to three such experiences, not under any pretence of exhausting their complexity, but merely in order to *begin* the task of exemplifying the various criteria which we have presented and of underscoring the range of historical possibilities which we have hinted at.

In the context of Southern Rhodesia, where the capitalist framework of colonialism was characterised by the existence of a significant settler farming community able to establish political dominance over the various forces contending for control, the ability of the local African population to develop cash-crop agriculture on a scale that would have allowed the growth of a class of non-peasant capitalist farmers was checked. In this specific situation only the development of tightly controlled small-scale cash farming has been permitted. The involvement of the peasantry has been forced into a pattern of subsistence agriculture with only small cash sales of agricultural produce on the one hand, and periods of paid employment for most males of working age as a means of meeting cash needs on the other. An attempt to stratify the peasantry by allowing the acquisition of small holdings with individual tenure through what was termed 'native purchase' has been on too small a scale to have significant structural effects. As population pressure on impoverished land increases and circular patterns of labour migration become more difficult to sustain, almost all African agriculturalists within Rhodesia have therefore to accept the fate of increased proletarianisation for at least some among their number, as well as a declining standard of living.[8] The alternative to this situation is a growth in consciousness about their class position and a revolutionary response to it.

In Ghana where, by contrast, there was no large-scale European farming community and hence a very different economic and political cast to the colonial situation, other patterns among the peasantry emerged. Thus in certain regions the cultivation of cocoa allowed the growth of large-scale cocoa farming by Ghanaian farmers. The peasants who developed these cocoa plantations were largely migrant farmers who quickly became capitalist farmers—to them we can hardly apply the term 'peasant'.[9] But their emergence profoundly affected the position of other peasants in the Ghanaian political economy. Certain areas not well-endowed with agricultural resources now developed labour-exporting peasantries, these travelling not only to some mines and to the cities, but also to the cocoa farming areas. A group of tenant farmers or debt farmers also emerged, and these can properly be seen as a peasantry, with a distinct class position.

Historically the capitalist cocoa farmers and wealthier peasants have been a politically conservative force, underpinning right-wing political parties as well as the post-Nkrumah military regime. In contrast, however, the lower peasantry was never fully and effectively enlisted into Nkrumah's movement, for the latter retained too many of the characteristics of a parasitic urban group to mobilise their support effectively. Market forces have therefore continued to chip away at the peasantry, albeit indecisively, for a deteriorating situation on the international market has sapped the power of cocoa to transform the rural economy, and neither the Nkrumah regime nor its successor has developed strategies for industrialisation which would provide an effective substitute. The peasantry's place has not therefore been eliminated by capitalist development, but neither have the abuses of incumbent elites proven a sufficient prod to generate its active intervention in the political arena.[10]

By contrast, Tanzania has not seen the development of one sizeable and homogeneous group of cash-crop farmers from its peasant ranks. In many different areas (in accordance with the environmental potential that existed) annual or perennial crops have been developed as marketable cash crops, and in each of these areas some degree of differentiation has emerged among farmers. This differentiation is expressed not simply in terms of economic status, but by differential involvement in cooperative organisations and other modern institutions and privileged access to the advantages which they make available.[11] Increasingly there have been for the early movers paths leading out of the peasantry into the farmer class. But once again the economic mobility of some agriculturalists changes the nature of the system in which others begin to move. Thus, the unhindered play of this process promises to result in a complex pattern of stratification, one marked by a number of strata of agriculturalists stretching all the way from capitalist farmer to landless labourer. In addition, regional differences which spring in part from the realities of different agro-ecological environments and marketing opportunities may give rise, as has happened elsewhere, to 'local' peasantries (sometimes wearing the cloak of tribalism) which have different structural positions, and conflicting interests, in the total system.

The Tanzanian government has been aware of the first stirrings of these possibilities and—almost alone among governments in sub-Saharan Africa—has chosen to confront the tasks of *pre-empting* them. So far this has involved only the tentative beginnings of that radicalisation of the political structure which might enlist the support and involvement of the mass of the rural population. But the leadership does argue for the possibility of a *socialist transformation* of the peasantries and has embarked upon a search for the modern collective forms appropriate to that end.[12] There has been some parallel attempt to redefine the nature of the country's relations with the international capitalist system and by so doing to effect a basic change in the peasants' structural position. Whether this attempt will withstand the opposition of those non-peasants (and advanced peasants) whose positions are threatened by such a strategy remains to be seen.

It is hoped that such 'case studies', though derisory in their brevity, will at least have indicated the importance of continuing the study of the African peasantry along some of the lines which we have indicated. It scarcely requires stating that a great deal of additional work in the spheres of conceptualisation and historicosociological investigation remains to be done.

Notes

1 E.R. Wolf, *Peasants*, Englewood Cliffs, N.J., 1966, p. 2.
2 Chayanov's theory of the peasant economy with its emphasis on the dual role of the peasant *household* as both a productive and a consumptive group is a valuable conceptual tool in any study of peasants. In much of Africa the concept needs to be extended to that of a *homestead* economy as a basic unit of analysis. The homestead, which is based on the joint property rights of an extended family, frequently has rights to farm land rather than rights to a particular farm. (A.V. Chayanov, *The Theory of Peasant Economy*, Chicago, 1966).
3 Pastoralists are an important category of the rural population in a number of African countries. Since these predominantly pastoral people are subject to the same kinds of political and economic forces as their predominantly agricultural breathren, and since their productive economy (in as much as it involves rights to, and control over, the family herds) is based on a similar kind of 'homestead' principle, they would fulfil our own limited criteria for peasants. We would thus include them in any study of African peasantries, however much this might offend 'peasant purists'.
4 L.A. Fallers, 'Are African Cultivators to be Called "Peasants"?', *Current Anthropology*, 2, 1961, pp. 108–10.
5 See A.G. Frank, *Capitalism and Underdevelopment in Latin America*, New York, 1967, and M. Harris, *Patterns of Race in the Americas*, New York, 1964, for two very different but illuminating studies which situate Latin American peasantries in historical and structural terms.
6 Our attention was drawn to the importance of seeing peasant aggregates in certain of these terms by an unpublished paper of D.L. Barnett, 'Three Types of African Peasantry', mimeo, n.d.
7 An important variable which we have not been able to explore here is the pressure of population upon the land. Taken as a whole African land resources are considerable but areas of 'population pressure' do exist and in these areas the options open to individual peasants are much more limited. There the growth of a farmer class tends to mean the proletarianisation of others.
8 A forthcoming study by Roger Woods on the 'Native Purchase Areas of Rhodesia' will elaborate upon these and related points.
9 P. Hill, *Migrant Cocoa Farmers of Southern Ghana*, London, 1963.
10 B. Fitch and M. Oppenheimer, *Ghana: End of an Illusion*, New York, 1966.
11 J.S. Saul, 'Marketing Cooperatives in a Developing Country', in P. Worsley, ed., *Two Blades of Grass*, Manchester, 1971.
12 J.K. Nyerere, *Socialism and Rural Development*, 1967, reprinted in Nyerere, *Freedom and Socialism*, Oxford, 1968.

7 The 'Labour Aristocracy' in Africa: Introduction to an Unfinished Controversy*

PETER WATERMAN

Introduction

There has been taking place amongst observers of labour problems in Africa a controversy about the role of wage-earners and their organisations. Much of this debate has been amongst socialists, and most of this centres on the Marxist concept of the 'aristocracy of labour'. The purpose of this paper is to identify and examine the three main positions that have so far emerged. These are, firstly, that the regularly-employed and unionised workers as a whole are a privileged and conservative aristocracy; secondly, that they are—on the contrary—the leading force for revolutionary change; and, thirdly, that whilst they cannot be categorised as a labour aristocracy, such a group exists amongst them.

My own position is that whilst the first two theses are demonstrably false or useless, the third opens the way to a solution of the problem. But even the third position has shortcomings—both conceptual and empirical—that must be recognised if such a solution is to be found.

Thesis 1: The Privileged Worker and his Conservative Union

In the debate over the role of workers and unions there has emerged a first position which, I believe, can be fairly summarised as follows.

> There exists within the modern economic sector in Africa an economically-privileged wage- and salary-earning stratum. This stratum is socially grouped with the rest of the urban elites. Its unions are generally self-interested and conservative, their policies and actions being opposed to the interests of the masses in general. They are an obstacle to the further development of the continent.

This case has been made by very different writers, some of whom are socialists and others of whom are not. If they are treated here together it is because of a strong family resemblance in their arguments which should reveal itself in the analysis below. Whilst some commentators have confined themselves to identifying the privileged solely in economic terms (incomes and conditions), most have shown social correlates (in terms of values and status) and political implications (in terms of group power vis-a-vis the state). Let us examine these elements in turn.

The economic element

For a classic statement of the basic economic argument, we may take this one from President Senghor:

> ... the annual income of an African civil servant is about 360 000 CFA francs: that of a wage-earner in the private sector is 180 000 francs:

*From *South African Labour Bulletin*, 2, 5 (1975), pp. 10–27.

whereas that of a peasant in the former French West Africa is 10 000 francs. The proletarian is not necessarily the one who claims the title.[1]
This income-differential point has been made by many. Thus the report of a recent Nigerian wages commission stated that whilst the annual income of the farmer ranged between £43 and £72, the minimum pay for the urban worker ranged between £84 and £108 per annum.[2] Commenting on this, Billy Dudley declared that 'Even at the lower figure, the urban worker is already earning almost three times the average per capita income'.[3]

To the income-differential factor there has been frequently added the widening-gap factor. Thus Kilby points out for Nigeria that 'real wages in the organised sector have increased at more than twice the rate of per capita GDP'.[4] And the Marxist, Arrighi, concludes that the 'main characteristics of the wage working class are: relatively static numbers and rising incomes'.[5] The narrowly economic argument is frequently broadened by stress on the 'privileges' of the regularly employed. Kilby writes thus:

Rather than being an exploited group, organised labour is already a highly-privileged minority. Whether initiated by modernising nationalists or the departing colonial benefactor, the full range of welfare measures contained in the ILO conventions ... have now been implemented in the unionised sectors of nearly all the countries of Latin America, Africa, Asia and the Middle East .... There is much *labour* unrest, but it has little to do with the absolute wage or conditions of work; rather it is, as in Nigeria, an expression of the relative deprivation of the 'haves' vis-a-vis the even smaller minority of the 'have-mores'.[6]

Elliot Berg writes of the more general benefits of city life.

... however low their income and welfare by some absolute yardstick African wage earners are in general a relatively privileged group in African society. They enjoy more of the benefits of modernisation and growth than any African social group. They have available more and better medical care, a larger share of the conveniences and amusements of modern life—from supermarkets to cinemas.[7]

The sociological element

Economic argumentation merely places the regularly-employed urban worker on a quantitative scale (higher than some, lower than others). Allied sociological arguments attempt to qualify him, to identify his relations with other social strata (identified with these, isolated from or opposed to those). The classic statement here is that of Fanon on the colonial working class.

In the colonial countries the working class has everything to lose;
in reality it represents that fraction of the colonised nation which is necessary and irreplaceable if the colonial machine is to run smoothly:
it includes tram conductors, taxi drivers, miners, dockers, interpreters, nurses and so on. It is these elements which ... constitute also the 'bourgeois' fraction of the colonised people.[8]

The argument has, again, been extended and deepened, this time by Arrighi when he speaks of the post-colonial period. Arrighi distinguishes within the urban sector between a 'semi-proletarianised peasantry' of unskilled labourers, too poor to cut its ties with the countryside, and the 'proletariat proper'. His proletariat consists of the skilled and semi-skilled manual and clerical working class demanded by the capital-intensive investments of international capitalism, and by the complex administrative apparatus taken over from colonialism. Arrighi asserts that the relatively high wages of this group unites them with the local elite and sub-elite in a group whose interests conflict with those of the semi-proletarianised peasantry and the peasantry proper. This is one group relationship. It leads to another with the international corporations. Here he finds a 'consistency between the interests of international capitalism and the African elite, sub-elite and *proletariat proper* [ie. excluding migrant labour], which we shall collectively refer to as the "labour aristocracy" of Tropical Africa'.[9]

A similar argument has been produced by the Africa Research Group, which includes within a 'middle class' the 'Nearly 40 per cent of Nigeria's wage-earners ... [who] consist of fairly typical white collar workers'.[10] In analogy with Arrighi, the ARG finds that this 'middle class itself is ... the primary vector of neo-colonial influence .... The historic mission of this middle class is to mediate between its own people's needs and the marketing system of the corporate economy'.[11]

The political element

These attempts to place the working class socially inevitably tend to qualify them politically also. But whilst the above assertions are limited to the role of the class (or sections of it), others deal specifically with the policies of their organisations. The classic statement comes again from Fanon.

> The workers, now that they have got their 'independence', do not know where to go from there. For the day after independence is declared the trade unions realise that if their social demands were to be expressed, they would scandalise the rest of the nation. ... any movement starting off to fight for the bettering of living conditions for the dockers and workmen would not only be very unpopular, but would also run the risk the provoking the hostility of the disinherited rural population.[12]

A more forceful one comes from Kaplinsky, referring to Ceylon and Zambia in particular.

> It is quite likely that there are unions in developing countries which are objectively progressive. But equally, there is no doubt that the majority of unions in high-wage, high-productivity industries are fundamentally reactionary .... Although these unions are prepared to press the system to get a larger share of the cake (or to maintain their share as prices and incomes rise), when a real threat to the distributive system arises they are quick to come out in active support for the existing balance of power. For if the existing balance were to be made more equal, there is little doubt that unionised labour, representing as it does the relatively privileged elements in society, will stand to lose.[13]

Arrighi draws similar implications for political attitudes out of the privileged position of his proletariat:

> ... even though the 'labour aristocracy' may not be opposed to state ownership and management of the means of production, it can be expected to resist that reallocation of the surplus on the part of the state which must be an essential component of the strategy for the transformation in the total situation of the societies of Tropical Africa.[14]

Antithesis: the Exploited Worker and his Radical Union

Unlike the first position, the second, in its strong form, is that of one scholar,

Jack Woddis, whose interpretation can be summarised as follows.

There exists within the modern economic sector in Africa an economically-exploited working class. This class is socially allied with the rest of the masses. Its unions have generally proven themselves socially-conscious and radical, their policies being opposed to the interests of the exploiting classes and oppressive regimes. They are the leading force for the further development of the continent..

In a number of works Woddis has polemicised against what he considers to be the 'denigration of the African working class' by both Fanonist socialists and conventional liberals.[15] His counter-attack covers three main areas, (1) income differentials, (2) the pre-independence role of the unions, and (3) the post-independence role of the unions.

(1) On the basis of much official evidence on low colonial wages, urban-rural income flows and inter-connections, and bad urban living conditions, Woddis concludes:

In the conditions of colonialism the overwhelming majority of African workers remained unskilled, casual, migrant, low-paid labourers who could in no sense be regarded as 'pampered'.[16]

(2) After describing trade union action against colonialism in 26 territories, he asserts that

In country after country the workers acted as pace makers of the national liberation struggle. They staged major confrontations with imperialism, organised strike struggles .... . General strikes became manifestations of national struggle and stirred millions into awareness of the total system of colonial oppression and discrimination, of the necessity to fight against it, and of the possibility of defeating it.[17]

He goes on to claim, reasonably, that if the workers had been so pampered and privileged as has been claimed, it would have been unnecessary for the colonial authorities to have spent as much energy as they did in holding them down and isolating them from the national independence movements.

(3) A description of trade union action in six post-colonial states follows. Woddis discovers a new shift to the offensive by unions around 1963. A new gap had opened up between the governments of the reactionary states and their peoples, a new round of conflict had begun, a key role being played by the unions, which thus showed that in Africa the political general strike could sometimes be 'the decisive action' to pull down unpopular governments.[18]

The error of those who extol other strata over the workers, Woddis has said earlier, is the failure to distinguish between 'what is the main force and what is the leading force'. The point is that 'the African countries will either become capitalist, in which case they will be led by the bourgeoisie; or they will advance to socialism, which requires a state led by the working class'.[19] However, the issue is not so much a question of class, as of the necessary ideology and party:

It is not so much a question as to who struggled most or longest being the measure of leadership ... but rather is it a question as to which ideology must assume leadership and on what decisive class force must this leadership be built if Africa is to advance from independence to socialism. This requires the creation of the necessary political weapon, the party of the working class.[20]

The third position is that of a number of socialist and radical writers who have been carrying out empirical studies on African workers and unions. Their position would seem to be the following.

> There exists within the modern economic sector in Africa an economically-exploited working class. This class is socially allied with the rest of the masses. Its unions have often shown themselves socially-conscious and radical, their policies often being opposed to the interests of the exploiting classes and oppressive regimes. But there exists amongst them economically-privileged groups. These are socially allied with the rest of the urban elites. They are self-interested and conservative, their policies being opposed to the interests of the rest of the workers and the masses as a whole. They provide a significant obstacle to the further development of the continent.

This position is apparently a combination of the first and second ones. It joins Woddis in rejecting the general argument of Arrighi, but joins Arrighi in recognising the existence and importance of a labour aristocracy. The economic, social and political elements of this position are, I think, brought out in the writings selected below.

The economic element

Chris Allen has made a detailed empirical and theoretical study of both the urban-rural income differential argument (URID), and the widening-gap one. Basing his argument on material taken from all over tropical Africa he concludes that the 'URID concept is weak, and is valueless for policy purposes',[21] and that there is no evidence of any widening gap except for the special case of Zambia, where it is due to high wages in a mining industry marked by demands for parity with white workers. But Chris Allen makes a significant qualification in his argument. He allows that

> persons earning well above the minimum wage (a category including a small group of skilled and experienced manual workers) can voluntarily move outside the system [of rural-urban economic interdependence], since they earn enough to create an urban extended family and client group or to save enough to provide for either retirement or a lucrative occupation such as trading, that can be run by relatives and employees.[22]

He also makes distinctions within the trade union movement, drawing lines between the rank-and-file, their shop-floor leaders and the union leaderships. Referring to the latter group, he cites a Ghanaian trade union official with a university degree and with an income of over £2 000 per annum.

The social element

In two studies of a major strike movement in Lagos, Adrian Peace denies the existence of a social gap between the urban workers and the rest of the urban and rural masses.

First, he argues that economic benefits to workers bring economic benefits to others.

> ... interdependence operates at a multiplicity of levels from the personal networks of permanently employed workers supporting less fortunate kinsmen to the broader interstrata level. With the greater part of low wages going on rent and foodstuffs, landlords and market

women constitute the major beneficiaries; craftsmen and supplies of other urban services come second through the higher prices which immediately follow general wage and salary awards (in itself a sound indication of non-wage earners' dependence on the employed sector). Gains made by the working class, then, are shared by an inestimably wider population.[23]

Secondly, he draws attention to the shared values and reference points of the Yoruba poor (who predominate in Lagos), whether these are farmers, traders, craftsmen or workers. Admiration for the private entrepreneur is shared by wage-earners and non-wage earners alike in Lagos society, and 'Values and sentiments attached to this wide range of roles promote unity ... between those inside and outside the industrial mode of production'.[24]

Finally, he argues that there are acts of 'interest identification' between protecting workers and protesting farmers, and of solidarity between workers and petty traders during strikes.[25]

Michael Burawoy is not concerned with the labour aristocracy debate in his study of the Zambian copper mines,[26] but he does directly take up the question of 'working-class conservatism' among a group that epitomises this aristocracy for many writers. There is, he shows, no evidence of deference by the copper miners to the new Zambians who (armed with nationalist and developmentalist rhetoric) have taken over control and supervision within the industry.

> The worker does not feel part of, or a genuine participant in, the bureaucratic machinery, which is not perceived as existing to advance the interests of the workers. What is important to the worker ... are the labour policies, wages, working conditions, general treatment, disciplinary procedures, etc., of management. In this respect the Zambian worker perceives his fellow Zambian supervisors and bureaucrats with distrust .... The worker considers that the newly 'arrived' Zambian in a high position will not be able to refrain from misusing his power to favour some and oppress others in more lowly positions .... The distrust shown by workers towards high-ranking Zambians reflects a class conflict in which the upper class is quite prepared to exploit the lower classes ruthlessly in a way the expatriate would not dare so long as he had no political base for support.[27]

However, another writer concerned to deny the privileged worker thesis has made a significant qualification. Analysing the social structure of Nigeria, Gavin Williams says that

> Clerical workers are often as concerned about the regrading of posts as about change in wage levels. Younger clerks look to further education as a means of advancement. They are often more concerned than are factory workers to seek the favour of their seniors (often determined or alleged to be determined by considerations of ethnicity and kinship rather than merit) insofar as their promotion structure is more favourable than that of factory workers. They also have greater security of tenure and better prospects of a gratuity which can be invested on early retirement in commercial activities.[28]

And Chris Allen argues for the necessity of distinguishing between different levels in the trade union movement, claiming that

> Socially ... union leaders differ from their members but not from the urban elite, and their ambition is very often to use their official positions to achieve at least the income of the elite, if not also member-

ship of it .... We may also note the widespread evidence of excessive salaries for, and of corruption by, union officials ....[29]

The political element

Richard Jeffries argues against the Fanonist position on the workers, insisting that they have in a number of countries been the main source of action against, and criticism of, elite wealth, corruption and authoritarianism. He examines the railway workers of Sekondi-Takoradi in order to show that, while not revolutionary, they persistently act in a radical democratic manner. Dealing specifically with the 1961 strike against both the 'radical' Nkrumah regime, and the 'radical' Ghana TUC, he shows that the strike was not inspired by political conservatism or economic self-interest. It sprang, rather, from a tradition of radical protest going back to colonial times, when the Sekondi-Takoradi workers and unions had acted as the back-bone of radical nationalism. Jeffries continues, 'The broader "symbolic" issue in the 1961 strike might be interpreted as that of protecting the increasingly elitist and authoritarian style of CPP government'.[30]

Adrian Peace, in his analysis of the spontaneous strikes in Lagos in 1970–71, goes even further, concluding that the local proletariat represents the 'political elite' of the masses, and that

> any attempt hitherto to examine the potential for a broader-based social movement towards a society organised in the interests of the mass of the people should acknowledge as a central element the rise of a politically sophisticated proletariat.[31]

But while he is arguing this point, Peace also insists on the existence of a membership-leadership gap in both the radical Communist-affiliated Nigerian Trade Union Congress, and the moderate Western-affiliated United Labour Congress. Although national headquarters were only five or ten miles away from the strike site (Nigeria's largest industrial estate at Ikeja), no national leaders approached it. He quotes the disparaging remarks of the workers and concludes that, 'Representatives of broader labour organisations such as the ULC or NTUC have marginal influence, being distrusted by local officials and workers alike'.[32]

Burawoy goes even further, arguing that officials of the miners' union in Zambia are part of the new upper class. He shows how the government has incorporated the Mineworkers' Union of Zambia, purging popular leaders and strengthening the bureaucracy. The closed shop and check-off provide a protected leadership with over $30 000 per month in dues. Membership dissatisfaction and apathy are marked:

> Workers are very conscious of the way the Union has been bureaucratised, with the leadership becoming increasingly remote. To many, in fact, the leadership appears as a privileged class which is given political support from the Government and management while deriving its wealth from the workers' subscriptions .... The workers see a grand alliance between the Union, the Government and the Companies.[33]

Assessment

Thesis one

It has been shown above that the 'privileged worker conservative union' thesis contains economic, social and political elements. Let me deal with these one by one.

(1) Only the economic element is based on an empirical footing and this, as the Woddis and Allen criticisms suggests, is a foot of clay.

(2) The social relations element is with Fanon a simple assertion, unsupported by any empirical evidence. While there is no behavioural evidence either for the assertions of Arrighi and the ARC, there is an attempt to base them on sociological analysis. For would-be Marxists, however, they produce particularly sloppy categories, borrowing eclectically from non-Marxist stratification theory and hardly bothering to relate analysis to relations of production. Thus Arrighi's 'elite' and 'sub-elite' are admitted to depend on concepts of 'status and prestige' that he does not even explain, far less justify. He then distinguishes among the mass of wage workers his 'semi-proletarianised peasants' and 'proper proletariat'. While the first of these categories is rooted in a detailed economic analysis (the most serious part of his paper), the second is *apparently* that group of workers which has an income high enough to support a family and to ensure its future, and which is thus able to abandon 'reciprocal obligations with the extended family in the traditional sector'.[34] Since the two categories he identifies 'only to some extent overlap' with his four skill categories (unskilled, semi-skilled, skilled, high-level), and since even these are nowhere measured, even approximately, the 'proper proletarian' is defined only according to his commitment to wage labour and a merely asserted relationship with a high-status and high-prestige elite and sub-elite.

(3) The assertions concerning union behaviour are of the same dubious quality. Fanon's are at least put in the conditional tense: the unions have not *yet* scandalised the rest of the nation nor provoked the hostility of the rural population.

Thesis two

The general shortcomings of Woddis' position are the same as they were some years ago:

> Woddis has failed to come to terms with the . . . great variation in the roles played by the working class and unions within given countries at different points of time, and between different countries at a given point of time. But the greatest shortcoming lies in his failure to prepare us for the very chequered experiences of even the most advanced trade unions in the post-colonial period.[35]

Where the labour aristocracy thesis dogmatically asserts the existence of an economic gap, social contradiction and political antagonism between the 'privileged workers' and the masses for which no convincing evidence is presented, Woddis dogmatically denies significance to evidence of economic heterogeneity, social distance and political divisions within the working class or between the working class and the rest of the masses. Thus, while some contradictory evidence is mentioned by Woddis, it is done as the exception that proves the general case. Let us take in turn his three pieces of evidence.

(1) Income levels. Woddis allows for the existence of some workers with a higher standard than most.

> This was true of some strata of Government employees and of that minority of workers who were able to acquire qualifications as skilled workers. But only a limited minority were so privileged.[36]

126

(2) Action against colonialism. Woddis allows for the existence of privileged trade union leaders—at least in the period of terminal colonialism.

> Admittedly, in most African territories in the final phase of direct colonial rule there were usually a group of trade union officials, mostly associated with the ICFTU, who were certainly 'pampered' and 'privileged'—but they were in no sense characteristic of the African working class as a whole.[38]

(3) Action against post-colonial regimes. Here Woddis gives no contrary evidence at all! Not one example is provided of a worker or a union or a union leader who in the post-colonial period failed to lead the struggle against neo-colonialism.

This is not a simple case of polemical over-kill. Nor is it simply the shortcoming of the heroic mode in which Woddis frequently writes. Woddis is, in fact, defending not any real African working class or trade union movement, but a theoretical (and, in the Marxist sense, ideological) 'working class'. This concept need only be applied by Woddis to a certain social group for it to be immediately and automatically imbued with the qualities of a 'leading force' in any and every situation. Faced with the non-revolutionary role of even his working class in some parts of Africa, and the total non-existence of it in other parts, Woddis falls back on futurology or on a problematic 'party of the working class' (see the quotations above).

Thesis three

Thesis three represents not so much a *synthesis* of the previous two as a theoretical negation of both. It draws on empirical research to destroy the position represented by the first group, but then creates a much more complex image of the working class and unions than that of Woddis. The workers can now be seen as emerging from the urban poor, sharing both egalitarian and entrepreneurial values with them, and yet being capable of playing a leadership role among them because of their special place in the social relations of production. The unions can be seen as complex, multi-level organisations, playing an ambiguous intermediary role (as in most countries at most times) between the workers and the employers or state. Those whose writings support this third position are also more rigorous theoretically. On the one hand they distinguish the industrial proletariat from the amorphous category of wage- and salary-earners. And on the other hand they do not build their conclusions about worker behaviour into their premises—even where they might agree that the working class must be the basis for a future socialist revolution and state.

However, this third group cannot be said to have solved the labour aristocracy problem. All they have demonstrated is that the industrial working class as a whole does not represent a class. Their statements about other groups among the working class are based neither on a firm conceptual basis, nor on empirical research. They are, so far, merely assertions.

Conclusion

An examination of the different arguments presented above shows that in discussing the privileged and conservative elements different groups are being referred to. Participants in the debate have referred variously to (1) the regularly-employed industrial working class as a whole; (2) a stratum of skilled and better-paid manual workers; (3) clerks and other salary-earners, whose proletarian status is problematic; and (4) paid trade union officials, who cannot be considered proletarian even if (as is rare in Africa) they are drawn from the proletariat. Writers in all groups have accepted the concept of the 'labour aristocracy'. Yet,

> There are few concepts in Marxist vocabulary which have been so inadequately studied and so frequently abused as that of 'labour aristocracy'. Popularised by Lenin, the term was never rigorously defined by him. Different passages from his writings can be used for widely contrasting versions of it—from the notion of a labour aristocracy as a small minority of skilled artisans and better-paid workers, to that of the permanent officialdom of reformist trade unions and parties, or finally even to that of the entire proletariat of the imperialist world, as allegedly benefiting from capitalist super-exploitation of the colonial and ex-colonial world. Only the first of these versions has received empirical investigation: none of them has ever been given a solid theoretical foundation. The notion of a 'labour aristocracy' has thus remained a politically and intellectually suspect one—an impatient short-cut through the real historical difficulties of uneven proletarian consciousness and industrial sectionalism.[38]

The article from which this statement is extracted suggests that the white South African workers might be the one contemporary case in which one section of the working class can be proven to be living on the surplus produced by another.

Yet it seems to me that there remains a real problem to be investigated. This is the problem of what I will for the time being call 'the active agents of conservatism among the working class'. 'Active' because we are concerned with those dominating or controlling leading positions. 'Among' because we are concerned, it seems to me, with those who dominate or control the working class, whether they are themselves workers or not.

The necessary research must therefore be both *theoretical*, defining the problem in relation to Marxist class theory, and *empirical*, investigating directly the agents and roots of this active conservatism.

Notes

1 Cited by J. Mohan, 'Varieties of African Socialism', in R. Miliband and J. Saville eds., *Socialist Register*, Merlin Press, London, 1966, p. 244.

2 S. Adebo, *Second and Final Report of the Wages and Salaries Review Commission 1970–71*, Federal Ministry of Information, Lagos, 1971, p. 17.

3 B. Dudley, 'The Politics of Adebo', *Quarterly Journal of Administration*, 6, 2 (1972), p. 133.

4 P. Kilby, *Industrialisation in an Open Economy: Nigeria 1945–66*, Cambridge University Press, London, 1969, p. 281.

5 G. Arrighi and J. Saul, *Essays on the Political Economy of Africa*, Monthly Review Press, New York, 1973.

6 Kilby, *op.cit.*, pp. 301–2.

7 E. Berg 'Major Issues of Wage Policy in Africa', in A.M. Ross ed., *Industrial Relations and Economic Development*, Macmillan, London, 1966, cited by C. Allen, 'Unions, Income and Development' in *Development Trends in Kenya*, Centre of African Studies, Edinburgh, 1972.

8 F. Fanon, *The Wretched of the Earth*, Penguin, 1967, p. 86.

9 Arrighi and Saul, *op.cit.*

10 African Research Group, *The Other Side of Nigeria's Civil War*, ARG, Cambridge, Mass., 1970, p. 5.

11 *Ibid.*

12 Fanon, *op.cit.*, 97.

13 R. Kaplinsky, 'Myths about the "Revolutionary Proletariat" in Developing Countries', *Institute of Development Studies Bulletin*, 3, 4 (1973), p. 21.

14 Arrighi and Saul, *op.cit.*

15 J. Woddis, *New Theories of Revolution*, Lawrence and Wishart, London, 1972, p. 170.

16 *Ibid.*, p. 113.

17 *Ibid.*, p. 115.

18 *Ibid.*, p. 148.

19 *Ibid.*, p. 171.

20 *Ibid.*, p. 174.

21 Allen, *op.cit.*, p. 73.

22 *Ibid.*, p. 76.

23 A. Peace, 'The Lagosian Proletariat as a Political Elite', 1974.

24 *Ibid.*

25 *Ibid.*

26 M. Burawoy, *The Colour of Class on the Copper Mines*, Institute of African Studies, University of Zambia, Zambian Papers, No. 7, 1972.

27 *Ibid.*, pp. 76–7.

28 G. Williams, 'The Political Economy of Colonialism and Neo-Colonialism in Nigeria', mimeo paper, Sociology Dept., University of Durham.

29 Allen, *op.cit.*, p. 82.

30 R. Jeffries, 'Urban Workers in Ghanaian Politics: The Political Culture of the Ghanain Railway Workers' Union', in R. Sandbrook and R. Cohen eds. *The Development of an African Working Class*, Longman, London, 1975, p. 264.

31 Peace, *op.cit.*

32 Peace, *op.cit.*

33 Burawoy, *op.cit.*, p. 79.

34 Arrighi and Saul, *op.cit.*

35 P. Waterman, 'Towards an Understanding of African Trade Unionism', *Présence Africaine*, 76, 1970.

36 Woddis, *op.cit.*, p. 113.

37 *Ibid.*, p. 123.

38 Introduction to R. Davies, 'The White Working Class in South Africa', *New Left Review*, 82, 1973, p. 38.

8 An Analysis of the Classes in South Africa*

SAM MHLONGO

To those who have taken for granted the preponderance of peasants in all the countries of Africa, Asia and Latin America, South Africa presents a unique spectacle. A population of 23 million people, 1 223 781 square kilometres in area, South Africa has no peasants.[1] A good deal of nonsense has been written on what has variously been referred to as 'semi-peasants', 'neither peasants nor workers', 'landless peasants', and so forth. The motive behind all this seems to be an attempt to impose the 'two-stage' theory of revolution on South Africa, ie. bourgeois revolution—intermission—proletarian revolution. In my view, this demonstrates a lack of understanding of the material process of history within which the correct questions and answers are concealed.

As long ago as 1848 Marx and Engels included in *The Communist Manifesto* an observation on capitalist development that is apparent even today, namely, that capitalism brings ruin to certain classes:

> The lower middle class, the small manufacturer, the shopkeeper, the artisan, the peasant, all these fight against the bourgeoisie to save from extinction their existence as fractions of the middle class . . . . If by chance they are revolutionary, they are so only in view of their *impending transfer into the proletariat.* [my italics][2]

It is difficult to see how a small manufacturer, peasant, or, for that matter, a ruined bourgeois, can continue to survive physically under capitalism unless the only commodity he has been left with, labour power, is sold to the possessor of money. 'Impending transfer into the proletariat' refers precisely to this phenomenon. The term 'landless peasant' is as meaningless as 'capital-less capitalist'. So far as the term 'semi-peasant' is concerned, there is no such thing, as I will try to demonstrate in this article. The other term, 'neither peasants nor workers', describes a state of non-existence and as such merits no examination.

Size and Distribution of the Population

South African censuses are indissolubly linked with the race ideology of the country, particularly when the geographical distribution of the population is considered. Having raised the 'black homelands' policy some twenty years ago to prevent the 'white areas' from being swamped by the blacks, the government soon found itself in a dilemma. That dilemma lay in capitalist development itself, since uneven economic and political development is an absolute necessity for capitalist accumulation and expansion. Since the present Nationalist regime came into office in 1948, the mass exodus of all racial groups from the country-side to the towns and cities has had no parallel in South African history. The main reason for this phenomenon was the post-1945 boom and the concerted

---

*From *Race and Class*, 16, 3 (1975), pp. 259–94.

efforts by the ruling class in South Africa to curtail the country's almost complete dependence on mining and agriculture. Hence, by 1971, manufacturing alone accounted for 23.6 per cent of the GNP, roughly equal to the contribution from mining and agriculture combined. With the mass exodus from the 'homelands' and the rural areas, government statisticians had to find a way round the rapidly declining numbers in these areas. How were the fundamentalists within the National Party going to extricate themselves from this impasse after their repeated electoral claims that South African cities were becoming whiter, thanks to the 'black homelands' policy? The following table and remarks from the South African Institute of Race Relations illustrate the tie up between race ideology and census.

Table 1. *South African Population, mid-1973*

	Totals	Percentage
African	16 217 000	70.6
White	3 958 000	17.2
Coloured	2 144 000	9.3
Asian	668 000	2.9

Source: *Survey of Race Relations in South Africa 1973*, Johannesburg, 1974.

The ministry of statistics also gave a further breakdown of distribution of the African population based on preliminary results of the 1970 census.

Table 2. *Distribution of African Population, 1970*

Urban	4 368 920
Rural	3 664 280
Homelands	7 003 160

Source: See Table 1.

It should also be borne in mind that some large towns inhabited by Africans are situated just within the boundaries of certain homelands. Although they are in effect dormitory suburbs of 'white' cities, their residents are included in the enumeration of the homeland population for census purposes.[3]

Thus, although thousands upon thousands of Africans permanently live and work outside the 'homelands', to satisfy the National Party (always white, since only whites have the franchise), government statistics include these Africans in the figure for the 'homelands'.

Social Classes in the Rural Areas

South Africa's own bourgeois social scientists, ie. those who have managed to lift their eyes above the horizons of National Party propaganda, have independently demonstrated one fact with regard to the 'homelands': so far as the sustenance of a family is concerned, the contribution from subsistence farming is negligible. So infertile and overcrowded are these areas (which constitute a mere 13 per cent of South Africa's land area) that despite the very low wages offered to migrant workers under the migratory labour system, and the stringent pass laws (615 075 Africans were arrested in a space of eleven months, July

1970–June 1971),[4] the towns exert an unopposed pull: the sheer unproductivity of subsistence farming leaves the worker no choice but to sell the only commodity he possesses—labour power.

The tendency to separate the 'homelands' from the rural countryside is without foundation except for the purpose of government propaganda which seeks to legitimise the concept of 'homelands', not only locally but also internationally. The people normally found in the 'homelands' are the old, the physically handicapped, the wives and children of migrant workers, farm labourers and prospective migrant workers, ie. those waiting their turn for work in the towns. Nowadays, the period of waiting is no more than three months, and many of these migrant workers spend approximately 80 per cent of their productive life (producing surplus value, that is) in the 'white' areas. But such prolonged stays in the towns and the cities encourage migrant workers to identify themselves more and more with the economic struggles of their permanently settled urban brothers. A series of strikes hit the mines in 1973 and 1974. In September 1973, one such strike ended with the shooting of eleven miners in Carletonville, near Johannesburg.[5] 'Unless the mines are to be crippled by discontent and repeated riots', commented the Johannesburg *Star,*

> something has to be done very quickly. That something is to provide African miners with opportunities for more—much more—technical training so that they will justify widening opportunities to make more money ... this in turn will presuppose a great reduction in the migratory labour factor, so that black miners will be stable enough and permanent enough to make their training worthwhile.[6]

Just as the separation of the 'homelands' from the rural areas is nonsensical, so is the separation of the modern South African urban migrant worker from the urban black proletariat. The two are now very closely bound up and constitute the urban black proletariat. And daily its numbers grow.

Having demonstrated the folly of regarding urban migrant workers as a fraction of the social classes in the rural areas, I shall now deal with those social classes which are 'permanent' in these areas. From now on I shall call the 'homelands' *rural ghettos,* since this is what they really are.

Rural landowners

In South Africa almost all significant agricultural production is carried out on white-owned farms. The agricultural sector, more than any other sector of the economy, is still characterised by formations peculiar to pre-capitalist societies. Under this system a number of African or Coloured families became tenant peasants on a white-owned farm. They paid their rent in the form of 90–180 days unpaid work on the white landowner's farm. In return, they had grazing rights for their livestock and subsistence farming rights on the particular farm. In South African terminology, these tenant peasants came to be known as squatters. In recent years, however, there has been a significant erosion of this kind of agricultural society because of the concentration and centralisation of capital in agriculture. In fact, the system has been so undermined that it has now reached an advanced stage of decomposition. Many of the farms are run on a cooperative basis, and those which have been classed unproductive have been, or are being, abandoned. The result has been the decline in the number of farms and farmers in South Africa.

The third and final report of the Commission of Enquiry into Agriculture has recommended that the Departments concerned should make a deliberate effort to make it easier for owners of uneconomic farms, in particular, to give up farming . . . This report indicated that between 1936 and 1967 the number of white farmers had decreased from some 132 000 to some 90 000 while the number of farming units had declined from some 105 000 to some 101 000.[7]

With regard to the tenant peasant system, the Government had this to say. At the end of 1969 there were 24 957 registered African labour tenants. During the year, 3 380 had been found redundant. The Government has continued to pursue its objective of abolishing the labour tenant system in favour of full-time labour . . . By the end of 1969, the system had been done away with in the whole of the Free State, 25 districts of the Transvaal, 3 in the Cape and 4 in Natal.[8]

On the whole, the farmers are opposed to these measures, which they look upon as revolutionary. The government and the capitalists have to tread very carefully, particularly the National Party, which relies heavily for its support on this conservative element in the countryside. But, however stubborn the resistance of these farmers, rural social relationships are being inexorably altered so that an agricultural labour market is becoming the norm. Some of the farmers who are not able to withstand the deep inroads which capitalism is making are forced, together with their children, to seek employment in the towns and cities, thus swelling the ranks of the white working class.

The landowning classes (the farmers) of South Africa, like similar classes before them in history, are more than conservative they are reactionary, and will go on resisting capitalist expansion and encroachment in favour of retaining in agriculture certain relationships peculiar to precapitalist societies. Land-ownership is all they have known for several generations and if this is threatened they will fight with the ferocity of a class faced with extinction. It is difficult to conceive that members of this class could comprehend the historical movement, and as a consequence break with the forces of reaction. In the face of these conclusions, the programme outlined by the Freedom Charter must be regarded as hopelessly out of touch with reality. The Charter, by declaring that 'South Africa belongs to all who live in it', is hopelessly utopian. The landowning class cannot be expected to support a move towards the extension of bourgeois democratic rights to black South Africa—as the Charter would have us believe. The agrarian problem in South Africa can only be solved by the revolutionary onslaught on the capitalist mode of production, primarily by the black labouring masses.

Farm Workers are drawn from all race groups living in the rural areas. By far the largest groups come from the Africans and the Coloureds, in that order.

Table 3. Distribution of Farm Workers in the Four Provinces

Race Group	Cape	Natal	Transvaal	OFS*	Totals
Africans	148 200	185 280	478 400	180 200	992 080
Coloureds	105 510	430	1 160	2 570	109 670
Whites	38 160	6 760	31 800	15 670	92 390
Indians	30	6 110	90	Nil**	6 230
			Sum total of all races		= 1 200 370

Source: *Survey of Race Relations in South Africa 1972*, Johannesburg, 1973.
* Orange Free State.
** Indians are forbidden by law from settling or working in this province.

Table 3 shows that 1 107 980 black (African, Coloured and Indian) workers are scattered through some 90 000 farms in various parts of the country, with only 92 390 white workers. The condition of the black agricultural workers is far worse than that of the other workers in the various sectors of the South African economy. In fact it has been shown that in many centres their real wages are below what they were in 1911.[10]

African rural workers

It is not possible from available data to calculate the rates of exploitation of African agricultural workers, since there are no whites performing comparable jobs in agriculture. But, bearing in mind that the wages in agriculture are the lowest of all sectors, then the rates of exploitation of African farm workers by far exceed those in the mining industry, which have been estimated at 181–415 per cent.[10]

In 1972 the Natal University Students Representative Council carried out a survey of the wattle-growing industry in Natal. This revealed that some of the foreign companies farming in South Africa (eg. Slater Walker) were paying average weekly rates ranging between R3.17 and R8.69 to their African workers. The survey concluded that the African workers were living at a subhuman level. A year later, in an expanded investigation, Adam Raphael of the *Guardian* was to confirm the students' findings over a wide area.[11] Raphael's findings, though limited to company farming under the control of British capital, could be taken as valid for all other farming concerns in South Africa.

Are these workers trapped in the agricultural sector? At first glance their position appears to be hopeless because the pass laws and the migratory labour system confine them to work in the rural areas and the agricultural labour market only. But not everyone working in agriculture is restricted in this way: the Coloureds are rapidly abandoning farm work in favour of employment in the other sectors of the economy where wages are higher. This is creating a serious labour shortage in the western Cape, traditionally a Coloured employment area, and the farmers are being forced to recruit workers from the rural ghettos—yet again demonstrating the failure of the government's 'homelands' policies. But can the rural Africans also improve their economic position? The answer lies in capitalist development itself.

Being agricultural migrant workers it is difficult for these workers to escape the police net in their attempts to join their relatively privileged brothers in the cities. But in the rural areas the increasing concentration of capital has brought ruin to small farmers and created a market for labourers, thereby pushing wages up. The following report in a South African newspaper illustrates this point with regard to farming and the development of the rural areas.

Zululand sugar farmers face their worst labour shortage in years. Higher wages being paid to Africans by developers in the Empangeni-Richards Bay area is the reason for this labour drift from the land. At an annual meeting of the South African Cane Growers' Association, in Durban, both the chairman and the vice-chairman of the association called for the improvement of wages and working conditions if their labour force was to be retained.[12]

It is not my intention to give the impression that African rural workers in South Africa receive wages adequate to meet their overall needs, let alone approximating to the wages of their urban counterparts. I simply cite this example to demonstrate that within the apparently impregnable 'granite walls' of apartheid, African workers can make moves to improve their economic condition. This is imperative if increased production and expansion are to occur.

Since agricultural workers are widely scattered among the farms in South Africa, a certain lack of organisation and an apathy towards the economic struggle have occurred. They have remained unmoved by the recent strikes in the urban areas. However, back in their respective rural ghettos they have demonstrated their ability to resist the government's 'homelands' policies by eliminating leading government collaborators. The history of the past twenty years is full of such examples: Zeerust, Sekhukuniland, Pondoland and the Transkei, to name but four. With the declining number of farming units and the concentration of capital in farming we may yet witness the birth of a 'Captain Swing' in rural South Africa. The Africans are denied trade union rights, but if the English agricultural labourers of the 1830s could organise themselves against the land-owning classes, then there is no reason why their South African counterparts cannot do so today. It has been said of the English agricultural labourers' movement that:

> A remarkable feature of the labourers' movement of 1830, distinguishing it from many others of its kind, was its multiformity. As we have seen, arson, threatening letters, 'inflammatory' handbills and posters, 'robbery', wages meetings, assaults on overseers, parsons and landlords and the destruction of different types of machinery all played their part . . . . Yet behind these multiform activities, the basic aims of the labourers were singularly consistent: to attain a minimum living wage and to end rural unemployment.[13]

With the periodic economic struggles of the urban African proletariat, the time may not be far off when the 'slumbering' rural proletarians will join in the struggles against capital. The situation is ripe for a brand new leadership that will place the proletariat in the centre of the stage and lead it to victory over all classes. But the proletariat will only begin to break out of the confines of an economic struggle, and enter the arena of political struggle, when it has a party of its own.

White rural workers

Numbering some 92 000, and scattered throughout the country on over 90 000 farms, the white rural workers are very few in proportion to the number of farms. If the number of the rural black proletarians is decreasing, that of the whites is doing so at a much faster rate. White farm workers are not directly concerned with the production of surplus value, they merely contribute to its realisation; some, it would be true to say, do not even contribute to the realisation of surplus value. They are mainly employed as technicians, mechanics, engineers, managers and overseers. Many of the overseers often have no knowledge of the work on the farm, and their job is done for them by the black foreman. The wages of these rural white workers closely follow those of their counterparts in the urban areas. No figures are available, but it is accepted that the gulf between their wages and those of the rural black workers is far wider than that found on the mines. In the mining industry the ratio of white to African wages is 20.6:1. Like their counterparts in the urban areas, the rural white workers have a high standard of living, thanks to the high rate of exploitation of the African proletariat. The white worker must be judged from this viewpoint when considering the position he is likely to adopt towards the African worker's struggle to narrow the wage gap and eventually be on a par with him. He cannot as yet be won over. He will support the forces of reaction until any hope of victory for these forces has been lost.

Indian and Coloured rural workers

Although relatively privileged in comparison with their African counterparts (a relic of British imperialism and the caste system), the working conditions and wage rates for Coloured and Indian rural workers fall far short of those for the whites.

Today, there are only 6230 Indian agricultural labourers, almost all of them in the province of Natal, where their slave ancestors were sent by the British in the mid-nineteenth century. Like their ancestors, many of these workers are in the sugar plantations.[14] What is the condition of the Indian agricultural labourer? He is not required to carry a pass, so it would appear that he is free to move from place to place. But in reality this is not the case. He is not allowed to move from the province of his birth, he is barred from entering the Orange Free State, except in transit, and is in general confined to the province of Natal. Despite these disabilities, the group exclusiveness of these workers is fostered and nurtured by the ruling classes and certain influential Indians from higher social strata who fear the inevitable fusion of these workers with their African counterparts. A survey in 1973 on wages stated: 'Asians and Coloureds were included in the survey for the first time and the most unexpected feature was that the worst-paid Asians received £8.13 a week—considerably less than their African counterparts'.[15] Although this survey was concerned with urban workers, the same could be said of the rural areas, of workers in agriculture in particular. Hence, the Indian agricultural labourer must be considered susceptible to a programme that would place him in the centre of the stage side by side with his African counterpart.

A few remarks have already been made about the Coloured agricultural workers. Although Coloureds are not required to carry passes, there are so many of them who are indistinguishable from Africans that they are forced to carry their identity cards lest they be charged under the pass laws. Psychologically, it is this type of Coloured who will have nothing to do with the African. He is comparable to what Malcolm X called the 'house-nigger', content to eat 'left-overs'. In some farms in the Cape, the Coloureds are just as exploited as their African and Indian counterparts, and the practice of giving these workers a small cash payment coupled with a bottle of wine still continues. The following extract will illustrate how badly some of these workers are paid.

> Winter rainfall had already achieved a relatively high level of production with mechanisation and labour, especially with Coloured labour
> ... the wages were much lower than those prevailing in industry ...
> in certain areas of the Cape, Coloured labourers earned 70 cents a day.[16]

Despite the apparent ambivalence of certain members of the Coloured labour force, and despite their century-old treatment as 'house-niggers' by the ruling class, there is a growing realisation that equality with white workers is unattainable. This tends to draw them closer to the African proletariat, and so they must be considered susceptible to a revolutionary programme in the same way as the Indians. If we accept, as we must, that a revolutionary programme is above other programmes, such as for civil rights, then the 'house-niggers' will see the futility of their position. In the USA the civil rights movement in 1964 ended the colour divisions among Afro-Americans. And in South Africa today the term non-white is being rejected in preference for the term black by the new and younger generation of Coloureds. In the towns and cities there is a growing opposition to government bodies such as the Coloured Person's Representative Council—a kind of 'homeland' council for the Coloureds. Consequently, the urban anti-Bantustan and 'anti-Colouredstan' movements have merged. With the emergence of a proletarian party, it is not inconceivable that certain sections of the Coloured working class will join it.

Rural black petty bourgeoisie

Because of uneven development, the rural trading and shopkeeping class is numerically greater than its counterpart in the towns and cities. Members of this class are in favour of rural ghettos since only there can they survive, away from competition with the bouregoisie. In the cities their counterparts are forced through competition to transfer to the rural areas. In addition, government policy has tended to favour the issuing of licences to those who wish to establish themselves in the rural ghettos—earning the government's self-congratulatory praise that its 'homelands' policies are working. This class, consequently, is growing in the rural areas. No reliable figures are available about its size, but as long ago as 1961 it was already more numerous in the rural ghettos than in the cities and towns.

I have so far maintained that rural ghettos ('homelands') only exist to satisfy the National Party functionaries and supporters that the whole thing is not a myth. All worthwhile reproductive activity (ie. reproductive activity in terms of labour power) for the African working class is impossible in the rural ghettos. Such activity only takes place in the towns, cities and rural areas. One chief executive of such a ghetto, himself a government appointee, protested to the government when 'his' people were being evicted from the 'white' areas and deported to the rural ghettos: 'the repatriation of urban Africans should be stopped. We must be realistic on this question. I do not see how we can possibly resettle these people now. They should stay where they are. We welcome back those who can start business.'[17]

In the past, before the present National Party had had time to legislate, promulgate and enforce its apartheid measures, many Indian and a few white traders were to be found in the rural ghettos. Their presence and their experience made life difficult for the African trader. Since the passage and enforcement of the Group Areas Act in 1957, the African trader has found himself in a relatively favoured position.

*Table 4. African Traders**

Rural Licences**	Number Granted in 1961
General dealers	2 166
Butchers	781
Bakers	98
Cafes & Restaurants	493
Millers	128
Grocers & Fruiterers	209
Miscellaneous	2 157
Total	6 032

Source: *The State of South Africa Yearbook 1963*, Johannesburg, 1964.
* No figures were given in the case of Coloureds. The figure for Indian traders was given as 18 888 for the country—except for the Orange Free State where Indians are forbidden to settle.
** The total number of licences issued to African traders in the urban areas was 5 968 in 1961.

Other social strata which form fractions of the rural petty bourgeoisie do exist. Even though they do not own small businesses, etc., their ideological position is that of the petty bourgeoisie: Government adjuncts and functionaries (collaborators, if you wish) in this policy of separate development are part of this class. Though not numerous, this group is of considerable importance in the rural ghettos when it comes to the allocation of civil jobs and trading licences. Of the educated and intellectual fraction, teachers form by far the largest group. In fact, a significant fraction of traders are themselves either retired teachers or teachers who register their shops under their wives' names. As yet there are very few doctors, lawyers and nurses in the rural ghettos, but the few there are belong to the petty bourgeoisie. Finally, the churches are an essential part of this class and ideological formation.

Like its counterpart in the urban areas, the rural black petty bourgeoisie aspires to the station of the bourgeoisie, which in South Africa is exclusively white. But there are many formidable obstacles in its path. Between it and the bourgeoisie stand the state and the white working class. Fearing the revolutionary potential of the black proletariat, yet facing opposition to its aspirations from the state and the white working class, the black petty bourgeoisie becomes extremely vacillating in its views. There are periods when its leading members are forced by conditions in South Africa to make a progressive stand. No revolutionary would condemn the stand taken by Chief G. Buthelezi during the 1973 Natal strikes. When 61 000 black workers had downed their tools for more pay, Chief Buthelezi appealed to unemployed blacks not to break the strike. A year later the Chief was found to retreat into a pact with the United Party, the official parliamentary white opposition party in South Africa. In substance there is no significant difference between the United Party and the governing National Party.

Deprived of any decisive significance, the black petty bourgeoisie necessarily runs full circle in search of classes it can lean on in the battle for democratic rights. True, from this class have come a few individuals who have raised themselves to the level of comprehending the developing historical movement, consequently cutting themselves adrift from their origins to join the proletarian movement. In the battle for democracy the black petty bourgeoisie will no doubt fight with the vigour of an oppressed class within the movement of opposition. But as soon as it becomes apparent that the black proletarian fraction of the opposition movement is breaking asunder, is forming an independent movement, the revolutionary vigour and enthusiasm of the petty bourgeoisie will strike a low point. Except for the petty bourgeois who has broken with his class origins to join the proletariat, the rest will almost certainly become counter-revolutionary at critical moments in the revolutionary struggle.

Social Classes in the Urban Areas

The discovery of gold in Johannesburg in 1886 gave birth to the South African bourgeoisie. This was scarcely seven years after the defeat of King Cetshwayo's Zulu armies by the reinforced British imperial armies. Although the war was not fought with the prospect of the discovery of gold in mind, the defeat of the Zulu and the loss of their lands paved the way for their rapid transformation, together with the other African peoples of South Africa, into wage labourers. If the Anglo-Zulu War of 1879 did not immediately give birth to capitalist entrepreneurs, the defeat of the Boers by British imperialism twenty-three years later in the Anglo-Boer War brought about the ascendancy of the mining capitalists, the forerunners of the present South African bourgeoisie. Henceforth, the Boers, whose agricultural societies were still pre-capitalist and archaic in form, were rapidly proletarianised. So, both the Boers (Afrikaners) and the Africans were converted into wage labourers at the same time. J.A. Hobson, a British liberal reformist and economist, wrote at the time:

> We must rather compare with the old tyranny of the Boer farmer [on the Africans] the new tyranny of the mining capitalist ... the Kaffir [derogatory term for African] with his family is to be placed in a position in which he cannot refuse his labour, and that of his family, for whatever wages the mines choose to offer.[18]

Contrary to the South African bourgeois economists' notion, that the low wages paid to African workers can be explained principally by recourse to subsistence farming, this extract demonstrates that the mining capitalists had made no such calculations.

South African bourgeoisie
Is the South African bourgeoisie united as a class? Does it hold any political sway in the South African parliament? The South African bourgeoisie is split into two factions or, rather, it is an amalgam of the rural landowning class and the industrial bourgeoisie. Of the two, the rural landowning class is by far the larger. While it can be said that the Republican Party in the USA and the Conservative Party in the UK are traditionally the parties of the national bourgeoisie, such a bold statement cannot be made in the case of South Africa. Following the defeat of the Boers by British imperialism in 1902, a period of uneasy calm descended upon the foundations of nascent capitalism. In the early years, though treading carefully between the industrial bourgeoisie and the white workers (but slightly tending to favour the latter), it can be said that the industrial bourgeoisie wielded more influence on successive regimes than the rural bourgeoisie. However, after the 1922 Rand White Miners' Revolt (many white miners were killed or wounded by the combined action of the army and air force), Premier Jan Smuts and the South African Party lost the 1924 general election. The root cause of the Rand Revolt was the crisis that faced international capital in the early 1920s. As a result, the mining companies announced in 1921 that they were going to give up some mining contracts and would replace a large number of the unskilled and semi-skilled white workers (who were very costly) by black miners (who were cheap.) The National Party (NP), formed in 1914 for the interests of the rural bourgeoisie, increased its representation in parliament but was not yet strong enough to form a government on its own. It had to find a partner. That partner was the Labour Party, and together they formed the Pact Government, with General J.B.M. Hertzog of the NP as Prime Minister. The two parties were united on one issue: they both felt very strongly about the need to strengthen the Industrial Colour Bar by further legislation. Both the NP and the Labour Party agreed that for the pact to function the NP was to drop its call for a republic and the Labour Party was to put in cold storage its programme of social democracy. For its part the Labour Party had proved itself back in 1911. Though very small then, it managed to secure legislation barring Africans and Indians from skilled jobs in the mines, in particular those jobs with higher rates of pay. The pact lasted until 1929 when the NP gained a clear-cut victory in that year's general election.

From 1929 onwards, with the exception of the uncertainty brought about by the Nazis' coming to power in Germany, the party of the landowners, the NP, was ascendant in South African politics. I have already stated that the landowning class is diminishing in number—yet its party continues to consolidate its power. How is this to be explained? The answer is that the NP has remained the trusted and reliable guardian of the white workers' interests. This dates back to the party's formation. It also explains the total elimination from the South African political scene of the Labour Party. Without white working class support, there is little doubt that the NP would decline as a political force in South Africa.

How does the South African industrial bourgeoisie view the situation? What about the international bourgeoisie? Politically they are not in a dominant position. Their actions are governed by their adherence to the erroneous notion that their society is in equilibrium and in harmony. Although they may find that they are in disagreement with, for example, the tendency of apartheid to distort labour market forces, so long as bourgeois equilibrium is not profoundly disturbed they are not going to be involved in a confrontation with the government. 'Dominant interests', as Ralph Miliband has said,

> do not necessarily manage to create dominant parties; but also this
> need not, given other means of influence and pressure, be particularly
> crippling. It is perfectly possible, for these interests at least, to achieve
> their purposes through parties which are not properly speaking their
> own, and through many other agencies.[19]

In the new industrialism of South Africa (ie. the fillip given to the manufacturing sector and the decreasing importance of agriculture and mining in terms of the GNP), Afrikaner capitalists (eg. Anton Rupert and others) have emerged. In the Afrikaner universities, too, Afrikaner bourgeois political economists are gradually making their impact felt, many of them now sitting on government economic commissions. These economists, many of whom are members of the NP, often come out with conclusions diametrically opposed to the interest of the 'founding fathers' of the Party—the rural landowners. I have already referred to the government's desire to end the remnants of pre-capitalist agrarian formations such as the squatter system. Leading members of the *Afrikaanse Handels Instituut*, an organisation for promoting the interests of the Afrikaner industrial capitalists, are interested in the development of more loopholes in the 'granite walls of apartheid'. Its president, P.B. Marais, said in 1970: 'It has become absolutely essential that reliable estimates of our labour resources and needs be made. *We must guard against the prevailing tendency to overprotect our people* [my italics]. It could be that job reservation removes the motivation of white workers to increase productivity.'[20]

The industrial bourgeoisie and the government have to tread very carefully since the white workers have the franchise, together with other bourgeois democratic rights that go with it. They must be seen to be doing their best in the interests of the white working class. That the white working class does feel this way is proved by the fact that despite the split in the NP into the *Verligtes* (enlightened and tending to listen to the growing influence of Afrikaner bourgeois economists) and the *Verkramptes* (traditionalists representing the rural landowners), it has returned the *Verligtes* to parliament in the recent election with an increased majority. Not a single hard-line *Verkrampte* was returned. There is little doubt that today's white workers would do exactly the same as their predecessors in the 1924 election, when they returned to parliament candidates of the ultra-right, should the present administration and the industrial bourgeoisie repeat the mistakes of 1922. If those mistakes were repeated today, the *Verkramptes* would sweep aside everything before them on their way to the legislative assembly in Cape Town. Unfortunately for the *Verkramptes*, all the political parties have learnt that lesson. Consequently, the industrial bourgeois cannot as yet be expected to enter into open conflict with the white workers so long as the black proletariat remains weak and unorganised as a class. Only at periods when the class struggle of the black proletariat assumes a glaring character will large sections of the industrial bourgeoisie, backed by international capital, enter the arena of open conflict with the white workers to prevent the revolution from becoming permanent.

Industrial bourgeois parties do exist in South Africa and, indeed, are represented in the legislative assembly in Cape Town. There are two such parties— the United Party and the Progressive Party. They constitute the 'opposition' in the South African parliament.

In bourgeois parliamentarism, opposition party implies an alternative party of government. In the South African context, however, it is meaningless. The white workers have found a home in the NP and their interests have been looked after more than satisfactorily ever since the Party was elected to office in 1948. It is for this reason that the NP has (except in one instance) increased its majorities at successive general elections. The fact that even if the United Party or the Progressive Party were to form the government, those aspects of the industrial colour bar which ensure white working class privilege would remain largely intact does not merit the attention of the South African white worker. He cannot equate the interests of the Oppenheimers in the Progressive Party with those of the emerging Afrikaner industrial bourgeoisie in the NP.

The super-exploitation of black workers based on the industrial colour bar is, given the South African superstructure, an absolute condition without which the South African bourgeoisie, both the landowners and the industrial capitalists, could not survive. Harry Oppenheimer, Chairman of the giant Anglo-American Corporation and a leading financial backer of the Progressive Party, is ostensibly aware of this fact. Let us suppose any government agreed with the bourgeoisie to 'dismantle' the foundations of the Industrial Colour Bar laws. The bourgeoisie and the government must be prepared to enter into open conflict with the white working class. Now why should any bourgeoisie bring about such a disruption in the absence of a powerful, organised and formidable threat from the black proletariat? The NP in any case is serving the Oppenheimers well by continually adapting to new conditions, even though this is done clandestinely for fear of possible and likely disruptions and demonstrations by white workers. Black workers may do 'white' skilled jobs but at lower rates of pay. This is occurring because white immigration, which would be expensive anyway, cannot match the rapidly expanding economy. Increasing numbers of blacks will be pushed into white jobs, but mostly at lower rates of pay. Harry Oppenheimer's comment in connection with that section of the white working class he feels is doing 'black' jobs is interesting. In toying with the idea of replacing these white workers with blacks, he said:

> It is impossible . . . to apply the 'rate for the job' by paying black workers at the rates that are directly related, comparing job content with job content, with the wages now paid to the white workers at the bottom end of the white wage scale . . . . What is to be done with these men [white workers]? They cannot be dismissed without proper provision for them nor can they reasonably be asked to pay in the form of lower wages and a reduced standard of living for the sins and mistakes of South African society as a whole . . . . Meantime they must continue to be employed at their old rates, even though black

workers who are being promoted into the same job categories are receiving lower pay. It is neither politically possible nor socially right to try to do justice to black workers at the expense of the security and established standard of certain classes of white workers.[21]

Clearly, Oppenheimer is not going to make white workers 'pay for the sins and mistakes of South African society', let alone pay the price himself. This leaves only one class of people to continue paying that price—the black proletariat. It cannot expect to obtain redress from the South African bourgeoisie, but will only do so by engaging in a revolutionary struggle to expropriate the bourgeoisie.

White urban working class

In dealing with the South African bourgeoisie, it was inevitable that the white working class should crop up again and again, because of the close tie-up between the two. The white working class in South Africa, like the working class of advanced capitalist countries, enjoys bourgeois democratic rights, ie. the right to vote, the right to have and belong to legally-recognised trades unions, and a host of other related bourgeois rights. This is what puts him in a uniquely favoured position in comparison with the black worker. To understand what the white worker has 'won', it is important to know what the black worker has lost and how.

When gold was discovered in Johannesburg, the Transvaal was still a Boer republic with Paul Kruger as president. 'South Africa' was still very underdeveloped, mainly made up of rural, pre-capitalist societies. Many Afrikaners could neither read nor write and, like the Africans, they were unskilled. It was for this reason that almost the entire skilled labour force was immigrant, mainly from the mining districts of Britain, during the formative years of South Africa's mining industry. In the Transvaal Paul Kruger sought ways and means to help the Afrikaners who were coming into the mining districts in large numbers from the farms. It was in 1893 that the Kruger administration passed legislation that was to eliminate competition for jobs between the two groups of unskilled workers—the African workers and the whites (Afrikaners). The mining companies were given firm instructions not to employ Africans as blasters. The African workers had no weapon to resist this colour bar legislation. The immigrant workers, themselves experienced in daily struggles against capitalists, remained aloof. Since they were all highly skilled workers, they were not threatened by the swarming numbers of African workers. The Afrikaner worker, lacking in skills, often illiterate and unable to speak the language of his employers (English), had only one weapon—the government of the day which he and his *volk* had supported against British imperialism from the days of the Great Trek (1836), was on his side.

Since gold mining was in the Transvaal and the Transvaal was a Boer republic until 1902 and not a British colony, the mining companies backed by British imperialism were all foreign—hence the term *uitlanders* used by the Boers at the time. These foreign companies did not raise a finger of protest at the industrial colour bar legislation of the Transvaal Republic. It paid them doubly: not only did they pay low black wages, which by raising the rate of exploitation meant fat profits, but their quiescence meant that they had a relatively easy time in procuring new leases and licences for prospecting from the Kruger administration. It is therefore not surprising that today foreign companies should act in the same way. Significantly, even after the defeat of the Boer republics by British imperialism in 1902, the colour bar statutes were left wholly intact. In fact successive governments were to strengthen the industrial colour bar. We have seen how the pressure by the small Labour Party on the Louis Botha government for a more effective colour bar in protecting white accers to skilled jobs paid off in 1911, and how the rise of the party of land-owners, the NP, depended on reactionary white working class support. When, in 1948, the NP finally got back into office, there was to be no turning back. With the other parties too weak and discredited in the eyes of the white working class, many members of this class have made the NP their home.

With the NP victory in 1948, the white working class was to receive more rewards in the form of more racially discriminatory legislation in employment. This had the effect of raising the rates of exploitation of the black working class in several job categories, a factor that enabled capitalists to pay the white workers much higher wages unrelated to their productivity. We have it on the authority of Oppenheimer himself that, 'the high wages paid to these white workers are only made economically possible by the relatively much lower wages paid to black workers'.[22]

When the Pact Government was formed in 1924, various racially discrimina-tory laws were passed. The most important was the Mines and Works Act of 1926, which reserved certain skilled and semi-skilled job categories in the mining industry for white workers. Both the NP and the Labour Party (the Pact Government formed in 1924) were opposed to European miners' immigration since this tended to slow down the training of the many poor, unskilled Afrikaner workers arriving on the labour market from the rural areas. With these early measures taken and effected in his favour, the Afrikaner worker left behind the African worker with whom he had been hurled simultaneously into the industrial scene. From then on the gulf in employment prospects and wages between the white and black workers widened. Further job discrimina-tory legislation had been passed since 1926, but in 1956 the J.G. Strydom administration rightly concluded that it was cumbersome and time-consuming to pass separate bits of law in connection with white job reservation. Rather than permanently trying to mop up a garden which was being water-logged because of a running hose, the more intelligent thing to do was to regulate the tap. It was under these circumstances that a new provision (section 77) was adopted and added to the Industrial Conciliation Act, ie. the Job Reservation Act. Under this Act all the minister had to do was act on a recommendation from an Industrial Tribunal (made up of five government-appointed members) and thus effect job reservation in any given area of employment. Government supporters, of course, will claim that the Act can be used in favour of any racial group, for example, in the rural ghettos. In these areas, however, the colour bar applies with the same effect as in 'white' areas. The Mines and Works Act, which reserves certain job categories for the white workers in the mining industry, is a good example. In the mines of the 'homelands', the African workers may not do the jobs that are reserved for white workers in the 'white' areas.

> Africans are not permitted to do such jobs as sampling, driving an underground diesel locomotive if whites are being conveyed, doing welding underground or even building a simple concrete wall under-ground. After blasting has taken place, gangs of Africans must wait, losing working time, until a white miner has inspected the stope.[23]

In the face of all this it is clear that the government does not see the rural ghettos as separate from the Republic of South Africa, nor do its supporters, the white workers, though at election time they are ready to believe that the blacks are being eliminated from the 'white' areas and are gaining independence in their own areas.

What is the attitude of the white trade unions to the industrial colour bar? Take, for example, the recent development of small-scale mining in the rural ghettos. On the one hand, the government is anxious to have the support of the chiefs in these areas by giving pusillanimous support to the notion that the blacks in 'their own' areas have more rights than 'foreigners' (ie., whites from the 'white' areas). But at the same time, it cannot afford to upset the white working class.

> ... the council of Mining Workers Unions, consisting of nine unions, had decided to support the stand of the Mine Workers' Union and to forbid members to train Africans to carry out semi-skilled or skilled works .... Two of the unions representing Boiler Makers and Iron Moulders, were also affiliated to the middle-of-the-road Trade Union Council of South Africa (TUCSA). A few days later TUCSA issued a statement saying ... it demanded the right to protect the interests of its members. It would not tolerate any changes in the black-white labour patterns without full consultation. There must be ... a clearly formulated policy to ensure the protection of white workers.[24]

Bourgeois and liberal economists will point out that apartheid is falling apart because of economic growth and expansion. They may point out (if they know it) that in one homeland, Lebowa, nineteen African mining assistants are now employed as blasters, drillers and testers and that a few more are undergoing training. But this was done only after the white miners had won a victory and had been bought off by the capitalists, since only in that way could conditions for extracting super-profits from the black workers be created. The following illustrates the point: 'Each of the men [the 19 supervisors] earned between R80 and R100 a month .... The white supervisors were earning between R660 and R700 a month (about R100 more than they did previously).'[25]

There are many other examples of discriminatory laws in employment and wages which various progressive agencies, such as the Anti-Apartheid Movement and others connected with the United Nations, have done much to publicise and condemn. I have only selected a few with a view to examining the position the white worker is likely to adopt regarding the unfolding South African class struggle. These show that there is no question regarding the stand he will adopt. He will fight fiercely on the side of the bourgeoisie until he realises that the forces he has been fighting for are losing the struggle. In fact, at that juncture the bourgeoisie will abandon him. Only then will he become susceptible to the proletarian socialist programme. Since the revolution will be permanent, it is quite conceivable that this same white worker on joining the proletarian party will turn and point his guns not only at his former allies, the white bourgeoisie, but also at the new allies of this bourgeoisie—the black petty bourgeoisie.

South Africa has no black bourgeoisie, only a petty bourgeoisie. Even the propertied classes among the Asian community in Durban could not be called a bourgeoisie as such because of the various legislative measures which prevent them from full participation in the process of accumulation and expansion. Among the Africans, and the Coloureds also, a search for a bourgeoisie yields no positive results. While the South African bourgeois needs both the white working class, principally as an ally, and the black working class, to super-exploit, the black petty bourgeois needs the black working class to accomplish his aim of conquering the commanding heights already occupied by the bourgeoisie.

Urban Indian petty bourgeoisie

The Indian trading class is, in relation to the total Indian population, very numerous in South Africa—particularly in the provinces of the Transvaal and the Cape. In some small towns in these areas, almost every Indian encountered belongs to a trading family. In Natal, however, the position is different, since it was there that the first shipment of Indian slaves arrived in 1860 to work in the sugar plantations. Their descendants are today's Indian proletariat, both rural and urban. From among the trading class has sprung the Indian professional group, including doctors, lawyers, teachers and intellectuals. Because of its economic position and educational attainment, coupled with the lack of organisation among the Indian working class, the Indian petty bourgeoisie has provided the leadership in the Indian community. I shall examine the interests of the various members of this class since 1948, when the NP came into office, and as a result of those interests what stand the leadership adopted.

Table 5. *Number of Indians affected by Group Areas Act since 1950*

	Natal	Transvaal	Cape
Number of licenses revoked	1 061	2 407	1 078
Number of renewed and resettled	231	181	135
Those not resettled, ie. ruined	830	2 226	943

Source: Tabulated from *1972 Survey of Race Relations in South Africa.*

I have already pointed out that the Group Areas Act brought ruin to many an Indian trader. Before this Act whites and Indians could trade in the African ghettos, whether rural or urban. In 1950, when the Act was passed, they both lost that right. There was very little opposition from the white trader who, in addition to the compensation he received, joined a privileged group of workers—the white working class. Almost without exception the white trader made no attempt to re-establish himself in the 'white' areas since he realised how rapidly he could be ruined by competition with the larger capitalists. For the ruined Indian trader, however, all the options were unfavourable. In the Transvaal and the Cape, where the Indian communities were small and scattered, the loss of trading rights in the densest population areas had a very deleterious effect. In the new Indian ghettos which the government was setting up, the populations were also scanty. In addition, many families now in these areas were traders before the Act was passed. There were simply too many prospective traders for this activity to be a viable proposition. The other alternative was to join the Indian working class, but therein lay the problem. Their wages were low and, unlike their former white counterparts, the Indian ex-traders were faced with the prospect of a drop in their standard of living once the meagre compensation they had received for their businesses had run out. But many of these former traders have had to join the ranks of the Indian proletariat. Table 5 gives some guide.

It is against this background that members of this class entered the movement of opposition with the same Gandhian tactics that their predecessors had used. From the moment the Act was passed they fought in the courts numerous orders from the state to leave the African or white areas. This was a losing battle from the start, but they had no option but to fight this way, if they were to fight at all, since they could not expect the proletariat come out on this issue. Eventually they were to form a pact in 1952 with members of the African and

Coloured petty bourgeoisie to fight the incessant race legislations of the D.F. Malan administration. The Indian fraction of this alliance was to push to the fore three demands. These were:

(1) An end to Provincial Barriers, since Indians could not settle in any province other than that of their birth, and as far as the Orange Free State was concerned, the Indians could not even be born there;

(2) An end to racial segregation in the trains, post offices and railway stations;

(3) Repeal of the Group Areas Act.

With such demands, it is hardly surprising that even though not as yet organised on a class basis, the Indian proletariat remained aloof, and none of these race laws have as yet been repealed today. Coupled with the lack of a whole host of political rights, it is these barriers—the Group Areas Act and the Provincial Bar—that severely hamper and postpone the graduation of the Indian petty-bourgeoisie into a bourgeoisie. The magazine *Fiat Lux* disclosed in April 1970 that in 1969 there were 527 Indian concerns which employed 9 500 Indian workers, largely in food processing, textile mills, clothing factories, timber undertakings, garages, furniture and upholstery business, printing works, and laundry and dry cleaning enterprises. Being Indian-owned they can only operate in Indian areas and with Indian labour. In addition, they may not expand beyond the confines of the province of their origin. Therefore, this class cannot be equated with any section of the South African bourgeoisie. Whether they support or oppose the government, the state is not run in their interests. The Indian petty bourgeois is hurled into the opposition movement because he realises his weak position. He joins the other petty bourgeois opposition forces where he claims to represent the interests of the entire Indian community (not classes, he does not use this term). The other numerically larger fractions of the movement of opposition, African and Coloured in that order, do not fare any better. They too claim to be there for the interests of their communities, 'class' being something foreign to their' people. The formation of the Black Consciousness Movement is a direct result of such petty bourgeois formations today.

Urban African petty bourgeoisie

Although a fraction of this class has already been dealt with in the section dealing with the rural areas, there is no distinction between the two, urban and rural. Indeed, the dynamics of apartheid are such that many of those who have trading licences in the rural ghettos are the same traders who are in the urban African ghettos.

Unlike their Indian counterparts they are not greatly affected by the Group Areas Act and the Provincial Bar is also of no consequence. In fact, the Group Areas Act which brought ruin to the Indian petty bourgeois, was a windfall to the African trader since it removed from the scene his experienced competitors. On these grounds it can be predicted that he will be reluctant to enter into a pact with the Indian petty bourgeoisie.

The other segments of this class—the intelligentsia, doctors, lawyers, teachers and nurses—are, however, prepared to fight on a wider platform with similar segments from the Indian and Coloured communities, for they do not, as separate groups, threaten each other. As professional classes with similar qualifications as whites, they feel a sense of revulsion at being paid lower wages. In addition, there is no opposition to their demands from similar professional groups among the whites. A good example is the support for equal pay by the

South African Medical Council—possible because paying black doctors the same as whites would not alter the racial bars that are in existence and there is no question of competition for jobs as in industry. It is interesting that it is mainly in those areas of employment which are not productive that white opposition to equal wages is almost absent. It was reported in 1973 that black doctors working for the Johannesburg City Council and those in the Transkei were being paid the same salaries.

It would be wrong to suggest that members of the African professional class (and their Indian and Coloured counter-parts) only set their sights on attaining equal wages. They all aspire to the position occupied by their white counter-parts. Because of their weakness numerically and politically, and their insignificance with regard to capitalist production, they search for classes to lean on. One example was the call made to black workers and white voters just before the 1958 general election. The black petty bourgeoisie asked the black proletariat to go on strike for three days in order to influence the white voters to vote for the ailing and declining United Party. An appeal was made to the white voters through the press: 'Remember that you vote not only for yourself but also on behalf of many fellow South Africans who are denied the franchise'.[26] Of course, the average white voter does not forget his fellow black South Africans the moment he reaches the polling booth. It is precisely because he has these black creatures in mind that he votes the way he does. It would also be typical of a petty bourgeois approach to expect the black proletariat to go on a three-day strike principally to help a reactionary white opposition party come into office. As was to be expected, judging by the 1948 and 1953 elections, the majority of white voters were increasingly finding a home in the NP; the United Party suffered a crushing defeat.

In his search for classes that he may lean on, the black petty bourgeois is forced back to make an appeal to the really decisive class—the black proletariat. But he is in a dilemma. He is not interested in the interests of the black working class, and yet he must mobilise this class if his own revolution is to take place. The petty bourgeois is necessarily a nationalist. He conjures up the spirits of the dead and is convinced that this will be enough to get workers out from the factory to fight. Others have put it this way.

> ... nationalism is invariably characterised by a high degree of political and ideological voluntarism. Simply because it is forced mass-mobilisation in a position of relative helplessness ... it is, in its immediate nature, idealistic. It always imagines an ideal 'people' (propped up by folklore studies, antiquarianism, or some surrogate for these) and it always searches urgently for vital inner, untapped, springs of energy both in the individual and the mass.[27]

Denying the existence of classes in African societies, African nationalists naturally view with hostility any attempts to analyse social classes in their societies. Their hostility assumes the character of an inferno when it becomes apparent that the method used in such an analysis has its basis in historical materialism. Anton Lembede, a founder of African nationalism in South Africa, said in 1947:

> African nationalism is to be pursued with the fanaticism and bigotry of religion .... The materialistic conception of History that conceives of Man as essentially an economic animal—Communist—and the biological interpretation that conceives of him as a Beast of Prey—Nazism—are false .... Africans are naturally socialistic as illustrated by their social practices and customs ... national liberation will

therefore herald or usher a new era, the era of African socialism.[28]
Lembede erred. His error had its roots in his ideological position. By rejecting
historical materialism, he failed to see the naked situation in front of him, ie.
even in the 1940s tribal formations had been grossly undermined by capitalist
development and had reached an advanced stage of decomposition. The conclusion that Africans are naturally socialistic is a rejection of scientific socialism.
Implicit in this is the notion that socialism is genetically transmitted and,
consequently, any conscious effort to achieve it is a waste of time.

Deprived of any real significance in the process of capitalist production,
and because of their numerical weakness, the black petty bourgeoisie cannot
on its own achieve the status of a bourgeoisie. Assistance is naturally sought
from the black proletariat. But the black proletariat has no interest in a bourgeois
revolution as a separate and distinct stage. The only way out for the petty
bourgeois is to study the historical movement developing in front of his very
eyes and make a break with his class. Failing this, it is not inconceivable that he
will remain in the service of international capital and imperialism at critical
periods in the revolution.

Urban black proletariat

I have explained how the discovery of gold in 1886 and, sixteen years later,
the defeat of the Boer republics, paved the way for the rapid transformation of
South Africa's African and· white (Boer) tribes into proletarians. By 1935
dispossession of these tribes and uneven development had reached such a high
level that the rural social relationships among the Africans and the Boer pre-
capitalist agrarian formations had been irrevocably undermined. This was
achieved in scarcely fifty years, far shorter than similar periods in Western
Europe. But, before I examine the significance of the black proletariat, what is
its size? Once again, government statistics, though incomplete and highly
unreliable, must be used.

Table 6 shows that the size of the black, ie. African, Coloured and Indian
proletariat, is 7 081 000, the Africans forming by far the largest group. Because
of the brief period of gestation leading to the birth of this proletariat, and by
skipping the feudal stage, through which the proletariat of the advanced
countries went, craft and guild traditions are noticeably absent from the African
proletariat. Only the Coloureds have some links with these traditions; just as
it was emerging, the African proletariat found itself face to face with international capital. And that was not all. There was an enormous concentration of
power in the state and, since this new proletariat had no political rights and no
experience in the economic struggle, the capitalists exploited these factors to
their advantage.

Table 6. Size of the Urban Workforce, 1972

Race	Number of Workers	Percentage of Workforce
African	6 130 000	70.5
White	1 607 000	18.5
Coloured	754 000	8.7
Asian	197 000	2.3
Total workforce	8 688 000	100.0

Source: 1973 Survey of Race Relations in South Africa.

148

The antagonisms between the white workers and the black workers have already been demonstrated, and I concluded that the white workers will remain for a long time the reliable allies of the bourgeoisie. What about the other small groups—the Coloureds and the Indians? Some of them belong to recognised trade unions which are mainly affiliated to the Trades Union Congress of South Africa (TUCSA). Like the white working class, unionised Coloured and Indian workers are opposed to the extension of trade union rights to African workers. But, as the figures show, they constitute only a small fraction of the labour force. Since the wages of the Coloured and Indian workers still fall far short of those for the whites, because of the Industrial Colour Bar, it would be reasonable to expect them to join with the African worker in his daily struggles against capital. Besides, as far as wages are concerned, there is so much overlap that there are groups of African workers who are paid more than some Coloured and Indian workers. Table 7 illustrates the gap between the Coloured, Indian and white wages, and also shows that in many cases there is not much of a gap between the Coloured and African wages.

Table 7. Relative Wages, May 1973

Industry	Race	Monthly average wage
Food	White	R355
	Asian	R120
	Coloured	R82
	African	R65
Tobacco	White	R359
	African	R86
	Coloured	R79
	Asian	not given
Electricity	White	R415
	Coloured	R105
	African	R80
	Asian	not given
Transport equipment	White	R380
	Asian	R153
	Coloured	R133
	African	R86

Source: *1973 Survey of Race Relations in South Africa.*

These figures are of course averages, and do not show the highest and lowest wages in each group. African workers, as a result of the pay increases won during the 1972–3 strikes, are now close on the heels of the Coloured and Indian workers. Under the impact of the growing militancy of the African workers, it is those wage gaps which are going to be sealed first. The Coloureds and the Indians cannot expect the white workers to come out in their support under the circumstances. They must be made to see that their only way out is to join the fraction which holds the initiative—the African working class.

I have discussed how the colour bar has created an artificial shortage of labour, and how both the government and the capitalists circumvent this in order to improve the conditions for the self-expansion of capital. Jobs, formerly reserved exclusively for whites, are reclassified black, and although skilled they now fall under the category semi-skilled at highly reduced rates of pay. The number of 'semi-skilled' workers is increased, the shortage of labour gradually subsides and the distorting effect due to apartheid is overcome. Job reclassification and the clandestine training of black workers for skilled jobs will continue to take place in South Africa as long as the Industrial Colour Bar is of mutual benefit to both the capitalists and the white workers. But it was those workers who were promoted to 'white' jobs, and saw some improvement in their wages, who were the most militant in 1973. In the apparently illegal set-up concerning black strike action, the African proletariat came out of their factories in 1972-3. It was estimated that by the end of 1973, 70 000 African workers had been involved in strike action for higher wages. All this was happening in the midst of 'highly concentrated state power' and 'rampant' capitalism.[29]

How class conscious is the African proletariat? These strikes, which are continuing in 1974, have proved that it is conscious enough to fight economic battles without legally recognised trade unions. African nationalists seek to mobilise the African working class on another basis—that its members are descended from a great people with a great fighting tradition, and as such must be armed and fight for their lost lands. Of course, it could not be otherwise for the African nationalists—their ideology being bourgeois. For them, dispossession is only peculiar to Africa, and only whites could bring it about. That the European working class is also descended from the land merits no consideration. In the last century Marx wrote,

> Thus were the agricultural people, first forcibly expropriated from the soil, driven from their homes, turned into vagabonds, and then shipped, branded, tortured by the laws grotesquely terrible, into discipline necessary for the wage system.[30]

Long before Marx, bourgeois historians and economists had described this phenomenon. On the question of lineage, we might add that the African worker may even be more aware than the nationalist that his great grandfather fought in the Anglo-Zulu War in 1879. This is to no avail. The African worker will not fight on this basis. The proletariat of Italy is descended from the famed Romans—but does that help it in its daily struggles against capital? We can see, therefore, how irrelevant to the worker the slogans of the petty bourgeois nationalists are in the face of the increased concentration of capital and state power.

The African proletariat has also escaped the biases associated with the handicraft guilds—which have had no role whatsoever in its development. But there is another psychological barrier in the minds of these workers, namely, that the development and entrenchment of the capitalist mode of production is the natural basis for existence. Marx wrote,

> The advance of capitalist production develops a working class, which by education, tradition, habit, looks upon the conditions of that mode of production as self-evident laws of Nature. The organisation of the capitalist process of production, once fully developed, breaks down all resistance.[31]

But if all resistance breaks down, one form of struggle commences—the daily struggle against capital by the workers. It is this kind of struggle that the worker is attuned to. Now a further point must be understood. The African working class, together with the other smaller fractions (Coloured and Indians) of the black proletariat, is unlikely to rise above the economic struggle. In the words of Lenin,

> Attention, therefore, must be devoted principally to raising the workers
> to the level of revolutionaries; it is not at all our task to descend to
> the level of the 'working masses' as the Economists wish to do.[32]

However, because the African worker has no political rights, coupled with the repressive and brutal nature of the state, the very moment he goes on strike he is breaking the law. His only form of struggle against the capitalists assumes a political character, and questions of politics are part of the everyday struggle of the worker. Tzarist Russia gives us a comparable situation,

> . . . the yoke of autocracy appears at first glance to obliterate all
> distinctions between the Social Democratic organisation and workers'
> associations . . . since the principal manifestation and weapon of the
> workers' economic struggle—the strike—is regarded as criminal (and
> sometimes even as a political) offence. Conditions in our country . . .
> strongly 'impel' the workers engaged in economic struggle to concern
> themselves with political questions.[33]

Conclusions

Against this background, it is clear that the South African revolutionaries face a mammoth task. With the defeat of Portuguese colonialism in Africa and the independence of Mozambique a *fait accompli*, there is a strongly held view among many in Africa that the struggle against white rule and oppression in Southern Africa will become much easier. Being nearer home, the lessons of Mozambique cannot be withheld from those blacks of Southern Africa still under white rule. The consummation of the national democratic revolution in Mozambique could in some respects be of tremendous value to the South African black proletariat. The existing contradictions within the South African superstructure could be sharpened manifold. Assuming that the new government does not stop the flow of migrant workers into South Africa, some interesting questions arise. Approximately 100 000 migrant workers in South Africa's mining industry are Mozambican. Being black, they are subject to Pass Law regulations and wage controls under the Industrial Colour Bar. But in addition, their wages are even below those of the South African black workers. Now, will a FRELIMO government, on coming into office in June 1975, demand from the South African capitalists 'white' wage rates for its migrant workers? Will it demand from the South African government the cessation of the application of the Pass Laws on these workers? Time will tell. If anything like this were to happen, it would represent a sharp break with the methods and independence traditions of the neighbouring black ruled states. Indeed, it would represent something unique even on an international scale.

The view that from now on the struggle in South Africa becomes much easier is largely prevalent among those who seek to subordinate the class struggle to a bush war away from the capitalists. It is imagined that such a bush or rural war will be fought both from outside and inside South Africa. It is perhaps significant that almost without exception, all white South African 'revolutionaries' subscribe to this view, perhaps because they have not as yet made a break with their roots in the 'white' areas. In my view, the struggle for proletarian ascendency in South Africa will be fought and won principally in the towns and cities where the proletariat and capital are concentrated. I do not rule out the rural areas, since it is obvious that a concurrent struggle in the countryside will have the effect of draining the already meagre manpower resources of the enemy from the urban areas.

Now, more than at any other time, the ideological unity of the South African revolutionaries needs to be seriously considered. To achieve it we need a revolutionary theory. Only pedantics will claim to have worked out a complete theory and tactic for the South African revolution. But ideological unity cannot be achieved without an organisation of revolutionaries in South Africa and abroad. More, it has to be worked for, and can only be achieved, within a precisely defined tendency. That tendency is scientific socialism as initially put forward by Engels and Marx, and later by Lenin and Mao Tse Tung. A consistent development of the ideas of scientific socialism in full view of all those who make revolution their daily business will enable the organisation to arrive at a clear political line for the revolutionary movement. For this to occur, open polemics or fundamental questions will need to be encouraged, not as dogma but as guides to action. While the capitalist factory produces an expert on economic battles, the organisation will concern itself with the task of raising this expert to the level of a revolutionary. To develop and disseminate the ideas of scientific socialism, the revolutionaries need a theoretical journal and a newspaper. Once these criteria are met, the politically-conscious and revolutionary proletariat, and the revolutionary intellectuals, will together help in the task of purging themselves of bourgeois ideas and prejudices. Soon the terms worker and intellectual must cease to have any meaning in the organisation, everyone being referred to as a revolutionary; and conditions in South Africa will impel members of this organisation to make it as secret as circumstances will allow.

Yet another question to be answered is the nature of the South African revolution. Which social classes can be said to be oppressed? My analysis of social class has, I hope, demonstrated that all blacks suffer oppression, manifested by the complete denial of democratic rights. This leads to the question: Can there be an amalgam of the oppressed social classes? Because of imperialism and its by-product, ie. white racism, and the super-exploitation of the entire black working class (African, Coloured and Indian), together with the complete absence of democratic rights, the movement of opposition in South Africa will be very broadly based. The rural and urban black proletariat on the one hand, and the rural and urban black petty bourgeois, on the other, will be found in this movement. Bourgeois and proletarian demands or slogans will be found inscribed on the same banner—eg. trades union rights, equal pay for equal work, equality of opportunity, free movement from within and from without South Africa, the ending of the residential colour bar—in short, the ending of apartheid. What are the chances of these demands being met under the circumstances? Nil. There is no doubt that the white working class will continue to stiffen its opposition with the support of the government and the industrial bourgeoisie. It is perfectly obvious, too, that these demands are bourgeois in character and in that respect the revolution is bourgeois. And yet we South African Marxists would be guilty of a serious tactical error if we dismissed as utterly irrelevant all these demands simply because they are bourgeois in character. The proletariat, by placing these demands side by side with its daily economic demands, grows in political stature. Under these conditions the work of the politically-conscious and revolutionary proletarians is improved manifold. The great merit of the politically conscious and revolutionary proletarians, and the intellectuals who join the proletarian wing of the movement of opposition, lies in their ability to distinguish what is bourgeois and what is not, and from this to synthesise the demands which are of greatest interest to the proletariat at various periods of the revolution.

Who will be the principal and decisive actors in this revolutionary drama? Unlike the French Revolution of 1789 and the Russian Revolution of 1905, the South African revolution does not seek to liberate a nascent bourgeoisie from the fetters and chains of pre-capitalist autocracy and feudal ownership. Conditions for extracting super-profits from black workers and rapid capitalist expansion already exist in South Africa. And, unlike in pre-Bolshevik Russia and in China before 1949, South Africa does not have social classes such as semi-peasants or semi-proletarians who, by definition, own or rent other means of production and therefore only sell a portion of their labour power to supplement these means. The Communist Party of South Africa (CPSA), largely because of its ties with the Stalin era and as a consequence its support for the petty bourgeois nationalist leadership of the African National Congress, has mechanically imported these terms in a crude attempt to impose the 'two-stage' theory of revolution on South Africa. Because of this mechanical approach to Marxism and Leninism, the CPSA sees South African society as an approximation of the societies which Lenin before 1905 and Mao Tse Tung in the 1930s analysed in their respective countries, and as a result advanced the 'two-stage' theory.[34] It is for these reasons that the 'two-stage' theory must be jettisoned, the bourgeoisie cannot be won over let alone the white workers. The principal actors in this revolutionary drama are the masses of the black proletarians. Consequently, in so far as its method is concerned, the South African revolution is not bourgeois but proletarian. Not only are black proletarians decisively important in the present mode of production, but they are also preponderant; hence questions regarding the application of scientific socialism will repeatedly come to the fore among the revolutionary proletarians as the revolutionary drama gathers momentum . . . .

The proletarian revolution in South Africa 'must not by any means be regarded as a single act . . . but a series of more or less powerful outbreaks rapidly alternating with periods of more or less complete calm'.[35] It is for that reason that South Africa is in urgent need of people who make revolution their daily business.

Notes

1 Sam Mhlongo, 'Black Workers' Strikes in Southern Africa', *New Left Review*, 83, January–February, 1974.

2 K. Marx and F. Engels, *Selected Works*, London, 1968, p. 44.

3 *1973 Survey of Race Relations in South Africa*, Johannesburg, 1974, p. 49. This is an annual publication of the South African Institute of Race Relations.

4 *1972 Survey of Race Relations in South Africa*, p. 161. The number of pass arrests is falling. In 1969, there were 1 019 629 arrests, as against 615 075 in the year 1970–1. Why the 'leniency'? The rapidly expanding manufacturing sector needs a skilled and permanently settled work force. The capitalists cannot afford the rapid turnover and waste of skilled, semi-skilled and trainee labour which would be the case if there were no 'leniency'. Because of the government's and the capitalists' alliance with the white working class, the training and urbanisation on a permanent basis of the black proletariat takes place clandestinely, by calculated deception and chicanery. Another reason for this 'leniency' is the spectre of Sharpeville.

5 Mhlongo, *op.cit.*

6 *Star* (Johannesburg), 18 June 1974.

7 *1972 Survey of Race Relations in South Africa*, p. 287.
8 *1970 Survey of Race Relations in South Africa*, p. 111.
9 M. Wilson and L. Thompson eds., *Oxford History of South Africa*, II, London, 1971, pp. 141, 161.
10 Robert Davies, 'The White Working Class in South Africa', *New Left Review*, 82, November–December, 1973.
11 *Guardian*, 12 March 1973.
12 *Star* (Johannesburg), 30 June 1972.
13 E.J. Hobsbawm and George Rude', *Captain Swing*, London 1969, p. 195.
14 In 1860 the British had no alternative but to import Indian slave labour, which was euphemistically referred to as indentured labour since slavery had been 'abolished' in the Empire in 1834. This arose because the Zulu refused to work in the plantations. At the time, the Zulu economic and military structures were still intact. Indeed, as late as 1879, the Zulus were inflicting serious defeats on a British army.
15 *The Star* (Johannesburg), 11 September 1973.
16 *1971 Survey of Race Relations in South Africa*, p. 226.
17 *Ibid.*, p. 36.
18 J.A. Hobson, *The War in South Africa*, London, 1900, p. 285. This deals with the Anglo-Boer War, 1899–1902. Because Hobson championed the Boer cause and was at the same time an apologist for British imperialism, he inferred very strongly that the war was fought for Jewish business interests. He said nothing about President Kruger's Industrial Colour Bar legislation of 1893.
19 Ralph Miliband, *The State in Capitalist Society*, London, 1973, p. 167.
20 *Financial Mail* (Johannesburg), 28 August 1970.
21 *Guardian*, 18 April 1973.
22 *Ibid.*
23 *1970 Survey of Race Relations in South Africa*, p. 151.
24 *Ibid.*, p. 153.
25 *1973 Survey of Race Relations in South Africa*, p. 174.
26 *Rand Daily Mail*, 11 April 1958. The statement was issued by A.J. Luthuli, then President of the African National Congress.
27 T. Nairn, 'Scotland and Europe', *New Left Review*, 83, January–February 1974, p. 65.
28 Tom Karis and G. Carter eds., *From Protest to Challenge*, II, Hoover Institution Press, pp. 126, 314–5, 318.
29 See Mhlongo, *op.cit.*, for further details about the strikes.
30 Karl Marx, *Capital*, I, Moscow, 1965, p. 737.
31 *Ibid.*, p. 737.
32 V. Lenin, *The Organisational Principles of a Proletarian Party*, Moscow, 1972, p. 81.
33 *Ibid.*, p. 78.
34 For the CPSA's adoption of the 'two-stage' theory of revolution see 'Road to Freedom', an *African Communist* pamphlet. (The *African Communist* is the CPSA's theoretical journal.)
35 V. Lenin, *op.cit.*, p. 82.

9 Commercial Capitalism in Nigeria: The Pattern of Competition*

TERISA TURNER

This study is concerned with the relationship between profit making and the Nigerian state. The overwhelming proportion of relations between countries are economic relations. Nigeria has an import-export economy and an indigenous business community engaged largely in commerce. By describing how this commercial system operates, I hope to go some way towards explaining the instability of the Nigerian state. I will outline the pattern of competition which characterises a commercial political economy such as that of Nigeria and shows how a policy of state intervention to promote economic development intensifies competition and introduces a new set of actors.

Profit-making

Contemporary political economies characterised by commercial capitalism are those which depend on foreign industrial production for virtually all locally-consumed manufactured goods. Although trade flourishes, there is little indigenous capitalist production of final consumer goods. In such an import-export economy, most business takes the form of commercial activity: importing, distribution and transport, wholesale, retail and petty trading. Agricultural primary products may be exported or foreign-based extractive industries may export minerals from an enclave. But for most local businessmen, profits are made predominantly through commerce: even in the local import-substitution sector, to the extent that it exists, profits stem more from market control than from value added through assembly and processing of largely imported inputs. The particular sub-group of commercial political economies of interest here is that comprised by oil-rich countries with a low level of industrialisation.

Much commercial activity takes the form of middlemanship. The local businessman organises the foreign seller's access to local markets. Final consumers constitute a market, but the state itself is becoming an important market especially if it can command vast incomes from oil. Now, more than during the colonial or pre-second world war period, access to national markets is restricted by the state. State control stems mainly from its role as a major buyer, but also from its regulatory powers over other commercial activities. Because the state controls opportunities to profit through commerce, politics becomes dominated by struggles for positions in the state or for access to those who have influence over government decisions.

The Triangular Relationship

The relationship between foreign businessmen and local actors from the national private and public sectors is called a 'commercial triangle' in this study, because

* From 'Commercial Capitalism and the 1975 Coup', in Keith Panter-Brick ed., *Soldiers and Oil: The Political Transformation of Nigeria*, Frank Cass, London, 1978, pp. 166–78.

it involves three parties to a buying or selling transaction. These parties are first, the businessman who represents the multinational corporation; second, the local middleman from the national private sector; and third, the state official who assists the foreign businessman in gaining access to the local market.

How does the triangular relationship work? A foreign businessman comes to the country to sell his firm's products. He hires a local citizen as a go-between with the state. If a contract materialises, the state official is usually rewarded with a payment arranged by the go-between or middleman. While its manifestations in real life take a great many forms (since the state not only awards contracts, but it sets terms for the sale of oil, crops or for the establishment of a business), the description which follows is meant to capture the commercial triad's essential features. Each member of the triangle can be described in turn.

The multinational corporation

In seeking business foreign firms are in competition for access to a country's economy. Competition is usually for markets, but it is also for opportunities to extract primary commodities or to use labour. The businessmen compete for access to state officials with the power and the inclination to give them government business on profitable terms. The greater the country's foreign reserves, the larger the number of businessmen and the more intense is the competition for government custom. Foreign businessmen sometimes deal directly with the state. But usually they approach government officials through middlemen who have privileged access to decision makers. The kickback or bribe, it is argued below, is an important means of securing competitive advantage in today's global marketplace.

The local middleman

The second member of the triangle is the local middleman who puts the businessman in touch with the market.[1] Those falling into the middleman group are sometimes expatriates themselves. For example, Levantines organise imports in some countries; the Indian or Chinese community does so in others. In the more formalised part of this 'intermediate' sector, businessmen act as importers, exporters, representative for foreign salesmen and marketing firms, representatives for foreign firms seeking a particular contract, job-finders, advisers, facilitators, intermediaries, brokers, agents, contact men and assistants of all varieties. For this intermediary service the middleman gets a retaining fee and usually a bonus when the contract or deal comes through. Some of this income is normally paid to officials in government who made the transaction possible. The middleman may conceptualise the state official's cut as part of his own 'expenses'. The relationship between the middleman and the state is emphasised by Adamu who writes of the Nigerian case that invariably the middleman is[2]

> ... either a front for a public servant, or an employee of a private company which would like to remain faceless and who has the opportunity to offer contracts to himself to be executed by himself. Or he receives contracts or import and export licences, only to present them to a waiting expatriate with the capital for a small fee called a commission for a civil servant who surcharged individuals for duties rendered.

Middlemen are dependent upon connections with the state and with foreign firms. Their dependent and intermediary role creates intensely competitive pressures within the local private sector and—because of the close interaction of the two—within the state. Since there are fewer state officials than there are aspiring middlemen, the bottleneck arises in getting access to the state. The middleman's usefulness to the foreign businessman is his special contacts and relationships with influential officials of state. Thus, the premium on establishing such contacts is high. Local businessmen compete intensely with each other for access to powerful government officials. Many aspiring intermediaries have little chance of succeeding and are bitter at patronage going to someone else.

In a commercial capitalist political economy, the dominant business class is not composed of capitalists who organise labour, capital, raw materials and energy to produce a product for the market. Among the reasons for the near absence of productive entrepreneurship are capital shortage, pre-emptive concentration of foreign firms[3] and more profitable alternatives. The absence of industrialisation is commonly explained by reference to a 'lack of appropriate technical skills and managerial know-how'.[4] This explanation fails to take into account the fact that many nationals with these technical and managerial qualities become middlemen, not capitalists. Many middlemen have professional qualifications as accountants, business administrators, lawyers, etc., and have been diverted from the practice of their professions by more promising opportunities in commerce. They find little incentive to produce when middlemanship requires little capital, when it complements and facilitates—but does not compete with—foreign capital, and most important, when it offers easy profits. It may be that the reasons for the perpetuation of commerce in certain political economies include its unparalleled success in enriching indigenees and foreign businessmen alike.[5]

The state comprador

The third actor in the commercial triangle is the state official whose position allows him to influence state spending and government policy, and who uses this position to assist foreign capital in its dealings with the state and indigenous society. 'Comprador', a Portuguese word for 'buyer' is used here to describe those state officials who perform the function of organising the foreign traders' access to local markets. With political independence of the European colonies and the expansion of trade after the Second World War, the state in these new countries became a major market and market regulator. With sovereignty, some state officials began to perform a kind of 'gatekeeper' function: they allow the entry and exit of goods and in the process may exact a 'toll' for performing the service of 'opening the gate'. In the following discussion, state officials who perform this function are called compradors, or alternatively, 'gatekeeper'.

It is useful to distinguish two different gatekeeper roles: where gatekeeper activity is of the indirect kind, a middleman is used. Gatekeepers who work in partnership with private local middlemen can be called 'collaborating compradors' because they and the middlemen join to carry out transactions which also include representatives of foreign firms. This triangular relationship is shown in the diagram of the commercial triad. However, the gatekeeper activity can also be direct, that is, the official deals directly with the foreign businessman. Instead of being triadic, the relationship is dyadic. Officials who deal directly with foreign businessmen can be called 'statist compradors' since they exclude the private national sector from transactions between the state and foreign multinationals. This direct relationship is shown in the diagram of the commercial dyad.

The exclusion of middlemen from taking part in transactions involving state officials and foreign businessmen is resisted by aspiring middlemen. This resistance is articulated in terms of opposition to state encroachment on the private sector's spheres of activity. Opposition to an enlargement of the state's role in the economy is at least partly a campaign to retain triads and the associated roles of middlemen in the face of pressures from foreign firms or state officials, in certain fields, to close out middlemen and set up exclusive dyads.

Comprador state officials are competitive. In countries in which the civil service has a prominant role in actually making, as well as in implementing decisions (as is often the case, for example, under military rule), much of the competition among compradors is struggle within the civil service to secure and retain positions with decision-making power. There is also a tendency to rationalise competition by reducing the number of officials involved and removing decisions from open forums. Since this tendency towards the concentration of power is a significant source of instability, it bears a little more discussion.

Competition among international firms is reproduced in the local context through the proliferation of triangular relationships. The triads increase in number depending both on the number of foreign suppliers interested, say, in winning a contract, and on the number of decision-makers within the state. For example, if a contract award is to be decided in the country's top decision-making forum, theoretically each of its members could form triangles with their respective middlemen and foreign firms and compete for the award. Such a situation may be insoluble. The work of arriving at a compromise is considerable, time goes by, foreign firms get impatient, market conditions change as do prices and the stakes are diluted by the larger numbers involved. This experience leads to the formation of cliques which can operate in particular spheres of interest. It also produces a strong impetus to limit the number of government officials who have access to and knowledge of these decisions—which as a result come to be made not in open forums but behind closed doors. The tendency towards monopoly of power and advantage within the state leads to suspicion and hostility from the out-groups not privy to decisions.

The political economy of a commercial capitalist society is defined largely by efforts to establish these triangular relationships and to operate them profitably. Instability is endemic in the struggle among middlemen for state patronage, and in the competition among officials of state for control of decisions. In these circumstances, politics is a form of business through which actors seek influence in the state, not in order to make and apply general rules, but in order to secure advantages.

The International Market

The basic source of competition among commercial triangles, and therefore of instability, is foreign business rivalry. The intense nature of this competition and its ultimate 'dog-eat-dog' character follow from the urgent need on the part of individual corporations to secure markets and raw materials, especially when jobs and balance of payments conditions in their home countries depend on making foreign sales. An efficient method of competing is through the purchase of favour with bribes. In 1916 Lenin argued that 'considerations' were an integral feature of a world market dominated by oligopoly or monopoly:[6]

> Finance capital has created the epoch of monopolies and monopolies introduce everywhere monopolist principles; the utilization of 'connections' for profitable transactions takes the place of competition on the open market.

The efficiency of bribes as a means of competition and the prevalence of oligopolies are interconnected. Bribe competition has none of the drawbacks of price competition which in an oligopolistic market can easily mean price war. Bribes are inexpensive and relatively easy to administer. Once a system of kickbacks and commissions is established, small firms and newcomers are subjected to pressure to conform if they are to do business. The commercial nexus between oligopolistic international firms and the state, now such a large economic concern in all countries, provides opportunity for the exercise of favour by compradors and the purchase of profitable terms by the corporate representative. Large firms among which there exists a high degree of oligopolistic world market control, obtain advantages through means other than price competition. One of the more prevalent and simplest methods of securing competitive advantage especially when dealing with the state, is the kickback.

While the means by which multinational firms seek profits can be identified as a fundamental source of political instability, the question of 'blame' is hardly relevant. The notion of moral business behaviour is vague; an act of bribery involves a giver and a receiver and international firms cannot be held responsible for adapting to a given business environment. A United States Conference Board study in February 1976 showed that even those businessmen who favoured a code of business ethics acknowledged that if 'faced with a problem of losing a major sale or not they would pay up and keep quiet about it'.[7]

It is useful to examine some of the determinants of buying decisions which predominate over what C. G. Tether calls 'normal considerations in international trade'.[8] A foreign businessman is a successful salesman not because he offers a competitive price, high quality produce, efficient service, or the commodity which best suits local needs. Oligopoly is a major factor which can make consideration of these sources of competitive advantage almost irrelevant. In most instances a businessman is successful because he has made contact with the right middleman and gets access to the right government official who finds the foreign firm's proposal attractive.[9] The main focus of competition, then, is for access to officials of state. Foreign salesmen of defence equipment, for example, make claims for their products which the buying government, and much less the local middlemen, usually have little ability or inclination to test. But clearcut competition can occur through inducements or bribes.

Bribe-bidding is a logical means of seeking competitive advantage. Furthermore, this pattern does coincide with what, impressionistically, would seem to be prevalent practice in several countries. As Tether observed, 'normal commercial considerations are clearly going to play a subsidiary role—if, indeed, they exercise any influence at all ... if orders are to go to producers [most effective in] greasing the palms of those who are well-placed to determine the final choice on the buying side ....'[10] The descriptions of bribes suggest that they are forms of competition: they are 'pay-offs' to 'promote the company's substantial sales' or 'gifts made to potential customers'.[11]

The foreign businessman is faced with the situation in which a major source of competitive advantage is the kickback. The choice to patronize one aircraft salesman over another appears to turn largely on the calculation of which deal is more profitable personally for the decision-maker. A report of the US Senate Subcommittee on Multinationals, published in February 1976, indicates that Lockheed, the US government's largest aero-space and defence contractor, admitted to bribing foreign officials over the last fifteen years and spending $22 million in kickbacks in the last five years in at least eight countries. Among these eight countries is Nigeria where, US Senate sources confirmed, Lockheed paid about \$3.6 million on a \$45 million deal.[12] The corporation's sales have been substantial and were projected to reach \$4 billion between 1975 and 1980. Not only Lockheed (which received \$195 million in US government loans between 1971 and 1976) but the total US defence industry has demonstrated its international competitiveness: Senator Proxmire reported that US arms manufacturers sold nine times as many arms as the French and fifteen times as many as the British in 1974. US military sales in 1976 were expected to reach \$10 billion, triple the level of 1972. The point of importance here is that the world predominance of Lockheed, or other corporations, depends on foreign sales. Therefore the methods by which sales are secured, in the face of competition from corporations based in other countries, are integrally a part of Lockheed's growth and survival. Given the importance of the defence contractor's products in the US military programme, the well-being of Lockheed can also be appreciated as a condition for United States military predominance on an international scale.[13]

Far from being an anomaly, the business bribe or commission is an essential element of the modern world system. Its centrality has to do with the profit-orientation of the corporate operation: it does not stem primarily from personal greed and lack of knowledge or planning on the part of the buyer. Corporations which are successful at profit-making have grown, squeezing out smaller firms and making the entry of new competitors increasingly difficult. Large multinational firms currently have oligopolistic control over certain industries. For example, the oil industry is dominated by seven major corporations and there are a similar number of major producers of cement for the international market. Aircraft and defence producers are even fewer in number. Firms in an oligopoly are reluctant to enter into price competition since a single price cutter can expect retaliation from other members of the oligopoly in other markets. A price war will only drive all members of the oligopoly into the red. Thus a premium is placed on securing contracts by offering inducements which may be large to the recipient, but which account for a small proportion of the firm's turnover, while keeping prices of a level agreeable to members of the oligopoly. For example, the \$68 million which Northrop, a defence equipment manufacturer, allegedly paid to Saudi Arabia's middleman Adnan Kashoggi, is only 2.83 per cent of the \$2.4 billion contract the US firm secured. Again, it is alleged that Grumman paid a commission of \$28 million or 1.27 per cent of an Iranian deal worth \$2.2 billion.[14]

Mention should also be made of small firms for which a single contract or concession could mean the difference between profit or collapse. These firms have a special incentive to offer kickbacks to secure a niche in a market dominated by large corporations. Finally, inducements are used not only to swing decision-makers over to a particular firm, but also to encourage the state to make purchases which would not otherwise have been made. US Senator Church emphasised how this method of expanding markets distorts the development programmes of poor countries by discouraging the optimum allocation of scarce (and often borrowed) resources.[15]

Since governments are responsible for a great deal of expenditure in poor countries, the full pressure of an oligopolistic market is brought to bear on state officials. Local intermediaries and foreign businessmen who are unable to gain access to the decision-makers of the moment look forward to their replacement. State officials who cannot obtain positions which allow them to influence decision-making similarly seek to unseat those in power. In this conflict-ridden context the power of guns and money plays an everyday role.

Technocrats and Economic Nationalism

Mention has been made of three sets of actors who participate in commercial triangles: foreign businessmen, local middlemen from the indigenous private sector, and state officials who carry out a gatekeeper or comprador function. In addition to these three groups, the political economies of commercial capitalist countries are influenced by another group of actors within the state—technocrats. Technocrats are those with professional training in some area of production who are employed in public corporations. Since they have professional education and jobs in production-oriented corporations, technocrats may also aspire to be state capitalists. That, is, they may be personally oriented towards engaging in capitalist production locally despite the predominance of commercial capitalist relations. But whether technocrats actually do perform the tasks of state capitalists depends on the relationship between the state corporation in which they are employed and the ministry or state institution which supervises the corporation. If a state corporation is controlled by a ministry headed by commercially-oriented gatekeepers, it is unlikely that the technocrats in the state corporation will be allowed to fulfil their potential of becoming state capitalists. This could give rise to frustration among technocrats, since they have been trained and hired by the state to engage in production. A public corporation which is under the direction of compradors in a ministry might be diverted from its potentiality for capitalist production, and become defunct or inefficient.

The key defining feature of technocratic state officials is their ability to produce commodities. This ability stems not only from training, but also from membership on a team of production-oriented professionals who are organized in a corporation in such a way as to make complex productive activities possible. Technocrats are often trained by foreign manufacturing and extractive firms and in institutions of education which service these industries. They have the potential of being state capitalists, but this potential can be realised only if the state corporation employing the technocrats is allowed to function as a profitable unit of capitalist production. Technocrats' jobs in the various public corporations involve combining technology, finance and managerial skills in a profit-making organization to produce a tangible result (a steel plant, an irrigation system). The division of labour in such an economic agency requires an inter-dependence among specialists, the success of which is measured firstly in terms of actual production and secondly in terms of profits. Individual technocrats, by virtue of their technical training and (for some) experience in foreign-based industry, are accustomed to rational, impersonal and universal criteria for making decisions and for assessing their own accomplishments. Professional standing, the grounds for job mobility, depends on getting results which in turn depends on co-operation with others in the production organisation.

Technocrats are capable of operating industrial concerns; gatekeeper state officials are not. Gatekeepers are committed to and engaged in facilitating commerce. The interests of these two strata of the local section of the world bourgeoisie are at variance, although both fundamentally support the option of private ownership of capital. Technocrats are relatively uncorrupt, not because they possess special moral qualities, but because they tend to see their function in terms of reducing dependence on imported products. In contrast, the gatekeeper role of mediating the entry and exit of goods tends to stand as an obstacle to industrialisation and to the realisation of technocratic plans.

Although the tensions between technocrats and compradors stem mainly from the conflicting strategies of productive capitalism on the one hand and commercial capitalism on the other, in practice it is likely that the form which production takes in hitherto unindustrialised countries (for example, the assembly and processing of imported components) would maintain national dependence on industrialised countries.

The policy of state-led capitalist development of production usually entails exclusive state control over certain sectors (the 'commanding heights') of the economy. Control is normally established through a state corporation which functions, ideally, as a profitable business operation. But it has been noted that if state corporations are under the control of ministries (the existence of which in most cases predates that of the corporations) then there is a tendency for those in charge of the Ministry to establish their own direct relationship with foreign firms. The more state corporations there are, the more opportunities exist for direct communication between compradors and representatives of foreign firms. In these direct relationships, 'statist' compradors are able to exclude middlemen from the local private sector, and in effect, replace some triangular relationships with bilateral ones.

Policies of economic nationalism and state-led development were manifest in the programmes of many non-industrialised countries by the 1970s. The new types of gatekeeper—the statist compradors—were appearing in the oil exporting commercial political economies just as oil incomes became significant in magnitude. Statist compradors are much more powerful than the earlier collaborators, given the former group's command of the revenues from oil and the associated projects for industrialisation which technocrats are hired to realize.

The policy of state intervention gives rise not only to a stratum of technocrats and to statist compradors but also to disaffected middlemen who are excluded from triangular relationships by the direct deals established in what are usually the most lucrative areas of the economy. In addition, aspirant compradors whose middle-rank positions mean that they are precluded from entering major bilateral deals also resist the policy of state monopoly in certain economic areas and align with middlemen in demanding private sector involvement in all economic activities.

Reference has been made to another type of tension which develops around issues of policy between technocrats and statist compradors—the two groups of civil servants in charge of implementing state-led capitalist production plans. Both oppose the involvement of middlemen in strategic areas and are therefore divided from local businessmen. Technocrats are hired to make functional ventures in state capitalism. But these are under the ultimate control of traditional comprador administrators who have the opportunity, with the new policy, to form bilateral relationships with foreign firms. In so doing, they threaten to divert the policy of economic nationalism from increasing local capabilities to intensifying links with foreign capital. Such a diversion leaves technocrats with little role to play and this in turn leads to frustration and opposition.

In sum, a commercial capitalist political economy in the 1970s is inherently unstable due to the triangular dynamic and to the policy divisions between comprador and technocratic factions within the state. To the competitive tensions generated by the drive to establish successful triangular relationships is added, in connection with state intervention in the economy, still more tensions. In this unstable situation a coup is possible any time and is more likely if some minimal level of cohesion is struck among members of the 'out group'.

Notes

1 On the powers of the independent Nigerian state to allocate profitable opportunities, see Gavin Williams, 'Nigeria: a Political Economy', in Gavin Williams ed., *Nigeria: Economy and Society*, Rex Collings, London, 1976, pp. 11–54.

2 Haroun Adamu, 'A Nation of Commissioners', *Sunday Times* (Lagos), 9 November 1975.

3 In the case of Nigeria, E.O. Akeredolu-Ale shows that the concentration of foreign firms in various economic activities leads Nigerians to either avoid those areas or to associate with the foreign operations. See his *Underdevelopment of Indigenous Entrepreneurship in Nigeria*, Ibadan University Press, Ibadan, 1973. On the obstacles to capitalist development see also Peter Kilby, *Industrialisation in an open economy: Nigeria 1945–66*, Cambridge University Press, London, 1969, and Akeredolu-Ale's review of Kilby, 'The competitive threshold hypothesis and Nigeria's industrialisation process', *Nigerian Journal of Economic and Social Studies*, 14, 1972.

4 S.A. Madujibeya, 'Economic enclaves, technology transfer and foreign investment in Nigeria', mimeo., London, November 1975, p. 2.

5 The *Third National Development Plan* (*1975–80*) states that 'In a country growing as rapidly as Nigeria, trading activities normally represent the quickest means of increasing income whereas manufacturing projects usually have long gestation periods'. Ministry of Economic Development and Reconstruction, Lagos, 1975, Vol. I, p. 152.

6 V. I. Lenin, *Imperialism, the highest stage of capitalism: a popular account*, Foreign Language Publishing House, Moscow, n.d., p. 108.

7 The Conference Board, *Unusual foreign payments: a survey of the policies and practices of U.S. companies*, United States Conference Board, New York, 1976, No. 682. Reviewed in the *Financial Times* (London), 16 February 1976.

8 C. Gordon Tether, 'The disregard of moral standard', Lombard Column, *Financial Times* (London), 11 February 1976.

9 S. Cronjé, M. Ling, G. Cronjé, *Lonrho: portrait of a multinational*, Penguin and Julian Friedmann, London, 1976, shows how the skills of Tiny Rowland in making contacts enabled his firm to grow rapidly into one of the more important multinationals operating in Africa.

10 C. Gordon Tether, 'The disregard of moral standards', Lombard Column, *Financial Times* (London), 11 February 1976. Jim Hougan stated that 'Northrop's corruption, for example, was a direct, *defensive* response to Lockheed's. Thus, as if by a variation of Gresham's law, bad business drove out the good'. 'The business of buying friends', *Harper's* (New York), December 1975, p. 45.

11 *Financial Times* (London), February 1976, various issues.

12 *Financial Times* (London), 16 and 17 February 1976. In November 1976, Brig. Garba, Commissioner for External Affairs, said of an investigation into the purchase of C-130 military transport aircraft by the Nigerian Airforce that the information made available to the Federal Government by the US Government was 'insufficient to warrant or justify the apprehension of any of the Nigerians who are known to be linked with Lockheed in his international scandal particularly as the exact nature and extent of benefits, if any, derived cannot be ascertained or determined'. Arrests were continuing with the aid of Interpol, according to the *West Africa* report of 29 November 1976, p. 1827. For comment on the difficulties of obtaining evidence, see Jim Hougan, *op.cit.*, pp. 44, 47.

13 *Financial Times* (London), 16 and 17 February 1976.

14 *Ibid.*, 16 February 1976. Theoretically, firms could use their oligopolistic power to eliminate kickbacks. By dividing international markets among themselves the need for competitive advantage would be reduced. In practice this level of agreement is too difficult to establish and maintain. Only the oil industry has been relatively successful. See John M. Blair, *The Control of Oil*, Pantheon Books, New York, 1976.

15 *Multinational corporations and U.S. foreign policy*, Part 12, (The Lockheed hearings), US Government Printing Office, Washington DC. See also Jim Hougan, 'The business of buying friends,' *op.cit.*, p. 45.

Part Three
The Culture of Dependency

Introduction and Select Bibliography
JOHN DANIEL

The culture of dependency refers to the kinds of attitudes engendered in a dependent people through their exploitation by a dominant people. It includes submission to domination as well as emulation by the dependent peoples of the attitudes and behaviour patterns of the dominant group. As the selections in this part reveal, this culture is seen as having been produced in Africa by the continent's integration into the nexus of international capitalism with its mechanisms of trade, slavery, conquest and repression accompanied by a process of political learning imposed upon the indigenes by the colonial state. It thus formed part of the colonial superstructure both legitimating and facilitating external control and indigenous submission; it is seen, too, as having survived into the post-colonial era, for its values were most strongly assimilated by the comprador class to whom the political instruments of state power were transfered at independence. It is this cultural factor which is seen as accounting in part for the minimal transformation effected to the metropole—satellite relationship, since independence for these assimilated values harmonise with those of the metropolitan bourgeoisie and provide the compradors with the ideological means to justify their continued close alliance with the metropole. The imposition of a culture of dependency upon a dominated people is regarded, therefore, as being fundamental to the establishment and survival of an imperial relationship[1] and, if one is to make any sense of contemporary African politics, then one must understand not just the political and economic dimensions of dependency but this vital cultural aspect too.

As was indicated above, cultural dependence did not come automatically to Africa in the colonial period. It did not just happen through some mystical transmission process but was learned; imposed upon and engendered into the African peoples through a political learning process referred to as political socialisation. The term refers to the processes and means by which an individual absorbs the 'norms, values, attitudes and behaviours accepted by the ongoing system'.[2] The media by which these values etc. are transmitted from generation to generation are many, but include the family, peer groups, church, school and university, social and business associations, and so forth. Socialisation is therefore a life-long process, though more intense and effective at different periods in every individual's life, probably the most effective being early childhood and adolescence, particularly years spent in a university environment.

However, a successful socialisation process does not merely transmit values over the generations; to be really effective each generation must not only absorb the values of the political system but also internalise them, ie. acquire more than just a cognitive awareness of the prevailing societal values but actually believe them and accept them as their own because they judge them to be good and proper ones. They must seem to be the only just and correct values in which one can believe. Thus, for example, in South Africa a highly effective socialisation system has not only propounded notions of white supremacy and black inferiority, but both whites and blacks have internalised these notions and come to believe in them. This factor enables the discriminatory system of apartheid to acquire a degree of legitimacy in the eyes of whites who can justify their privilege not only because they see themselves as superior but, because they believe blacks are inferior, they can argue that their control of the polity is actually to the benefit of the black populace. Such racist ideological super-structural values enable whites to obscure the unpalatable reality that apartheid is a system rooted in material privilege. Conversely, the internalisation by blacks of notions of their own inferiority is a clear example of cultural subordina-tion and its utility for the dominating group. Few who are familiar with the political history of South Africa can deny that, in a manifestation of cultural dependency, black political organisations displayed an almost instinctive de-pendence upon their white allies and allowed them an influence in their organisations disproportionate to their numbers. It was only with the emergence of the black consciousness ideology in the late 1960s that young black South Africans revealed a determination to break out of this cultural cul-de-sac. In recognition of the political importance of this development, an article on Black Consciousness is included in this section of the readings.

In the last decade a large body of material has appeared on the political socialisation process in Western capitalist nations. Our concern in this section is to examine that process in the African context and, in particular, to understand how three related cultural phenomena contributed to the emergence of cultural dependence. They are (1) *Capitalism*, with its distinctive economic and cultural value systems; (2) *Colonialism*, with its racist supremacist values; and (3) specific *European* behaviour patterns and values.

The first of five selections in this section focuses upon two of the cultural phenomena mentioned above—colonial capitalism—revealing how their partic-ular values contributed to the distortion and suppression of Africa's indigenous cultures and the emergence of the culture of dependency. Daniel then assesses the impact of this latter culture upon the self-image of the African and its impact in terms of class formation, arguing that the assimilation of the cultural values of the West by the African petty bourgeoisie played no less a part in Africa's transition to neo-colonialism than did the metropole's control of 'the command-ing heights' of Africa's economy. He goes on to examine Africa's post-colonial response to cultural dependence, arguing that most of sub-Saharan Africa's ruling classes have been so steeped in European culture that they have failed to see it as a problem and have consequently done little for the cause of cultural emancipation. His view is that nothing short of a wholesale re-socialisation campaign, including a rejection of many of the elitist and material values of the West, and a massive overhaul of the transplanted educational systems, will sever the links of cultural oppression; the Mozambican efforts are examined in this light. While not explicit in his article, it is clear that Daniel believes that it is only in those countries where the expulsion of the colonial foreigners was effected by armed struggle that true liberation can come about and that, where there was no such struggle and power was transferred to hand-picked moderates, continued class struggle against the petty bourgeoisie is necessary so that power can be seized by those classes not linked by an umbilical cord of privilege to the metropolitan ruling class.

The second selection amplifies upon some of the themes developed by Daniel. Though published as long ago as 1965, and set in the context of North Africa, Albert Memmi's *The Coloniser and the Colonised* has a universal validity as a chronicle of colonial oppression everywhere. Moreover, its analysis of the settler mode of colonialism has a particular relevance to the Southern African situation, the major area of conflict in contemporary Africa. In the excepts included in this book, Memmi describes the mythical view the coloniser develops of those they colonised, revealing how these myths serve the historic, cultural and economic needs and goals of the coloniser. He examines the impact of these myths upon the self-view of the African and shows how the internalisation of these myths alienates him from his history and culture, producing a sense of shame about the indigenous way of life—what Fanon has described as a colonial mentality of dependency. This is the zenith of colonial oppression and exploitation.

However, analysis reveals that there is a dialectic in the relationship between the coloniser and colonised. The colonial relationship carries within it the seeds of its own destruction, for there will come a time when the colonised will realise that 'assimilation has turned out to be impossible', and will tire 'of the exorbitant price which he must pay and which he never finishes owing'.[3] Rejection now sets in, and the colonised will strive to recover his self, his pride and his history. From that moment, colonialism is on the defensive.

This is the stage which the South African situation has entered, for with the capture of mainstream black political thought by the Black Consciousness ideology the colonised black South African has entered the period of rejection. This concept of rejection forms the core of the philosophy. It is reflected in the Black Consciousness Manifesto which describes its major tenet as being a rejection of 'all value systems that seek to make him [the blackman] a foreigner in the country of his birth', and which result in him being 'defined by others' and not 'as self-defined'.[4] This same theme of rejection runs though the article published in this section, while another early theoretician, Thami Zani, described black consciousness as a 'rejection by the black man of being seen as an aberration of the normal which is White'.[5] In rejecting white values, black consciousness summons blacks to stand on their own, to come together as a group and mobilise their political and economic power. Its political prescription is to advocate group cohesion and black solidarity but, while the philosophy has had an enormous political impact in South Africa, it is less a political programme than an attempt to snap the chains of cultural dependency which mentally enslave blacks. This is reflected in the Manifesto which contains the classic Fanonist dictate that 'liberation of the blackman begins first with liberation from psychological oppression'.[6] This is essentially what the theory intends to achieve.

The philosophy is not one rooted solely in the experiences of black South Africans. Many of its insights are drawn from the common experiences of black and oppressed peoples everywhere, and many of its ideas are borrowed from thinkers who wrote on these experiences. Thus, one finds in it distinct strains of the Negritude philosophy of the 1930s, as well as notions derived from the writings of Frantz Fanon and from the 'black power' theoreticians of the 1960s in the United States. It builds, too, upon notions developed earlier by two of the seminal thinkers among black South Africans, Anton Lembede and Robert Sobukwe.[7] But it took a third great seminal thinker to weave these notions into a coherent philosophy and to initiate the black South Africans march away from dependency upon whites and towards their ultimate liberation. He was the late Steve Biko, a brilliant and charismatic one-time medical student cruelly murdered by South Africa's security police. In this action the police robbed black South Africans of a great leader and South Africa of a great future leader. In including here an article on Black Consciousness by Harry Nengwekhulu, a 'disciple' of Biko, we are not only stressing the importance of this ideology but also expressing our tribute to a courageous man.

Biko may be dead but his legacy is the resurgence of confidence, pride and militancy among black South Africans, attitudes reflected in the Soweto uprising in 1976, a rebellion that spread far beyond Soweto to most other urban centres, into the black colleges and schools all over the country and even into rural reserves and so-called 'homeland' areas. It is reflected, too, in the near total rejection of the dummy black institutions created by the regime and of their leaders, particularly the Bantustan leaders who are scorned as 'apartheid's puppets'. But black consciousness alone will not liberate South Africa. It is freeing the minds of black South Africans from subservience, but this is only a step on the road to freedom. What is required is a link-up between black consciousness as a prescription for a cultural revolution in South Africa and a coherent political programme for armed struggle from within and without the country—a strategy for total liberation that was successfully applied in Mozambique.

Appropriately then our fourth selection deals with Mozambique. It consists of a policy statement on education in post-colonial Mozambique delivered to the 1976 Unesco Conference of African Ministers of Education. This statement is analysed in some detail in Daniel's article, for this new educational programme forms part of an attack on the culture of dependency which developed in Mozambique. It is clearly education for re-socialisation, and is by far and away the most comprehensive of all such programmes to have been developed in independent Black Africa. Its goal is to produce a new Mozambican personality which is first and foremost African and one 'free from all complexes of supe-riority and inferiority, free from superstitious beliefs, self-reliant and ready to make his scientific knowledge the basis of the new society based on unity and equality'.[8] The statement contains a critique of the colonial system of education which, it contends, was aimed at the destruction of all that was African and the production of deformed personalities destined to serve and not to govern. It then goes on to announce sweeping and revolutionary changes to the system and syllabi, including the introduction of political instruction (in the principles of Marxist-Leninism) and manual labour in the community. It abolishes all forms of religious teaching, and concludes with an affirmation that the new state's priority is to serve the needs of the working class and rural masses and to end discrimination against women.

Our final selection is also set in the context of former Portuguese Africa and is also illustrative of how a conscious programme of political education can change deep-rooted cultural traditions. Stephanie Urdang's article is based on personal observations derived from several months spent on a walking tour of the liberated zones of Guinea-Bissau during the late stages of the armed struggle. She examines (1) the role played by women in the struggle, and (2) the impact of that role upon the traditional role structures of women and their levels of political consciousness. She shows how the political involvement of women in the liberation struggle paved the way for the emancipation of women from oppressive institutions—lack of divorce rights, arranged and forced marriages, and polygamy. This, in turn, led women to challenge their traditional role in the mode of production where divisions of labour were based on sex. Today in Guinea-Bissau traditionally assigned roles of 'men's work' and 'women's work' are breaking down, and the social relations of production are being democratised. Urdang argues that this change has its roots in the ideological and educational programme of the PAIGC, the political party that spearheaded the armed struggle. It illustrates yet again how such programmes are a *sine qua non* for the elimination of cultural tutelage in Africa and the struggle for complete freedom from foreign control.

Notes

1 The term 'imperial' is an abstract concept that describes an unequal relationship of domination and subordination. Such a relationship can, *inter alia*, exist between individuals, between a teacher and his pupils and between nations. The term does not refer to the physical domination of a nation by another—that is colonialism, and represents only one form that an imperial relationship between nations can take. The other is indirect control, ie. neo-colonialism. An imperial relationship between nations therefore manifests itself in one of two forms, colonialism or neo-colonialism.

2 Roberta Sigel, *Learning About Politics*, Random House, New York, 1970, p. xii.

3 Albert Memmi, *The Colonizer and the Colonized*, Beacon Press, Boston, 1965, p. 123.

4 'Black Consciousness Manifesto', *SASO Newsletter*, 5, 2 (1975), p. 21.

5 Thami Zani, 'Black Consciousness', *Daily Dispatch*, 14 March 1977.

6 'Black Consciousness Manifesto'.

7 Anton Lembede was a co-founder in 1943 of the Youth League of the African National Congress of South Africa and its acknowledged leading thinker and ideologue. He died in 1946 but his ideas, as expressed in numerous documents, were carried forward by his fellow members of the Youth League who captured control of the senior party in 1949. One of these was Robert Sobukwe, a Fort Hare Graduate and Lecturer at Witwatersrand University in Johannesburg. He broke with the ANC in 1958 and established the Pan-Africanist Congress of South Africa in 1959, in part because he saw the ANC as having strayed from the ideas of Anton Lembede into a crippling alliance with white and Asian communists, a fact which, he argued, could only perpetuate the inferiority complexes of Africans. He died in 1978, after spending the last 18 years of his life either in prison or confined to his home as a 'banned' person. Lembede's writings can be found in Thomas Karis and Gwendolin Carter, *From Protest to Challenge: Documents of African Politics in South Africa, 1882–1964*, II, Stanford University Press, 1973. Sobukwe's writings and speeches can be found in the same volume and also in volume III. Also see *Sobukwe: The Man who still walks Tall*, Pan-Africanist Congress of Azania, London, 1973.

8 'Education Policy in the People's Republic of Mozambique', *The Journal of Modern African Studies*, 14, 2 (1976), p. 333.

Select Bibliography

1 The Culture of Dependency and Political Socialisation

Aime Cesaire, *Discourse on Colonialism*, Monthly Review Press, New York and London, 1972.

R.E. Dawson and K. Prewitt, *Political Socialisation*, Little, Brown and Co., Boston, 1969.

Frantz Fanon, *The Wretched of the Earth*, Grove Press, New York, 1961.

———, *Toward the African Revolution*, Grove Press, New York, 1964.

———, *Studies in a Dying Colonialism*, Grove Press, New York, 1967.

———, *Black Skin, White Masks*, Grove Press, New York, 1968.

C. Geertz ed., *Old Societies and New States*, Free Press, Glencoe, 1963.

H. Hyman, *Political Socialisation*, Free Press, Glencoe, 1959.

D. Jaros, *Socialisation to Politics*, Thomas Nelson, London, 1973.

K.P. Langton, *Political Socialisation*, Oxford University Press, London, 1969.

O. Mannoni, *Prospero and Caliban: The Psychology of Colonialism*, Praeger, New York, 1964.

R. Sigel, ed., *Learning About Politics*, Random House, New York, 1970.

B. Stacey, *Political Socialisation in Western Society*, Edward Arnold, London, 1978.

Renate Zahar, *Frantz Fanon: Colonialism and Alienation*, Monthly Review Press, New York and London, 1974.

2 Political Education and Cultural Revolution

Barbara Barnes, 'Creating a National Culture: An Overview', *Issue*, 8, 1 (1978).

Henry Bienen, 'State and Revolution: The Work of Amilcar Cabral', *The Journal of Modern African Studies*, 15, 4 (1977).

Amilcar Cabral, *Revolution in Guinea*, Monthly Review Press, New York, 1969, esp. 'The Weapon of Theory'.

———, *Return to the Source: Selected Speeches of Amilcar Cabral*, Monthly Review Press, New York and London, 1973, esp. 'National Liberation and Culture'.

Onuoha Chukunta, 'Education and National Integration in Africa: A Case Study of Nigeria', *The African Studies Review*, 21, 2 (1978).

David Court, 'The Education System as a Response to Inequality in Tanzania and Kenya', *The Journal of Modern African Studies*, 14, 4 (1976).

Carole Collins, 'Mozambique: Dynamizing the People', *Issue*, 8, 1 (1978).

Gerhard Grohs, 'Difficulties of Cultural Emancipation in Africa', *Journal of Modern African Studies*, 14, 1 (1976).

Adele Jinadu, 'Some African Theorists of Culture and Modernisation: Fanon, Cabral and some Others', *The African Studies Review*, 21, 1 (1978).

Lansine Kaba, 'The Cultural Revolution, Artistic Creativity, and Freedom of Expression in Guinea', *Journal of Modern African Studies*, 14, 2 (1976).

Thomas Kanza, *Evolution and Revolution*, Rex Collings, London, 1971.

Bryan Langlands, 'Students and Politics in Uganda', *African Affairs*, 76, 1977.

Richard Marvin, 'Economic Baba—Is this a Satisfactory Explanation of Why African Parents Value Schooling?', *The Journal of Modern African Studies*, 13, 2 (1975).

Ali A. Mazrui, *Cultural Engineering and Nation Building in East Africa*, North-western University Press, Evanston, 1972.

Ahmed Mohiddin, 'Towards Relevant Culture and Politics in Africa', *Africa Development*, 2, 4 (1977).

Julius K. Nyerere, 'Education for Self-Reliance', in J.K. Nyerere, *Ujamaa: Essays on Socialism*, Oxford University Press, London, 1968.

K. Prewitt ed., *Education and Political Values: An East African Case Study*, East African Publishing House, Nairobi, 1971.

Chris Searle, '"Escola Nova": The New Secondary School in Mozambique', *Issue*, 8, 1 (1978).

N.J. Small, 'Social Engineering in a New State', *African Affairs*, 77, 1978.

Stephanie Urdang, 'Precondition for Victory: Women's Liberation in Mozambique and Guinea-Bissau', *Issue*, 8, 1 (1978).

————, *Fighting Two Colonialisms: Women in Guinea-Bissau*, Monthly Review Press, New York, 1979.

Tanzania African National Union, 'Directive on the Implementation of Education for Self-Reliance', reprinted in *The African Review*, 6, 1 (1976).

3 Black Consciousness in South Africa

Heribert Adam, 'The Rise of Black Consciousness in South Africa', *Race*, 15, 2 (1973).

Manas Buthelezi, 'The Christian Challenge of Black Theology', in *Black Renaissance*, Ravan Press, Johannesburg, 1975.

James Cone, 'Black Consciousness and the Black Church: An Historical Theological Interpretation', in *Black Renaissance*, Ravan Press, Johannesburg, 1975.

Gail Gerhart, 'The Southern African Students' Organisation, 1968–1975', *Paper presented to the Annual Conference of the African Studies Association*, San Francisco, October–November, 1975.

————, *Black Power in South Africa*, University of California Press, Los Angeles, 1978.

C.J. Gerwel, 'Black Power: SA', *South African Outlook*, 103, July 1973.

Mafika Gwala, 'Towards the Practical Manifestation of Black Consciousness', in *Black Renaissance*, Ravan Press, Johannesburg, 1975.

Bennie Khoapa, 'Black Consciousness', *South African Outlook*, 102, June–July 1972.

————, 'The New Black' in B.S. Biko ed., *Black Viewpoint*, Spro-Cas Black Community Programme, Durban, 1972.

Bhekie Langa, 'Black Consciousness and the Black Community', *SASO Newsletter*, 5, 1 (1975).

S.M. Motsuenyane, 'Black Consciousness and the Economic Position of the Black Man in South Africa', in *Black Renaissance*, Ravan Press, Johannesburg, 1975.

Richard Turner, 'Black Consciousness and White Liberals', *Reality*, 4, 3 (1972).

10 The Culture of Dependency and Political Education in Africa

JOHN DANIEL

In the introduction to this part the culture of dependency was defined and the argument advanced that the distortion of Africa's indigenous cultural systems and their eclipse by alien cultural values formed an important, indeed essential, part of the system of colonial domination. It was also suggested that the survival of these values after the formal granting of independence smoothed the way to Africa's transition from a state of colonial to neo-colonial dependency. In this paper I examine these arguments in detail, describing how a culture of dependency was created in Africa and the instrumental ends that it served for the metropolitan powers. Finally, I discuss Africa's response to the persistence of this subordinate culture, focusing on political education programmes designed to re-socialise the populace to values, attitudes and goals seen as being more compatible with Africa's contemporary needs. The programme in Mozambique will be used as an illustration of these re-socialising efforts.

A culture of dependency began to develop in Africa with its incorporation into the 'North Atlantic Capitalist System', to use Samir Amin's term. Elsewhere in this volume, Amin[1] describes the mechanics of this process and the long-term political and economic consequences for Africa. It must be remembered, however, that capitalism is not just a political and economic system. It is also a cultural system with a distinctive set of values whose absorption are no less essential to the effective functioning of the system than the construction of the economic organisation it propounds. Amin does not discuss this cultural factor and this paper is designed to fill the gap.

Capitalism's fundamental values are those of acquisitiveness, competitiveness and individualism; they are antithetical to the corporate and communal values of pre-capitalist or traditional Africa. Africa's penetration by capitalism therefore precipitated a large-scale cultural encounter between two sets of contradictory value systems, and initiated a relentless and multi-faceted assault upon Africa's non-capitalist values. The assault took both a conscious and unconscious form, and those who undertook it did not necessarily do so with a malicious or self-serving intent; rather their attack upon African culture was prompted by their ideological stance which regarded European culture 'as the ultimate refinement and repository of all human excellence, virtue and industry'.[2]

Nonetheless their onslaught was no less effective for this perception. The primary actor in this assault was naturally the colonial regime operating in collusion with such auxiliaries as the missionary, the trader and the educator. Ahmed Mohiddin[3] has described how these functionaries were assigned the task of socialising Africans to the capitalist incursion and to altering their mode of economic behaviour and social thought so that they would undertake the labour roles assinged to them.

The missionary, both in the role of preacher and of educator, attacked virtually every aspect of African culture: African religion was branded as barbaric, ancestral beliefs were condemned as witch-craft, social customs like polygamy were regarded as pagan and evil, while African economic behaviour was scorned as lazy and inefficient.

Simultaneously the missionary promoted the social relations and values of colonial capitalism, extolling the imperatives of labour and obedience and stressing the virtues of 'private property, frugality and the need to save and to accumulate'.[4] In short, the missionary propagated a new set of spiritual and material values for the African. Complementing the missionary was the trader who exposed the African to new goods and tastes which, in time, altered his perception of his material needs and aspirations. These could be realised only through the possession of a commodity that could be acquired only in the capitalist market place—money. Thus, the African entered the capitalist market economy as either a wage labourer or cash-crop producer. However, lest the above should create the impression that this entrance into the market was entirely voluntary, it should be stressed that the peasantisation and/or proletarianisation of the subsistence producer was invariably initiated and then accelerated by the colonial governments' imposition of taxes of various kinds and of increasing severity.

Cast in a similar role to the twin agents discussed above was the educator. This individual operated from within an educational system which, as Memmi illustrates in the following chapter,[5] was largely irrelevant to the local society, teaching the African of a world only peripherally reminiscent to his own. However, it was a system that served two of the ends of colonial capitalism. First, it separated the African from his past, distorting or denying him knowledge of his own history and culture, his legends and his customs. What it taught him alienated him from his community and transformed him into an individual in the mould of the coloniser, one receptive to new values and attitudes. Second, like the church, the school propounded capitalist values while also imparting the basic literacy and simple technical skills required for the servicing of the lower echelons of the economy and administrative superstructure.

Other features of this superstructure reinforced the above socialising forces and impressed upon the African notions of his own inferiority and of European superiority. The official colonial policies of the metropolitan powers, in particular the assimilationist theories of the French and Portuguese, taught the African that he could only attain a sense of status and with it limited civil rights if, in effect, he became less African through the attainment of certain property and/or educational qualifications laid down by the European. He had to adopt the European's religion, master his language, acquire a knowledge of the rivers and mountains, kings and queens etc. of the European metropole—in other words, a knowledge of Africa became irrelevant to his acquisition of status. Yet even those who did acquire such status could not escape from the humiliating 'boy-girl syndome' common to all colonial societies, whereby even adult and professional Africans were reduced to an infantile status of being described as 'boys' or 'girls', even by the children of the colonised.

Elsewhere in the courts and in the economy the African learned that his life and his property was of a lesser value than that of the European coloniser. The educator may have taught him that the law was sacred and neutral but, in its application, he soon realised that there was a double standard in that the same offences committed by Africans and Europeans were judged differently. Rape of a European woman by an African was frequently a capital offence, but rarely when the roles were reversed. Likewise, in the allocation of labour roles the African found that the most menial, degrading and most poorly paid slots in the economy were reserved for him, while even the individuals with skills and qualifications were rarely allowed to assume a position of authority over European workers.

What then was the cumulative effect of this assault by colonial capitalism upon the African's sense of self-esteem and his set of cultural values? For the purposes of this paper two general consequences need to be highlighted, one in terms of the African's self-image and his cultural identity, and the other in terms of class formation in the colonial period.

With reference to the first of these perspectives, a passage from Kenneth Clark's *Dark Ghetto* seems applicable to the African situation, even though he was writing in of the black American context. He writes,

> Human beings who are forced to live under ghetto conditions and whose daily experience tells them that almost nowhere in society are they respected and granted the ordinary dignity and courtesy accorded to others will, as a matter of course, begin to doubt their own worth. Since every human being depends upon his cumulative experiences with others for clues as to how he should view and value himself, children who are consistently rejected understandably begin to question and doubt whether they, their family, and their group really deserve no more respect from the larger society than they receive. These doubts become the seeds of a pernicious self and group hatred, the Negro's complex and debilitating prejudice against himself.[6]

In other words, the African came to believe in his own inferiority. He developed a sense of shame about his cultural heritage and turned his back on it. Instead, he embraced the values of an alien culture and began to ape the white man, emulating specific aspects of his life-style: dress, eating and drinking habits, music, cosmetics, even exaggerating the particular accents of the coloniser's language. As Memmi has noted, his ambition was 'to become equal to that splendid model and to resemble him to the point of disappearing in him'.[7]

With reference to the second consequence, class formation, Mohiddin has noted that 'by encouraging consumerism, acquisitiveness and individualism, colonial capitalism transformed what was essentially a communitarian society into an acquisitive and stratified one'.[8] This statement could be misleading if one was to infer from it that colonial capitalism initiated the process of social stratification in Africa. But, as Mohiddin goes on to show, social divisions were present in pre-capitalist times; what colonial capitalism did was to exacerbate the process of class formation. In Amin's 'Africa of the Colonial Trade Economy' (former Anglophone and Francophone West and Sahelian Africa), large numbers of subsistence agriculturalists were peasantised, and in 'Africa of the Labour Reserves' (Southern and Eastern Africa) they were proletarianised into first the mining and then the industrial labour force.[9] Throughout the continent a small but not insignificant number of Africans did, to a certain extent, break through colonial barriers to acquire a petty-bourgeois (and even in rare cases a bourgeois) status as civil servants, professionals, shopkeepers and farmers. It was this stratum that most decisively rejected its cultural roots, becoming what some have termed 'Afro-Saxons' or 'white blackmen'. It constituted the elite of the colonised world but its members were really 'nowhere people', alienated from their own people and socially shunned by the world of the European.

Politically, too, this stratum was impotent and ignored until after World War Two, when all but the Portuguese colonialists saw in it the answer to their post-war dilemma of how to withdraw from Africa while protecting their economic and strategic interests. Suddenly the petty bourgeoisie, who had so thoroughly assimilated the cultural, political and economic values of Europe, was recognised as being politically safe, a special breed 'different and seperate from the rest of the masses with special roles to perform'.[10] And so constitutions were devised, elections manipulated, and occasionally even troublesome radical deviants eliminated, to ensure the transfer of power to this class. The colonial system was Africanised and a 'bridgehead of dependency'[11] developed between the metropole and former colony with its African infrastructure manned by a comprador class, one which thorough acculturation to alien values saw the world through the eyes of their former rulers. The culture of dependency had performed a vital task from the point of view of the metropole, ensuring that the independence of their former colonies meant virtually nothing in terms of their essential interests.

The Post-Colonial Response

How has post-colonial Africa responded to the debasement of its cultural heritage, and what efforts have the ruling classes made to revive this heritage and restore pride in it?

Generally, in the area of culture two somewhat contradictory trends are discernible. On the one hand, certain social habits introduced in the colonial era have intensified so that social behaviour in Africa increasingly resembles that of the consumer societies of the industrialised world (preferences for large and costly European automobiles, expensive tastes in Western fashions, high cost European liquor etc.). Furthermore, these consumer habits have spread well beyond the petty bourgeoisie to all but the poorest of the citizenry. On the other hand, attempts are underway to resuscitate or re-legitimise some aspects of the traditional cultures (polygamy, the use of traditional medicines, are examples), and increasingly scholars are attempting either to rediscover, rewrite or reinterpret African history, art, music, languages, anthropology etc. The state, however, has done little to encourage these efforts, providing only minimal capital resources for cultural efforts. Calls for a cultural renaissance are only lip-service pronouncements, a fact that should cause little surprise when one considers how steeped in European values are those who control the state apparatus, be they civilian or military.

If an indigenous and independent culture is to develop again in Africa, a wholesale re-socialisation of the people must be undertaken, and an initial step in this task should be a thorough-going reconstruction of the inherited educational systems. But what has been Africa's record in this respect? It would not be an exaggeration to assert that as a general rule what has been done amounts to little more than cosmetic tinkerings. The school systems remain European-oriented, with the focus still being competitive examinations on the European model. Indeed, in former Anglophone Africa some school systems still write British certificate examinations and, where local examining boards have been established, they are mere carbon copies of these British systems (such as the East and West African Examination Councils). The curricula continue to stress the skills required by the bureaucratic sector while the desperately-needed vocational and technical skills receive insufficient attention.

In that part of the continent with which I am most familiar (Botswana, Lesotho and Swaziland) the educational systems of the colonial days survive virtually intact. In Swaziland, primary and secondary curricula units have been established to rewrite the school syllabi but, in their very creation, the ruling class has only re-emphasised its dependency syndrome, for the task has been assigned to a hotch-potch collection of expatriates—individuals with the best of intentions but hopelessly ignorant of local conditions and who must of necessity spend most of their contracts undergoing familiarisation. The whole operation functions like a shuttle-service as 'experts' come and go, some for as little as eight weeks. Not surprisingly, after five years little has been achieved. The goal of a coherent, Swazi-oriented school programme remains a distant prospect.

Few attempts have been made to develop full-scale re-socialisation programmes in sub-Saharan Africa. Mozambique, Tanzania and Guinea from 1959 to 1968[12] stand out as the exceptions. Elsewhere a political dimension has been introduced into school programmes, but with the limited goal of forging a sense of national unity out of situations of multi-ethnic loyalties. This is a noble goal but of itself does nothing to attack the roots of cultural dependency or to transform the metropole-satellite relationship. Furthermore, studies have shown that nowhere (neither in Nigeria, Ghana, Kenya nor Cameroon) have these programmes succeeded.[13]

The political education programme in Mozambique has no such limited goal. It amounts to an all-out assault upon the socialising influences of the colonial period with the intention of producing a new Mozambican personality, purged of all the negative and debilitating features of both the traditional and colonial cultures. Since its inception, Frelimo has regarded education and culture as weapons for revolutionary change. Cultural seminars were held periodically during the war of liberation, the first at the end of 1970, and repeatedly Frelimo members stressed that their struggle was more than just a political revolution, but a cultural one as well. In his address on the occasion of the installation of Mozambique's provisional government in 1974, President Machel took up this theme, pledging the state to 'an unyielding struggle against the vestiges of colonialism, decadent values, erroneous ideas, the attitude of uncritically imitating foreigners'.[14] The struggle for independence, he argued, had not been fought for the expulsion of the foreign dominators 'but also to reconquer our Mozambican personality, to bring about the resurgence of our culture and create a new mentality, a new society'.[15] The school was assigned the vanguard role in this struggle. Schools, Machel stated, must be

> centres for wiping out the Colonial-capitalist mentality and the negative aspects of the traditional mentality. Superstition, individualism, selfishness, elitism and ambition must be fought in them. There should be no place in them for social, racial or sexual discrimination. Above all, the masses must have both access to and power in the schools, Universities and culture .... At school level we must be able to introduce collective work and create an open climate of criticism and self-criticism .... Our schools must truly be centres for the propogation of national culture and political, technical and scientific knowledge.[16]

These sentiments were given policy expression in a statement to the conference of African Ministers of Education in 1976, a document reprinted in chapter 16. This statement depicted the goal of the colonial education system as having been to teach the Mozambican scholar 'to deny his true self, to constantly strive to emulate the Portuguese way of life, and to be a useful intermediary between the colonialists and the illiterate mass of his fellow countrymen ... [to become] little black Portuguese, the docile instrument of colonialism, whose ambition was to live like a settler, in whose image he was created'.[17] In the attainment of these objectives, the Catholic Church was depicted as a primary instrument.

Not surprisingly, one of Frelimo's first acts was to place all church, mission and private schools under state control, abolish religious instruction and replace it with political instruction and manual work, the latter undertaken in the community throughout the year, including throughout two of the three school-holiday months. It is intended that the school's teachers and pupils will thereby become an energising force in the community, transmitting knowledge to the world around it as it is absorbed, and not storing it away for use in distant years ahead. The undertaking of manual tasks with the community's workers is also designed to prevent the development within the school of elitist, individualistic notions.

Abolished along with religious teaching were all the old Portuguese textbooks, but this raised the problem of developing alternative materials. A further problem faced by the new educational planners was not simply the lack of teachers, and the poor quality of their training, but even more crucially, that the bulk had been socialised into absorbing the now redundant values of the colonial era. To overcome these problems the three commissions mentioned in the document were established, and these have tackled the tasks of retraining the teaching cadre, developing new teaching materials and finding new 'ways of evaluating academic performance in a system that puts the major emphasis on group work ... of measuring such important qualities as political awareness and work'.[18] This latter commission will generate a revolutionary change to the usual African practice of evaluating knowledge according to European standards.

Since the release of this policy statement further changes have been made to the school system, including a requirement that teachers and pupils spend non-classroom time in neighbourhood *Alfabetizacao* centres teaching basic literacy. But perhaps the most dramatic changes of all are occurring within the schools themselves, where a democratic revolution is under way.[19] The colonial school was an oppressive institution where unquestioning obedience was expected of pupils who were given no voice at all in the decisions that affected their lives. Now students elect representative bodies (*turma*) where school problems are examined and discussed and where cultural and service activities are planned. From among the *turma*, a representative is elected to attend the *Conselho da Escola*, where teachers discuss student affairs. The teachers themselves have been liberated from past oppression by their administrators and now they elect from among themselves a *Comissao Directive*, the highest internal authority in the school. Operating alongside these bodies is the *Grupe Dynamizador*, composed or the most militant students, teachers and other workers in the school. This group gives the school its political direction and represents Frelimo within the school. In time this democratic process will eradicate the habits of submissiveness and notions of helplessness whereby the colonial state socialised its people into docility. They will, as Searle has indicated, also 'give the student the necessary apprenticeship in collective discussion and decision-making—so essential to the foundations of a Socialist society'.[20]

What has been going on in the schools is only part of a greater cultural transformation in society. In 1977, a 'Cultural Offensive of the Worker and Peasant Classes' was launched with the goal of mobilising the whole society in a cultural renaissance. To this end, cultural groups have been formed at all levels—schools, factories, government offices, communal villages.[21] These groups plan their own cultural activities with the idea of raising the nation's cultural consciousness and developing a revolutionary cultural expression. Additionally, brigades are scouring the country 'to gather songs, musical instruments, carvings, stories',[22] recording on tape the latter. The Offensive is directed by the National Institute for Culture within the Ministry of Education and Culture. The Institute has working-parties within it for each of the art forms, which examine its state and study ways of developing it. In the Offensive, the Institute works through *Casas da Cultura* (Houses of Culture) which are described as 'formative centres where dancing, singing and poetry-reading and other cultural manifestations take place'.[23] They also constitute meeting-places for artists and the citizenry and a forum for the exchange of ideas. This cultural campaign links up with Frelimo's political programme through the *Grupe Dynamizadore*. At a centre for Cultural Studies in Maputo, individuals are trained in ways of stimulating political and cultural consciousness in the schools, factories etc.

It is premature to attempt an assessment of this cultural revolution but, in this ambitions re-socialisation programme, Mozambique and all of Africa face enormous obstacles. One, is the lack of resources at the disposal of the state. The mass media are not highly developed. Radio and television services frequently do not penetrate beyond the major urban centres. Even in one of Africa's tiniest nations—Swaziland—and a full decade after independence, the national radio service does not reach more than half of the country. Likewise, Africa's newspapers tend to circulate only within the urban areas, while the use of the press as a socialising agent is limited by Africa's high rate of illiteracy.

A second problem pertains to the use of the school as a socialiser. Most African students simply do not stay in school long enough for re-socialisation programmes, where they exist, to be effective. Over and above that, the primary school teacher is often the most poorly trained of the teaching corps and therefore the least equipped for the crusade against colonial values.

A third set of problems lies in the fact that in every African nation there exist powerful countervailing forces that interrupt the smooth transmission of new values. The older generations, for example, were socialised into the values of colonialism, and they often impart contradictory messages to their offspring, thereby undermining the re-socialisation effort and creating a sense of confusion among the young. In Africa's multi-ethnic societies there also survive parochial political cultures linked to the tribe and these too may sabotage the efforts of the state. Lastly, the international mass media, which penetrate all of Africa, are controlled by the advanced capitalist nations and present the developed world's perspective on news events, frequently distorting of misinterpreting developments in the Third World. In Swaziland this is a particular problem for, because of the inadequacy of the radio services and the lack of a nationally-controlled daily newspaper, most Swazi rely on the government-controlled, pro-apartheid radio service of South Africa for information, while the conservative English-language newspapers of South Africa are the mostly widely-read organs of the press.

Finally, re-socialisation programmes are often sabotaged by the ruling classes themselves. In the public arena, they preach frugality and sacrifice on the part of the people, proclaim the need to revive indigenous cultural values and traditions and yet, in their lifestyles, often fail to practise what they preach, emulating the conspicious consumptive habits of the West with large cars, expensive residences and frequent excursions beyond their borders. Disillusionment with their national political leaders among the youth of countries is increasing, as was shown in the attack by University of Dar es Salaam students on the decision by the Chama Cha Mapinduzi of Tanzania to raise substantially the salaries of MPs. The students objected to this action at a time when workers and peasants were being required to tighten their belts, and they accused the Party of not being serious about building socialism. Tanzania's parliament was described as 'a state instrument whose function is to enact laws which promote the interests of the exploiters and which suppress the interests of the workers and peasants. The parliament is not an instrument of the downtrodden, it is a part of the state whose major function is to oppress the downtrodden'.[24] Over 300 students were expelled from the University for their role in this protest, an action likely only to increase the students' sense of alienation.

Twenty years ago African liberation was interpreted as meaning political emancipation from foreign tutelage. Independence occurred, but little changed. Only later did Africa's consciousness of neo-colonialism develop, and attention shifted to means of attaining economic independence. But the neo-colonial chains that bind Africa to the metropole are not simply economic, they are cultural too. To attain a true state of emancipation, Africa must experience a cultural revolution in the wake of the overthrow of the comprador ruling classes who are content to remain in, and benefit from, the neo-colonial orbit. It is for this reason that the Mozambique effort merits close examination. Its wholesale rejection of the imported colonial model, and its multi-faceted assault upon every manifestation of dependence, makes it Africa's best hope for achieving a new, assertive and progressive African consciousness from the ashes of the colonial state.

Notes

1 See Samir Amin, 'Underdevelopment and Dependence in Black Africa-Origins and Contemporary Forms', in Part One of this volume.
2 Ahmed Mohiddin, 'Towards Relevant Culture and Politics in Africa', *Africa Development*, 2, 4 (1977), p. 58.
3 *Ibid.*, pp. 55–69.
4 *Ibid.*, p. 58.
5 See Albert Memmi, 'The Coloniser and the Colonised', in Part Three of this volume.
6 Kenneth Clark, *Dark Ghetto*, Harper and Row, New York, 1965, pp. 63–4.
7 Memmi, *The Coloniser and the Colonised*, Beacon Press, Boston, 1965, p. 120.
8 Mohiddin, *op.cit.*, p. 59.
9 See Amin, *op.cit.*
10 Mohiddin, *op.cit.*, p. 60.
11 The concept of the 'bridgehead of dependency' has been developed by Johan Galtung in his article 'A Structural Theory of Imperialism', *The African Review*, 1, 4 (1972), pp. 93–138, and by Susanne Bodenheimer in her article 'Dependency and Imperialism: The Roots of Latin American Underdevelopment', in K.T. Fann and Donald C. Hodges eds., *Readings in US Imperialism*, Porter Sargent Publishers, Boston, 1971, pp. 155–81.
12 The cultural revolution in Guinea is discussed in an article by Lansine Kaba, 'The Cultural Revolution, Artistic Creativity, and Freedom of Expression in Guinea', *The Journal of Modern African Studies*, 14, 2 (1976), pp. 201–18. Kaba argues that after 1968 Guinea's cultural revolution degenerated into an uncreative and oppressive crusade to develop a personality-cult about the figure of President Sekou Touré.
13 For a discussion of the efforts in these countries see Onuoka Chukurta, 'Education and National Integration in Africa: A Case Study of Nigeria', *The African Studies Review*, 21, 2 (1978), pp. 67–76.
14 Samora Machel, 'Message from Samora Machel', *SASO newsletter*, 5, 2, p. 16.
15 *Ibid.*
16 *Ibid.*
17 'Education Policy in the People's Republic of Mozambique', *Journal of Modern African Studies*, 14, 2 (1976), p. 332.
18 *Ibid.*, p. 338.
19 This information and that dealing with the democratisation of the school are derived

from Chris Searle, '"Escola Nova": The New Secondary School in Mozambique', *Issue*, 8, 1 (1978), pp. 32–4.

20 *Ibid.*, p. 34.
21 This information on the Cultural Offensive is derived from Barbara Barnes, 'Creating a National Culture: An Overview', *Issue*, 8, 1 (1978), pp. 35–8.
22 *Ibid.*, p. 36.
23 *Ibid.*
24 Memorandum of the University of Dar es Salaam Students to Chama Cha Mapinduzi (CCM), 5 March 1978, reprinted in *Review of African Political Economy*, 10, September–December 1977, pp. 104–5.

11 The Coloniser and the Colonised*

ALBERT MEMMI

Mythical Portrait of the Colonised

Just as the bourgeoisie proposes an image of the proletariat, the existence of
the coloniser requires that an image of the colonised be suggested. These
images become excuses without which the presence and conduct of a coloniser,
and that of a bourgeois, would seem shocking. But the favoured image becomes
a myth precisely because it suits them too well.

Let us imagine, for the sake of this portrait and accusation, the often-cited
trait of laziness. It seems to receive unanimous approval of colonisers from
Liberia to Laos, via the Maghreb. It is easy to see to what extent this description
is useful. It occupies an important place in the dialectics exalting the coloniser
and humbling the colonised. Furthermore, it is economically fruitful.

Nothing could better justify the coloniser's privileged position than his
industry, and nothing could better justify the colonised's destitution than his
indolence. The mythical portrait of the colonised therefore includes an un-
believable laziness, and that of the coloniser, a virtuous taste for action. At the
same time the coloniser suggests that employing the colonised is not very
profitable, thereby authorising his unreasonable wages.

It may seem that colonisation would profit by employing experienced
personnel. Nothing is less true. A qualified worker existing among the colonisers
earns three or four times more than does the colonised, while he does not
produce three or four times as much, either in quantity or in quality. It is more
advantageous to use three of the colonised than one European. Every firm needs
specialists, of course, but only a minimum of them, and the coloniser imports or
recruits experts among his own kind. In addition, there is the matter of the
special attention and legal protection required by a European worker. The
colonised, however, is only asked for his muscles; he is so poorly evaluated
that three or four can be taken on for the price of one European.

From listening to him, on the other hand, one finds that the coloniser is
not so displeased with that laziness, whether supposed or real. He talks of it
with amused affability, he jokes about it, he takes up all the usual expressions,
perfects them, and invents others. Nothing can describe well enough the
extraordinary deficiency of the colonised. He becomes lyrical about it, in a
negative way. The colonised doesn't let grass grow under his feet, but a tree,
and what a tree! A eucalyptus, an American centenarian oak! A tree? No, a
forest!

But, one will insist, is the colonised truly lazy? To tell the truth, the question
is poorly stated. Besides having to define a point of reference, a norm, varying
from one people to another, can one accuse an entire people of laziness? It can
be suspected of individuals, even many of them in a single group. One can
wonder if their output is mediocre, whether malnutrition, low wages, a closed
future, a ridiculous conception of his role in society, does not make the colonised

---

*From *The Coloniser and the Colonised*, The Beacon Press, Boston, 1965, pp. 79–104,
119–41. © Viking Press Inc. and Editions Buchet.

uninterested in his work. What is suspect is that the accusation is not directed solely at the farm labourer or slum resident, but also at the professor, engineer or physician who does the same number of hours of work as his coloniser colleagues; indeed, all individuals of the colonised group are accused. Essentially, the independence of the accusation from any sociological or historical conditions makes it suspect.

In fact, the accusation has nothing to do with an objective notation, subject to possible changes, but of an institution. By his accusation the coloniser establishes the colonised as being lazy. He decides that laziness is constitutional in the very nature of the colonised. It becomes obvious that the colonised, whatever he may undertake, whatever zeal he may apply, could never be anything but lazy. This always brings us back to racism, which is the substantive expression, to the accuser's benefit, of a real or imaginary trait of the accused.

It is possible to proceed with the same analysis for each of the features found in the colonised.

Whenever the coloniser states, in his language, that the colonised is a weakling, he suggests thereby that this deficiency requires protection. From this comes the concept of a protectorate. It is in the colonised's own interest that he be excluded from management functions, and that those heavy responsibilities be reserved for the coloniser. Whenever the coloniser adds, in order not to fall prey to anxiety, that the colonised is a wicked, backward person with evil, thievish, somewhat sadistic instincts, he thus justifies his police and his legitimate severity. After all, he must defend himself against the dangerous and foolish acts of the irresponsible, and at the same time protect him against himself! It is the same for the colonised's lack of desires, his ineptitude for comfort, science, progress, his astonishing familiarity with poverty. Why should the coloniser worry about things that hardly trouble the interested party? It would be, he adds with dark and insolent philosophy, doing him a bad turn if he subjected him to the disadvantages of civilisation. After all, remember that wisdom is Eastern; let us accept, as he does, the colonised's wretchedness. The same reasoning is also true for the colonised's notorious ingratitude; the coloniser's acts of charity are wasted, the improvements the coloniser has made are not appreciated. It is impossible to save the colonised from this myth—a portrait of wretchedness has been indelibly engraved.

It is significant that this portrait requires nothing else. It is difficult, for instance, to reconcile most of these features and then to proceed to synthesise them objectively. One can hardly see how the colonised can be simultaneously inferior and wicked, lazy and backward.

What is more, the traits ascribed to the colonised are incompatible with one another, though this does not bother his prosecutor. He is depicted as frugal, sober, without many desires and, at the same time, he consumes disgusting quantities of meat, fat, alcohol, anything; as a coward who is afraid of suffering and as a brute who is not checked by any inhibitions of civilisation, etc. It is additional proof that it is useless to seek this consistency anywhere except in the coloniser himself. At the basis of the entire construction, one finally finds a common motive; the coloniser's economic and basic needs, which he substitutes for logic, and which shape and explain each of the traits he assigns to the colonised. In the last analysis, these traits are all advantageous to the coloniser, even those which at first sight seem damaging to him.

The point is that the colonised means little to the coloniser. Far from wanting to understand him as he really is, the coloniser is preoccupied with making him undergo this urgent change. The mechanism of this remoulding of the colonised is revealing in itself. It consists, in the first place, of a series of negations. The colonised is not this, is not that. He is never considered in a positive light; or if he is, the quality which is conceded is the result of a psychological or ethical failing. Thus it is with Arab hospitality, which is difficult to consider as a negative characteristic. If one pays attention, one discovers that the praise comes from tourists, visiting Europeans, and not colonisers, ie. Europeans who have settled down in the colony. As soon as he is settled, the European no longer takes advantage of this hospitality, but cuts off intercourse and contributes to the barriers which plague the colonised. He rapidly changes palette to portray the colonised, who becomes jealous, withdrawn, intolerant and fanatical. What happens to the famous hospitality? Since he cannot deny it, the coloniser then brings into play the shadows and describes the disastrous consequences.

This hospitality is a result of the colonised's irresponsibility and extravagance, since he has no notion of foresight or economy. From the wealthy down to the fellah, the festivities are wonderful and bountiful: but what happens afterward? The colonised ruins himself, borrows and finally pays with someone else's money! Does one speak, on the other hand, of the modesty of the colonised's life? Of his not less well-known lack of needs? It is no longer a proof of wisdom but of stupidity—as if, then, every recognised or invented trait had to be an indication of negativity.

Thus, one after another, all the qualities which make a man of the colonised crumble away. The humanity of the colonised, rejected by the coloniser, becomes opaque. It is useless, he asserts, to try to forecast the colonised's actions ('They are unpredictable!', 'With them, you never know!'). It seems to him that strange and disturbing impulsiveness controls the colonised. The colonised must indeed be very strange, if he remains so mysterious after years of living with the coloniser.

Another sign of the colonised's depersonalisation is what one might call the mark of the plural. The colonised is never characterised in an individual manner; he is entitled only to drown in an anonymous collectivity ('They are this', 'They are all the same'). If a colonised servant does not come in one morning, the coloniser will not say that she is ill, or that she is cheating, or that she is tempted not to abide by an oppressive contract. (Seven days a week; colonised domestics rarely enjoy the one day off a week granted to others.) He will say, 'You can't count on them'. It is not just a grammatical expression. He refuses to consider personal, private occurrences in his maid's life; that life in a specific sense does not interest him, and his maid does not exist as an individual.

Finally, the coloniser denies the colonised the most precious right granted to most men: liberty. Living conditions imposed on the colonised by colonisation make no provision for it; indeed, they ignore it. The colonised has no way out of his state of woe—neither a legal outlet (naturalisation) nor a religious outlet (conversion). The colonised is not free to choose between being colonised or not being colonised.

What is left of the colonised at the end of this stubborn effort to dehumanise him? He is surely no longer an *alter ego* of the coloniser. He is hardly a human being. He tends rapidly toward becoming an object. As an end, in the coloniser's supreme ambition, he should exist only as a function of the needs of the coloniser, ie. be transformed into a pure colonised.

The extraordinary efficiency of this operation is obvious. One does not have a serious obligation toward an animal or an object. It is then easily understood that the coloniser can indulge in such shocking attitudes and opinions. A colonised driving a car is a sight to which the coloniser refuses to become accustomed; he denies him all normality. An accident, even a serious one, overtaking the colonised almost makes him laugh. A machine-gun burst into a crowd of colonised causes him merely to shrug his shoulders. Even a 'native' mother weeping over the death of her son or a 'native' woman weeping for her husband reminds him only vaguely of the grief of a mother or a wife. Those desperate cries, those unfamiliar gestures, would be enough to freeze his compassion even if it were aroused. An author was recently humorously telling us how rebelling 'natives' were driven like game toward huge cages. The fact that someone had conceived and then dared build those cages, and even more, that reporters had been allowed to photograph the fighting, certainly proves that the spectacle had contained nothing human.

Madness for destroying the colonised having originated with the needs of the coloniser, it is not surprising that it conforms so well to them, that it seems to confirm and justify the coloniser's conduct. More surprising, more harmful perhaps, is the echo that it excites in the colonised himself. Constantly confronted with this image of himself, set forth and imposed on all institutions and in every human contact, how could the colonised help reacting to his portrait? It cannot leave him indifferent and remain a veneer which, like an insult, blows with the wind. He ends up recognising it as one would a detested nickname which has become a familiar description. The accusation disturbs him and worries him even more because he admires and fears his powerful accuser. 'Is he not partially right?' he mutters. 'Are we not all a little guilty after all? Lazy, because we have so many idlers? Timid, because we let ourselves be oppressed.' Wilfully created and spread by the coloniser, this mythical and degrading portrait ends up by being accepted and lived with to a certain extent by the colonised. It thus acquires a certain amount of reality and contributes to the true portrait of the colonised.

This process is not unknown. It is a hoax. It is common knowledge that the ideology of a governing class is adopted in large measure by the governed classes. Now, every ideology of combat includes as an integral part of itself a conception of the adversary. By agreeing to this ideology, the dominated classes practically confirm the role assigned to them. This explains, *inter alia*, the relative stability of societies; oppression is tolerated willy-nilly by the oppressed themselves. In colonial relationships, domination is imposed by people upon people but the pattern remains the same. The characterisation and role of the colonised occupies a choice place in colonialist ideology; a characterisation which is neither true to life, nor in itself incoherent, but necessary and inseparable within that ideology. It is one to which the colonised gives his troubled and partial, but undeniable, assent.

There is only a particle of truth in the fashionable notions of 'dependency complex', 'colonisability', etc. There undoubtedly exists—at some point in its evolution—a certain adherence of the colonised to colonisation. However, this adherence is the result of colonisation and not its cause. It arises after and not before colonial occupation. In order for the coloniser to be the complete master, it is not enough for him to be so in actual fact, but he must also believe in its legitimacy. In order for that legitimacy to be complete, it is not enough for the colonised to be a slave, he must also accept this role. The bond between coloniser and colonised is thus destructive and creative. It destroys and re-creates the two partners of colonisation into coloniser and colonised. One is disfigured into an oppressor, a partial, unpatriotic and treacherous being, worrying only about his privileges and their defence; the other, into an oppressed creature, whose development is broken and who compromises by his defeat.

Just as the coloniser is tempted to accept his part, the colonised is forced to accept being colonised.

Situation of the Colonised

Since the colonised is presumed a thief, he must in fact be guarded against (being suspect by definition, why should he not be guilty?). Some laundry was stolen (a frequent incident in these sunny lands, where the laundry dries in the open air and mocks those who are naked), and who but the first colonised seen in that vicinity can be guilty? Since it may be he, they go to his home and take him to the police station.

'Some injustice!', retorts the coloniser. 'One time out of two, we hit it right. And, in any case, the thief is a colonised; if we don't find him in the first hut, he'll be in the second one'.

It would have been too good if that mythical portrait had remained a pure illusion, a look at the colonised which would only have softened the coloniser's bad conscience. However, impelled by the same needs which created it, it cannot fail to be expressed in actual conduct, in active and constructive behaviour.

This conduct, which is common to colonisers as a group, thus becomes what can be called a social institution. In other words, it defines and establishes concrete situations which close in on the colonised, weigh on him until they bend his conduct and leave their marks on his face. Generally-speaking, these are situations of inadequacy. The ideological aggression which tends to de-humanise and then deceive the colonised finally corresponds to concrete situations which lead to the same result. To be deceived to some extent already, to endorse the myth and then adapt to it, is to be acted upon by it. That myth is furthermore supported by a very solid organisation; a government and a judicial system fed and renewed by the coloniser's historic, economic and cultural needs. Even if he were insensitive to calumny and scorn, even if he shrugged his shoulders at insults and jostling, how could the colonised escape the low wages, the agony of his culture, the law which rules him from birth until death?

Just as the colonised cannot escape the colonialist hoax, he could not avoid those situations which create real inadequacy. To a certain extent, the true portrait of the colonised is a function of this relationship. Reversing a previous formula, it can be stated that colonisation creates the colonised just as we have seen that it creates the coloniser.

The most serious blow suffered by the colonised is being removed from history and from the community. Colonisation usurps any free role in either war or peace, every decision contributing to his destiny and that of the world, and all cultural and social responsibility.

It is true that discouraged citizens of free countries tell themselves that they have no voice in the nation's affairs, that their actions are useless, that their voice is not heard, and that the elections are fixed. Such people claim that the press and radio are in the hands of a few, that they cannot prevent war, or demand peace, or even obtain from their elected representatives that for which they were sent to parliament. However, they at least immediately recognise that they possess the right to do so; the potential if not the effective power;

that they are deceived or weary, but not enslaved. They try to believe they are free men, momentarily vanquished by hoaxes or stunned by demagogy. Driven beyond the boiling point, they are seized by sudden anger, break their paper chains and upset the politicians' little calculations. These people proudly remember those periodic and just storms! Thinking it over, they may feel guilty for not revolting more often; after all, they are responsible for their own freedom and if, because of fatigue or weakness or scepticism, they do not use it, they deserve their punishment.

The colonised, on the other hand, feels neither responsible nor guilty nor sceptical, for he is out of the game. He is in no way a subject of history any more. Of course, he carries its burden, often more cruelly than others, but always as an object. He has forgotten how to participate actively in history and no longer even asks to do so. No matter how briefly colonisation may have lasted, all memory of freedom seems distant; he forgets what it costs or else he no longer dares to pay the price for it. How else can one explain how a garrison of a few men can hold out in a mountain post? How a handful of often arrogant colonisers can live in the midst of a multitude of colonised? The colonisers themselves are amazed, and it follows that they accuse the colonised of cowardice. Actually, the accusation is too easy; they know very well that if they were in danger, their lonely position would quickly be changed. All the resources of science— telephone, telegraph, and air-plane—would be placed at their disposal and, within a few minutes, terrible weapons of defence and destruction. For each coloniser killed, hundreds or thousands of the colonised have been, or would be, exterminated. That experience has occurred often enough—perhaps incited— for the colonised to be convinced of the inevitable and heinous punishment. Everything has been brought into play to destroy his courage to die and face the sight of blood.

It is even more clear that if it is really a matter of inadequacy involved, born of a situation and of the will of the coloniser, it is only that and not some congenital inability to assume a role in history. The severity of the laws attest to the difficulty of conditioning the colonised to feel inadequate. While it is pardonable for the coloniser to have his little arsenals, the discovery of even a rusty weapon among the colonised is cause for immediate punishment. The Arab *fantasia* has become nothing more than the act of a trained animal which is asked to roar, as he used to, to frighten the guests. But the animal roars extremely well; and nostalgia for arms is always present, and is part of all ceremonies in Africa, from north to south. The lack of implements of war appears proportional to the size of the colonialist forces; the most isolated tribes are still the first to pick up their weapons. That is not a proof of savagery, but only evidence that the conditioning is not sufficiently maintained.

That is also why the experience of the last war was so decisive. It did not only, as has been stated, imprudently teach the colonised the technique of guerilla warfare, but also it reminded them of the possibility of aggressive and free action. The European governments which, after that war, prohibited the showing of certain movies of resistance in colonial theatres were not wrong from their point of view. In objection to this, it was stated that American Westerns, gangster pictures and war propaganda strips had already shown how to use a revolver or tommy-gun. That argument was not enough. The significance of resistance films is entirely different. They show that poorly armed or even unarmed oppressed people did dare attack their oppressors.

When the first disturbances broke out in the colonies, those who did not understand their meaning were consoled by the fact that there were so few active fighters. The colonised, it is true, hesitates before taking his destiny in his hands. But the meaning of the event was so much greater than its arithmetical weight! The rebels were laughed at because of their insistence on wearing khaki uniforms. Obviously, they hoped to be considered soldiers and treated in accordance with the rules of war. There is profound meaning to this emphatic desire, as it was by this tactic that they laid claim to and wore the dress of history; and, unfortunately, history today wears a military uniform.

As mentioned before, the same goes for community affairs. 'They are not capable of governing themselves', says the coloniser. 'That is why', he explains, 'I don't let them and will never let them, enter the government'.

The fact is that the colonised does not govern. Being kept away from power, he ends up by losing both interest and feeling for control. How could he be interested in something from which he is so resolutely excluded? Among the colonised few men are suitable for government. How could such a long absence from autonomous government give rise to skill? Can the coloniser succeed in barring the colonised from future participation in government by cheating him from this role in the present?

Since the colonised's organisations have nationalistic claims, it is often concluded that the colonised are chauvinistic. Nothing is less true. What is involved, on the contrary, is an ambition and a form of mob psychology which appeals to passionate motives. Except among the militants of this national renaissance, the usual signs of chauvinism—aggressive love for the flag, use of patriotic songs, fervent feeling of belonging to the same national organisation —are rare among the colonised. It is repeated that colonisation precipitated the awakening of national consciousness of the colonised. One could state equally well that it moderated the tempo of this awareness by keeping the colonised apart from the true conditions of contemporary citizenship. It is not a coincidence that colonised peoples are the last to awaken to national consciousness.

The colonised enjoys none of the attributes of citizenship; neither his own, which is dependent, contested and smothered, nor that of the coloniser. He can hardly adhere to one or claim the other. Not having his just place in the community, not enjoying the rights of a modern citizen, not being subject to his normal duties, not voting, not bearing the burden of community affairs, he cannot feel like a true citizen. As a result of colonisation, the colonised almost never experiences nationality and citizenship, except privately. Nationally and civically he is only what the coloniser is not.

This social and historical mutilation gives rise to the most serious consequences. It contributes to bringing out the deficiencies in the other aspects of the colonised's life and, by a counter-effect which is frequent in human processes, it is itself fed by the colonised's other infirmities.

Not considering himself a citizen, the colonised likewise loses all hope of seeing his son achieve citizenship. Before long, renouncing citizenship himself, he no longer includes it in his plans, eliminates it from his paternal ambitions, and allows no place for it in his teachings. Nothing therefore suggests to the young colonised the self-assurance or pride of his citizenship. He will expect nothing more from it and will not be prepared to assume its responsibilities. (Obviously, there is likewise nothing in his school education, in which references to the community and nation are always in terms of the colonising nation.) This educational void, a result of social inadequacy, thus perpetuates that same inadequacy, damaging one of the essential dimensions of the colonised individual.

Later, as an adolescent, it is with difficulty that he conceives vaguely, if at all, of the only way out of a disastrous family situation: revolt. The ring is tightly sealed. Revolt against his father and family is a wholesome act and an indispensable one for self-achievement. It permits him to start his adult life—a new unhappy and happy battle—among other men. The conflict of generations can and must be resolved by social conflict; conversely, it is thus a factor in movement and progress. The young generations find the solution to their problems in collective movements. By choosing a movement, they accelerate it. It is necessary, of course, that that movement be possible. Now, into what kind of life and social dynamic do we emerge? The colony's life is frozen; its structure is both corsetted and hardened. No new role is open to the young man, no invention is possible. The coloniser admits this with a now classical euphemism: he respects, he proclaims, the ways and customs of the colonised. And, to be sure, he cannot help respecting them, albeit by force of circumstances. Since any change would be against the interests of colonisation, the coloniser is led to favour the least progressive features. He is not solely responsible for this mummification of the colonised society; he demonstrates relatively good faith when he maintains that it is independent by its own will. It derives largely, however, from the colonial situation. Not being master of its destiny, not being its own legislator, not controlling its organisation, colonised society can no longer adapt its institutions to its grievous needs. But it is those needs which practically shape the organisational face of every normal society. It is under their constant pressure that the political and administrative face of France has been gradually changing over the centuries. However, if the discord becomes too sharp, and harmony becomes impossible to attain under existing legal forms, the result is either to revolt or to be calcified.

Colonised society is a diseased society in which internal dynamics no longer succeed in creating new structures. Its century-hardened face has become nothing more than a mask under which it slowly smothers and dies. Such a society cannot dissolve the conflicts of generations, for it is unable to be transformed. The revolt of the adolescent colonised, far from resolving into mobility and social progress, can only sink into the morass of colonised society—unless there is a total revolution. But we shall return to that later.

Sooner or later then, the potential rebel falls back on the traditional values. This explains the astonishing survival of the colonised's family. The colonial superstructure has real value as a refuge. It saves the colonised from the despair of total defeat and, in return, it finds confirmation in a constant inflow of new blood. The young man will marry, will become a devoted father, reliable brother, responsible uncle and, until he takes his father's place, a respectful son. Everything has gone back into the order of things. Revolt and conflict have ended in a victory for the parents and tradition.

But it is a pyrrhic victory. Colonised society has not taken even half a step forward; for the young man, it is an internal catastrophe. He will remain glued to that family which offers him warmth and tenderness but which simultaneously absorbs, clutches and emasculates him. Doesn't the community require the full duties of citizenship? Wouldn't it refuse them to him if he should still try to claim them? Doesn't it grant him few rights and prohibit him from participating in all national life? Actually, he no longer desperately needs them. His correct place, always reserved in the soft warmth of clan reunions, satisfies him. He would be afraid to leave it. With good grace now, he submits, as do the others, to his father's authority and prepares to replace him. The model is a weak one. His universe is that of the vanquished. But what other way out is there? By a curious paradox, his father is simultaneously weak and possessive.

The young man is ready to assume his role of the colonised adult—that is, to accept being an oppressed creature.

The same goes for the indisputable hold of a deep-rooted and formal religion. Complacently, missionaries depict this formality as an essential feature of non-Christian religions. Thus they suggest that the only way to escape from one would be to pass over to the next closest one. Actually, all religions have moments of coercive formality and moments of indulgent flexibility. It remains to be explained why a given group, at a given period in its history, goes through a certain stage. Why such hollow rigidity in the religions of the colonised?

It would be useless to construct a religious psychology which is peculiar to the colonised or to invoke that all-explaining nature which is attributed to them. While they give a certain amount of attention to religion, one seldom notices excessive religious zeal among the colonised. It seems to me that the explanation is parallel to that of family control. It is not an original psychology which explains the importance of the family, nor is it the intensity of family life which explains the state of social structures. It is rather the impossibility of enjoying a complete social life which maintains vigour in the family and pulls the individual back to that more restricted cell, which saves and smothers him. At the same time, the entire condition of the colonised institutions takes into account the excessive weight of religion.

With its institutional network, its collective and periodic holidays, religion constitutes another refuge value, both for the individual and for the group. For the individual, it is one of the rare paths of retreat; for the group, it is one of the rare manifestations which can protect its original existence. Since colonised society does not possess national structures and cannot conceive of a historical future for itself, it must be content with the passive sluggishness of its present. It must withdraw even that present from the conquering invasion of colonisation which gives it prestige with the young generations. Formalism, of which religious formality is only one aspect, is the cyst into which colonial society shuts itself and hardens, degrading its own life in order to save it. It is a spontaneous action of self-defence, a means of safeguarding the collective consciousness without which a people quickly cease to exist. Under the conditions of colonial dependence, religious emancipation, like the break-up of the family, would have involved a serious risk of dying by itself.

The calcified colonised society is therefore the consequence of two processes having opposite symptoms; encystment originating internally and a corset imposed from outside. Both phenomena have one common factor, contact with colonisation. They converge in the social and historical catalepsy of the colonised.

As long as he tolerates colonisation, the only possible alternatives for the colonised are assimilation or petrifaction. Assimilation being refused him, as we shall see, nothing is left for him but to live isolated from his age. He is driven back by colonisation and, to a certain extent, lives with that situation. Planning and building his future are forbidden. He must therefore limit himself to the present, and even that present is cut off and abstract.

We should add that he draws less and less from his past. The coloniser never even recognised that he had one; everyone knows that the commoner whose origins are unknown has no history. Let us ask the colonised himself: who are his folk heroes, his great popular leaders, his sages? At most, he may be able to give us a few names, in complete disorder, and fewer and fewer as one goes down the generations. The colonised seems condemned to lose his memory.

Memory is not purely a mental phenomenon. Just as the memory of an individual is the fruit of his history and physiology, that of a people rests upon its institutions. Now the colonised's institutions are dead or petrified. He scarcely believes in those which continue to show some signs of life and daily confirms their ineffectiveness. He often becomes ashamed of these institutions, as of a ridiculous and overaged monument.

All effectiveness and social dynamics, on the other hand, seem monopolised by the coloniser's institutions. If the colonised needs help, it is to them that he applies. If he does something wrong, it is by them that he is punished. When a man of authority happens to wear a tarboosh, he has an evasive glance and abrupt manners, as though he wanted to forestall any challenge, as though he were under the coloniser's constant surveillance. Suppose the community has a festival. It is the coloniser's holiday, a religious one perhaps, and is celebrated brilliantly—Christmas and Joan of Arc, Carnival and Bastille Day. It is the coloniser's armies which parade, the very ones which crushed the colonised to keep him in his place.

Naturally, by virtue of his formalism, the colonised observes all his religious holidays. These holidays are located at the beginning of history, rather than in history. From the time they were instituted, nothing else has happened in the life of that people. That is, nothing peculiar to their own existence which deserves to be retained by the collective consciousness and celebrated. Nothing except a great void.

Finally, the few material traces of that past are slowly erased, and the future remnants will no longer carry the stamp of the colonised group. The few statues which decorate the city represent (with incredible scorn for the colonised who pass by them every day) the great deeds of colonisation. The buildings are patterned after the coloniser's own favourite designs; the same is true of the street names, which recall the faraway provinces from which he came. Occasionally, the coloniser starts a neo-Eastern style, just as the colonised imitates European style. But it is only exoticism (like old guns and antique chests) and not a renaissance; the colonised himself only avoids his own past . . . .

The Two Answers of the Colonised

The body and face of the colonised are not a pretty sight. It is not without damage that one carries the weight of such historical misfortune. If the coloniser's face is the odious one of an oppressor, that of his victim certainly does not express calm and harmony. The colonised does not exist in accordance with the colonial myth, but he is nevertheless recognisable. Being a creature of oppression, he is bound to be a creature of want.

How can one believe that he can ever be resigned to the colonial relationship; that face of suffering and disdain allotted to him? In all of the colonised there is a fundamental need for change. For the colonisers to be unconscious of this need means that either their lack of understanding of the colonial system is immense, or that their blind selfishness is more than readily believable. To assert, for instance, that the colonised's claims are the acts of a few intellectuals or ambitious individuals, of deception or self-interest, is a perfect example of projection: an explanation of others in terms of one's own interests. The colonised's refusal resembles a surface phenomenon, but it actually derives from the very nature of the colonial situation.

The middle-class colonised suffers most from bilingualism. The intellectual lives more in cultural anguish, and the illiterate person is simply walled into his language and re-chews scraps of oral culture. Those who understand their fate become impatient and no longer tolerate colonisation. They only express the common misfortune. If not, why would they be so quickly heard, so well understood and obeyed?

If he chooses to understand the colonial system, he must admit that it is unstable and its equilibrium constantly threatened. He can be reconciled to every situation, and the colonised can wait a long time to live. But, regardless of how soon or how violently the colonised rejects his situation, he will one day begin to overthrow his unlivable existence with the whole force of his oppressed personality.

The two historically possible solutions are then tried in succession or simultaneously. He attempts either to become different or to reconquer all the dimensions which colonisation tore away from him.

The first attempt of the colonised is to change his condition by changing his skin. There is a tempting model very close at hand—the coloniser. The latter suffers from none of his deficiencies, has all rights, enjoys every possession and benefits from every prestige. He is, moreover, the other part of the comparison, the one that crushes the colonised and keeps him in servitude. The first ambition of the colonised is to become equal to that splendid model and to resemble him to the point of disappearing in him.

By this step, which actually presupposes admiration for the coloniser, one can infer approval of colonisation. But by obvious logic, at the very moment when the colonised best adjusts himself to his fate, he rejects himself with most tenacity. That is to say that he rejects, in another way, the colonial situation. Rejection of self and love of another are common to all candidates for assimilation. Moreover, the two components of this attempt at liberation are closely tied. Love of the coloniser is subtended by a complex of feelings ranging from shame to self-hate.

The extremism in that submission to the model is already revealing. A blonde woman, be she dull or anything else, appears superior to any brunette. A product manufactured by the coloniser is accepted with confidence. His habits, clothing, food and architecture are closely copied, even if inappropriate. A mixed marriage is the extreme expression of this audacious leap.

This fit of passion for the coloniser's values would not be so suspect, however, if it did not involve such a negative side. The colonised does not seek merely to enrich himself with the coloniser's virtues. In the name of what he hopes to become, he sets his mind on impoverishing himself, tearing himself away from his true self. The crushing of the colonised is included among the coloniser's values. As soon as the colonised adopts those values, he similarly adopts his own condemnation. In order to free himself, at least so he believes, he agrees to destroy himself. This phenomenon is comparable to Negrophobia in a Negro, or anti-Semitism in a Jew. Negro women try desperately to uncurl their hair, which keeps curling back, and torture their skin to make it a little whiter. Many Jews would, if they could, tear out their souls—that soul which, they are told, is irremediably bad. People have told the colonised that his music is like the mewing of cats, and his painting like sugar syrup. He repeats that his music is vulgar and his painting disgusting. If that music nevertheless moves him, excites him more than the tame Western exercises, which he finds cold and complicated, if that unison of singing and slightly intoxicating colours gladdens his eye, it is against his will. He becomes indignant with himself, conceals it from strangers' eyes or makes strong statements of repugnance that are comical. The woman of the bourgeoisie prefer a mediocre jewel from Europe to the purest jewel of their tradition. Only the tourists express wonder before the products of centuries-old craftsmanship. The point is that whether Negro, Jew or colonised, one must resemble the white man, the non-Jew, the coloniser. Just as many people avoid showing off their poor relations, the colonised in the throes of assimilation hides his past, his traditions, in fact all his origins which have become ignominious.

Those internal convulsions and contortions could have attained their goal. At the end of a long, painful process, one certainly full of conflict, the colonised would perhaps have dissolved into the midst of the colonisers. There is no problem which the erosion of history cannot resolve. It is a question of time and generations. There is, however, one condition—that it not contain contradictory ideas. Within the colonial framework assimilation has turned out to be impossible.

The candidate for assimilation almost always comes to tire of the exorbitant price which he must pay and which he never finishes owing. He discovers with alarm the full meaning of his attempt. It is a dramatic moment when he realises that he has assumed all the accusations and condemnations of the coloniser, that he is becoming accustomed to looking at his own people through the eyes of their procurer. True, they are not without defects, nor even without blame. There is concrete foundation for his impatience with them and their values. Almost everything in them is out of style, inefficient and derisory. But what is this? They are his own people, he is and has never ceased to be one of them at heart! Those rhythms balanced for centuries, that food which fills his mouth and stomach so well, they are still his own; they are still himself. Must he, all his life, be ashamed of what is most real in him, of the only things not borrowed? Must he insist on denying himself, and, moreover, will he always be able to endure it? Must his liberation be accomplished through systematic self-denial?

Nonetheless, the major impossibility is not negating one's existence, for he soon discovers that, even if he agrees to everything, he would not be saved. In order to be assimilated, it is not enough to leave one's group, but one must enter another; now he meets with the coloniser's rejection.

All that the colonised has done to emulate the coloniser has met with disdain from the colonial masters. They explain to the colonised that those efforts are in vain, that he thereby only acquires an additional trait, that of being ridiculous. He can never succeed in becoming identified with the coloniser, nor even in copying his role correctly. In the best of circumstances, if he does not want to offend the colonised too much, the coloniser will use all his psychological theories. The national character of peoples is incompatible; every gesture is subtended by the entire spirit, etc. If he is more rude, he will say that the colonised is an ape. The shrewder the ape, the better he imitates, and the more the coloniser becomes irritated. With that vigilance and a smell sharpened by malice, he will track down the tell-tale nuance in clothing or language, the 'lack of good taste' which he always manages to discover. Indeed, a man straddling two cultures is rarely well-seated, and the colonised does not always find the right post.

Everything is mobilised so that the colonised cannot cross the doorstep, so that he understands and admits that this path is dead and assimilation is impossible.

This makes the regrets of humanists in the mother country very hollow, just as their reproach directed to the colonised is unjust. How dare he refuse that wonderful synthesis in which he can only win? It is the colonised who is the first to desire assimilation, and it is the coloniser who refuses it to him.

Now that colonisation is reaching its end, tardy expressions of good will are heard asking whether assimilation was not the great opportunity missed by colonisers and mother countries. 'Ah, if we had only agreed to it! Can't you imagine!', they daydream. 'A France with one hundred million Frenchmen?' It is not forbidden to re-imagine history, and it is often consoling, but only on the condition that you discover another meaning to it, another hidden rationale.

Could assimilation have succeeded? Perhaps it could have at other periods of history. Under the conditions of contemporary colonisation, apparently not. It may be a historical misfortune, and perhaps we should all deplore it together. Not only did it fail, but it appeared impossible to all parties concerned.

In the final analysis, its failure is due not only to the coloniser's bias but also to the colonised's backwardness. Assimilation, whether carried out or not, is not a question of goodwill or psychology alone. A sufficiently long series of happy circumstances can change the fate of an individual. A few of the colonised almost succeeded in disappearing into the coloniser group. It is clear, on the other hand, that a collective drama will never be settled through individual solutions. The individual disappears in his lineage and the group drama goes on. In order for assimilation of the colonised to have both purpose and meaning, it would have to affect an entire people; ie., that the whole colonial condition be changed. However, the colonial condition cannot be changed except by doing away with the colonial relationship.

We again meet with the fundamental relationship which, dynamically meshed one with another, unites our two portraits. We see once again that it is useless to hope to act upon one or the other without affecting that relationship, and therefore, colonisation. To say that the coloniser could, or should, accept assimilation and, hence, the colonised's emancipation, means destroying the colonial relationship. If not, it implies that he can proceed by himself to a complete overthrow of his status by condemning colonial privileges and the exorbitant rights of colonists and industrialists—paying colonised labour fairly, assuring juridical, administrative and political promotion of the colonised, industrialising the colony, etc. In other words, the end of the colony as a colony, and the end of the mother country as a mother country. To put it bluntly, the coloniser would be asked to put an end to himself.

Under the contemporary conditions of colonisation, assimilation and colonisation are contradictory.

What is there left then for the colonised to do? Being unable to change his condition in harmony and communion with the coloniser, he tries to become free despite him: he will revolt.

Far from being surprised at the revolts of colonised people, we should be, on the contrary, surprised that they are not more frequent and more violent. Actually, the coloniser guards against them in many ways: by continuous incapacitation of the leaders and periodic destruction of those who, despite everything, manage to come forward; by corruption or police oppression; by aborting all popular movements and causing their brutal and rapid destruction. We have also noted the doubts of the colonised himself, the inadequacy of the aggressiveness of a vanquished who admires his conqueror despite himself, the long maintained hope that the almighty power of the coloniser might bear the fruit of infinite goodness.

However, revolt is the only way out of the colonial situation, and the colonised realises it sooner or later. His condition is absolute and cries for an absolute solution; a break and not a compromise. He has been torn away from his past and cut off from his future, his traditions are dying and he loses the hope of acquiring a new culture. He has neither language, nor flag, nor technical knowledge, nor national or international existence, nor rights, nor duties. He possesses nothing, is no longer anything and no longer hopes for anything. Moreover, the solution becomes more urgent every day. The mechanism for destroying the colonised cannot but worsen daily. The more oppression increases, the more the coloniser needs justification. The more he must debase the colonised, the more guilty he feels, the more he must justify himself, etc. How can he emerge from this increasingly explosive circle except by rupture, explosion? The colonial situation, by its own internal inevitability, brings on revolt. For the colonial condition cannot be adjusted to; like an iron collar, it can only be broken.

We then witness a reversal of terms. Assimilation being abandoned, the colonised's liberation must be carried out through a recovery of self and of autonomous dignity. Attempts at imitating the coloniser required self-denial; the coloniser's rejection is the indispensable prelude to self-discovery. That accusing and annihilating image must be shaken off; oppression must 'be attacked boldly since it is impossible to go around it. After having been rejected for so long by the coloniser, the day has come when it is the colonised who must refuse the coloniser.

There can be no unconditional desire for assimilation if there is to follow a complete rejection of the model. At the height of his revolt, the colonised still bears the traces and lessons of prolonged cohabitation (just as the smile or movements of a wife, even during divorce proceedings, remind one strangely of those of her husband). The colonised fights in the name of the very values of the coloniser, uses his techniques of thought and his methods of combat. It must be added that this is the only action that the coloniser understands.

Henceforth, the coloniser adopts a negative approach. In particular, he is negatively induced by the active attitude of the colonised. He is challenged at every moment with respect to both his culture and his life, including his motherland. He is suspected, challenged and opposed in the least significant actions. With fury and ostentation, the colonised begins to show a preference for German cars, Italian radios and American refrigerators. He does without tobacco if it bears the colonialist's stamp! These are pressure methods and economic sanctions, but they are, equally, sacrificial rites of colonisation. They continue until the terrible days of the coloniser's fury or the colonised's exasperation, which in turn culminate in hatred and explode into a bloody revolt. Then day-by-day living begins again, but a little more dramatically, more irremediably . . . more contradictory.

It is in this context that the colonised's xenophobia and even a certain racism, must make their return.

Considered *en bloc* as *them, they* or *those*, different from every point of view, homogeneous in a radical heterogeneity, the colonised reacts by rejecting all the colonisers *en bloc*. The distinction between deed and intent has no great significance in the colonial situation. In the eyes of the colonised, all Europeans in the colonies are *de facto* colonisers, and whether they want to be or not, they are colonisers in some ways. By their privileged economic position, by belonging to the political system of oppression, or by participating in an effectively negative complex toward the colonised, they are colonisers. Furthermore, Europeans in Europe itself are potentially colonisers. All they need do is set foot on the colonised's land. Perhaps they even receive some benefit from colonisation. They are supporters, or at least unconscious accomplices, of that great collective aggression of Europe. By their whole weight, intentionally or not, they contribute to the perpetuation of colonial oppression. If xenophobia and racism consist of accusing an entire human group as a whole, condemning each individual of that group, seeing in him an irremediably noxious nature, then the colonised has, indeed, become a xenophobe and a racist.

All racism and all xenophobia consist of delusions about oneself, including absurd and unjust aggression toward others. Included are those of the colonised —the more so when they extend beyond the colonisers to everything which is not strictly colonised. When, for example, they are carried away by enjoyment of the misfortunes of another human group simply because it is not in slavery, they are guilty of xenophobia. However, it must be noted at the same time that the colonised's racism is the result of a more general delusion: the colonialist delusion.

Being considered and treated apart by colonialist racism, the colonised ends up accepting this Manichaean division of the colony and, by extension, of the whole world. Being definitely excluded from half the world, why should he not suspect it of confirming his condemnation? Why should be not judge it and condemn it in his turn? The racism of the colonised is then neither biological nor metaphysical, but social and historical. It is not based on a belief in the inferiority of the detested group but on the conviction, and in large measure on the observation, that this group is truly an aggressor and dangerous. Furthermore, while modern Europen racism hates and scorns more than it fears, that of the colonised fears and also continues to admire. In brief, it is not aggressive but defensive racism.

Thus, it should be relatively easy to appease. The few European voices raised during these past few years to repudiate this exclusion and inhumanity of the colonised, did more than all the good works and philanthropy in which segregation remained subjacent. That is why one can say that though the xenophobia and racism of the colonised undoubtedly contain enormous resentment and are a negative force, they could be the prelude to a positive movement, the regaining of self-control by the colonised.

However, at the beginning, the colonised's claim is narrowly limited and conditioned by the colonial situation and the requirements of the coloniser.

The colonised accepts and asserts himself with passion. But who is he? Surely not man in general, the holder of universal values common to all men. In fact, he has been excluded from that universality, both in word and in fact. On the contrary, what makes him different from other men has been sought out and hardened to the point of substantiation. He has been haughtily shown that he could never assimilate with others; he has been scornfully thrown back toward what is in him which could not be assimilated by others. Very well, then! He is, he shall be, that man. The same passion which made him admire and absorb Europe shall make him assert his differences; since those differences, after all, are within him and correctly constitute his true self.

Now, the young intellectual who had broken with religions, internally at least, and ate during Ramadan, begins to fast with ostentation. He who considered the rites as inevitable family drudgery, re-introduces them into his social life, gives them a place in his conception of the world. To use them better, he re-explains the forgotten messages and adapts them to present-day needs. He then discovers that religion is not simply an attempt to communicate with the invisible, but also an extraordinary place of communion for the whole group. The colonised, his leaders and intellectuals, his traditionalists and liberals, all classes of society, can meet there, reinforce their bonds, verify and re-create their unity. Of course, their is a considerable risk that the means become the end. Assigning attention to the old myths, giving them virility, he regenerates them dangerously. They find in this an unexpected power which makes them extend beyond the limited intentions of the colonised's leaders. We see a true return to religion. It may even happen that the sorcerer's apprentice, the intellectual or liberal bourgeois, to whom secularisation appeared to be the condition for all intellectual and social progress, might be attracted to those neglected traditions, that his pressured mind . . . .

However, all that which seems so important in the eyes of an outside observer, and which is so perhaps for the general welfare of the people, is basically secondary to the colonised. He has now discovered the motivating principle of his battle. He must bolster his people and affirm his own solidarity with it. Obviously, his religion is one of the constituent elements of that people. At Bandung, to the astonishment and embarrassment of leftists all over the world, one of the two fundamental principles of the conference was religion.

Likewise, the colonised no longer knew his language except in the form of a lowly dialect. In order to emerge from the most elementary monotony and emotions, he had to borrow the coloniser's language. In recovering his auton-omous and separate destiny, he immediately goes back to his own tongue. It is pointed out to him that its vocabulary is limited, its syntax bastardised. It would be comical to hear a course in higher mathematics or philosophy in it. Even the left-wing coloniser is surprised by this unnecessary challenge which is more costly in the long run to the colonised than to the coloniser. Why not go on using Western languages to describe motors or teach abstract subjects?

Again, there exist other urgent matters for the colonised besides mathematics and philosophy and even technology. To this self-rediscovery movement of an entire people must be returned the most appropriate tool; that which finds the shortest path to its soul, because it comes directly from it. That path is words of love and tenderness, anger and indignation, words which the potter uses when talking to his pots, and the shoemaker to his soles. Education will come later, and so will the humanities and sciences. These people have learned all too well how to wait. Besides, is it certain that this language which stammers today is unable to develop and become rich? Thanks to him, it is already discovering forgotten treasures. It is beginning to see a possible continuity with a past which is not inconsequential. No more hesitation and half-measures! On the contrary, one must know how to break through, one must know how to forge ahead. He will even choose the greatest of all difficulties. He will go so far as to prohibit any additional conveniences of the coloniser's tongue; he will replace it as often and as soon as he can. Between the vulgar tongue and scholarly language, he will give preference to the scholarly, running the risk of making the sought-after communion more arduous. The important thing now is to rebuild his people, whatever be their authentic nature; to reform their unity, communicate with it and to feel that they belong.

This must be done no matter what the price paid by the colonised. Thus he will be nationalistic but not, of course, internationalistic. Naturally, by so doing, he runs the risk of falling into exclusionism and chauvinism, of sticking to the most narrow principles, and of setting national solidarity against human solidarity—and even ethnic solidarity against national solidarity. But to expect the colonised to open his mind to the world and be a humanist and inter-nationalist would seem to be ludicrous thoughtlessness. He is still regaining possession of himself, still examining himself with astonishment, passionately demanding the return of his language.

Moreover, it is remarkable that he is even more ardent in asserting himself as he tries to assume the identity of the coloniser. Is it a coincidence that so many colonised leaders contracted mixed marriages, or that the Tunisian leader Bourguiba, the two Algerian leaders Messali Hadj and Ferhat Abbas, and several other nationalists who have devoted their lives to leading their own people, chose a wife from among the colonisers? Having penetrated the coloniser's experience to the highest limit, to the point of finding it un-livable, they withdrew to their own bases. Whoever has not left his country and his people will never understand to what extent those are dear to him. Now they know that their salvation coincides with that of their people, and that they must cling as closely as possible to them and to their traditions.

The necessity of self-renewal is as obvious as the ambiguity involved. While the colonised's revolt is a clear attitude in itself, its contents may be muddled; for it is the result of an unclear situation—the colonial situation.

First, by taking up the challenge of exclusion, the colonised accepts being separate and different, but his individuality is that which is limited and defined by the coloniser.

Thus he embodies religion and tradition, ineptitude for technology of a special nature which we call Eastern, etc. Yes, that is quite right, he agrees with it. A black author did his best to explain to us that the nature of the blacks, his own people, is not compatible with mechanised civilisation. He drew a curious pride from that. So then, no doubt provisionally, the colonised admits that he corresponds to that picture of himself which the coloniser has thrust upon him. He is starting a new life but continues to subscribe to the colonisers' deception.

To be sure, he does not arrive at it by a purely ideological process; he is not only defined by the coloniser, but his situation is shaped by colonisation. It is obvious that he is reclaiming a people that is suffering deficiencies in its body and spirit, in its responses. He is restored to a not very glorious history pierced through with frightful holes, to a moribund culture which he had planned to abandon, to frozen traditions, to a rusted tongue. The heritage which he eventually accepts bears the burden of a liability which would discourage anyone. He must endorse notes and debts, the debts being many and large. It is also a fact that the institutions of the colony do not operate directly for him. The educational system is directed to him only haphazardly. The roads are open to him only because they are pure offerings.

But to go all the way with his revolt, it seems necessary to him to accept those inhibitions and amputations. He will forego the use of the coloniser's language, even if all the locks of the country turn with that key; he will change the signs and highway markings, even if he is the first to be inconvenienced. He will prefer a long period of educational mistakes to the continuance of the coloniser's school organisation. He will choose institutional disorder in order to destroy the institutions built by the coloniser as soon as possible. There we see, indeed, a reactive drive of profound protest. He will no longer owe anything to the coloniser and will have definitely broken with him. But this also involves a confused and misleading conviction: everything that belongs to the coloniser is not appropriate for the colonised. That is just what the coloniser always told him. Briefly, the rebellious colonised begins by accepting himself as something negative.

A second point is that the negative element has become an essential part of his revival and struggle, and will be proclaimed and glorified to the hilt. Not only does he accept his wrinkles and his wounds, but he will consider them praiseworthy. Gaining self-assurance, offering himself to the world just as he is, he can hardly propose criticism of himself at the same time. While he knows how to overthrow the coloniser and colonisation, he cannot cause the end of what he truly is and what he so disastrously acquired during colonisation. He offers himself as a whole and agrees that he is what he is—that colonised being which he has become. Suddenly, exactly to the reverse of the colonialist accusation, the colonised, his culture, his country, everything that belongs to him, everything he represents, become perfectly positive elements.

We shall ultimately find ourselves before a counter-mythology. The negative myth thrust on him by the coloniser is succeeded by a positive myth about himself suggested by the colonised—just as there would seem to be a positive myth of the proletarian opposed to a negative one. To hear the colonised and often his friends, everything is good, everything must be retained among his customs and traditions, his actions and plans; even the anachronous or disorderly, the immoral or mistaken. Everything is justified because everything can be explained.

The colonised's self-assertion, born out of protest, continues to define itself in relation to it. In the midst of revolt, the colonised continues to think, feel and live against and, therefore, in relation to the coloniser and colonisation.

It must also be said that the colonised recognises this, revealing it in his conduct, and even admitting it at times. Realising that these attitudes are essentially reactions, he suffers from the pangs of bad faith.

Uncertain of himself, he gives in to the intoxication of fury and violence. In fact, he asserts himself vigorously. Uncertain of being able to convince others, he provokes them. Simultaneously provocative and sensitive, he now makes a display of his contrasts, refuses to let himself be forgotten as such, and becomes indignant when they are mentioned. Automatically distrustful, he assumes hostile intentions in those with whom he converses and reacts accordingly. He demands endless approval from his best friends, of even that which he doubts and himself condemns. Frustrated by history for too long, he makes demands all the more imperiously as he continues to be restless. He no longer knows what he owes to himself and what he can ask, what others actually owe him and what he must pay in return. He complicates and confuses, *a priori*, his human relationships, which history has already made so difficult. 'Oh, they are sick!', wrote one black author. 'They are all sick!'

So goes the drama of the man who is a product and victim of colonisation. He almost never succeeds in corresponding with his true self.

Colonised painting, for instance, is balanced between two poles. From excessive submission to Europe resulting in depersonalisation, it passes to such a violent return to self that it is noxious and esthetically illusory. The right balance not being found, the self-accusation continues. Before and during the revolt, the colonised always considers the coloniser as a model or as an antithesis. He continues to struggle against him. He was torn between what he was and what he wanted to be, and now he is torn between what he wanted to be and what he is making of himself. Nonetheless, the painful discord with himself continues.

In order to witness the colonised's complete cure, his alienation must completely cease. We must await the complete disappearance of colonisation—including the period of revolt.

12 The Meaning of Black Consciousness in the Struggle for Liberation in South Africa*

RANWEDZI NENGWEKHULU

The Meaning of Black Consciousness: An Overview

A proper analysis of Black Consciousness should, we believe, begin with its adequate and comprehensive definition, which would serve as a context within which we could then begin an exposition of the philosophy and ideology which are the basic tenets of Black Consciousness.

The 1972 Policy Manifesto of the South African Students' Organisation (SASO) defines Black Consciousness as 'an attitude of mind, a way of life whose basic tenet is that the black must reject all value systems that seek to make him a foreigner in the country of birth and reduce his basic human dignity'. The concept of Black Consciousness therefore implies an awareness of and pride in their blackness by black people and implies that black people should and must appreciate their value as human beings.

Black Consciousness also means that black people should be aware of the significance and importance of their own value systems, ie. their socio-economic, political and cultural values. Implied in this appreciation of their value systems is the need to reject those foreign, alien values that were forced down black people's throats as part of the oppressor's logic of maintaining and perpetrating his brutal system of exploitation and emasculation.

Thus the essence of this search for our indigenous value systems is the need to redefine ourselves and our value systems which are today engulfed in the foreign, alien, exploitative and oppressive values which have been imposed upon us, both physically and psychologically, by our oppressors in order to make us malleable to subjugation. The challenge of Black Consciousness for any black man in South Africa today is the need for a new and incisive redefinition, reidentification and reappraisal of the black totality in the context of a capitalist, racist and exploitative South Africa, presided over by a self-appointed white minority acting as the missionary of international capitalism and finance capital.

Another significant aspect of Black Consciousness is the call for cohesive group solidarity, ie. black solidarity. Thus the quintessence of Black Consciousness is the realisation and acceptance of blacks in South Africa that, in order to play a positive role in the struggle for liberation and emancipation, they must effectively employ the concept of group power and thereby build a strong base from which to counter the oppressor's policy of divide and rule. The philosophy of Black Consciousness therefore means group pride and determination by black people in South Africa to rise together from the death-bed of oppression and exploitation.

---

*Paper circulated by the United Nations Centre Against Apartheid, Department of Political and Security Council Affairs, July 1976. The author worked as a full-time organiser for the South African Students' Organisation between 1971 and 1973.

At the heart of Black Consciousness is also the realisation by blacks that the most potent and effective weapon of oppression and exploitation in the hands of the oppressor is the mind of the oppressed. In South Africa, the oppressor has attempted to twist and manipulate our minds to make us mentally and psychologically pliable to his exploitation and manipulation.

Black Consciousness therefore calls for a psychological revolution in the black community; this will be a revolution which is directed towards the elimination of all stereotypes by blacks about themselves, and one which is directed towards the complete eradication of the slave mentality and feelings of inadequacy characteristic of an oppressed and exploited society. The basic logic inherent in Black Consciousness is that no people can wage a meaningful war of liberation unless and until they have effectively eradicated their slave mentality and accepted themselves as full human beings who have a role to play in their own salvation.

Black Consciousness therefore forces black people to see themselves as full human beings, complete, full and total in themselves, and not as extensions of others.

Some people have accused proponents of Black Consciousness of rejecting and spurning a coalition between white liberals and the blacks. However, assessment and evaluation of the history of the involvement of the white liberal establishment in the black struggle have convinced us that white liberals have indeed been criminally responsible for arresting and aborting the struggle by playing the role of a bulwark, a kind of buffer zone between the blacks and the white system which has been oppressing us for centuries. In fact, to us, the white liberal establishment is part and parcel of the white system; indeed, the driving force behind the white liberal establishment's involvement in the black struggle is its desire to kill the revolutionary zeal of the black masses by promising them a 'controlled' change which will result in some mystical, 'mosaic' multi-racialism. This multi-racialism is never defined precisely lest it reveal to blacks that it is nothing but a polished and sophisticated version of the racist system which has been responsible for the dehumanisation of blacks in South Africa.

Implications of Community Projects in the Context of Black Consciousness in South Africa

One of the basic tenets of Black Consciousness which SASO has emphasised is the development of socio-political awareness among blacks in South Africa, ie. to activate the black community into thinking seriously and positively about the socio-economic and political problems that beset them in their country, and to seek solutions to emancipate themselves from these dehumanising shackles.

This aim is to be achieved chiefly through community projects, which, as devised and run by the Black Consciousness movement in South Africa, is designed 'to heighten the sense of awareness and encourage blacks to become involved in the political, economic and social development of the black people'.

Thus SASO sees itself as a training ground for future black leaders who will relate to the black community and will be capable of assessing and directing the attitudes, goals and aspirations of the black community.

Vicious white racism and massive economic exploitation have placed upon black people a psychological yoke of despondency, helplessness and dependency which kills the initiative, originality and will of a people. The creative instincts and skills of black people have not surfaced primarily because of lack of opportunities, but also because they have come to rely on whites who, ironically, are their oppressors and who would not open avenues for the social and political development of their victims. We have, indeed, shockingly perhaps, come to rely on whites even for our own salvation.

It is for this reason that SASO and other Black Consciousness movements saw fit to take as its ideology one which heightens the awareness and consciousness of black people, and confronts them with the realities of their situation, ie. their oppression and exploitation. Only in this way will it be possible to redirect black energies towards the goal of black liberation and emancipation.

The concept of Black Consciousness implies the awareness by black people of the power they wield as a group, both economically and politically. Hence group cohesion and solidarity are important elements of that ideology, all the more so in view of the 'divide and rule' colonial strategy practised by the white establishment. Our endeavour, therefore, is to try to arouse the entire black community to strive for its liberation.

Thus the main aim of our community development projects is to inculcate in our people a sense of self-reliance, initiative and solidarity that is essential in our struggle to free ourselves from white racism, capitalism, colonialism and psychological servitude instilled in us during all these centuries of colonial emasculation.

One must, however, also be patient when one is involved in community development geared towards raising consciousness and political awareness. One should never assume that it is easy to eradicate psychological attitudes which took the oppressor centuries to cultivate.

Another problem we face in our community development projects is in the area of communication between the community and students. Perhaps one of the ugliest aspects of oppression is that the oppressor systematically cuts off meaningful communication among the oppressed. In fact it is one of the essential aspects of the oppressor's strategy to keep the oppressed divided and not to allow communication among them lest they plot against him.

Thus, police harassment, intimidation, banning orders and other means are employed to make it difficult for the oppressed to organise themselves. One must constantly fight against fear—a ubiquitous factor in the black community that handicaps even the most ardent exponent of Black Consciousness.

It is fear founded on the realities of the situation—fear of finding oneself on Robben Island or banned—that has led to the frightening silence in the black community in South Africa. The regime wastes no time in sustaining and perpetuating this fear in order to preserve and perpetuate the *status quo*. Indeed, all the factors that create this epidemic of fear in our community have become integral parts of the entire societal structure in South Africa.

Black people know that the whole structure is against them. Hence it is not the individual white they are afraid of. It is the entire racist monolithic white structure that has lynched, maimed and exploited them.

One is thus faced with the problem of convincing our people that, despite the real and great hazards, we must do something positive about our fate: we have to fight for our liberation.

This is why we try to communicate with our people through community projects rather than inviting them to a political discussion, which they would often be afraid to attend. In this way we develop rapport between them and ourselves. Once confidence has been built up it becomes easier to talk about more fundamental issues of liberation.

Indeed, the basic rationale behind our community projects is that community development is inherently liberating because it enables a person to become aware of the inadequacy of his present situation and, moreover, it enables him to act or respond in such a way that he will be able to bring about change in his situation.

We are aware of the fact that the greatest danger inherent in all community development projects designed to bring about change in the community, and to instil a sense of self-reliance, is that these projects may potentially become welfare projects. The basic difference between welfare projects and projects oriented towards social action and self-reliance is that the former are based on the principle of helping the victims to survive in the very situation that is responsible for their condition, rather than attempting to assist the victims to help themselves. In other words, the main purpose of welfare projects is to alleviate suffering rather than to eradicate the source of evil. Welfare projects have never created a revolution, and they are not likely to ignite one; in fact, they destroy and annihilate all elements necessary for a revolution.

Our community development projects on the other hand are designed to instil a sense of self-reliance and initiative in our people. Thus the aim of our community development programme is to politicise and revitalise black individuals to help them to deliver themselves from the situation.

When we talk of community development projects, we mean projects that will revolutionise and transform the entire colonial capitalist society in which we live, and thereby to destroy forever the economic exploitation and dependency of our people.

We have designed our community projects as means of assisting our people to find themselves, and also to create a conducive climate for creative rapport and communion between black students and the black community as a whole, a communion that is essential for our liberation.

One of the most important and essential aspects of our community development projects is a programme of leadership training both for the students and the community. In this way we try to give the participants the basic theoretical and practical skills of leadership in dealing with an oppressive and exploitative situation. This is in fact political education. It also has the aim of minimising the chances of our projects becoming simply welfare projects.

What we always keep in mind is that the project must always involve the community it is intended to assist ie., we must work *with* the community rather than *for* the community.

The Black Political Climate in the 1960s and the Formation of SASO

The outlawing of the African National Congress (ANC) and the Pan-Africanist Congress (PAC) in 1960 and the Sharpeville massacre of the same year brought about a certain amount of political quietness in the black community for the major part of the 1960s. This quietness was perhaps understandable when one takes into consideration that there were no political organisations around which black people could rally. Other black organisations like the Non-European Unity Movement (NEUM) did not have a large following.

With the banning and outlawing of the ANC and PAC, the Sharpeville massacre and the subsequent mass arrests, trials, detention and imprisonment of black leaders, blacks began to feel that it was futile for them to become involved in politics. Fear and frustration therefore was the dominant mood of the 1960s, even though a number of blacks continued to be arrested and tried for their political activities. It was particularly on the student level, however, that there was still some political activity, and a number of black student associations were formed after the banning of the ANC and PAC.

These black student associations, however, formed along sectional political lines. For example, students who owed allegiance to the ANC formed the African Students Association (ASA) and those loyal to the PAC formed the African Students Union of South Africa (ASUSA). Students whose ideological affiliations were those of NEUM formed the Durban Students Union (Natal) and the (Cape) Peninsula Students Union; these two later merged to form the Progressive National Students Organisation.

These associations saw themselves as national organisations and, as such, concerned themselves with national issues. However, the ideological differences of the ANC, PAC and NEUM were so acute as to preclude any idea of cooperation or amalgamation. Their differences also stemmed from relationships with the National Union of South African Students (NUSAS). Both ASUSA and the Progressive National Students Organisation were fanatically opposed to any cooperation with whites. Perhaps the fact that for a long time black students never attained any strong and viable solidarity on the campuses was attributable to these divided loyalties.

This also led to a damaging lack of coordination and progress in the articulation of the interests and aspirations of black students. Furthermore, NUSAS was by no means a spent force among black students and commanded an appreciable following. Eventually, the differences between ASA, ASUSA and the Progressive National Students Organisation coupled with intimidation and harassment of the leadership of these associations by university authorities and the police led to the collapse of both ASA and ASUSA.

With the establishment of separate universities for blacks, a period of isolation ensued for black students. Furthermore, none of these universities was allowed to have any contact with NUSAS, the only student association which assumed the role of a spokesman for the plight of black students. Dogged by fear of victimisation by university authorities and of harassment by the security police and colonies of informers, and in view of the general political apathy pervading the entire black community, many black students resigned themselves to tolerate the situation pertaining on the campuses and in the country as a whole.

There was also growing disillusionment and disenchantment with NUSAS. Concern was expressed that such organisations as NUSAS and the University Christian Movement were white-dominated and, as such, paid very little attention to the particular problems of the black student community. In fact, some people began to doubt the very competence of a pluralistic group to examine without bias problems affecting one group, especially where the unaffected group is from the oppressor camp. It was felt that a time had come when blacks had to formulate their own thinking unpolluted by ideas emanating from a group with a good deal at stake in the *status quo*.

By 1967 there was a noticeable resurgence of political interest among black students, while in the general black community the word 'politics' was still considered a taboo. This then was the political climate in the black community in 1968, when the South African Students' Organisation (SASO) was formed.

The Impact of Black Consciousness on the South African Political Scene

The advent of Black Consciousness is South Africa has had a tremendous impact on both whites and blacks. For whites, the Black Consciousness movement represents the imminent unleashing of a black avalanche that is about to engulf them and thereby upset the *status quo*. Whites fear that the 'beautiful' and 'healthy' society which they believe they have so painstakingly built around the 'virtues' and 'values' of a 'superior' Western civilisation and culture will be destroyed.

Even the white liberal establishment, traditionally assumed to be the friend, ally and comrade of the oppressed blacks, has been shocked by the birth and growth of Black Consciousness. To the white liberal establishment, Black Consciousness is 'bad' because it has destroyed the basis of the society they claimed they were attempting to build. The Black Consciousness movement has destroyed the whole pseudo-philosophy of the so-called multi-racialism. Perhaps the anger and frustration of the white liberal establishment and its hostile, though somewhat subdued, reaction towards the Black Consciousness movement is understandable if one looks at it from the point of view of an advocate of multi-racialism.

Indeed the first main focus of the attack by the Black Consciousness movement was the white liberal establishment itself because we believed that it was the cause of the frustrations that have characterised our struggle. Before the advent of Black Consciousness the white liberal establishment, with a certain amount of arrogance, abrogated to itself the role of the natural leader and pace setter of the black struggle in South Africa. The Black Consciousness movement has completely destroyed this myth. There is no doubt that the black struggle will never again experience the pangs inflicted by this group of arrogant white 'messiahs'. We have always been convinced that we do not need white liberals to further our struggle.

The impact of Black Consciousness on the general white community was on the whole even more devastating because to them it was inconceivable that blacks could organise themselves so effectively without the assistance of the white liberals who had always run the affairs of blacks, claiming to be the champions of the black cause which, in any case, they never understood and they can never understand.

Generally-speaking, the reaction of the white community, including the white liberal establishment, has been characterised by the desire and determination to destroy the black consciousness movement. There are certain individual whites, however, who have tried to accommodate themselves to the existence of the movement, if only because they realised that black consciousness had come to stay.

The failure of the white community to uproot black consciousness has been reflected in the massive arrests of its exponents and the trials and persecutions which are going on at present in South Africa.

The impact of black consciousness on the black community has also been tremendous. There is no doubt that black consciousness is accepted by the vast majority of black people. Although initially the response of the black community was mixed, we now enjoy massive support among our people. The popularity of black consciousness today is also reflected in the fact that even the regime's stooges and puppets in the Bantustans are paying lip-service to Black Consciousness because they realise that they lack the power and resources to counter its growing popularity.

Indeed the popularity and the support enjoyed by the movement is understandable because it was the only viable movement to emerge in the aftermath of the Sharpeville massacre and the outlawing of the PAC and ANC. We are convinced that despite the present persecutions by the regime, the Black Consciousness movement will survive to witness the birth of Azania in South Africa.

We have been attacked by certain organisations and individuals, but we are convinced that we are on the right track in our desire to create a society in which there will not be any exploitation of man by man and consequent alienation of man from himself.

Another point which should be mentioned is that the Black Consciousness movement has played, and continues to play, an important role in the reactivation of political awareness among the black people of South Africa. This role has been underplayed internationally. Black Consciousness has come to stay and has become a political force to reckon with. All the strikes that have occurred in the country since 1970 are a reflection of the role being played, directly or indirectly, by the movement.

Finally, we wish to affirm our belief that radical change and transformation, and the creation of an egalitarian society in South Africa and the birth of a proud Azania, can only come about by blacks coming together and uniting to form a black solidarity movement; this is the objective we have set for ourselves. The rejection and exclusion from our movement of all members from the enemy camp is a precondition for this solidarity. In our endeavour to build this solidarity, we will also bear in mind that the black stooges who are furthering the regime's Bantustan policy and the balkanisation of our country have chosen to become appendages of the white oppressive power structure and, as such, they have no place in this black solidarity.

So we in the Black Consciousness movement are determined to march forward until we achieve our goal. Time is on our side and victory assuredly ours.

13 Education Policy in the People's Republic of Mozambique*

The People's Republic of Mozambique is a very new member of the international community of independent and sovereign states, having gained its independence on 25 June 1975. We have much to learn, which is what we hope to do at this Conference, and have many new challenges to face. But at the same time we have the benefit of ten years of armed liberation struggle, and the wide experience of organising and administering vast areas of our country which were gradually freed from Portuguese colonial domination.

During these years we forged a tool, moulded through months and years of hard people's fight for the construction of a new society: we have a solid political line, and a vanguard movement with the organisation and discipline to ensure the implementation of this line. When we speak of educational policy we are then talking about Frelimo's political line as it is manifested in this sector. The commitment to build a new society, based on equality and the elimination of the exploitation of man by man, and the definition of the enemy as being capitalism and imperialism, indicate immediately the kind of education we do not want in our country and the kind of educational system we must introduce.

Traditional and Colonial Education

Though differing in method, the kinds of education provided both by our own traditional society and by Portuguese colonialism shared similar objectives and characteristics: the perpetuation of the existing oppressive system of class divisions by the inculcation of passive subservience, the stifling of initiative, and the fostering of superstitious beliefs in supernatural forces that control man and his environment. Since it was the colonial educational system that we have encountered in an institutionalised form, we would like to examine its workings in a little more detail, while pointing out that the negative aspects of traditional education still exist and have to be equally vigorously combatted.

The aim of colonial education was the strengthening of Portuguese colonialism through the implantation of Portuguese cultural, social, and political values, and the destruction of all that was African: our society, our culture, and our personality. At school a Mozambican pupil was taught to deny his true self, to constantly strive to emulate the Portuguese way of life, and to be a useful intermediary between the colonialists and the illiterate mass of his fellow countrymen.

All the programmes came from Portugal, all the books, all the administrators, all the qualified teachers, all the examinations. Mozambique existed as a far-flung European island, cut off from its own history and geographical perspective, and as effectively isolated from the rest of its African continent as if the miles

* Statement by the Delegation from Maputo to the Conference of Ministers of Education of African Member States of UNESCO held in Lagos from 27 January to 4 February 1976. Official Government Paper reprinted in *Journal of Modern African Studies*, 14, 2 (1976), pp. 331–9.

that separated Mozambique from Portugal in fact separated Mozambique from Africa.

Our colleagues here today are, we know, only too familiar with such a situation, which was effectively directed to the needs of the European settlers In Mozambique, however, it was considerably reinforced by the Roman Catholic Church, which in 1940 was handed all responsibility for the education of the 'indigenous', as we were called. The Church's interpretation of its duties in this respect were clearly defined in 1960 by the Cardinal Patriarch of Lisbon when he said:

> We try to reach the native population . . . reading, writing and arith-
> metic, not to make 'doctors' of them . . . . To educate and instruct
> them . . . [in] the path of good sense and of political and social security
> for the province . . . schools are necessary, yes, but schools where we
> teach the native . . . the grandeur of the nation which protects him.

This so-called education had religion as the dominant factor, with literacy and Portuguese so as to be able to read the Bible, and some maths so as to calculate better the compulsory quota of cotton production, or to be more lucrative 'boss-boys' in South African mines. Our children grew up with a deformed picture of the world composed of those destined to govern and those destined to serve, where the educated work with their heads and despise the uneducated who perform with their hands the lowest form of work, physical labour. Instead of being the agent of change of his society and environment, man was the subservient recipient of divine will.

Divided by tribes, divided by religions, divided into those who had assimilated 'civilised' ways and those who had not, divided into those from the towns and those from the countryside—all and every tactic was used to prevent our people from seeing that they had everything in common, that they were a people with a national identity, suffering from the same exploitation and forming the same class.

These divisions even extended to the teachers, and we have inherited five or six different categories of primary-school staff—for example, each with different preparation, salaries, and privileges. Obviously, the most poorly trained, poorly paid, and overworked are the African Mozambicans.

The state schools were reinforced by an extensive network of private institutions for those who wanted and could afford what they considered to be a better education for their children. This was but a logical consequence of a system rooted in class distinction, competition, and individualism, where the 'haves'—who can mobilise the most financial resources and show the most ruthless egoism—benefit most, and the 'have-nots' remain that way.

In sum, beyond the boundaries of the areas liberated by Frelimo, all schools were based on racism, divisionism, elitism, individualism, obscurantism, and contempt for everything Africa. Many a Mozambican who managed to surmount the enormous obstacles to secondary or higher education, did so at the cost of turning himself into a little black Portuguese, the docile instrument of colonialism, whose ambition was to live like a settler, in whose image he was created.

It was this system, with all its implications and consequences implanted over some 40 years, that we encountered with independence.

Frelimo's Educational Policy

In Mozambique we have been waging a revolutionary struggle—and, despite political independence, we still are—against all forms of exploitation, for a new society where political and economic power is in the hands of the people. It follows then that the educational process must also serve the entire nation.

Some may claim that this is the aim of almost any African government; that universal education is an obvious necessity if a country wants to develop its full potential, and that this is always the ideal, if not necessarily always attainable. But this is to confuse objectives with strategy. Most capitalist countries now have universal education, but the use to which this is put is the strengthening of the capitalist system.

For us, an education that serves the people is one where those who receive it use their knowledge to benefit others, not to exploit nor oppress them. Thus, it is not an ideal, nor is it just a pragmatic solution to a social problem. It is an important basic political principle. In the words of our President, Samora Moises Machel: 'He who has studied should be the match that comes to light the flame that is the people'.

The new revolutionary education is aimed at forming a Mozambican African personality, a New Man, free from all complexes of superiority and inferiority, free from superstitious beliefs, self-reliant and ready to make his scientific knowledge the basis of the new society based on unity and equality. In sum, education for us is the principle instrument for our liberation, for our real political, economic, social, and cultural independence.

Given the objective conditions of our country the strategy to attain these objectives must include the provision of a basic scientific education for our illiterate population. It follows that a high priority must be given to adult and primary education.

The many tasks we face in national reconstruction in independent Mozambique present very similar problems to those that confronted us during the war—notably a shortage of trained cadres who are consequently called upon to do all and everything. The solutions we defined then are equally valid today. Continuous education is a luxury we cannot necessarily afford in all spheres. Instead, education must be permanent and progressive: permanent in that it provides possibilities for people to constantly raise their knowledge through specialised, intensive courses and seminars; and progressive in that a pupil does not continue straight from kindergarten to university but advances in stages, and at the end of each goes out to work, to increase his knowledge through practice, to use his knowledge for the benefit of the nation, only later returning to the point where he left off.

As we said during the war: 'We cannot wait to form generals to wage the battle'—we learn as we do and by doing. To give one example: comrades in the liberated areas who had *segunda classe* taught *primeira classe*, developing their knowledge and skills through constant meetings with other teachers in the district where they discussed and prepared lessons together. They then passed on to teaching even *terçeira classe*, constantly following the same method. Meetings and seminars at provincial level were also frequent to refresh our knowledge and to exchange experiences on the basis that if we draw together the little knowledge we have the sum total will be important.

At the national level too we met and discussed, despite all the difficulties inherent in a war situation. In September 1967 a special commission submitted its report on the definition of a national education policy. At the end of 1968 there took place the first conference of the Department of Education and Culture (DEC) of Frelimo which defined the objectives and role of education in the revolution. October 1970 saw the second conference of DEC, and in January

1972 the first national cultural seminar. A year later a national pedagogic seminar analysed our programmes and teaching methods, and in April and May 1974 teachers from all the liberated areas came together to discuss policies and methods in our first literacy seminar.

Higher cadres are also necessary, but in view of the great responsibilities that await them it has always been our guiding principle to select candidates as much for their political consciousness and capacity for work as for their intellectual ability. The courses they follow, and the way they use their advanced skills, must always serve the revolutionary process. We cannot afford the luxury of graduate research in aerodynamics when our secondary schools have no physics textbooks and 95 per cent of our people cannot write their own name or read a newspaper. Anyone who has knowledge must communicate it and put it at the service of the people. To quote our President again: 'If the seed is locked in the drawer we can never harvest the fruit'.

Another important aspect of our educational strategy is the symbiotic relationship between study and physical work. The watchword of our pupils has been: Study, Produce, Fight—a permanent reminder that we must always combat isolationist academic elitism, that study without practical application is worthless. When everyone participates in productive manual work on the basis of complete equality, each learns from the other, and the barriers between intellectual and illiterate, between teacher and pupil, are removed by the hoe and the shovel. We all put our knowledge to the practical test, we make mistakes and learn from them. In the revolution manual work is praised, not despised, for it helps us to develop our sense of class, it makes us aware of the class we come from and that we represent; and by working together we get to know each other, thus contributing to our greater unity. It is also the practical and effective manifestation of our spirit of self-reliance.

The methods and programmes we use are defined by our objectives. A capitalist, individualist, competitive society produces—and it is the product of —a capitalist, individualist, competitive mentality. In order to break this vicious circle, society must change our mentality through practice—the practice of collective work and study, of democratic participation, of working out new kinds of relations between people.

Ten pupils with adequate marks who help each other and study collectively are worth much more to us than one 'genius' who works on his own. However, collective study must be organised and disciplined, part of a structured system, if it is to show positive results and not provide a refuge for the lazy or a vehicle for the smart.

Our schools are democratic centres, structured in such a way as to incorporate all the workers there—pupils, teachers, and employees—in running the school together. The base units are study groups which form sections which form one class. Running vertically through the school are sections of activity covering culture, production, hygiene etc, which send representatives to a management committee that works with the headmaster. It is in the practice of assuming responsibility that our youth learn to be responsible and to develop their creative initiative.

It is also the means by which we learn to develop new relations of mutual respect, assistance, and confidence between us, supported by a constant process of criticism and self-criticism, where we learn to recognise our errors and those of others. A revolutionary teacher is not one who can quote a series of revolutionary tracts, but one who learns from his pupils and is open to criticism from everyone—including them—who fights for the new values and the new mentality through his own example. Similarly, the revolutionary pupil is conscious that to study is a task confided by the people with a much more noble purpose than the simple acquisition of diplomas.

The programmes and structures we developed in the liberated areas, and which are now being implemented through the rest of the country, are the direct result of this close comradely pupil-teacher relationship. For ten years we lived together the revolutionary process of practice, theory, practice—or, in other words, of acting, formulating, putting to the test, analysing, reviewing, and developing further.

Transition and Independence

The principles and policies that brought us independence have not changed in the post-independence period. Clearly we are facing many new·problems and on a national scale, but because our political line is correct it is as valid now as then. We cannot permit our schools to remain diploma-giving factories that generate social and economic divisions. The people built the schools, colleges, and the university, and they must reap the benefits.

In the sixteen months since the Lusaka Agreement and the formation of the transitional government, when Frelimo took office for the first time, we have continued to apply our collective methods of work to the solution of problems. One of our first priorities was the reactionary and alienatory school programme. We called teachers from all over the country to come and fuse their many experiences and ideas through a national education seminar into a single experience. At the beginning, the fact that the teachers had never previously questioned the content of the lessons they taught showed in their work, revealing their stifling background. Either they expected the Frelimo participants to tell them what to do, just as the colonial government had done, or they thought it was sufficient to simply·substitute the word Mozambique for Portugal.

However, through collective discussion they' soon realised that much more was involved. They began to see that teaching geography did not mean learning by heart the principal rivers and mountains in Mozambique, but showing how man is the agent of change of his environment, how and why our country is as it is—because of the economic requirements of the colonial power—and how it must be changed. Teaching Portuguese correctly is not just a question of grammar and syntax, but of the content of the text too. Perhaps, most important of all, our teachers learned that although the sciences are concerned with verifiable concrete facts this does not mean that what is taught is universally the same. The selection of material and the way it is communicated always reflects the prevailing ideology. Books—such as existed in Mozambique— which claim that the difference between animal and man is that the latter has a soul, implant an unreal view of the world and the role of science in the minds of our children.

These few examples show what we mean by the imperative necessity to relate what is taught in our schools to the practical realities of our life.

The new programmes were immediately put into effect in the middle of the academic year. Religious instruction was removed from the school, and political instruction and productive manual work were introduced, to form together the motive force in the mobilisation and formation of a new mentality among our students. The politics studied in the classroom are put into practice in daily school life, in particular through the political administrative structures, also reviewed and improved in the seminar.

This presents yet another challenge for teachers. Accustomed to simply giving lessons in the classroom, they now have not only to build new kinds of relations with their pupils, but also to incorporate their teaching, their educating, within the community at large. The school must be the dynamic factor in the community, and its pupils and teachers must be in permanent contact with the local population, must learn from them, must work with them, and in this way must never forget why it is they are studying and teaching.

To this end the long vacation is considered an opportunity to rest through a change of task rather than just doing nothing. Two of the three holiday months are spent working in organised groups, either on school improvements or on productive activities in the community: technical students must work with the municipal electricity authority, commercial students go to the central registry office, primary-school pupils tend their gardens or mend their furniture, teams of university students work on rural development projects. All put their knowledge to practical use.

The old textbooks were prohibited because they reflected a way of life and ideas completely alien to our own. Although initially ill-prepared, both technically and psychologically, the teachers in each school are working in subject groups preparing their own texts and exercises for every lesson, while at the national level parallel groups are producing what we have called 'support texts' to be distributed by the Ministry—the modest beginning of our new textbooks.

Some people may consider that we would have done better to maintain at least some of the Portuguese books for the time being. Our answer is that the immediate problems created by the absence of textbooks are much less prejudicial to our future development than to use literature based on criteria completely opposed to our situation and objectives.

Recently, another seminar gathered together teachers and senior representatives of the ministries concerned to discuss how to bring technical training in line with national priorities. As usual, the work began with an analysis of technical education in the past, and revolutionary education as developed by Frelimo, so as to better understand our current difficulties and find solutions to them.

In addition to the ills already cited, the seminar identified sexual discrimination, the inappropriate location of schools (dictated by the needs of the dominant class), the overwhelming theoretical content of the courses, and their proliferation and duplication. Thus the guiding principles for new programmes and structures included the end of discrimination against women, the definition of more suitable sites, and the preparation of courses oriented towards productive practice, with theory as their complementary and dynamic factor. Within each branch (technical proper, commercial, and agricultural) courses must be of a polivalent nature so that pupils are capable of resolving a variety of technical problems as and when they arise. Moreover, courses should be scaled so that pupils will have mastered certain specific operations that they might be called upon to perform before the end of each year. Studies should be specifically directed towards the needs of the working class, and consequently all should have as their point of reference the needs of rural development and communal villages; there should also be flexible entrance requirements and different types of courses (for example, by correspondence) that match the various needs of workers at each phase of our development.

The second national literacy seminar has also been held to define objectives and methods. After each of these gatherings, the participants return home and organise smaller meetings at provincial, or even district level, to disseminate their experiences and the new orientations as widely as possible.

We mentioned earlier that intensive courses must also figure high on our list of priorities. We have begun with the largest and most poorly qualified group of teachers: the primary-school *monitores*. Ten training centres have been established—one in each province—where the 10 000 *monitores* must pass through six-week refresher courses during the long vacation. By mid-February 1976 we shall have retrained 3 000. This is the short-term solution to resolve an immediate problem. Between vacations the centres will start tackling the longer-term questions by the formation of better trained and more highly qualified *monitores* with the aim of gradually reducing the six categories of primary teachers to just two: the less qualified *monitores* produced in large numbers, and the post-secondary school two-year trained teachers in more reduced numbers.

Another important course just ended was aimed at forming the new Ministry's administrators at the provincial level. The majority of the participants were ordinary school teachers with little or no administrative experience, but who were selected on the basis of their sense of responsibility, initiative, and loyalty to the people. So what they lack in administrative skills is more than compensated by their understanding of the people's problems and difficulties, which will ensure that they do not become ivory-towered bureaucrats isolated from the people.

There are, of course, still many urgent problems that we have not yet been able to resolve in this way, and which require profound study over a long period. The restructuring of the Ministry of Education and Culture which has just been completed reflects these preoccupations and priorities. To give you some idea of our future plans we would like to mention just three of the new organisations that have been set up. The Commission for the Formation of Cadres is responsible for all training and refresher courses, seminars, etc, at every level, from the preparation of kindergarten teachers to a national meeting of chemistry teachers. The Commission on School Materials has the task of matching our local self-reliance with self-sufficiency at the national level too. Apart from defining the minimum equipment and materials necessary for each educational establishment, its main task is to generate the local manufacture and production of all that is now imported. Finally, the Commission for the Evaluation of Knowledge was established on the grounds that we need to study more effective and just ways of evaluating academic performance in a system that puts the major emphasis on group work. Moreover, even on a collective basis intellectual capacity alone is not enough, and we must find ways of measuring such important qualities as political awareness and work.

Our most powerful blow to date against the old system was undoubtedly the nationalisation of all private educational establishments one month after independence. More than 1 000 ordinary and mission schools—primary, secondary, technical, and teacher-training—passed under governmental control. Education in Mozambique is no longer a question of who can pay and who can't. It was an important and essential step that had to be taken, despite the enormous financial burden it brings and the subsequent exodus of teachers it provokes. As the President said when he announced the decision to the nation:

> We can withstand a shortage of teachers for two or three years if,
> when the time comes for us to have our own teachers, they . . . eliminate
> ignorance and illiteracy and develop the Mozambican people so that

they can stand firmly on their own two feet.

This summary of educational developments in Mozambique and our policy guidelines would not be complete without a brief mention of the focal point of all our national development priorities. Our policies dictate that our major efforts must be directed to the rural areas, where the mass of the people live. Their standard of living must be raised by the introduction of a new way of life organised on a collective not an exploitative basis: communal villages. Only then will it be possible to stop the drift to the towns and the consequent urban unemployment. So the whole weight of the present town-based educational system must be switched to the rural areas, and in particular to the communal villages.

We think we have made a reasonable start although aware that there are many more problems as yet untouched. We are certain that we are on the right path because it is the only one that produces firm political results. We will not be intimidated or blackmailed by anyone or anything—be it a shortage of foreign technicians, or some mythical international standards that our University must maintain—that demands compromises in our political line.

During the war we were not intimidated by the superior firepower of Portugal and her NATO allies, nor by its assassination of our leaders. If necessary we will mark time, or even take a step backwards, if this ensures that in the future we continue along the right lines. In 1968, despite the tremendous shortage of trained cadres, we did not hesitate to close down our only secondary school when it suffered enemy infiltration which fomented the elitist notion that the educated study while the rest fight. Similar things happened at other points in our struggle. But in fact these were never considered setbacks; for they confirmed that we knew what we were doing, where we were going, and how we wanted to get there.

In the People's Republic of Mozambique we are building a socialist society, and consequently the responsibility of the educational system, and all of us who work in it, is to turn our schools into the bases that prepare the people to take power. A *luta continua*.

14 Fighting Two Colonialisms: The Women's Struggle in Guinea-Bissau*

STEPHANIE URDANG

The sixties will be remembered as the decade of independence for most of Africa, independence won for the most part at the negotiating table. All too frequently the parties negotiating on behalf of African countries were a carefully cultivated elite who simply replaced the colonial administrators and set the stage for the growth of neo-colonialism, coups, and counter-coups. Unlike Britain and France, Portugal, until its 1974 revolution, refused to relinquish its colonies in Africa—Guinea-Bissau, Mozambique, and Angola.[1]

Guinea-Bissau, a small country on the west coast of Africa, had been a colony of Portugal for 500 years. For most of this period the relationship was one of trading. Portugal was not interested in political control so long as it had access to slaves and other goods. But with the 'scramble for Africa' at the end of the nineteenth century Portugal changed its attitude. Africa was being greedily divided up by the imperial powers, and Portugal realised that unless it entrenched its presence and took political control it might lose out altogether. With the coming to power of Salazar and a fascist dictatorship in Portugal in 1926, the control became both brutal and complete.

In 1956 the African Party for the Independence of Guinea and Cape Verde (PAIGC) was founded by Amilcar Cabral and a few country people. At first PAIGC's goal was to organise workers in the towns, hoping that through demonstrations and strikes they would convince the Portuguese to negotiate for independence. It soon became clear that this was not going to happen. Each demonstration was met with violence, until the 1959 massacre of fifty dockworkers holding a peaceful demonstration at Pidgiguiti. This was a turning point for PAIGC; they realised that independence could not be won without an armed struggle, one that had to be based on the mass participation of the people. They turned their focus to the countryside and to mobilising the peasants, who represented 95 per cent of the population.

The war of liberation began in January 1963, after a two-year intensive and successful campaign of political mobilisation. It lasted eleven-and-a-half years, ending soon after the coup in Portugal on 24 April 1974, which overturned the Caetano government. On 24 September of the same year the Republic of Guinea-Bissau, self-proclaimed one year earlier, celebrated its first anniversary in victory.

A colonial power had been forced to withdraw as a result of a guerrilla war. But another dimension of this struggle against Portuguese colonialism makes it particularly important. PAIGC saw the armed struggle not as an end in itself, but as part of a movement to establish the foundation for a completely new society. 'Liberation of the people', said Cabral,[2] 'means the liberation of the productive forces of our country, the liquidation of all kinds of imperialist or colonial domination in our country, and the taking of every measure to avoid any new exploitation of our people. We don't confuse exploitation with the colour of one's skin. We want equality, social justice and freedom . . . '.[3] PAIGC proceeded to transform theory into practice with the programme of social and

---

*From *African Studies Review*, 18, 3 (1975), pp. 29–34.

national reconstruction in the liberated areas.[4]

Firmly entrenched in this ideology is the belief that the liberation of women must be an integral part of the overall programme for building a new society, a society without exploitation of any kind. According to Cabral, 'we cannot have a successful revolution without the full participation of women'. This was reflected in PAIGC's programme both for the armed struggle and the building of a new society. A party directive of the early 1960s stated:

> Defend women's rights, respect women (children, youth and adults) and make them respected; but convince the women of our country that their liberation should be their own achievement, by their work, attachment to the Party, self-respect, personality and steadfastness before everything that could be against their dignity.[5]

The involvement of women in the revolution, a goal from the very beginning, was not an afterthought brought about through necessity (as was the case in the Algerian revolution, for example). When the first mobilisers went into the countryside in 1959–60, the programme of political education for which they were trained by Cabral included raising the consciousness of both women and men about the oppression of women and the need to fight against it. At first few women attended the meetings called by the mobilisers; those who did relayed the message to the women of their village and encouraged them to attend. Attendance by women slowly increased. By the time I visited the country just over a decade later, men and women were attending meetings of the population in equal numbers. Half the speakers that I heard were women, who told me of their participation in the revolution and who spoke with confidence before hundreds of people.

Some of the first people mobilised in the sixties were women. Among these was Bweta N'dubi, a Balante[6] peasant who lived on the south front of the country. She had never had any formal schooling and could not read or write. At the time of my visit she held a position of responsibility in the local government, that of regional deputy to the National Assembly, acting as liaison between the people in her areas and the members of the Assembly. (Deputies and members are elected by the population.) I interviewed her at length. Despite the double language barrier—what she said in Balante was translated into Creole[7] and then into English—her strong and vibrant personality came through.

'I first heard about women's rights at the beginning of mobilisation', she told me. 'I understood what was being said immediately, that equality is necessary and possible. Today I work together with men, having more responsibility than many men. This is not only true for me. I understand that I have to fight together with other women against the domination of men. But we have to fight *twice*, once to convince women and the second time to convince men that women have to have the same rights as men.'

Bweta N'dubi was a member of the first elected village council. These councils were established in areas immediately after liberation to deal with the daily village organisation and provide war support. They were elected by the members of the village and replaced the traditional councils or chiefs. Two stipulations were made regarding those who could run for election to the council. First, the candidates had to show genuine opposition to Portuguese colonialism, and, secondly, at least two of the five members had to be women.

In this way women were included in the political leadership at a grassroots level. Up until then politics and decision-making, and hence power—as many women in Guinea-Bissau told me—had been the domain of men, a situation repeated throughout much of Africa. It was the men who had made the political decisions in the villages as chiefs or on councils of elders. Strong traditions against the participation of women in politics had to be circumvented in order for women to be elected.

As each member of the council was charged with a specific task, women were at first made responsible for providing rice (the staple diet of the country) for the guerrillas. As an extension of 'women's work' men could not, and no doubt would not, do it. So they supported the inclusion of women on the council. Once on the council, women took part in collective decision-making and were encouraged to play an active role. Now there are women presidents and vice-presidents in the party, as well as women who have taken on responsibility outside the village, Bweta N'dubi being a striking example.

The fact that food production was made a political task is in itself important. Provision of food is vital in any society. In Africa, although it is done largely by women, and despite its importance, women have derived little power or status from it. Women would have had to organise the provision of rice for the guerrillas, given the division of labour in the community, regardless of whether they were on the village council or not. By making it a task performed by councillors it became a political task, and its status was increased.

There were other ways in which PAIGC helped pave the way for increased freedom of women. Three traditional customs felt to be most detrimental and oppressive to women, lack of divorce, forced marriage, and polygyny, were singled out to be eradicated, in keeping with PAIGC policy on 'detrimental traditions'. A party directive states: 'Oppose without violence all prejudicial customs, the negative aspects of the beliefs and traditions of our people'. Lack of divorce for women and forced marriage were seen as the most oppressive of the three, and efforts were quickly made to decrease their practice; the result has been that they have virtually disappeared.

In the past men could repudiate their wives if they felt that they were unsatisfactory for any reason. A wife accused of disobedience or laziness could be sent back to her parents in disgrace. A man could beat his wife and generally maltreat her, but she had no redress. From the beginning of the struggle divorces were granted to women, and I was told that many women joined the party in order to procure a divorce from their husbands, men who for the most part had been chosen for them by their parents. Once the People's Courts were elected in each village, they took on the responsibility of granting divorces.

Forced marriages are now illegal, and the People's Courts can intervene if a daughter requests it. Again, young women joined the party to escape forced marriage, for husbands were often chosen for them in infancy, and under traditional law they would have been unable to avoid their fate. I was told that forced marriage is virtually non-existent now in the liberated areas,[8] and all the young women I met in the villages I visited had married men of their own choosing.

Fighting polygyny is a slower process. PAIGC obviously could not demand that men divorce all but one of their wives. Their position on polygyny was explained to my by Fidelis Almada, the Commissioner of Justice. 'The party is against polygyny in principle. But you cannot change the customs of the people overnight, or they will turn against you. It is not only a question of the pleasure of having two or three wives. Wives work in the rice fields. They are an economic necessity. We have to move, but we have to move slowly.'

Hence polygyny has not been outlawed. However, with the possibility of divorce, a woman who is unhappy in a polygynous marriage has the option to leave. In addition, young women are demanding more and more that their husbands do not marry more than one wife. One limitation imposed in the villages is that if a man loses one of his wives through death or divorce he cannot automatically replace her, as would have been possible under the traditional system. Further, polygyny is ruled out for party members, even if they are practising Muslims.

The lives of peasant women have changed radically since the beginning of the war. Besides the measures mentioned above, services such as health, education and trading stores have helped to free women from the burdens resulting from living under the yoke of colonialism. It is far too early, after one decade, to expect a complete change and equality of the sexes. As the party continues to push towards its goal and the women continue to 'fight twice', in the words of Bweta N'dubi, the peasant society will continue its transformation. However, I felt that the next quantitative step in this direction could only occur when the actual mode of production is changed, when men are no longer 'helping' women in their work. The heavy burden of production must be moved to straddle more equally the shoulders of both men and women.

The present division of labour based on sex is still entrenched in the economy of the village. Given the conditions of armed struggle, and the relatively short time that liberated zones existed, this changed little during the war. Of course, it would not be sufficient to change only the mode of production, as this would not necessarily alter the relative positions of women and men. Unless there is a struggle to permit women to enter all fields of work, the field of politics in particular, the division of labour based on sex could simply be perpetuated later in a different form. Both these issues—the economic and the political— have to be tackled. The question of the change of mode of production still has to be implemented now that the country is independent, and steps are being taken in this direction.

Education is seen by PAIGC as the key to the future, and a bridge between the traditional society and the new, a bridge too between the traditional woman and the new woman of Guinea-Bissau. Soon after the first areas were liberated, schools were established with the intention that all children should attend. One of the first problems confronted was that fathers resisted sending their daughters to school. In their view girls should get married as young as possible, so why should they go to school? Furthermore, they were needed at home to help their mothers, and this was an economic necessity that could not easily be overlooked. The party consistently fought against these attitudes. A nineteen-year-old woman director of one of the main schools of the country, Jacinta Mendosa de Sousa told me: 'Our party places great emphasis on the children because they are the future of our country. Political workers go to the villages and explain why education is so important, particularly for girls. They stress that we want to reconstruct a free society, a society without sex discrimination.' Female students averaged 25 per cent of the enrolment of the schools I visited, with the exception of the Pilot School in Conakry, the secondary school from which students went abroad to study. There the proportion of girls was 33 per cent of the total enrolment.

Time is set aside each week in all the schools for political education. In these sessions the issue of women's rights and the need to fight for liberation is regularly discussed. 'We especially insist on the rights of women to the boys', Jacinta de Sousa said, 'so that they understand that what they have learnt in their own homes regarding women is not true. The boys come to school with the opinion that "I am a boy, she is a girl, therefore I am superior".'

PAIGC theory on the need for the liberation of women to be a necessity for a successful revolution seems from my observations to have been borne out in practice. However, demands by the party will get nowhere in the long run unless the women take up the struggle themselves. This happened almost instantly once mobilisation and work for the armed struggle began. Most of the young women I spoke to, who had joined the party and left the villages, insisted that in order for a women's struggle to achieve its goals it had to be waged by women themselves and not by the party. They saw the party and belonging to the party as being very important in the process, but ultimately it was their own struggle. 'In Guinea-Bissau we say that women must fight against two colonialisms. One against the Portuguese, the other against men', Carmen Pereira told me. She is one of the leaders of PAIGC and a member of the State Council of the new Republic. This concept was repeated to me again and again.

I got a glimpse of the future from the young women about 19 and 20 years old who had grown up in the revolution and from slightly older women who had joined the struggle when it began and they were then about 17 years of age. Most had had some education, though even the younger women were too old to have benefited from the full PAIGC programme of education. The women I spoke to were articulate, spirited and militant. They seemed to have a lucid and uncomplicated view of the future, a future which they did not doubt was one without sex discrimination, though they knew full well that the journey to that future was to be marked with much fighting. While all spoke about the need to fight the attitudes of men who treated them as inferior, the older women had found this fight more acute. Teodora Gomes, 17 years old when she joined PAIGC, recalled how Cabral had been very outspoken against these attitudes. 'Women are not like shirts', he would chastise the young men, 'so that you put on one today, another tomorrow'. He told the young men that if they treated women in this way, he would insist—as long as the women were agreeable—on them getting married. 'There were many, many marriages at the beginning of the struggle', Teodora added with a hearty laugh. Women like Fina Crato reached the age of 17 and hence womanhood almost ten years later. For her this was not a particular problem. Though conscious of the need to assert herself when necessary, she felt that in general men treated the women they worked with as comrades and equals. I saw a number of examples of this and felt generally that these 'put-downs' by men would have transgressed the language barrier. One example was Jacinta da Sousa, who had to correct a lesson being taught by a teacher who was male and older than she. This was done with authority and warmth on her part, and taken without resentment by the teacher, who changed the lesson accordingly.

Young women spoke to me as well about the need to change their lives personally. 'There is no point in fighting for political independence if we do not also fight for personal independence', said Francisca Pereira, one of the leaders of PAIGC and a member of the delegation to the United Nations. One woman with whom I spent quite a lot of time told me that although she had a three-year-old son she was not married; quite unselfconsciously she said that she had not loved the father so why should she marry him. She had wanted the child; she said she had not been ostracised by any of their friends and even her parents accepted it. 'There is a war. They have got used to a new way of life.'

One of the measures of the success of such a struggle is whether women are entering what was traditionally 'men's work' or participating in the new society in non-traditional areas that in other African countries have become 'men's work'. Again, after a decade it is too early to expect to see women and men entering the different areas of work on an equal basis. The traditions of the society which treated women as inferior, as only fit for certain tasks, as not being able to enter the field of politics and leadership, are still strong. Nevertheless, important gains have been made. For instance, each of the three fronts had a political worker who is responsible for the programme of social reconstruction and political education for the whole front. As far as work within the country is concerned, these positions were the most important politically. Two of the three political workers were women.[9] The director of the secondary school in Conakry is a woman, as are two directors of the higher grade schools within the liberated areas. There were regional *responsables*[10] for health and political work, as well as heads of hospitals and chief nurses. Many of these women had come from peasant families. Women who begin to take the first steps towards greater responsibility are encouraged very strongly to become more fully involved and to move to higher positions. People commented to me that women cadres have to work harder than men, as they must work with other women, as well as do their own work for the party and the struggle.

There was one area of work in which women were not encouraged to play an equal role: this was in the military. I seldom saw women armed. Those who were, were generally cadres of the party who were armed for self-defence, rather than soldiers in the army. At the beginning of the war there had been many women fighters in the militia. However, with the reorganisation of the army into a national and local army, women were encouraged to become nurses or radio communications people. PAIGC reasoning was as follows: Guinea-Bissau was a small country where there were more men who wanted to join the army than were needed. Therefore, unlike armed struggles being waged elsewhere—in Mozambique and Vietnam, for instance—it was not necessary for women to take part in combat. In order to include women in combat, the traditions of the society had to be overcome. This would have taken a long time, and the ousting of the Portuguese colonialists had to have the first priority. They could not slow down the war in order to involve women. They would continue to fight these traditions in other ways. There was some indication that PAIGC felt, too, that through their experience—for at the beginning women did fight in combat to some extent—women did not keep up with men in combat. There were many women who had had military training and were part of the village defence units.

This question of women in the military, however, should be seen in the broader context of the overall revolution. PAIGC emphasises strongly that the war was transitory and that the ultimate goal for the country was the building of a new society. This goal transcends the armed struggle, which is seen as one part of achieving that goal, not an end in itself. They try not to attach heroic importance to the role of the guerrilla fighter. Rather, they emphasise that all work that contributes to the new society is of equal importance, and that the work of the soldier is no more important than any other. Cabral stressed this in an address to a meeting of peasants in 1966:

> There is no point to our struggle if our only goal is to drive out the Portuguese. We want to drive out the Portuguese and build a new society . . . . Every man and woman must learn that work is their first duty, and that all workers in the country are useful to the cause . . . .
> The armed struggle is very important but the most important thing of all is an understanding of our people's situation. Our people support the armed struggle. We must assure them that those who bear arms are the sons of our people and that arms are no better than the tools of

labour. Between one man carrying a gun and another carrying a tool, the more important of the two is the man with the tool.

Nonetheless, the fact that women were not armed is potentially problematic. Guns and power are often equated. I wondered, seeing guns everywhere, whether this might have an effect on the girls and boys growing up in the society. On the other hand, now the war is over, and women have become vigilant about men's attempts to dominate them, it is to be hoped that this determination will counter-act the fact that women have not been armed as men have been.

The success thus far of the women's struggle in Guinea-Bissau has been due to the interrelationships between party ideology on the issue to women's rights and the striving by women themselves for their own independence. Both of these are essential ingredients for any revolution or process of social change, if it is to be ultimately successful. Unfortunately, there are few examples of the women's struggle having been a conscious facet of the broader process of social change.

Though the war is over, the fight for a new society is not. 'When we are independent', said Amilcar Cabral, 'that is when our struggle *really* begins'. Women have told me that the fight for the liberation of women will go on long after the Portuguese colonialists have left the shores of Guinea-Bissau. Portuguese colonialism has been defeated. The fight against the other colonialism continues.

Notes

1 In April and May of 1974, I spent four weeks inside the liberated areas of Guinea-Bissau and another four weeks with PAIGC in the Republics of Guinea and Senegal. I spent three weeks in the South Front accompanied by a regional political worker, Teodora Gomes, who holds a high position in the party. I spent one week in the East Front accompanied by a young cadre of the party, Fina Crato. (The country was divided into three fronts—South, North, and East.) The focus of my visit was the role of women in the struggle against Portuguese colonialism and their own struggle for liberation—the subject of a book I am writing.
2 Amilcar Cabral was the Secretary-General of PAIGC until he was assassinated in January 1973 by agents of Portuguese colonialism. He was an outstanding theoretician as well as leader. His death was a loss, not only to his country, but to Africa and the Third World as well.
3 From a speech given in London, October 1971.
4 By the end of the war, two-thirds of the country had been liberated by PAIGC. In these areas schools, hospitals, clinics, people's stores, a system of justice, and a system of local government had been established, providing the fundamentals for a self-sufficient state.
5 From a PAIGC document, 'Report on the Politico-Socio-Economic Role of Women in Guinea and the Cape Verde Islands'.
6 The Balante are the largest ethnic group in Guinea-Bissau, comprising 30 per cent of the population of 800 000. They are predominantly animist. Twenty per cent of the total population, the largest group of which are the Fula, are Islamised.
7 Creole is spoken throughout the country. It is a mixture of Portuguese and African languages.
8 When I discuss the changes that have taken place since the beginning of the war, I am referring to the two-thirds of the country which had been liberated from the Portuguese colonial control when I was there. Now the whole country is independent and PAIGC has begun to implement its programme and policies throughout the country.

9 Titina Silla, who was the political worker for the North Front, was killed in an ambush by the Portuguese while crossing a river on her way to Amilcar Cabral's funeral in January 1973. The other was Carmen Pereira, for the South Front.

10 *Responsable* is a term used for party members who are responsible for a particular area of work: hence there are health *responsables*, *responsables* for education, for justice, for economy, etc.

Part Four
Strategies for Development and Change

Introduction and Select Bibliography
JOHN DANIEL

There is probably no other topic more frequently or more fiercely debated in the literature on Africa than the one of development and change. Edition after edition of both the serious academic journals as well as the popular mass-circulation magazines contain either details of the currently favoured strategy, or an analysis of the latest failed 'development' project or a prescription for the road ahead, one which will avoid the pitfalls of previous efforts. Along with this proliferation of published materials, there has been a veritable 'invasion' of Africa by an 'army' of expatriate specialists from either the development agencies of the donor nations, or the myriad of international organisations that have mushroomed in the so-called field of development.

And what has all this achieved? The record is not impressive and is actually one that is indicative of developing impoverishment rather than of economic progress. Of the world's 26 poorest nations, half are in Africa, six of those occupying the 'top' (or is it the 'bottom') ten positions. Despite the efforts of legions of health and family specialists, agricultural experts, urban planners, industrial and educational consultants etc., one finds in Africa (a) an overall death rate, like the illiteracy rate, higher than anywhere else in the world; (b) some of the world's highest birth rates; (c) a rural exodus that is producing a chaotic and uncontrolled population explosion in Africa's major cities so that by the year 2 000, at present rates, at least a dozen of these cities will be as uninhabitable as Calcutta is today; and (d) a declining rate of food production in even some of the agriculturally dependent nations and a consequent rising level of imports of basic foodstuffs. To top this catalogue, and in a classic instance of misplaced priorities, Africa as a whole spent in 1976 $5.9 billion on military hardware as against only $2.5 billion for public health and $5.3 billion for education.

This by no means exhaustive chronology of failure is as much a legacy of Africa's exploitation by colonial capitalism as it is an indicator of how development programmes formulated within the framework of international capitalism exacerbate Africa's condition of dependency rather than reduce it. It highlights too the enormity of the problem facing the continent's development planners.

How can this downward spiral to disaster be reversed? The perspective of this volume is that strategies which see no alternative but that of accommodation to the international capitalist framework only heighten the problem, rather than offer any solution. It is for this reason that three of the five readings in this section propound either a non-capitalist strategy or one of integrating Africa's economies as the most effective means of radically altering the existing capitalist relations of production and exchange. The fourth selection deals with another critical problem of change in Africa, namely, the struggle to overthrow the minority colonial regime of South Africa through armed struggle, while the final selection debates the question as to whether the African peasantry constitute an obstacle to, or powerful agent of, change, and examines the conditions under which it can be shaped into a force for revolutionary change in Africa. This challenge is critical to the success of the armed struggle in South Africa for, as the histories of the liberation struggles in Mozambique, Guinea-Bissau and Zimbabwe reveal, the mass mobilisation of the peasantry is crucial not just for the victory of the liberation forces but also for the task of socialist transformation. While the proletarianisation of the South African peasantry is advanced, there are still in the rural reserves 'millions of impoverished, land-hungry and unemployed Africans',[1] and among them the guerilla army must established powerful bases, as it must among the urban proletariat.

None of the selections offers any details of a development strategy along capitalist lines, so a brief outline of such a strategy is presented here. The capitalist theorist regards the major obstacles to Africa's development as being its lack of capital, technology and knowledge. To rectify this these factors must be imported, and the task of the state in an African capitalist strategy is to provide a conducive atmosphere for their inflow so that capital can perform its role as the primary engine of growth. To encourage the inflow of outside capital the state must perform a number of functions, for example, (a) provide incentives in the form of tax concessions, guarantees against either expropriation or the imposition of severe curbs on the remittance of surplus; and (b) construct an infrastructure for the inflow and effective functioning of capital in the form of modern communication facilities (roads, railways, telecommunications), and housing, educational and health services for the foreign personnel of a standard to which they are accustomed in their home countries. The state must therefore give priority to the needs of foreign capital over local demands, even if that requires the diversion of resources away from pressing domestic problems.

The state in such a capitalist strategy is not therefore non-interventionist, but the point is that it does not act against the interest of capital. What it does is intervene in order to enable the process of capital accumulation to proceed unhindered, to the extent even of intervening against the interest of local trade unions, not necessarily destroying them but at least curbing their independence so that 'normal' capital—labour relations are maintained. This has occured in virtually all of Africa's capitalist-oriented nations such as Kenya, Ghana, Botswana and Swaziland. The advocates of this strategy argue that, through the process of capital accumulation, the material means will be created for the development of an adequate, and gradually improving, rise in the standard of living in the country as a whole—jobs will be created, prosperity will rise, and there will be a horizontal and vertical spread of this prosperity. They accept that this strategy will produce and reproduce in Africa the class structures of the advanced capitalist nations, but this is seen as a positive factor because the emergence of a capital-holding national bourgeoisie is seen as vital to the success of such a strategy. It is this class which, given its self-interested motives of accumulation, and a free rein with which to operate, will build an increasingly efficient and productive economic system which will be to the ultimate benefit of all the citizenry.

Our first two documents reflect a development policy opposed to the capitalist strategy. Both are blueprints of the Tanzanian government and express a dedication to the principles of socialism and determination to reconstruct the economy along non-capitalist lines. The first is the *Arusha Declaration*, perhaps the most important, certainly the most widely examined, statement of state policy to have emerged from post-colonial Africa. Issued in 1967, the Declaration was the first in a series of pronouncements which seemed to set Tanzania firmly on a socialist path, and to many scholars Tanzania stands out as one of a handful of African nations genuinely determined to refashion its links with international capitalism. Of late, however, a more critical group of scholars have emerged, among whom Issa Shivji, himself a Tanzanian, has perhaps been the most influential. In a recent study of Tanzania,[2] he is sharply critical of its ruling class and the Tanzanian brand of socialism, which he dismisses as 'mere manipulation', although some progressive strands of Tanzanian policy, such as its support for Southern African liberation movements, is acknowledged. The Arusha Declaration is itself attacked, and depicted not in its usual terms of enunciating genuine socialist principles, but rather as representing the culmination of the efforts by the bureaucratic stratum of the petty bourgeoisie to acquire an economic base in order to transform itself into a fully-fledged bureaucratic bourgeoisie, a class fraction seen as being anti-popular and with a primary motive of consolidating its control over the nation's resources for accumulation on its own behalf. Thus, while some interpret the nationalisation measures announced a few days after the issuance of the Declaration as a decisive attack on metropolitan capital, to Shivji they represented a victory for the upper-levels of the petty bourgeoisie in their struggle to decimate the Asian commercial bourgeoisie, through the nationalisation of the import-export trade sector. These views of Shivji are critically discussed by John Saul in an article in Part Two of this volume.

The second Tanzanian document published here is the *TANU Guidelines on Guarding, Consolidating and Advancing the Revolution of Tanzania, and of Africa* (usually, and hereafter, referred to as the *Mwongozo*). Published in 1971, the Mwongozo is less well known than the Arusha Declaration but is no less important. It was prompted by the overthrow of the Obote regime in Uganda in January 1971 and the Portuguese-sponsored invasion of the Republic of Guinea in the previous year.

Both events were interpreted by TANU as the efforts of imperialist forces with internal African accomplices to topple Africa's progressive regimes and, thereby, thwart the African revolution. The document is divided into four sections: the first identifies the major goals of, and dangers to, the struggle to liberate Africa from imperialist exploitation; the second outlines the policies necessary for overcoming these dangers; the third details the steps necessary for the defence and security of Tanzania's independence; the fourth discusses economic issues.

Three features of the Mwongozo require emphasis. The first is that this document's content represented a marked change from previous expressions of official policy in Africa. Gone are optimistic expressions about Africa's bright and prosperous future with heady references to 'development decades'. Instead there is a more mature and sober analysis of the enormity and complexity of the task of overcoming the exploitative heritage of neo-colonialism. The reality of neo-colonial dependency is recognised, as is the need for radical structural change to Africa's political and economic institutions.

Secondly, at a time when all over Africa the political party as an instrument of change was in decline, it is interesting to note that it is to TANU to whom the spearhead role is assigned of concretising and consolidating the transformation of the colonial superstructure, of organising, educating and guiding the masses, and of directing the nation's socio-economic life. The third, and possibly the most interesting aspect of the Mwongozo, is to be found in those sections where relations between the masses and their leaders are discussed. Here there seems to be a recognition that, if the Tanzanian socialist revolution is to be advanced,

223

then the political relations between the people and their leaders must be democratised and the economic relations of production socialised. A true socialist state, the document argues, cannot exist where only the means of production are socialised: it requires also the elimination of the 'colonial working habits' of the nation's leaders—habits of arrogance, elitism, contempt and oppression. It requires the formation of people's militias, establishment of TANU branches in factories, offices and places of work, a nation-wide campaign of political education, and greater recognition for workers' committees and workers' councils designed to democratise the economic life of the proletariat.

The publication of the Mwongozo was therefore a landmark event, but it must also be observed that today (nine years after its appearance) it remains only a paper pronouncement. Virtually nothing has been done to put its programme into effect. In fact, almost from the moment of its publication the Tanzanian state bureaucracy acted in a manner directly contrary to the guidelines. Publication was followed closely by a rash of strikes and workers' challenges to management throughout Tanzania's industrial sector. As Pascal Mihyo has documented,[3] the workers, using Mwongozo as an ideological weapon to attract support from the state, attacked the arrogance of their managers, trade unions and government officials, seized control of some privately owned factories and converted them into producer cooperatives. In certain rare cases the state endorsed the worker's actions but generally the workers were denounced as 'saboteurs' and 'wreckers', their efforts crushed and their leaders goaled. These actions by the state more than any other prompted the more critical evaluation of Tanzanian socialism to which reference was made earlier. From the perspective of the late 1970s, it is clear that the appearance of the Mwongozo represented the high-water mark in the struggle for socialism in Tanzania. Most of the seventies have been marked by a retreat from that goal towards an accommodation with international capital. From the perspective of the socialist ideologue, Tanzania is today a major disappointment.

The third reading in this section propounds a strategy of confronting the damaging effects of neo-colonialism, not through socialism, but through the continental integration of Africa's economies, something which is seen as being the most viable path to effecting 'radical economic changes in the structures of production and international economic relations'.[4] Reginald H. Green and Ann Seidman make the case for pan-African economic unity. Though their book *Unity or Poverty: The Economics of Pan-Africanism* was published more than a decade ago, it is still an important and relevant text and their concluding ten-page summary case for economic unity is as compelling an argument as any available. It opens with a brief outline of the dominant characteristics and limitations of Africa's national economies leading to a presentation of the four main advantages of continental economic integration, concluding with a gradualist strategy for achieving that goal. While the collapse of the East African Community has been a setback for the proponents of economic pan-Africanism, it in no way affects the plausible logic of Green and Seidman's case and neither should it be regarded as a paralysing setback to further efforts at economic integration in Africa. Indeed, the continuing deterioration in the international terms of trade for most Third World nations leaves them with few alternatives but to attempt a pooling of their resources and/or bargaining abilities. Third World nations have recognised this fact and some 70 of them have in recent years joined forces to form the Association of African, Caribbean and Pacific Nations (ACP), something which has given them a bargaining tool of greater effectiveness than anything any one of the member states could have devised on their own. Furthermore, the recent formation of the 15-member Economic Community of West African States (ECOWAS) is a step forward which may revive the momentum towards the economic integration of all of Africa.

The realisation of that aim will be a daunting task, but no more than the challenge to which we turn in our fourth selection—the overthrow of minority rule in South Africa. The situation in South Africa parallels, in many respects, the colonial situations in Kenya, Algeria, Zimbabwe and former Portuguese Africa. In each of these territories, a minority of settler origin ultimately acquired a near monopoly of the instruments of political power and the colonies' wealth. This latter task was achieved through the seizure of the nation's productive assets, including all of its high yield land. In the process they violently dispossessed the indigenes of most of the land and then converted them into a labour proletariat whom they forced to work at the cheapest possible rate. In addition, the settlers entwined the colonial economy in a web of monopolies, protecting them from indigenous competition and giving them monopoly rights over, or access to, the best crops, mineral resources, communications, credit, government services, transportation etc. Not surprisingly, in this environment the settlers developed for themselves a lifestyle of leisure and immense privilege, one which only a tiny minority of Africans shared.

Heribert Adam has described colonies in terms of two types, those of exploitation and those of settlement.[5] The distinguishing feature is that in the latter the settlers decide to stay. They stop regarding themselves as temporary sojourners and look upon themselves as indigenes. They develop interests distinct from those of the metropole, and a desire develops on their part to change, or sever, their ties to the motherland. Each of the colonies mentioned above were colonies of settlement, and in them the metropole ultimately transferred internal political power to the settlers, who then ceased to be the agents of an imperial power and became a ruling class on their own. In each of these colonies the power of this ruling class was broken only after protracted and bloody campaigns of armed violence.

Does this mean that armed struggle represents the only viable strategy for change in South Africa in favour of the black majority? In our view this is the case, even though success for that strategy remains a distant prospect. This view is based on the fact that, while South Africa retains most features of the settler model described above, it has also developed a variant of the model. This variant was produced by the fact that, in its evolution from the exploitative to the settler pattern, South Africa was granted juridical independence in 1910 with power vested in the hands of the white minority and, thereafter, that power came increasingly to be concentrated in the hands of the Afrikaner, the one group within the ruling establishment with no ties of kith and kin to either the metropole or any other nation; in short, a group which saw itself as indigenous, with cultural roots nurtured in the soil of a land selected for them by God, with their own particular philosophy, religion and language forged in a struggle for survival against hostile elements in their 'promised land'. To the Afrikaners the colony became the motherland, so that while the French Algerians or the Portuguese colonisers or the British of Kenya, Zimbabwe and South Africa could always look to an external mother country as a sanctuary of last resort, the Afrikaner could not. His survival is seen as being at stake, and only his perpetual dominance of the polity can guarantee that survival.

This variant is perhaps best described as domestic settler colonialism and its characteristic feature is the geographical unity of both the metropole and the colony. This unique feature, and the survival complex of the Afrikaner, seem to us to render the task of the armed insurgents that much greater than it was anywhere else in Africa. Additionally, South Africa is Africa's economic and military giant with a capacity for destruction greater than the rest of the continent combined. Furthermore, the fact that she is the repository of some of the planet's most valuable and strategically most important raw materials enables South Africa's rulers to solicit considerable overt and covert assistance from western capitalist nations. Internally, South Africa has constructed a massive security apparatus and given it awesome legal powers to crush internal dissent. She has mentally prepared her white citizenry for a fight to the finish, while she has taken the offensive in the struggle against the forces of African nationalism in South Africa. Through the creation of ethnic homelands she has fragmented nationalist unity and deflected it along ethnic lines and away from common national goals. The acceptance of South Africa's brand of independence by the carefully selected leaders of these homelands has provided white South Africa with black allies in the developing armed struggle, for these homeland leaders have as much to fear from the liberation army as do the nation's white rulers.

All of the above factors are recognised in the article by Slovo, himself a veteran of the South African liberation struggle. While noting the obstacles, Slovo correctly observes 'that the material strength of the enemy is by no means a decisive factor',[6] and he points out that there are factors which operate in favour of the liberation forces. One of these would not seem to be the physical environment but, again as Slovo notes, the presence of mountainous jungle terrain is not a *sine qua non* for a successful armed insurgency. While some environments are more favourable than others, guerrilla warfare can be and has been waged in many different terrains; the challenge to the South African guerrillas is to adapt their tactics to the varying topography of South Africa's advanced urban areas and the underdeveloped nature of much of the country's rural environment where most of the black populace reside. The armed struggle in South Africa will have to link up the rural and urban centres and mobilise both the black urban proletariat and the rural dwellers.

It is in this context that John Saul's article on the African Peasant and Revolution is included as the final selection. He analyses the role of the African peasantry as an agent for revolutionary change in Africa, not mere change *per se* but radical, anti-imperialist and socialist change. The article opens with a useful survey of how theorists have conceptualised the political potential of the peasantry. Reference is made to both Marx's scepticism about, and Fanon's romanticisation of, their radical potential. Saul takes a guarded but positive attitude towards the contribution the African peasantry can make to the revolutionary process. While acknowledging their potential, he is aware of the inherent limitations in their political consciousness. His view is that for peasants to be mobilised in a progressive direction they require organisation and ideological politicisation. Like Amilcar Cabral, whom he quotes approvingly, Saul assigns primacy to 'hard political work' by dedicated cadres drawn from the non-peasant classes. Theirs is the vanguard role.

But politicisation alone will not persuade the peasant into joining the armed struggle. The 'ideal' is a combination of both attitudinal factors and concrete structural conditions. By the latter is meant conditions of cruel oppression and exploitation such as were to be found in Mozambique under Portuguese rule. Such conditions facilitate the task of the vanguard cadre. Hence, Saul argues, in his contrasting case studies of Tanzania and Mozambique, that Frelimo had the less difficult task in mobilising the peasantry for revolutionary action in

Mozambique than the politicians in Tanzania, where the peasants have experienced a lesser degree of exploitation. This is one factor which favours the South African liberation movement, for the oppression of apartheid is virtually without parallel. As the peasantry of Mozambique and Zimbabwe have shown, the rural peasantry of Southern Africa constitutes a major force for revolutionary change.

Notes

1 Joe Slovo, 'South Africa—No Middle Road', in B. Davidson, J. Slovo and A. Wilkinson, *Southern Africa: The New Politics of Revolution*, Penguin, London, 1976, p. 202.
2 Issa Shivji, *Class Struggles in Tanzania*, Heinemann, London, 1976.
3 Pascal Mihyo, 'The Struggle for Workers' Control in Tanzania', *Review of African Political Economy*, 4, November 1975.
4 Reginald Green and Ann Seidman, *Unity or Poverty? The Economics of Pan-Africanism*, Penguin, London, 1968, p. 346.
5 Heribert Adam, *Modernizing Racial Domination: The Dynamics of South African Politics*, University of California Press, Berkeley, pp. 42–5.
6 Slovo, *op.cit.*, p. 197.

Select Bibliography

1 Official strategies for development
Republic of Botswana, *First (1970–75) and Second (1977) National Development Plans*, Government Printer, Gaborone, 1972 and 1977.
Republic of Ghana, *The Seven Year Plan for 'Work and Happiness'*, Government Printer, Accra, 1962.
Republic of Kenya, *African Socialism and its Application to Planning in Kenya*, Government Printer, Nairobi, 1965.
Republic of Uganda, *The Common Man's Charter*, Milton Obote Foundation, Kampala, 1969.
The Dakar Declaration and Action Programme, 1974, reprinted in *The African Review*, 5, 1 (1975).
The Cocoyoc Declaration, 1974, reprinted in *The African Review*, 5, 3 (1975).

2 Commentaries on development strategies
Samir Amin, 'In Praise of Socialism', *African Development*, 2, 4 (1977).
R.W. James, 'Implementing the Arusha Declaration—The Role of the Legal System', *The African Review*, 3, 2 (1973).
Paul Kennedy, 'Indigenous Capitalism in Ghana', *Review of African Political Economy*, 8, January–April 1977.
Steve Langdon, 'The State and Capitalism in Kenya', *Review of African Political Economy*, 8, January–April 1977.
Bismarck Mwansusu, 'Commentary on Mwongozo wa TANU, 1971', *The African Review*, 1, 4 (1972).
H.N. Mwesu, 'Nigeria's Third National Development Plan 1975–80; Major Problems to Implementation', *Africa Today*, 24, 4 (1977).
Nyongoo, Anyang. 'Liberal Models of Capitalist Development: Ivory Coast', *Africa Development*, 3, 2 (1978).
Oculi Okello, 'The Issue of Participation and the Common Man's Charter', *Mawazo*, 2, 2 (1969).

3 Development in Tanzania
Lionel Cliffe and J.S. Saul eds., *Socialism in Tanzania*, Vol. I *Politics*, and Vol. II *Policies*, East African Publishing House, Nairobi, 1972 and 1973.
Andrew Coulson, 'Agricultural Policies in Mainland Tanzania', *Review of Africa Political Economy*, 10, September–December 1977.
William Duggan and John Civille, *Tanzania and Nyerere: A Study of Ujamaa and Nationhood*, Orbis Books, Maryknoll, 1976.
J. Loxley and J. Saul, 'Multinationals, workers and parastatals', *Review of African Political Economy*, 2, January–April 1975.
Pascal Mihyo, 'The struggle for Workers Control in Tanzania', *Review of African Economy*, 4, November 1975.
K. Nsari, 'Tanzania: Neo-Colonialism and the Struggle for National Liberation', *Ibid.*
Julius K. Nyerere, *Freedom and Development: A Selection of Writings and Speeches, 1968–1973*, Oxford University Press, Nairobi, 1974.
Cranford Pratt, 'Nyerere and the Transition to Socialism in Tanzania', *The African Review*, 5, 1 (1975).
P. Raikes, 'Ujamaa and Rural Socialism', *Review of African Political Economy*, 3, May–October 1975.

Walter Rodney, 'Tanzania Ujamaa and Scientific Socialism', *The African Review*, 1, 4 (1972).

J.F. Rweyemanu, *Underdevelopment and Industrialisation in Tanzania*. East Africa Publishing House, Nairobi, 1973.

J.D. Saul, 'Tanzania's transition to Socialism', *Canadian Journal of African Studies*, 11, 3 (1977).

Issa Shivji, *Class Struggles in Tanzania*, Heinemann, London, 1976.

G. Tschannerl, 'Periphery Capitalist Development: The Tanzanian Economy', *Utafiti*, 1, 1 (1976).

Michaela Von Freyhold, 'The Post-Colonial State and its Tanzanian Version', *Review of African Political Economy*, 8, January–April 1977.

4 Regional and continental integration

Johan Galtung, 'The Lomé Convention and Neo-Capitalism', *The African Review*, 5, 1 (1975).

Immanuel Geiss, *The Pan-African Movement*, Methuen, London, 1974.

H. Green, 'The Lomé Convention: updated dependence or departure towards Collective Self-reliance', *The African Review*, 6, 1 (1976).

Arthur Hazlewood, *Economic Integration: An East African Experience*, Heinemann, London, 1975.

Ras Makonnen, *Pan-Africanism from Within*, Oxford University Press, Nairobi, 1973.

S. Okechukura Mezu, ed., *The Philosophy of Pan-Africanism*, Georgetown University Press, Georgetown, 1965.

B.W.T. Muthanka, 'Mutinational Corporations in Regional Integration: The African Experience', *The African Review*, 5, 4 (1975).

Kwame Nkrumah, *African must Unite*, International Publishers, New York, 1970.

F.I. Nixson, *Economic Integration and Industrial Location: East African Case Study*, Longman, London, 1973.

Agyeman Opoku, 'The Osagyefo, the Mwalimu, and Pan Africanism: a Study in the Growth of a Dynamic Concept', *Journal of Modern African Studies*, 13, 4 (1976).

Paul Saenz, 'The Organisation of African Unity in the Subordinate African Regional System', *African Studies Review*, 13, 2 (1970).

Aguibou Yansane, 'The State of Economic Integration in North West Africa South of the Sahara: The Emergence of the Economic Community of West African States (ECOWAS)', *African Studies Review*, 20, 2 (1977).

5 Armed struggle, peasants and revolution

Hamza Alavi, 'Peasants and Revolution', in Ralph Miliband and John Saville eds., *The Socialist Register*, *1965*, Merlin Press, London, 1965.

Henry Bernstein, 'Notes on Capital and Peasantry', *Review of African Political Economy*, 10, September–December 1977.

Malcolm Caldwell, 'The Revolutionary Role of the Peasant—2', *International Socialism*, 41, December–January 1969–70.

G. Chailand, *Armed Struggle in Africa*, Monthly Review Press, New York, 1969.

Basil Davidson, 'African peasants and revolution', *Journal of Peasant Studies*, I, 3 (1974).

————, *The Liberation of Guinea*, Penguin, London, 1969.

————, *In the Eye of the Storm: Angola's People*, Penguin, London, 1975.

Basil Davidson, J. Slovo and A. Wilkinson, *Southern Africa: The New Politics of Revolution*, Penguin, London, 1976.

Frantz Fanon, *Towards the African Revolution*, Grove Press, New York, 1967.

Nigel Harris, 'The Revolutionary Role of the Peasants', *International Socialism*, 41, December–January 1969–70.

E.J. Hobsbawn, 'Peasants and Politics', *Journal of Peasant Studies*, I, 1 (1973).

Sheridan Johns, 'Obstacles to Guerrilla Warfare—A South African Case Study', *Journal of Modern African Studies*, 2, 2 (1973).

Samora Machel, 'The People's Republic of Mozambique: The Struggle Continues', *Review of African Political Economy*, 4, November 1975.

John Marcum, *The Angolan Revolution*, Vol. I, M.I.T. Press, Cambridge, 1969.

———, 'The Exile condition and Revolutionary Effectiveness: Southern African Liberation Movement', in C. Potholm and R. Dale, eds., *Southern Africa in Perspective: Essays in Regional Politics*, The Free Press, New York, 1972.

Kees Maxey, *The fight for Zimbabwe. The Armed Conflict in Southern Rhodesia since U.D.I.*, Rex Collings, London, 1975.

Eduardo Mondlane, *The Struggle for Mozambique*, Penguin, London, 1969.

N. Perinbam, 'Fanon and the Revolutionary Peasantry—The Algerian Case', *Journal of Modern African Studies*, 2, 3 (1973).

Issa Shivji, 'Peasants and Class Alliances', *Review of African Political Economy*, 3, May–October, 1975.

Joe Slovo, 'Southern Africa—Problems of Armed Struggle', *The Socialist Register*, Merlin Press, London, 1974.

Eric Wolf, *Peasant Wars of the Twentieth Century*, University of Chicago Press, Chicago, 1969.

15 The Arusha Declaration, 5 February 1967

TANZANIAN AFRICAN NATIONAL UNION

Part One: The TANU Creed

The policy of TANU is to build a socialist state. The principles of socialism are laid down in the TANU Constitution and they are as follows:
Whereas TANU believes:

(a) That all human beings are equal;
(b) That every individual has a right to dignity and respect;
(c) That every citizen is an integral part of the nation and has the right to take an equal part in government at local, regional and national level;
(d) That every citizen has the right to freedom of expression, of movement, of religious belief and of association within the context of the law;
(e) That every individual has the right to receive from society protection of his life and of property held according to law;
(f) That every individual has the right to receive a just return for his labour;
(g) That all citizens together possess all the natural resources of the country in trust for their descendants;
(h) That in order to ensure economic justice the state must have effective control over the principal means of production; and
(i) That it is the responsibility of the state to intervene actively in the economic life of the nation so as to ensure the well-being of all citizens, and so as to prevent the exploitation of one person by another or one group by another, and so as to prevent the accumulation of wealth to an extent which is inconsistent with the existence of a classless society.

Now, therefore, the principal aims and objects of TANU shall be as follows:

(a) To consolidate and maintain the independence of this country and the freedom of its people;
(b) To safeguard the inherent dignity of the individual in accordance with the Universal Declaration of Human Rights;
(c) To ensure that this country shall be governed by a democratic socialist government of the people;
(d) To cooperate with all political parties in Africa engaged in the liberation of all Africa;
(e) To see that the government mobilises all the resources of this country towards the elimination of poverty, ignorance and disease;
(f) To see that the government actively assists in the formation and maintenance of cooperative organisations;
(g) To see that wherever possible the government itself directly participates in the economic development of this country;
(h) To see that the government gives equal opportunity to all men and women irrespective of race, religion or status;
(i) To see that the government eradicates all types of exploitation, intimidation, discrimination, bribery and corruption;
(j) To see that the government exercises effective control over the principal

means of production and pursues policies which facilitate the way to collective ownership of the resources of this country;

(k) To see that the government cooperates with other states in Africa in bringing about African unity;

(l) To see that government works tirelessly towards world peace and security through the United Nations Organisation.

Part Two: The Policy of Socialism

1 Absence of exploitation

A truly socialist state is one in which all people are workers and in which neither capitalism nor feudalism exists. It does not have two classes of people, a lower class composed of people who work for their living, and an upper class of people who live on the work of others. In a really socialist country no person exploits another; everyone who is physically able to work does so; every worker obtains a just return for the labour he performs; and the incomes derived from different types of work are not grossly divergent.

In a socialist country, the only people who live on the work of others, and who have the right to be dependent upon their fellows, are small children, people who are too old to support themselves, the crippled, and those whom the state at any one time cannot provide with an opportunity to work for their living.

Tanzania is a nation of peasants and workers, but it is not yet a socialist society. It still contains elements of feudalism and capitalism—with their temptations. These feudalistic and capitalistic features of our society could spread and entrench themselves.

2 The major means of production and exchange are under the control of peasants and workers

To build and maintain socialism it is essential that all the major means of production and exchange in the nation are controlled and owned by the peasants through the machinery of their government and their cooperatives. Further, it is essential that the ruling party should be a party of peasants and workers.

The major means of production and exchange are such things as: land; forests; minerals; water; oil and electricity; news media; communications; banks, insurance, import and export trade, wholesale trade; iron and steel, machine-tool, arms, motor-car, cement, fertiliser, and textile industries; and any big factory on which a large section of the people depend for their living, or which provides essential components of other industries; large plantations, and especially those which provide raw materials essential to important industries.

Some of the instruments of production and exchange which have been listed here are already owned or controlled by the people's Government of Tanzania.

3 The existence of democracy

A state is not socialist simply because its means of production and exchange are controlled or owned by the government, either wholly or in large part. For a country to be socialist, it is essential that its government is chosen and led by the peasants and workers themselves. If the minority governments of Rhodesia or South Africa controlled or owned the entire economies of these respective countries, the result would be a strengthening of oppression, not the building of socialism. True socialism cannot exist without democracy also existing in the society.

4 Socialism is a belief

Socialism is a way of life, and a socialist society cannot simply come into existence. A socialist society can only be built by those who believe in, and who themselves practise, the principles of socialism. A committed member of TANU will be a socialist, and his fellow socialists—that is, his fellow believers in this political and economic system—are all those in Africa or elsewhere in the world who fight for the rights of peasants and workers. The first duty of a TANU member, and especially of a TANU leader, is to accept these socialist principles, and to live his own life in accordance with them. In particular, a genuine TANU leader will not live off the sweat of another man, nor commit any feudalistic or capitalistic actions.

The successful implementation of socialist objectives depends very much upon the leaders, because socialism is a belief in a particular system of living, and it is difficult for leaders to promote its growth if they do not themselves accept it.

Part Three: The Policy of Self-Reliance

We are at war

TANU is involved in a war against poverty and oppression in our country; the struggle is aimed at moving the people of Tanzania (and the people of Africa as a whole) from a state of poverty to a state of prosperity.

We have been oppressed a great deal, we have been exploited a great deal and we have been disregarded a great deal. It is our weakness that has led to our being oppressed, exploited and disregarded. Now we want a revolution— a revolution which brings to an end our weakness, so that we are never again exploited, oppressed, or humiliated.

A poor man does not use money as a weapon

But it is obvious that in the past we have chosen the wrong weapon for our struggle, because we chose money as our weapon. We are trying to overcome our economic weakness by using the weapons of the economically strong— weapons which in fact we do not possess. By our thoughts, words and actions it appears as if we have come to the conclusion that without money we cannot bring about the revolution we are aiming at. It is as if we have said, 'Money is the basis of development. Without money there can be no development.'

That is what we believe at present. TANU leaders and government leaders and officials, all put great emphasis and dependence on money. The people's leaders, and the people themselves, in TANU, NUTA, Parliament, UWT, the cooperatives, TAPA, and in other national institutions think, hope and pray for *money*. It is as if we had all agreed to speak with one voice, saying, 'If we get money we shall develop, without money we cannot develop'.

In brief, our Five-Year Development Plan aims at more food, more education, and better health; but the weapon we have put emphasis upon is money. It is as if we said, 'In the next five years we want to have more food, more education, and better health, and in order to achieve these things we shall spend £250 000 000'. We think and speak as if the most important thing to depend upon is *money* and anything else we intend to use in our struggle is of minor importance.

When a Member of Parliament says that there is a shortage of water in his constituency and he asks the government how it intends to deal with the problem, he expects the government to reply that it is planning to remove the shortage of water in his constituency—*with money*.

When another Member of Parliament asks what the government is doing about the shortage of roads, schools or hospitals in his constituency, he also expects the government to tell him that it has specific plans to build roads, schools and hospitals in his constituency—*with money*.

When a NUTA official asks the government about its plans to deal with the low wages and poor housing of the workers, he expect the government to inform him that the minimum wage will be increased and that better houses will be provided for the workers—*with money*.

When a TAPA official asks the government what plans it has to give assistance to the many TAPA schools which do not get government aid, he expects the government to state that it is ready the following morning to give the required assistance—*with money*.

When an offical of the cooperative movement mentions any problem facing the farmer, he expects to hear that the government will solve the farmer's problems—*with money*. In short, for every problem facing our nation, the solution that is in everybody's mind is *money*.

Each year, each ministry of government makes its estimates of expenditure, ie. the amount of money it will require in the coming year to meet recurrent and development expenses. Only one minister and his ministry make estimates of revenue. This is the minister for finance. Every ministry puts forward very good development plans. When the ministry presents its estimates, it believes that the money is there for the asking but that the minister for finance and his ministry are being obstructive. And regularly each year the minister for finance has to tell his fellow ministers that there is no money. And each year the ministries complain about the ministry of finance when it trims down their estimates.

Similarly, when Members of Parliament and other leaders demand that the government should carry out a certain development, they believe that there is a lot of money to spend on such projects, but that the government is the stumbling block. Yet such belief on the part of ministries, Members of Parliament and other leaders does not alter the stark truth, which is that government has no money.

When it is said that government has no money, what does this mean? It means that the people of Tanzania have insufficient money. The people pay taxes out of the very little wealth they have; it is from these taxes that the government meets its recurrent and development expenditure. When we call on the government to spend more money on development projects, we are asking the government to use more money. And if the government does not have any more, the only way it can do this is to increase its revenue through extra taxation.

If one calls on the government to spend more, one is in effect calling on the government to increase taxes. Calling on the government to spend more without raising taxes is like demanding that the government should perform miracles; it is equivalent to asking for more milk from a cow while insisting that the cow should not be milked again. But our refusal to admit that calling on the government to spend more is the same as calling on the government to raise taxes shows that we fully realise the difficulties of increasing taxes. We realise that the cow has no more milk—that is, that the people find it difficult to pay more taxes. We know that the cow would like to have more milk herself, so that her calves could drink it, or that she would like more milk which could be sold to provide more comfort for herself or her calves. But knowing all the things which could be done with more milk does not alter the fact that the cow has no more milk!

What of external aid?
One method we use to try and avoid a recognition of the need to increase taxes if we want to have more money for development, is to think in terms of getting the extra money from outside Tanzania. Such external finance falls into three main categories.

(a) *Gifts* This means that another government gives our Government a sum of money as a free gift for a particular development scheme. Sometimes it may be that an institution in another country gives our government, or an institution in our country, financial help for development programmes.

(b) *Loans* The greater portion of financial help we expect to get from outside is not in the form of gifts or charity, but in the form of loans. A foreign government or a foreign institution, such as a bank, lends our government money for the purposes of development. Such a loan has repayment conditions attached to it, covering such factors as the time period for which it is available and the rate of interest.

(c) *Private Investment* The third category of financial help is also greater than the first. This takes the form of investment in our country by individuals or companies from outside. The important condition which such private investors have in mind is that the enterprise into which they put their money should bring them profit and that our government should permit them to repatriate these profits. They also prefer to invest in a country whose policies they agree with and which will safeguard their economic interests.

These three are the main categories of external finance. And there is in Tanzania a fantastic amount of talk about getting money from outside. Our government, and different groups of our leaders, never stop thinking about methods of getting finance from abroad. And if we get some money or even if we just get a promise of it, our newspapers, our radio, and our leaders, all advertise the fact in order that every person shall know that salvation is coming, or is on the way. If we receive a gift we announce it, if we receive a loan we announce it, if we get a new factory we announce it—and always loudly. In the same way, when we get a promise of a gift, a loan, or a new industry, we make an announcement of the promise. Even when we have merely started discussions with a foreign government or institution for a gift, a loan, or a new industry, we make an announcement—even though we do not know the outcome of the discussions. Why do we do all this? Because we want our people to know that we have started discussions which will bring prosperity.

Do not let us depend upon money for development
It is stupid to rely on money as the major instrument of development when we know only too well that our country is poor. It is equally stupid, indeed it is even more stupid, for us to imagine that we shall rid ourselves of our poverty through foreign financial assistance rather than our own financial resources. It is stupid for two reasons.

Firstly, we shall not get the money. It is true that there are countries which can, and which would like to, help us. But there is no country in the world which is prepared to give us gifts or loans, or establish industries, to the extent that we would be able to achieve all our development targets. There are many needy countries in the world. And even if all the prosperous nations were willing to help the needy countries, the assistance would still not suffice. But in any case the prosperous nations have not accepted a responsibility to fight world poverty. Even within their own borders poverty still exists, and the rich individuals do not willingly give money to the government to help their poor fellow citizens.

It is only through taxation, which people have to pay whether they want to or not, that money can be extracted from the rich in order to help the masses. Even then there would not be enough money. However heavily we taxed the citizens of Tanzania and the aliens living here, the resulting revenue would not be enough to meet the costs of the development we want. And there is no World Government which can tax the prosperous nations in order to help the poor nations; nor if one did exist could it raise enough revenue to do all that is needed in the world. But in fact, such a World Government does not exist. Such money as the rich nations offer to the poor nations is given voluntarily, either through their own goodness, or for their own benefit. All this means that it is impossible for Tanzania to obtain from overseas enough money to develop our economy.

Gifts and loans will endanger our independence
Secondly, even if it were possible for us to get enough money for our needs from external sources, is this what we really want? Independence means self-reliance. Independence cannot be real if a nation depends upon gifts and loans from another for its development. Even if there was a nation, or nations, prepared to give us all the money we need for our development, it would be improper for us to accept such assistance without asking ourselves how this would affect our independence and our very survival as a nation. Gifts which increase, or act as a catalyst, to our own efforts are valuable. But gifts which could have the effect of weakening or distorting our own efforts should not be accepted until we have asked ourselves a number of questions.

The same applies to loans. It is true that loans are better than 'free' gifts. A loan is intended to increase our efforts or make those efforts more fruitful. One condition of a loan is that you show how you are going to repay it. This means you have to show that you intend to use the loan profitably and will therefore be able to repay it.

But even loans have their limitations. You have to give consideration to the ability to repay. When we borrow money from other countries it is the Tanzanian who pays it back. And as we have already stated, Tanzanians are poor people. To burden the people with big loans, the repayment of which will be beyond their means, is not to help them but to make them suffer. It is even worse when the loans they are asked to repay have not benefited the majority of the people but have only benefited a small minority.

How about the enterprises of foreign investors? It is true we need these enterprises. We have even passed an Act of Parliament protecting foreign investments in this country. Our aim is to make foreign investors feel that Tanzania is a good place in which to invest because investments would be safe and profitable, and the profits can be taken out of the country without difficulty. We expect to get money through this method. But we cannot get enough. And even if we were able to convince foreign investors and foreign firms to undertake all the projects and programmes of economic development that we need, is that what we actually want to happen?

Had we been able to attract investors from America and Europe to come and start all the industries and all the projects of economic development that we need in this country, could we do so without questioning ourselves? Could we agree to leave the economy of our country in the hands of foreigners who would take the profits back to their countries? Or supposing they did not insist upon taking their profits away, but decided to reinvest them in Tanzania; could we really accept this situation without asking ourselves what disadvantages our nation would suffer? Would this allow the socialism we have said it is our objective to build?

How can we depend upon gifts, loans, and investments from foreign countries and foreign companies without endangering our independence? The English people have a proverb which says, 'He who pays the piper calls the tune'. How can we depend upon foreign governments and companies for the major part of our development without giving to those governments and countries a great part of our freedom to act as we please? The truth is that we cannot.

Let us repeat. We made a mistake in choosing money—something we do not have—to be the big instrument of our development. We are making a mistake to think that we shall get the money from other countries; first, because in fact we shall not be able to get sufficient money for our economic development; and secondly, because even if we could get all that we need, such dependence upon others would endanger our independence and our ability to choose our own political policies.

We have put too much emphasis on industries

Because of our emphasis on money, we have made another big mistake. We have put too much emphasis on industries. Just as we have said, 'Without money there can be no development', we also seem to say, 'Industries are the basis of development, without industries there is no development'. This is true. The day when we have lots of money we shall be able to say we are a developed country. We shall be able to say, 'When we began our development plans we did not have enough money and this situation made it difficult for us to develop as fast as we wanted. Today we are developed and we have enough money'. That is to say, our money has been brought by development. Similarly, the day we become industrialised, we shall be able to say we are developed. Development would have enabled us to have industries. The mistake we are making is to think that development begins with industries. It is a mistake because we do not have the means to establish many modern industries in our country. We do not have either the necessary finances or the technical know-how. It is not enough to say that we shall borrow the finances and the technicians from other countries to come and start the industries. The answer to this is the same one we gave earlier, that we cannot get enough money and borrow enough technicians to start all the industries we need. And even if we could get the necessary assistance, dependence on it could interfere with our policy on socialism. The policy of inviting a chain of capitalists to come and establish industries in our country might succeed in giving us all the industries we need, but it would also succeed in preventing the establishment of socialism unless we believe that without first building capitalism, we cannot build socialism.

Let us pay heed to the peasant

Our emphasis on money and industries has made us concentrate on urban development. We recognise that we do not have enough money to bring the kind of development to each village which would benefit everybody. We also know that we cannot establish an industry in each village and through this means effect a rise in the real incomes of the people. For these reasons we spend most of our money in the urban areas and our industries are established in the towns.

Yet the greater part of this money that we spend in the towns comes from loans. Whether it is used to build schools, hospitals, houses or factories, etc., it still has to be repaid. But it is obvious that it cannot be repaid just out of money obtained from urban and industrial development. To repay the loans we have to use foreign currency which is obtained from the sale of our exports. But we do not now sell our industrial products in foreign markets, and indeed it is likely to be a long time before our industries produce for export. The main aim of our new industries is 'import substitution'—that is, to produce things which up to now we have had to import from foreign countries.

It is therefore obvious that the foreign currency we shall use to pay back the loans used in the development of the urban areas will not come from the towns or the industries. Where, then, shall we get it from? We shall get it from the villages and from agriculture. What does this mean? It means that the people who benefit directly from development which is brought about by borrowed money are not the ones who will repay the loans. The largest proportion of the loans will be spent in, or for, the urban areas, but the largest proportion of the repayment will be made through the efforts of the farmers.

This fact should always be borne in mind, for there are various forms of exploitation. We must not forget that people who live in towns can possibly become the exploiters of those who live in the rural areas. All our big hospitals are in towns and they benefit only a small section of the people of Tanzania. Yet if we have built them with loans from outside Tanzania, it is the overseas sale of the peasants' produce which provides the foreign exchange for repayment. Those who do not get the benefit of the hospitals thus carry the major responsibility for paying for them. Tarmac roads, too, are mostly found in towns and are of especial value to the motor-car owners. Yet if we have built those roads with loans, it is again the farmer who produces the goods which will pay for them. What is more, the foreign exchange with which the car was bought also came from the sale of the farmers' produce. Again, electric lights, water pipes, hotels and other aspects of modern development are mostly found in towns. Most of them have been built with loans, and most of them do not benefit the farmer directly, although they will be paid for by the foreign exchange earned by the sale of his produce. We should always bear this in mind.

Although when we talk of exploitation we usually think of capitalists, we should not forget that there are many fish in the sea. They eat each other. The large ones eat the small ones, and small ones eat those who are even smaller. There are two possible ways of dividing the people in our country. We can put the capitalists and feudalists on one side, and the farmers and workers on the other. But we can also divide the people into urban dwellers on one side and those who live in the rural areas on the other. If we are not careful we might get to the position where the real exploitation in Tanzania is that of the town dwellers exploiting the peasants.

The people and agriculture
The development of a country is brought about by people, not by money. Money, and the wealth it represents, is the result and not the basis of development. The four prerequisites of development are different; they are (a) people; (b) land; (c) good policies; (d) good leadership. Our country has more than ten million people and its area is more than 937 500 square kilometres.

Agriculture is the basis of development

A great part of Tanzania's land is fertile and gets sufficient rain. Our country can produce various crops for home consumption and for export.

We can produce food crops (which can be exported if we produce in large quantities) such as maize, rice, wheat, beans, groundnuts, etc. And we can produce such cash crops as sisal, cotton, coffee, tobacco, pyrethrum, tea, etc. Our land is also good for grazing cattle, goats, sheep, and for raising chickens, etc.; we can get plenty of fish from our rivers, lakes, and from the sea. All of our farmers are in areas which can produce two or three or even more of the food and cash crops enumerated above, and each farmer could increase his production so as to get more food or more money. And because the main aim of development is to get more food, and more money for our other needs, our purpose must be to increase production of these agricultural crops. This is in fact the only road through which we can develop our country—in other words, only by increasing our production of these things can we get more food and more money for every Tanzanian.

The conditions of development

(a) *Hard Work*   Everybody wants development; but not everybody understands and accepts the basic requirements for development. The biggest requirement is hard work. Let us go to the villages and talk to our people and see whether or not it is possible for them to work harder.

In towns, for example, wage-earners normally work for seven and a half or eight hours a day, and for six or six and a half days a week. This is about 45 hours a week for the whole year, except for two or three weeks leave. In other words, a wage-earner works for 45 hours a week for 48 or 50 weeks of the year.

For a country like ours these are really quite short working hours. In other countries, even those which are more developed than we are, people work for more than 45 hours a week. It is not normal for a young country to start with such a short working week. The normal thing is to begin with long working hours and decrease them as the country becomes more and more prosperous. By starting with such short working hours and asking for even shorter hours, we are in fact imitating the more developed countries. And we shall regret this imitation. Nevertheless, wage-earners do work for 45 hours per week and their annual vacation does not exceed four weeks.

It would be appropriate to ask our farmers, especially the men, how many hours a week and how many weeks a year they work. Many do not even work for half as many hours as the wage-earner does. The truth is that in the villages the women work very hard. At times they work for 12 or 14 hours a day. They even work on Sundays and public holidays. Women who live in the villages work harder than anybody else in Tanzania. But the men who live in villages (and some of the women in towns) are on leave for half of their life. The energies of the millions of men in the villages and thousands of women in the towns which are at presented wasted in gossip, dancing and drinking, are a great treasure which could contribute more towards the development of our country than anything we could get from rich nations.

We would be doing something very beneficial to our country if we went to the villages and told our people that they hold this treasure and that it is up to them to use it for their own benefit and the benefit of our whole nation.

(b) *Intelligence*   The second condition of development is the use of intelligence. Unintelligent hard work would not bring the same good results as the two combined. Using a big hoe instead of a small one; using a plough pulled by oxen instead of an ordinary hoe; the use of fertilisers; the use of insecticides; knowing the right crop for a particular season or soil; choosing good seeds for planting; knowing the right time for planting, weeding, etc.; all these things show the use of knowledge and intelligence. And all of them combine with hard work to produce more and better results.

The money and time we spend on passing on this knowledge to the peasants are better spent and bring more benefits to our country than the money and great amount of time we spend on other things which we call development.

These facts are well known to all of us. The parts of our Five-Year Development Plan which are on target, or where the target has been exceeded, are those parts which depend solely upon the people's own hard work. The production of cotton, coffee, cashew nuts, tobacco and pyrethrum has increased enormously for the past three years. But these are things which are produced by hard work and the good leadership of the people, not by the use of great amounts of money.

Furthermore the people, through their own hard work and with a little help and leadership, have finished many development projects in the villages. They have built schools, dispensaries, community centres, and roads; they have dug wells, water channels, animal dips, small dams, and completed various other development projects. Had they waited for money, they would not now have the use of these things.

Hard work is the root of development

Some Plan projects which depend on money are going on well, but there are many which have stopped and others which might never be fulfilled because of lack of money. Yet still we talk about money and our search for money increases and takes nearly all our energies. We should not lessen our efforts to get the money we really need, but it would be more appropriate for us to spend time in the villages showing the people how to bring about development through their own efforts rather than going on so many long and expensive journeys abroad in search of development money. This is the real way to bring development to everybody in the country.

None of this means that from now on we will not need money or that we will not start industries or embark upon development projects which require money. Furthermore, we are not saying that we will not accept, or even that we shall not look for, money from other countries for our development. This is *not* what we are saying. We will continue to use money; and each year we will use more money for the various development projects than we used the previous year because this will be one of the signs of our development.

What we are saying, however, is that from now on we shall know what is the foundation and what is the fruit of development. Between *money* and *people* it is obvious that the people and their *hard work* are the foundation of development, and money is one of the fruits of that hard work.

From now on we shall stand upright and walk forward on our feet rather than look at this problem upside down. Industries will come and money will come but their foundation is *the people* and their *hard work*, especially in *agriculture*. This is the meaning of self-reliance.

Our emphasis should therefore be on: (a) the land and agriculture; (b) the people; (c) the policy of socialism and self-reliance; and (d) good leadership.

(a) *The Land* Because the economy of Tanzania depends and will continue to depend on agriculture and animal husbandry, Tanzanians can live well without depending on help from outside if they use their land properly. Land is the basis of human life and all Tanzanians should use it as a valuable investment for future development. Because the land belongs to the nation, the government has to see to it that it is used for the benefit of the whole nation and not for the benefit of one individual or just a few people.

It is the responsibility of TANU to see that the country produces enough food and enough cash crops for export. It is the responsibility of the government and the co-operative societies to see to it that our people get the necessary tools, training and leadership in modern methods of agriculture.

(b) *The People* In order properly to implement the policy of self-reliance, the people have to be taught the meaning of self-reliance and its practice. They must become self-sufficient in food, serviceable clothes and good housing.

In our country work should be something to be proud of, and laziness, drunkenness and idleness should be things to be ashamed of. And for the defence of our nation, it is necessary for us to be on guard against internal stooges who could be used by external enemies who aim to destroy us. The people should always be ready to defend their nation when they are called upon to do so.

(c) *Good policies* The principles of our policy of self-reliance go hand in hand with our policy on socialism. In order to prevent exploitation it is necessary for everybody to work and to live on his own labour. And in order to distribute the national wealth fairly, it is necessary for everybody to work to the maximum of his ability. Nobody should go and stay for a long time with his relative, doing no work, because in doing so he will be exploiting his relative. Likewise, nobody should be allowed to loiter in towns or villages without doing work which would enable him to be self-reliant without exploiting his relatives.

TANU believes that everybody who loves his nation has a duty to serve it by co-operating with his fellows in building the country for the benefit of all the people of Tanzania. In order to maintain our independence and our people's freedom we ought to be self-reliant in every possible way and avoid depending upon other countries for assistance. If every individual is self-reliant the ten-house cell will be self-reliant; if all the cells are self-reliant the whole ward will be self-reliant; and if the wards are self-reliant the District will be self-reliant. If the Districts are self-reliant, then the Region is self-reliant, and if the Regions are self-reliant, then the whole nation is self-reliant and this is our aim.

(d) *Good leadership* TANU recognised the urgency and importance of good leadership. But we have not yet produced systematic training for our leaders; it is necessary that TANU Headquarters should now prepare a programme of training for all leaders—from the national level to the ten-house cell level—so that every one of them understands our political and economic policies. Leaders must set a good example to the rest of the people in their lives and in all their activities.

Part Four: TANU Membership

Since the party was founded we have put great emphasis on getting as many members as possible. This was the right policy during the independence struggle. But now the National Executive feels that the time has come when we should put more emphasis on the beliefs of our party and its policies of socialism.

That part of the TANU constitution which relates to the admission of a member should be adhered to, and if it is discovered that a man does not appear to accept the faith, the objects, and the rules and regulations of the Party, then he should not be accepted as a member. In particular, it should not be forgotten that TANU is a party of peasants and workers.

Part Five: The Arusha Resolution

Therefore, the National Executive Committee, meeting in the Community Centre at Arusha from 26 January 1967 to 29 January 1967 resolves:

1 The Leadership
(a) Every TANU and government leader must be either a peasant or worker, and should in no way be associated with the practices of capitalism or feudalism.
(b) No TANU or government leader should hold shares in any company.
(c) No TANU or government leader should hold directorships in any privately-owned enterprise.
(d) No TANU or government leader should receive two or more salaries.
(e) No TANU or government leader should own houses which he rents to others.
(f) For the purposes of this Resolution the term 'leader' should comprise the following:
Members of the TANU National Executive Committee; Ministers; Members of Parliament; senior officials of organisations affiliated to TANU; senior officials of para-statal organisations; all those appointed or elected under any clause of the TANU Constitution; councillors; and civil servants in the high and middle cadres. (In this context 'leader' means a man, or a man and his wife; a woman, or a woman and her husband.)

2 The Government and other institutions
(a) Congratulates the government for the steps it has taken so far in the implementation of the policy of socialism.
(b) Calls upon the government to take further steps in the implementation of our policy of socialism as described in Part Two of this document without waiting for a Presidential Commission on Socialism.
(c) Calls upon the government to put emphasis, when preparing its development plans, on the ability of this country to implement the plans rather than depending on foreign loans and grants as has been done in the current Five-Year Development Plan. The National Executive Committee also resolves that the Plan should be amended so as to make it fit in with the policy of self-reliance.
(d) Calls upon the government to take action designed to ensure that the incomes of workers in the private sector are not very different from the incomes of workers in the public sector.
(e) Calls upon the government to put great emphasis on actions which will raise the standard of living of the peasants, and the rural community.
(f) Calls upon NUTA, the cooperatives, TAPA, UWT, TYL, and other government institutions, to take steps to implement the policy of socialism and self-reliance.

3 Membership
Members should get thorough teaching on party ideology so that they may understand it, and they should always be reminded of the importance of living up to its principles.

16 TANU Guidelines on Guarding, Consolidating and Advancing the Revolution of Tanzania, and of Africa*

Introduction

1 Today our African continent is a hot-bed of the liberation struggle. This struggle is between those who have for centuries been exploiting Africa's natural resources and using the people of this continent as their tools and as their slaves, and the people of Africa who have, after realising their weakness and exploitation, decided to engage in the struggle to liberate themselves.

It is both a bitter and continuing struggle: at times it is a silent one, occasionally it explodes like gunpowder, at other times the successes and gains achieved by the people slip away.

This has been the history of Africa since 1960 when many African states obtained flag independence. Since that year many legitimate African governments have been forcefully toppled and new governments established. Recently, sudden changes have been brought about by force in Uganda, where puppet Amin and a group of fellow soldiers have rebelled against the government of the revolutionary UPC led by President Obote.

The majority of the armed forces do not accept the rebellion and many of them, particularly senior officers, have been killed by the puppets. It is obvious that those who hail the rebellion are those who opposed the UPC policy of bringing about unity and socialism and eradicating tribalism and exploitation.

This is why our party has the duty to spell out the aims of the Tanzanian and the African revolution, and to identify the enemies of this revolution, in order to set out policies and strategies which will enable us to safeguard, consolidate and further our revolution.

2 Revolutions are quick social changes, changes which wrest from the minority the power they exploited for their own benefit (and that of external exploiters) and put it in the hands of the majority so that they can promote their own well-being. The opposition of a revolution is a counter-revolution: that is, quick and sudden changes which wrest power from the majority and hand it over to the minority with the aim of stopping the progress of the masses.

3 The greatest aim of the African revolution is to liberate the African. This liberation is not sent from heaven, it is achieved by combating exploitation, colonialism and imperialism. Nor is liberation brought by specialists or experts. We who are being humiliated, exploited and oppressed are the experts of this liberation. There is no nation in the world which can teach the Africans how to liberate themselves. The duty of liberating ourselves lies with us, and the necessary expertise will be obtained during the struggle itself.

4 Furthermore, the present situation in Africa shows that there is no people

---

* From *The African Review*, 1, 4 (1972), pp. 1–8 © Chama Cha Mapinduzi.

in any African state which has achieved the stage of total liberation. Africa is still a continent of people suffering from the weakness inherent in being exploited and humiliated. That is why revolutionary political parties in independent African countries, such as TANU, are still in fact liberation movements.

5 The African revolution, whose aim is the true liberation of the African, is in conflict with policies of exploitation, colonialism, neo-colonialism and imperialism. The object of colonialism, neo-colonialism and imperialism is to ensure that Africa's wealth is used for the benefit of the capitalists of Europe and America, instead of benefiting the African countries themselves. Therefore, participating in the African revolution is participating in the struggle against colonialism and imperialism.

6 The imperialist countries which have been exploiting and oppressing Africa for centuries are those in Western Europe, particularly Britain, France, Portugal, Belgium and Spain. These countries are the ones really confronting the African people on the question of liberating Africa. Different attempts to distort the progress of the African revolution stem from the plots of European imperialists who are bent on maintaining and continuing their old exploitation.

7 For Tanzania it must be understood that the imperialist enemies we are confronting are British imperialism, Portuguese colonialism, the racism and apartheid of South Africa and Rhodesia. For historical, geographical and political reasons these imperialists will be ready to attack us whenever they have an opportunity.

8 The Portuguese invasion of the Republic of Guinea is a big lesson for us. Guinea was invaded by the Portuguese imperialists firstly because of its policy of equality and its opposition to exploitation, and secondly because of its genuine stand in supporting the freedom fighters in Guinea-Bissau and Africa. For similar reasons the imperialists may attempt to attack Tanzania one day. But Guinea has also taught us that when the people and the army stand solidly together, no imperialist will be able to subvert their independence.

9 The lesson we draw from Uganda is one of treachery and counter-revolution. It shows that, instead of invading the country to overthrow the revolutionary government, imperialism prefers to use local puppets to overthrow the legitimate government and replace it with a government of 'foremen' or puppets. Such a government will allow the imperialists to exploit national wealth in partnership with the local bourgeoisie.

The people must learn from the events in Uganda and those in Guinea that, although imperialism is still strong, its ability to topple a revolutionary government greatly depends on the possibility of getting domestic counter-revolutionary puppets to help in thwarting the revolution.

10 We Tanzanians value our national independence because it is from that point that our liberation, and our aspirations for a liberation struggle in conjunction with other African people, begin. For this reason, we have the duty to take all necessary steps to enable us to guard our independence in order to further our revolution and thus make Tanzania a true example of the African revolution.

The Party

11 The responsibility of the party is to lead the masses, and their various institutions, in the effort to safeguard national independence and to advance the liberation of the African. The duty of a socialist party is to guide all activities of the masses. The government, parastatals, national organisations, etc. are instruments for implementing the party's policies. Our short history of independence reveals problems that may arise when a party does not guide its instruments. The time has now come for the party to take the reins and lead all the people's activities.

12 The first task of the leadership is to spell out the national goal. This is understood and the party has already fulfilled this duty. Our aim is to build socialism in Tanzania. But to attain this objective the party must offer policies and guidelines concerning different aspects of the people's activities. The party has already given guidelines on socialism in rural areas, education for self-reliance, etc. There is still the need to clarify the party's policies on other matters, such as housing, workers, money and loan policies, etc.

13 But the charting of objectives and policies does not by itself constitute good leadership. Leadership also means organising the people. It is the party which decides on the structure of government, various institutions, the army, etc. In addition, the party should provide guidelines on work methods and attitudes, and decision-making.

The truth is that we have not only inherited a colonial governmental structure but also adopted colonial working habits and leadership methods. For example, we have inherited in the government, industries and other institutions the habit in which one man gives the orders and the rest just obey them. If you do not involve the people in work plans, the result is to make them feel a national institution is not theirs, and consequently workers adopt the habits of hired employees. The party has a duty to emphasise its leadership on this issue.

14 In addition to organising the people, leadership involves supervising the implementation of the party's policy. Ways must be found to ensure that the party actively supervises the activities and the running of its implementing agencies. Leadership also entails reviewing the results of implementation. It is the party's duty to ensure that it assesses the effects of the policy implementation undertaken by its agencies. This is the only way to establish whether people participate in devising solutions to their problems in offices, institutions, the army, villages, industries, etc.

15 Together with the issue of involving the people in solving their problems, there is also the question of the habits of leaders in their work and in day-to-day life.

There must be a deliberate effort to build equality between the leaders and those they lead. For a Tanzanian leader it must be forbidden to be arrogant, extravagant, contemptuous and oppressive. The Tanzanian leader has to be a person who respects people, scorns ostentation and who is not a tyrant. He should epitomise heroism, bravery, and be a champion of justice and equality.

Similarly, the party has the responsibility to fight the vindictiveness of some of its agents, such actions do not promote socialism but drive a wedge between the Party and the government on the one side and the people on the other.

16 There are presently some leaders who do not fulfil these conditions. They disregard and cleverly avoid the leadership code. The time has come for the party to supervise the conduct and the bearing of the leaders.

Foreign policy

17 Our foreign policy is one of non-alignment. We are ready to cooperate in a friendly manner with any country that wishes us well, be it from the East or West. The second important aspect of our foreign policy is to strengthen relations with, and cooperate in supporting, genuine liberation movements in Africa. We have said earlier that our own party is still a liberation movement.

At the moment in Africa the liberation movements are in the vanguard of the struggle against colonialism and imperialism. By strengthening our co-operation, in the knowledge that their war is our war, we shall double our strength in bringing about the total liberation of Africa. The Party must take the necessary steps to establish this revolutionary relationship with revolutionary movements of Africa, Asia and Latin America.

Similarly it is our duty to establish fraternal and revolutionary relations with those American citizens fighting for justice and human equality.

18 In addition, we have the obligation to strengthen cooperation and solidarity with revolutionary African countries because all of us are in the same boat and our destination is one. With unity and cooperation, our enemies will not be able to destroy us one by one as is now their habit.

19 At the United Nations and other international organisations, there is need to stress cooperation with all friendly, socialist revolutionary countries in Africa, Asia, and Latin America.

Uganda and the East African Community

20 We value the political and economic benefits derived from the cooperation that exists among the partner states of the East African Community. Therefore, the present situation created by the puppet Amin in subverting the legitimate government of UPC greatly disturbs us, because it has given rise to difficulties in co-operation and in running the activities of the Community.

If the situation continues as it is it may make the progress and the activities of the Community extremely difficult to maintain, and will weaken East African cooperation. The party supports the government's stand on Uganda and the East African Community. Although it is for the people of Uganda to decide on matters relating to Uganda's liberation, it is the duty of the Tanzanian people to support the efforts of their Ugandan brothers to liberate themselves.

Defence and Security

21 The basis of Tanzania's development is the people themselves—every Tanzanian—in particular each patriot and each socialist. Tanzania's defence and security depend on Tanzanians themselves—every Tanzanian, in particular each patriot, each socialist.

22 Had our party been forced to wage a liberation war, every TANU member would have been a soldier, either in the army or wherever he was. A TANU member would have been a soldier and a soldier a TANU member. It is not only the party which would have been a liberation movement, but the army

also would have been a liberation army—fist and shield of the liberation movement.

23 Our party was not forced to fight a liberation war. It was a liberation movement without a liberation army. But since 1964 we have been building the Tanzanian People's Defence Forces. And just as TANU is still a liberation movement, the Tanzania People's Defence Force is the liberation army of the people of Tanzania.

TANU's relations with TPDF should be those of a people's party and a people's army. It is up to TANU to ensure that the people's army is the army for both the liberation and the defence of the people. It is TANU's responsibility to ensure that the army's main task in peacetime is to enable the people to safeguard their independence and their policy of socialism and self-reliance.

24 The National Executive Committee stresses the implementation of the Arusha Declaration and particularly the need to arouse political consciousness so that every Tanzanian understands our national environment and the importance of safeguarding the security and the lives of the people, and of safeguarding our policies, our independence, our economy and our culture.

25 Political education must make the people aware of our national enemies and the strategies they employ to subvert our policies, our independence, our economy and our culture. To enable the people to confront the enemy, it is necessary to make them aware of the enemy's strength in all spheres, such as their army, their commercial enterprise, their life and habits, and the way these conflict with our convictions and aspirations.

26 In order that they be able to oppose our enemies, the people must know that it is they who are the nation's shield. This means that defence and security matters must be replaced in the hands of the people themselves. We do not have the means to establish large permanent armies to guard the whole country. Our army must be the people's army, used in teaching the people how to defend themselves in their localities and to enable them to report on matters of national security. Therefore it is imperative to start training a militia for the whole country. Since the militia will spread through the country, in cooperation with the regular army, they will have the duty to defend our territorial borders, our air space and to expose traitors and enemies, all in cooperation with our regular army.

The party leads the army
27 The registration of the militia and the army must be scrutinised very carefully, and supervised by the party. Ensuring cooperation between the army and the militia, and providing for political enducation to both, must be a prime responsibility of the party. The party must establish a sub-committee of the central committee to look into defence and security.

Economics and Progress

Progress of the people
28 For a people who have been slaves or have been oppressed, exploited and humiliated by colonialism or capitalism, 'development' means 'liberation'. Any action that gives them more control of their own affairs is an action for develop-

ment, even if it does not offer them better health or more bread. Any action that reduces their say in determining their own affairs or running their own lives is not development and retards them even if the action brings them a little better health and a little more bread.

To us development means both the elimination of oppression, exploitation, enslavement and humiliation, and the promotion of our independence and human dignity. Therefore, in considering the development of our nation and in preparing development plans, our main emphasis at all times should be the development of people and not of things. If development is to benefit the people, the people must participate in considering, planning and implementing their development plans.

The duty of our party is not to urge the people to implement plans which have been decided upon by a few experts and leaders. The duty of our party is to ensure that the leaders and experts implement the plans that have been agreed upon by the people themselves. When the people's decision requires information which is only available to the leaders and the experts, it will be the duty of leaders and experts to make such information available to the people. But it is not correct for leaders and experts to usurp the people's right to decide on an issue just because they have the expertise.

29 In order that the people shall be enthusiastic in the defence of their country, it is of first importance for the TANU government to place a lot of emphasis on improving their conditions.

The inherited economic structure which has kept many people out of the economic mainstream must be replaced immediately by programmes designed to boost the development expenditure and to spread investment to all districts. The Regional Development Fund has helped to arouse economic activities and has thus brought visible benefits to the people. It will be beneficial to increase allocations to the fund and to give this expenditure special priority when appropriating government finances. The party must stress the participation of the people in the various nation-building projects.

Savings
30 It is also the party's duty to educate the people on the importance of saving through national institutions such as the Savings Bank and the National Bank of Commerce, instead of just hoarding their money.

National economy
31 In consolidating the people's development, there is now a need to build and promote the internal economy. Although this was touched upon in the Second Five-Year Development Plan, its implementation has not been stressed, and therefore results have not been seen. The things that are produced in this country must also be protected from unnecessary foreign competition.

Foreign trade
32 In our external trade, we must avoid using our foreign reserves in buying items that do not help our economy. The government and its corporations must be an example—a thing that is not now being done. Our importing agencies must be given guidelines appropriate to our policy of socialism and self-reliance, and the guidelines must be adhered to. It is the duty of every Tanzanian, and particularly a leader, to remember that shortage of foreign exchange weakens our economy and endangers our national independence.

Parastatal institutions

33 The conduct and activities of the parastatals must be looked into to ensure that they help further our policy of socialism and self-reliance. The activities of the parastatals should be a source of satisfaction and not discontent. The party must ensure that the parastatals do not spend money extravagantly on items which do not contribute to the development of the national economy as a whole.

Surpluses

34 The government must supervise and guide the expenditure of surpluses accruing from the economic activities of the parastatals.

35 'We have been oppressed a great deal, we have been exploited a great deal and we have been disregarded a great deal. It is our weakness that has led to our being oppressed, exploited and disregarded. Now we want a revolution—a revolution which brings to an end our weakness, so that we are never again exploited, oppressed, or humiliated.'

17 Towards Economic Unity*

REGINALD H. GREEN and ANN SEIDMAN

Independent Africa has inherited fragmented, retarded, virtually undeveloped economies. Small-scale agricultural and craft production and local trade afford subsistence incomes for the bulk of the population. Colonial economic growth was all but entirely limited to export-import enclaves. Profits and interest on investment by foreign firms remitted overseas consumed the bulk of potential investible surpluses.

Specialising in the exploitation of a few mineral and forest resources, tropical products and cheap unskilled labour, the colonial export sectors of African territories could not produce national economic structures capable of sustained increases in *per capita* productivity. They could not even sustain growth in total production and exports. Relatively short periods of rapid growth alternated with stagnation and retrogression. There is little reason to assume that the spurt of growth in the basically colonial export-import enclaves which began after 1945 will continue much longer; indeed in many African states where the 1945–60 growth was most pronounced, stagnation has already reappeared in the traditional export sectors. While African economies remain dependent on foreign markets and sources of supply, African exports and markets have remained peripheral and without significant bargaining force in the world economy.

Economic advance and structural change

Economic independence and higher living standards require sustained advances in *per capita* output which can only be achieved through radical changes in the structure of African economies. Modern technology and human skills must be employed throughout. Qualitatively new stages and kinds of industry and agriculture are needed to attain sustained increases in productivity. Processing of primary products, the manufacture of complex consumer goods and the development of intermediate and capital goods industries are vital. Production for national markets must be increased. Individual productive enterprises must be planned in relation to each other so as to establish poles of growth. Economic planning must seek to maximise growth, reinforcing and spreading linkages among productive sectors. Production of exports, especially in processed form, should be expanded to augment the size of modern sectors and increase investible surpluses. But the primary focus of economic activity should be redirected from world markets and sources of supply to the national economy.

Essential structural changes do not take place automatically. African states have, in general, accepted the need to initiate planning and create appropriate economic institutions to ensure that such planning is put into effect.

The attainment of African command over all vital economic decisions is essential to the achievement of economic reconstruction. African states must find the means of exercising control over the foreign firms which dominate the strategic export-import sectors of their economies. These firms are often

*From *Unity or Poverty? The Economics of Pan-Africanism*, Penguin, 1968, pp. 343–520.

economically as large as, or larger than, the African governments themselves. Within the context of planned economic policy directed to African goals, foreign economic units might play a constructive role in the early stages of national economic reconstruction. But if they are not subject to direction and control by the African state, they will affect the patterns of economic change in ways most unlikely to serve African ends.

Most African governments realise that 'market forces'—especially when dominated by foreign private or public interests—will not provide incentives for the structural changes sought. The objectives of private economic interests, whether African or foreign, often differ from those held by the majority of the African people. Therefore most African states have sought to formulate and implement economic policies and programmes designed to assure that private decisions contribute to the fulfilment of national goals. Most have expressed their determination to build mixed economies, with the public sector playing a significant or even dominant role. Several have taken steps to create socialist economies. Almost all have accepted the responsibility for substantial public investment in productive sectors. Many have initiated programmes to limit private luxury consumption as well as remittances abroad so as to assure direction of individual savings to increased national output. A significant number have recognised that consistency and efficiency in the pursuit of national economic reconstruction require an overall coordination and harmonisation of projects, which is possible only in the framework of serious national economic planning, involving priority in the use of public revenues.

Limitations of African national economies

Individually, however, the plans of separate African states for economic reconstruction are for the most part doomed to total or partial frustration. Existing African states are severely limited in their capacity for planned economic change and rapid development by the limited range of national resources available to each state; the small size of their national markets (none of which reaches the minimum efficient size range of $30–40 billion); the lack of capital needed to provide large-sized efficient industrial complexes (a single one of which costs as much as $20–50 billion); and the inequalities imposed by their small economic size in bargaining with foreign interests. At best, national economic planning is difficult, limited and frustrating. At worst, it is a delusion and a farce.

Eur-Africa: a mirage

Eur-African proposals, exemplified by EEC-Associate Status, will not give African participants the significant control over export prices, the access to markets or the guarantees of investment flows they seek. Instead, they discriminate against other African, Asian and Latin American countries, and, on balance, retard structural change and national planning. An artificial network of price subsidies and tariff preferences for unprocessed exports and over-priced imports has been established. Investment has been allotted almost solely to expanding the mining-plantation sectors and supporting infrastructure which cannot result in a rational productive pattern designed to meet African needs. Concentrated dependence on the EEC and its members for markets, capital and high level manpower has substantially limited freedom in selecting economic strategies and policies.

African unity and economic size

The need for radical economic changes in the structure of production and international economic relations, combined with the near-impossibility of attaining them within economic units as small as the present states, forms the basic economic case for African political unity. Economic unity would enhance the possibility of achieving rapid continental growth in four major respects:

First, the range of natural resources available to a continental African economy would be such as to permit the production of most major agricultural and industrial products required by a modern economy. The merger of agricultural and mineral resources together with the joint use of major power and water supplies could create a significantly more effective natural resource base than the sum of resources divided among separate states.

Second, investments could be concentrated on efficient large-scale plants and specialisation in related industries, leading to rapid increases in productivity at reduced costs.

Third, an economic unit encompassing all free African states would be able to exert significant bargaining power on the world market. A unified African economy would be considerably larger than even the largest foreign private concern. Although it would still be economically smaller than the USSR, EEC, CMEA or EFTA, it would be roughly the same order of income size as India and potentially more influential because of its larger extra-continental trade. A unified Africa could take leadership in a way open to no single African state in formulating united bargaining and policy decisions among the 'low-income' countries of Asia, Africa, the Middle East and Latin America.

Finally, comprehensive economic planning would be much more practicable on a continental or, transitionally, semi-continental scale than for individual African states. Production, markets and investible surpluses could be planned and implemented on a consolidated basis. External trade could be treated as an integral element of the continental economy, rather than dominating production decisions, policy implementation and plan fulfilment.

Towards continental planning

There is widespread agreement on the advantages of continental economic integration. Complete unification of critical areas of economic policy, planning and implementation cannot be achieved in full immediately. Nevertheless, agreement should be attainable now on the fundamental principle that continental economic unity is desirable. A continental planning agency can then be established to coordinate state plans and formulate a minimum set of multinational projects. Continental institutions for coordinated specific purposes such as the African Development Bank can be created, and specific measures of economic coordination in production, trade and transport put into operation. Once initiated, this programme would demonstrate the value of unification and lay the basis for broadening its scope. At the same time such an approach would allow relative freedom of action to less convinced states. All partial approaches should, however, be evaluated not only in terms of their short-run benefits and costs, but of their contribution to, or hindrance of, further progress toward the creation of a unified African economy.

The continental planning agency could initially devote its attention to coordinating state plans in such a way as to promote multinational river-basin projects and industrial complexes that can assure significant poles of growth in every African state and region, so attaining harmonised and mutually reinforcing national economic growth. State planners would be aided in attaining markets and sources of supply, to stimulate the greatest possible development in their own state within a larger framework. Continental planning should include specific measures to create unified markets for designated products, both those traditionally involved in intra-African trade and the output of newly planned large-scale projects. Ranges of minimum and maximum supplies and prices would need to be adopted for the inter-state trade in these designated products. As rapidly as possible, these markets would be expanded to include all 'African produced' output. The continental planning agency would coordinate state plans to assure the creation of the necessary intra-African transportation and communication links.

The establishment of a continental planning agency would facilitate the formulation of a united continental policy on exports, designed to earn the greatest possible amounts of foreign exchange for the import of essential capital goods and equipment to promote new industry, agriculture transport and power projects.

Finally, continental integration should include establishment of monetary institutions to promote intra-African economic relations and achieve greater monetary autonomy. Creation of a continental clearing and payments union is important to facilitate intra-African trade. The longer-run goal should be an All-African monetary authority, essentially a continental central bank, which could, in cooperation with the continental planning agency, devise monetary policies to stimulate economic development and establish the basis for the ultimate creation of a continental currency. Backed by continental planning, the African Development Bank, too, could become far more effective in its tasks of mobilising continental investment surpluses as well as of bargaining with foreign interests for loans, grants and investment in strategic multinational projects.

The economic logic of political unification

While full continental economic unity can be approached rather gradually, its achievement requires the parallel establishment of permanent political relationships, embodied in some form of African continental government, with substantial decision-making powers least in the field of economic policy.

The creation of the initial programme for economic union will require a parallel set of decisions and institutions of a basically political nature. The formulation and implementation of a significant portion of economic policies cannot be entrusted to an autonomous technical body, but only to one responsible to African governments. It is impossible to blueprint the precise nature of the agency for the necessary political control, but it must meet two criteria: (1) It must be responsible to member governments; and (2) it must be capable of formulating broad policies and supervising their implementation competently and expeditiously. Neither annual meetings of Heads of State nor *ad hoc* Ministerial committees meet these requirements. An institutionalised council or parliament, with a constitution defining its powers and obligations, adopted by all member states, is essential. The importance of an agreed political framework for action directed towards economic unification is clear not only because major economic decisions are among the most vital of all political decisions, but also because without such a framework to insure permanence, the commitment of substantial resources to union-oriented economic activity would be extremely hazardous. This is true for the following reasons:

First, creation of a unified economy to achieve rapid structural change requires unification of planning strategy and implementation through a continental planning agency. The decisions of the planning body will be of crucial political as well as economic importance to each state. Quite clearly, no state can entrust powers to make and enforce basic economic-political decisions to a body over which it does not have political control. No single state could expect to control any decision or expect to agree fully with each; but it would require all decisions to be made in a framework of agreed socio-political goals and economic strategies, adopted as the underlying basis for specific economic decisions.

Second, continental economic integration requires a permanent political structure on strictly economic grounds. No African state can afford to tie its plans to, or invest its scarce resources in, intra-African specialisation of production and trade unless it is absolutely confident that the new structural pattern will be permanent.

Only after the basic political decision has been taken to create a permanent economic framework, including an acceptable political body for formulating continent-wide economic action, can African states proceed with confidence to coordinate their state plans through a continental planning body. The many economic policies and institutions which they have in common will provide the foundation for the minimum agreements required in strategic areas to assure dynamic continental economic growth. At the same time, such agreements may be so devised as to assure each state of the opportunity to pursue its own political-economic option for internal development.

The need to act on an initially limited front and build from it has been cogently argued by President Nyerere, in his address to the UAR National Assembly on 9 April 1967:

> Like-mindedness even on major social and economic issues is not likely to be achieved even after Unity; it will never be achieved before.
>
> To imagine a merger of sovereignties will automatically solve inter-African conflicts is to invite disaster. Unity will simply change the context in which these problems can be tackled. The socialist policies of our own countries must be safeguarded, the African-orientated policies of non-socialist [African] states will also have to be safeguarded.

The need for deliberate haste

African economic unification cannot be allowed to remain in the realm of pure speculation and debate on desirable long-term policy. Immediate steps towards economic unification are imperative. If the case for African economic unity on the grounds of promoting development is valid, the continued failure of African economies to unite must lower their rates of growth and inhibit development of structurally sound patterns of production and trade. The growth rate of investible surplus as well as of consumption, education and social services will remain lower than it could be with unification. The gap between Africa and the industrialised states will continue to widen both absolutely and relatively.

Not only will growth be less rapid than it could be with continental planning, but it will continue to be, of necessity, either totally dependent on extra-continental trade or developed along national autarchic lines. No African state can afford to act as if economic union existed, until it is really achieved; and each will necessarily undertake projects and programmes on the basis of a national plan quite different from and inferior to, its potential place in an all-African plan. Further investment in these patterns will limit the ultimate scope of policy for the optimum location of continental projects. Every sub-optimal assembly plant or factory built not only decreases the benefits to be derived from ultimate African territorial specialisation, but also creates vested public and private interests opposed to joint planning and industrial specialisa-tion. In time, the growth of such interests, often linked with those of foreign investors and neo-colonial governmental policies, may become insuperable obstacles to African unity.

If existing negative tendencies arising from autarchic planning are to be halted and reversed, deliberate haste is critical. The urgency is sharply exposed by the fact that, should the industrial and agricultural targets of all the African plans initiated in the 1960s be carried out on an autarchic basis, the momentum towards narrow nationalist economic policies will probably prevent any serious moves towards economic unification for several decades. On the other hand, formulation of industrial location and market development agreements in the next four to six years, covering twenty to thirty key industries, could create the basic momentum necessary for cementing continental African economic and political union within this decade.

In the words of President Nyerere's 1967 Cairo lecture, quoted above:

... the problems which threaten to overwhelm us individually become containable in a wider context. The people of Africa are the only justification for African unity and they are the only means through which it will be attained. Africa must be free. And Africa's freedom will come only through united action. Any step to unity is a help provided that the ultimate goal of a united Africa is not precluded.

Proposed institutions, strategies, and policies must meet two tests: first, are they realistic and widely acceptable enough to be adopted and implemented, thereby creating growing gains from a broadening area of unification; second, are they consistent with the basic goal of African union, building up forces and reasons for, rather than objections and obstacles to, its attainment?

The choice confronting the peoples and governments of Africa seems clear. Either they unite, in a political framework, to plan the continental economic growth that is essential to economic independence and higher living standards; or they are doomed to increasing separate sacrifices with no more result than a general stagnation. The longer the decision to unite is postponed, the harder it will be to make, because of the growth in uneconomic autarchic production. Initiation *now* of positive measures towards continental unification is imperative, if dynamic economic development is to be attained, and the huge human need of Africa is ever to be met.

18 Perspectives of Armed Struggle in South Africa*

JOE SLOVO

It is clear that the South African liberation movement's endeavour to lay a basis for sustained armed struggle is perhaps the most difficult on the whole African continent. The enemy here is in stable command of a rich and varied economy, which can finance a massive military budget, of £594 million in 1975, even at the stage when it is not required to extend itself. It has a well-trained army and para-military police force. It can draw on considerable manpower resources from among the overwhelming majority of the four million privileged whites, who can be expected to fight with great ferocity and conviction to sustain their privileges. In addition it has rich and influential allies to help build its military and economic potential. It faces an unarmed people historically deprived of opportunities to learn the skills of modern warfare. And it has one of the most sophisticated repressive security machines in the world. If then the employment of force is a subjective imperative, what about these objective difficulties?

The recent history of guerrilla struggle has underlined the fact that the material strength of the enemy is by no means a decisive factor. Witness the resources at the disposal of the French in Algeria; at the height of the fighting, 600 000 troops were supplied and serviced by a leading industrial nation from an economic base quite outside the reach of military operations. Consider the unsurpassed superiority of pure material strength and almost limitless resources of the USA in Vietnam? Yet neither modern industrial backing, technical know-how nor fire-power swayed the balance in favour of the invaders. Grivas and his Cyprus group challenged the British Army with forty-seven rifles, twenty-seven automatic weapons and seven revolvers. ('It was with these arms and these alone that I kept the fight going for almost a year without any appreciable reinforcements'.)[1]

Guerrilla warfare, almost by definition, posits a situation of vast imbalance in material and military resources between the opposing sides. It is designed to cope particularly with a situation in which the enemy is infinitely superior in every conventional factor of warfare. It is supremely the weapon of the materially weak against the materially strong. With a populace increasingly supporting and protecting it whilst opposing and exposing the enemy, a people's army is assured of survival and growth by skilful exercise of tactics. Surprise, mobility and tactical retreat make it difficult for the enemy to bring its superior firepower into play in any decisive battles. No individual battle is fought under circumstances unfavourable to the guerrilla. Superior force can be harassed, weakened and, in the end, destroyed.

The absence of an orthodox front of fighting lines; the need of the enemy to attenuate his resources and lines of communication over vast distances; his need to protect the widely scattered installations on which his economy is dependent (because the guerrilla pops up now here, now there); these are among the factors which serve, in the long run, to compensate the guerrillas

---

*From 'South Africa—No Middle Road', in Basil Davidson, Joe Slovo and A. Wilkinson, *South Africa: The New Politics of Revolution*, Penguin, London, 1976, pp. 196–206.

for their disparity in initial strength. I stress the words 'in the long run' because it would be idle to dispute that for a long time the enemy has considerable military advantages from his high level of industrialisation, his ready-to-hand reserves of manpower and his excellent roads, railways and air transport which facilitate swift manoeuvre and speedy concentration of personnel.

But over a period of time, many of these very factors could begin to operate in favour of the liberation force. The resources, including food production, depend overwhelmingly upon black labour which will not remain docile and cooperative if the struggle grows in intensity. The white manpower resources, adequate initially, must become dangerously stretched as guerrilla warfare develops. The mobilisation of a large force for a protracted struggle would place a further burden on the workings of the economy. The South African Director-General of Strategic Studies, General J.H. Robertze, stressed the vulnerability of the South African economy in a paper on the strategic implications of recent developments in South Africa, presented to an international conference in Paris in early 1975.[2] He apprehensively predicted the establishment of 'active guerrilla bases' in both Angola and Mozambique. Of South Africa's agricultural production, he declared that, 'in the event of civil war or generalised violence this intricate economic machinery will be disrupted or destroyed'. Many installations, vital power and water supplies might be disrupted with disastrous effects; mines could be flooded. All this, General Robbertze maintains, could lead directly to a virtual paralysis of industrial activity in the country.

In contrast to many other major guerrilla struggles (Cuba was one of the exceptions), the enemy's economic and manpower resources are all situated within South Africa, the theatre of war. There is no economic base area which can remain safe from sabotage, mass action and guerrilla strikes. In an underdeveloped country, the interruption of supplies to any given region may be no more than a local setback. But in a highly sensitive modern economic structure of the South African type, the successful interruption of transport to any major industrial complex would inflict immense damage on the whole economy and on the morale of the enemy. The South African forces would have the task of keeping intact about 48 300 kilometres of railway lines spread across an area of over 1 000 000 square kilometres.

One of the more popular misconceptions concerning guerrilla warfare is that a physical environment which conforms to a special pattern is indispensable: thick jungle, inaccessible mountain ranges, swamps, and so forth. The availability of such terrain is, to be sure, of enormous advantage to the guerrillas, especially in the early non-operational phase when training and other preparatory steps are undertaken, and no external bases are available for this purpose. However, when the operations commence, the guerrilla cannot survive, let alone flourish, unless he moves to areas where people live and work and where the enemy can be engaged in combat. If he is fortunate enough to have behind him a friendly border or areas of difficult access which can provide temporary refuge, it is of course advantageous; although it sometimes brings with it its own set of problems, connected mainly with supplies. But guerrilla warfare can, and has been, successfully waged in every conceivable type of terrain; in deserts, in swamps, in farm fields, in built-up areas, in plains, in the bush and in countries without friendly borders.

The sole question is one of adjusting survival tactics to the sort of terrain in which operations have to be conducted. In any case, in the vast expanse that is South Africa, a people's force will find a multitude of variations in topography; deserts, mountain forests, veld, and swamps. There might not be a single impregnable Sierra Maestra or impenetrable jungle, but the country abounds in terrain which in general is certainly no less favourable for guerrilla operations than some of the terrain in which the Algerians or the resistance movements in occupied Europe operated. Tito, when told that a certain area was 'as level as the palm of your hand and with very little forests', retorted: 'What a first-class example it is of the relative unimportance of geographical factors in the development of a rising'.

In particular, South Africa's great size will make it extremely difficult, if not impossible, for the ruling power to keep the whole of it under armed surveillance in strength and in depth. Hence, an early development of a relatively safe (though shifting) rear is not beyond the realm of possibility. The undetected existence of a SWAPO training camp inside Namibia for over a year and, more especially, the survival for years in the mountains and hills in the Transkei of the leaders of 'Intaba' during the military occupation of the area after the 1960 Pondo Revolt, support this possibility.

A look ahead

But, theory aside, the stark reality is that after more than ten years of effort, there is as yet no evidence of any form of military engagement inside the country. Critics of the liberation movement's strategy during this period have attributed its lack of success to a combination of organisational mistakes and formidable objective obstacles. They point to the fact that since the immediate post-Sharpeville low, the regime has shown a relative economic and political stability, has strengthened its external ties, and has not faced a crisis of the proportions which normally precedes a revolutionary breakthrough. They question whether there are 'grounds for declaring that (the people) prefer death to oppression, the finality of annihilation to the indeterminacy of existence',[3] and ask whether there is a psychological readiness and a motivation among the Africans to use violence.[4]

Some academic analysts also conclude that the people's readiness to seek a solution by force seems minimal since, 'in spite of the structural violence embodied in South African society, individual violent reactions against this situation have been remarkably limited'.[5] Doubt is expressed whether there are present in South Africa the very specialised conditions in which armed revolutions have made headway elsewhere.[6] It is also suggested that the 'reformist option' persisted 'long past the point in time when a decision to shift from non-violent struggle might have stood a remote chance of possible success'.[7]

In one form or another, all the critics stress the difficulties of an unarmed people, deprived of opportunities to learn the skills of modern warfare, engaging a powerful and highly industrialised enemy; a factor aggravated by the absence of friendly border states. Most also allude to the negative effects of exile politics in a period in which internal national leadership had been distroyed.

To recognise the validity or partial validity of some of these assessments does not imply that the armed tactic has no place in South Africa's future liberation strategy. Indeed, the ANC and its allies continue to regard the introduction of force as one of the main foundations of such a strategy. They do so for a number of reasons. In the first place the struggle for majority rule in South Africa today has no realistic backing without it. To abandon the armed tactic is to abandon the people to forces willing to settle for the scraps of power and not its substance. However long the struggle still takes and however many lessons there are still to be learnt, it is unthinkable for South African revolutionaries, in this era, to return to struggle for reforms only within the white framework; for this is the only alternative.

The obstacles facing the liberation movement in pursuit of its strategy may have disappointed earlier hopes and defied some of the more optimistic predictions. But the defeatist conclusions of many academic analysts are static in their conception and show an onlooker's separation from the demands and processes of active revolutionary struggle. Was there any demonstrable evidence in Mozambique in 1962, when FRELIMO charted the armed path, that the mass preferred 'death to oppression' or that they were psychologically ready to use violence? Were there any more individual reactions against violence in pre-1958 Guinea-Bissau than there are in South Africa? Were the French occupiers of Algeria or the Portuguese occupiers of Angola passing through an identifiable moment of economic or political collapse when the liberation forces in these territories launched their own armed activities? Did the Cubans have a friendly border? Did none of these movements make serious tactical mistakes and were they not also, for a time, dogged by the exile syndrome?

The combination of favourable and unfavourable conditions in which each of these struggles had to be launched was different in each territory. South Africa, too, is a special case. But what is common to them all is that a people which has exhausted the 'reformist option' responds to the revolutionary one when the feasibility of hitting the enemy has been demonstrated by deeds as well as words.

Experiences have been gained and lessons learnt by the ANC and its allies. Against the background of the changing external and internal situations, a more hopeful basis is emerging for the success of a strategy which includes the factor of organised force.

Inside the country there are once again signs of a significant upswing in political awareness and militancy. This will gain momentum as the system remains incapable of overcoming the ever-recurring financial and economic crises inherent in the capitalist mode of production, and more especially as the special contradictions which flow from its internal racialist-colonialist character intensify. The efforts to slow down and reverse the process of permanent black urbanisation has not succeeded, and white dependence on black labour is growing inexorably.[8] This, together with the depressed state of black wages, has already triggered off economic struggles in the recent period which are giving the workers a renewed consciousness of their collective strength. The mining industry, so dependent on foreign labour, faces severe difficulties of labour supply and is being forced to reconsider its migratory labour policies. The creation of a more permanent black work force would, for obvious reasons, strengthen the potential for class-based economic and political pressures.

In the Reserves a situation with enormous explosive potential is being created by the crowding into its limited area of more and more millions of impoverished, land-hungry and unemployed Africans.[9]

The working and student youth, in particular, are in search of a strategy which will begin to lay the basis of the struggle for power. At the universities and in the schools the mood is one of growing hostility to white rule. Organisations such as SASO have not only challenged government policy at the educational institutions but have involved themselves in wider political struggles.

Government attempts to gain Coloured and Indian acceptance of relatively powerless communal institutions as a substitute for direct political representation have made little headway. The Coloured Labour Party, in particular, has once again (in the March 1975 elections) won overwhelming support for its rejection of differential institutions. Indian workers in Natal showed an impressive degree of solidarity with the striking Africans, and many Indian youths have begun to play an active role in newly formed black organisations with militant anti-apartheid postures. New attempts have been made to revive the Indian Congress movement.

But in all these areas of reawakening, it is already clear that police harassment and intimidation set a limit to the activity and growth of purely legal mass structures. Beyond the struggle for 'moderate' reforms within the framework of continuing white domination, there hovers the state's legal and administrative hatchet. Thus the renewed awareness can no longer express itself, as it could during the 1950s, in sustained mass demonstrations. Nor can the struggle for power be mounted by mass legal pressures alone, although these constitute an essential ingredient in the unfolding of the struggle. Without the direct or indirect backing of offensive and defensive force and effective underground mass leadership, the limits are self-evident; but, with it, this ferment once again sets a more hopeful scene for radical political advances.

If the elusive psychological factor is to be given its place in the projection of future responses to armed activity, there can be no doubt that it has become more favourable for South Africa's liberation movement. The armed victories in the former Portuguese territories and the perceptible progress of armed actions in Zimbabwe and in the Caprivi Strip have had a great inspirational impact on South Africa's black people: because, unlike other such victories, they have happened and are happening next door. And, as already emphasised, these events have also driven home to South Africa's ruling class the growing likelihood of internal insurgency in the not too distant future.

But the people's expectations and the enemy's fears aside, there can be no doubt that the dramatic transformation which has taken place in southern Africa has eliminated one of the most serious obstacles in the path of people's insurgency. South Africa is no longer cushioned by states actively hostile to the South African liberation movement. This is not to belittle South Africa's internal strength, which is shored up by direct and behind-the-scenes support from the West. Nor can we dismiss the continued possibility of 'some independent African states taking a leading part in championing the cause of what amounts to collaboration with the counter-revolution'.[10] But despite these factors, both the internal and external balance of forces have become much more favourable to liberation endeavours. The changes that have taken place, especially on South Africa's borders, provide the more militant lobby in the OAU with renewed incentives to oppose the trend of compromise perceptible in the Lusaka Manifesto and in the recent dialogue manoeuvres.

But at the end of the day, the tendencies to support the liberation drive will only become lasting realities through the efforts of the liberation movement itself and its support groups throughout the world. Above all, the extent to which the world translates its verbal condemnation of the racist regime into significant action against it and more direct support for the liberation movement, will depend upon events inside the country.

The liberation movement recognises that well-planned activities by its armed wing is not the only immediate perspective of struggle in South Africa. Mass political mobilisation of people in the urban and rural areas is a vital ingredient and requires a combination of all methods: legal, semi-legal and clandestine. The muscle power of the black working class needs to find stronger organisational expression through the building of a powerful trade union movement. The Bantustan deception must be exposed and fought both inside and outside the so-called 'homelands'. The struggle can no longer be centred on pleas for civil rights or for reforms within the framework of white dominance; it is a struggle for people's power, in which mass ferment and the growing importance of the armed factor go hand in hand. The liberation movement points to this as the only path which can be trodden by the oppressed mass if it is not to submit permanently to white overlordship. An underground leadership presence within the country itself is the most vital element in the phase ahead, and there are signs that this is closer than at any time since the pre-Rivonia period.

All this does not mean that the revolution is around the corner. It rather signifies that conditions for its unfolding are perhaps more favourable today than at any time this century.

Oliver Tambo, the Acting President-General of the ANC, in a speech delivered in June 1973, said:

> In South Africa, the long stalemate since Rivonia is undeniably over. Everywhere in Southern Africa our struggles are gathering a new momentum and our people are striking out in several directions against the Apartheid and colonialist regimes. There is no peace for the enemy. They live in a state of apprehension, doubt and fear. They no longer strut about with arrogant confidence in the permanence of their power. Instead they are now frantically directing their energies into repairing the floodgates which menacingly threaten to burst open in revolution throughout the Southern African region.[11]

When Tambo spoke these words, the situation seemed on the surface less promising than he claimed. FRELIMO, MPLA and PAIGC were still locked in struggle with Portuguese colonialism; Smith, with Vorster's backing, still clung arrogantly to his belief in the permanence of white rule in Zimbabwe; Namibia was still a routine item on the UN agenda; and Vorster seemed unthreatened in his racialist fortress. But the turbulence below, which Tambo so correctly sensed, was to surface dramatically. Within a year Portuguese colonialism was no more. Smith was talking a less assured language while Zimbabwean guerrillas cut deep into his territory. Vorster was frantically making his gestures on 'petty apartheid' and Namibia. Although these and other gestures were of little substance, they nevertheless marked the measure of his apprehension of things to come.

This dramatic lunge forward in the sub-continent's history was the fruit of protracted endeavour and sacrifices by the liberation movements. The unexpectedly swift change was, however, triggered off by an event thousands of miles away: the overthrow of the fascist dictatorship in Portugal. But the apparently 'accidental' trigger of Lisbon's April *coup* was, like all such 'so-called accidents', merely 'the form behind which necessity lurks'.[12]

In South Africa too, struggle in the new conditions sets the scene for the fulfilment of its historical necessity—the early achievement of liberation and freedom from exploitation.

Notes

1 *The Memoirs of General Grivas*, Longman, London, 1964, p. 22.
2 *Rand Daily Mail*, 22 March 1975.
3 Leo Kuper, 'Non-Violence Revisited', in Robert I. Rotberg and Ali A. Mazrui eds.,

Protest and Power in Black Africa, Oxford University Press, London, 1970, p. 797.

4 Fatima Meer, 'African Nationalism—Some Inhibiting Factors', in Heribert Adam ed., *South Africa: Sociological Perspectives*, 1971, pp. 121–57.

5 Heribert Adam, *Modernising Racial Domination: South Africa's Political Dynamics*, University of California Press, 1971, p. 116.

6 J. Bowyer Bell, *The Myth of the Guerrilla: Revolutionary Theory and Malpractice*, New York, 1971; and 'The Future of Guerrilla Revolution in Southern Africa', *Africa Today*, Winter 1972. Also see Lewis H. Gann, 'No Hope for Violent Revolution: A strategic Assessment', *Africa Report*, 17 February 1972.

7 Sheridan Johns, 'Obstacles to Guerrilla Warfare—a South African Case Study', *Journal of Modern African Studies*, No. 2, 1973, pp. 296–7. Johns's is perhaps the most informative discussion of the period in question.

8 According to Dr Cyril Wyndham, of the Chamber of Mines Human Sciences Laboratory, by 1980 South Africa will have an economically active population of 10.4 million of which only 1.7 million will be white, *Financial Mail*, 2 August 1974, p. 408.

9 The Government's Tomlinson Commission (1956) talked of the need to create 500 000 new jobs over a ten-year period in and around the Reserves if progress were to be made in the implementation of apartheid. According to the Government-supporting Afrikaanse Handels Instituut (*Rand Daily Mail*, 18 August 1973) only 8 000 new jobs had been created in all the Bantustans in the previous ten years. In the 'border' regions the figure for the $11\frac{1}{2}$ years from June 1960 to December 1972 is 78 451. Tomlinson also claimed that the Reserves, which now have a population of 7 million, could only reasonably support life for 2.3 million people even if his recommendations for development investment were carried out.

10 Declaration of ANC Executive Committee, 17–20 March 1975.

11 *Sechaba*, September 1973, p. 19.

12 F. Engels, 'Ludwig Feuerbach and the End of German Classical Philosophy', in K. Marx and F. Engels, *Selected Works* (3-volume edition), Progress Publishers, Vol. 3, p. 363.

19 African Peasants and Revolution*

JOHN S. SAUL

In the past many social scientists have been reluctant to utilise the term peasant with reference to African cultivators. More recently a body of literature has emerged which, in seeking to theorise the most important trends in rural Africa, has found the notion of the peasantry to be a particularly illuminating one. Some brief reference to this latter emphasis, and to the rationale which sustains it, will need to be made here. But the main thrust of this paper lies elsewhere—in a discussion of the conditions (socio-economic, ideological, organisational) under which the African peasantry, so identified, becomes a force for radical transformation of the status quo of colonialism and neo-colonialism in contemporary Africa. It is worth emphasising at the outset that the latter is no mere academic concern. In the two concrete situations which we shall explore—these being the Portuguese colony of Mozambique and the independent country of Tanzania—it is the conscious attempt to engage the peasants in precisely such revolutionary activity that has been one of the most striking features of recent political and socio-economic developments there. In Mozambique, the success of this strategy has been crowned by the presentation of a particularly dramatic challenge to Portuguese colonial hegemony. In Tanzania, the ultimate effectiveness of that country's challenge to neo-colonialism is more open to doubt, but the intense interest of the effort to construct a new, socialist Tanzania on a popular base of active and self-conscious 'workers and peasants' cannot be denied.

Peasants and Revolution

Revolutionary theory has evinced much scepticism concerning the peasantry—a scepticism rooted in the classics of Marxism and, most dramatically, in Marx's own often quoted description of the peasants as being merely like a 'sack of potatoes', divided and demobilised.[1] Yet peasants in the twentieth century have become a revolutionary force in ways that Marx, necessarily, could not predict. There are those who cling steadfastly to the classical view, of course—arguing that the proletariat, by virtue of its participation in the centralising and collectivising logic of modern industry, remains the sole and indispensable guarantor of genuine revolution. Those who, like Nigel Harris, press the point most fiercely, are aided in doing so by a definition of socialism (the end-product of any such genuine revolution) which excludes every existing country from that category.[2] Others, less concerned to ignore the claims of, say, a country like China to revolutionary achievement are, concomitantly, more charitable towards the peasantry. Indeed, Malcolm Caldwell, vigorously criticising Harris's position and making, among other points, 'the simple factual assertion that the peasantry played the decisive role in the Chinese Revolution', has gone so far as to conclude:

> ... we may be sure that the peoples of Africa, Asia, and Latin America themselves alone can transform their own lives. Since the vast majority

*From *Review of African Political Economy*, 1, 1974, pp. 41–68.

of these people are peasants, the future must lie in their hands, whether
it accords with one's preconceived theories or not . . . . In the world
of today, the poor, the dissatisfied and the unprivileged are peasants:
therefore 'the peasants alone are revolutionary for they have nothing
to lose and everything to gain'.[3]

It is not necessary here to exhaust the general debate being rehearsed (and, it
would seem, unduly polarised) in the exchange between Harris and Caldwell.
As a first approximation, it is sufficient to remind ourselves of Trotsky's
dictum: 'Without a guiding organisation the energy of the masses would
dissipate like steam not enclosed in a piston box. But nonetheless what moves
things is not the piston, or the box, but the steam.'[4] For one cannot examine
the course of recent history without affirming that peasants have provided
much of the steam for revolutionary challenge to the status quo in this century.
Why should this be so? Many Marxists emphasise that the expansion of the
international capitalist system into less developed areas of the world has been
such as to displace certain crucial contradictions of that system from its centre
to its periphery.[5] And even a growing number of non-Marxist thinkers seek
for answers to such a question in an understanding of imperialism. Thus, Eric
Wolf, summarising the lessons drawn from a careful survey of peasant wars
of the twentieth century, concludes that the historical experience which situates
such wars, 'constitutes, in turn, the precipitate in the present of a great overriding cultural phenomenon, the world wide spread and diffusion of a particular
cultural system, that of North Atlantic capitalism'.[6] Moreover, we shall see that
it is precisely a concern with the historical emergence and further evolution of
capitalist imperialism which is crucial to an identification of the peasantry (and
other relevant actors) in an African setting.

Nonetheless, many misgivings expressed by Marx and others about the
peasantry's likely contribution to revolution, also have some validity. Parochial-
ism cuts deep in the rural areas; the outlines of the broader exploitative
environment, world-wide and territorial, which oppresses him, are not easily
perceived by the peasant and as a result 'the aggregate of small producers'
constitute themselves only with difficulty as a group capable of 'a shared
consciousness and joint political action as a class'.[7] Even if peasant political
action (rather than apathetic resignation and/or preoccupation with quasi-
traditional involvements closer to home) is forthcoming, it may still prove either
to be quite localised and isolated in its spontaneous expression, or else be
forced too easily into channels of mere regional and ethnic self-assertiveness by
a territorial leadership which divides in order that it may continue to rule.
Moreover, most twentieth century revolutionaries aim at some kind of socialist
transformation of the existing system, this being, ultimately, the only effective
response to imperialism. The peasants' temptation to seek a resolution of the
contradictions which confront him either by shoring up 'traditional' aspects of
the peasant economy or by attempting 'petty bourgeois' solutions which would
further service his isolation—a redistribution of land designed to guarantee
his own individual tenure and possible economic aggrandisement on that basis,
for example—may make him a risky ally for such an enterprise.

This seems all the more likely to be the case when one considers the findings
of Wolf and of Hamza Alavi—that it is the middle peasant rather than the poorest
of peasants who is 'initially the most militant element of the peasantry'.[8] Yet
counter-revolutionary results are not inevitable. Alavi does observe that 'when
the movement in the countryside advances to a revolutionary stage they (the
middle peasants) may move away from the revolutionary movement' since

'their social perspective is limited by their class position'. Nonetheless, he suggests that this is only true 'unless their fears are allayed and they are drawn into the process of cooperative endeavour'. Moreover, poorer peasants, who have an even greater stake in structural transformation, gradually can become mobilised for action as well—and carry the revolutionary process further.[9] Indeed, what is demonstrated by the introduction of various qualifications to the more rosy picture of the peasantry painted by Caldwell is merely the need to avoid falling back on romantic illusions about the inevitable and unequivocal spontaneity of peasant involvement in revolution. It becomes clear that if peasant action is to service such a revolution—to manifest full confidence and a sense of efficacy, to acquire effectively national focus, and to set in train a comprehensive transformation of society—political work must come to mediate it and help to define its thrust.

We return by this route to Trotsky's metaphor: a 'piston box' is also necessary in order to harness the steam of peasant discontent. Again, one of Wolf's formulations is suggestive: 'Peasants often harbour a deep sense of injustice, but this sense of injustice must be given shape and expression in organisation before it can become active on the political scene; and it is obvious that not every callow agitator will find welcome hearing in village circles, traditionally suspicious of outsiders'. Like Wolf, we must be 'greatly aware of the importance of groups which mediate between the peasants and the larger society of which he forms a part'. However, this emphasis too would be misleading if the capacity of the peasants to play an active role in the process of politicising their grievances were to be understated. In fact, the vital contradiction between organisation/ leadership on the one hand, and participation/spontaneity on the other, is not one that can be evaded or suppressed—both aspects are essential. If effective methods of political work are used, it is merely a contradiction which can be resolved, over time, in a manner that contributes to further revolutionary advance.

In recent times, 'people's war' has been the technique which has most satisfactorily realised this goal, this effective blending of both leadership from above and spontaneity from below. Selden has stated this point clearly with reference to Vietnam and China, and his formulation is worth quoting at length.[10]

> Out of the ashes of military strife which enveloped China and Vietnam in protracted wars of liberation emerged a radically new vision of man and society and a concrete approach to development. Built on foundations of participation and community action which challenge elite domination, this approach offers hope of more *humane* forms of development and of effectively overcoming the formidable barriers to the transformation of peasant societies. In the base areas and consolidated war zones in which the movement enjoyed its fullest growth, the redefinition of community began in the resistance to a foreign invader and continued in the struggle to overcome domestic problems of poverty and oppression. People's war implies more than a popular guerrilla struggle for national independence; it impinges directly on the full scope of rural life. In the course of a people's war, local communities defined in response to the imperatives of defence and social change may be effectively integrated in national movements. The very intensity of the war-time experience contributes to rapid development of consciousness and organisation. In people's war peasants cease to be the passive pawns of landlords and officials or to fatalistically accept the verdict of a harsh natural environment. Where

the primary resource of insurgent movements in man [*sic*], and where active commitment is the *sine qua non* of success, the sharing of common hardships and hopes creates powerful bonds among resisters and between leaders and led. In the new institutions which emerge locally in the course of the resistance, to an unprecedented degree peasants begin to secure active control of their economic and political destinies.

We shall see that this is precisely the pattern that has emerged in Mozambique in the course of the liberation struggle against Portuguese colonialism. In Tanzania the situation is more complicated. There the leadership (or one section of it) has also made some effort to forge 'new bonds of unity in which the very definitions of leader and led are recast and the beginnings of a new social base are created'. But it is doing so in cold blood as it were—from within the framework of established structures, rather than in the heat of a convulsive upheaval. It is obvious that the making of a peasant-based revolution under such circumstances presents anomalies—and, as we shall see, it is indeed proving to be a difficult task.

African Peasantries

Who are the peasants in Tanzania and Mozambique then? Indeed, 'are African cultivators to be called peasants?', as a well-known article on rural Africa once asked.[11] It is worth noting that this has been a subject of some controversy in the literature, though it is a controversy which easily degenerates into a mere word game. In the first instance, the debate has seemed most concerned with the nature of 'traditional' Africa; moreover, the latter has all too often been ossified and discussed by social scientists as some kind of 'anthropological present' in a manner which can foreclose discussion of the real present of colonialism and neo-colonialism. Even with reference to pre-contact Africa, there may have been more peasant-like dimensions of the rural situation than has sometimes been assumed.[12] But the more immediately relevant argument of a number of recent writers is that, whatever the case for an earlier Africa, the incursion of imperialism and particularly of formal colonialism has gradually forced a large proportion of rural dwellers in Africa to take on the characteristics of a peasantry. As Woods and I have argued elsewhere,[13] this way of construing the majority of rural Africans is important, firstly because it fits neatly within the kind of broad analytical framework which seems best suited to identifying and explaining the overall patterns of change and development in contemporary Africa. Secondly, the concept quite accurately pinpoints characteristics of rural Africans which bear a family resemblance to peasant characteristics as identified elsewhere; it thus enables students of Africa, and political activists there, to collect data and theorise experience alongside others concerned about the problematic of the peasantry in other parts of the world. These two points can be briefly documented.

The key historical factor in defining the shape of contemporary Africa has been its forced insertion, as a dependency, within the broader Europe-centred imperial system.[14] And, as Woods and I wrote, 'despite the existence of some pre-figurings of a peasant class in earlier periods, it is more fruitful to view the creation of an African peasantry ... as being primarily the result of the interaction between an international capitalist economic system and traditional socio-economic systems, within the context of territorially defined colonial political systems'. Ken Post has described the process of 'peasantisation' in

West Africa in similar terms, citing Trotsky's 'Law of Uneven and Combined Development' and emphasising the economic, the political and the cultural dimensions of the process which subordinates 'communal cultivators and such pre-colonial peasants as there were' to that broader system:

> Whatever their differences, it is true to say that all the colonial powers in Western Africa greatly extended the market principle to the point where the impersonal forces of the world market dominated the lives of millions and imposed a state where none had been before or to supersede indigenous ones. The African quest for western education and the issue of assimilation amply demonstrate the presence of a new 'great' culture. It would appear, then, that many of the conditions for the existence of a peasantry were suddenly created, but from outside and quite independently of the processes of internal differentiation in origin, though the internal factors had important influences upon the final form of these conditions.

In validating this perspective, Post is particularly concerned to demonstrate that 'surplus' is extracted from the African rural population within such a structure by the 'levying of taxes and other dues by the state', for example, and by unequal terms of exchange for agricultural produce.[16] Finally, Derman has made closely related points—with reference in particular to the role of the state in peasantising cultivators—when he criticises the views of those anthropologists who continue to withhold the term 'peasantry' from such rural dwellers and instead see them as 'subsistence oriented cultivators in the process of becoming farmers'! In Derman's view, this ignores the fact that 'the state—both colonial and post-colonial—remains highly exploitative of the rural peasants or cultivators. African peasants are coming to form an increasingly subordinate segment of the population, a trend which began during the colonial era'. This too is a suggestive perception—and is entirely accurate.

Balancing the fact of such structural subordination within the wider political and economic systems of Africa is a second feature, one which is equally necessary in order to confirm the peasant character of such cultivators (particularly in comparative terms): 'the importance to the peasantry of the family economy'. Woods and I wrote:

> Thus peasants are those whose ultimate security and subsistence lies in their having certain rights in land and in the labour of family members on the land, but who are involved, through rights and obligations, in a wider economic system which includes the participation of non-peasants. The fact that for peasants ultimate security and subsistence rests upon maintaining rights in land and rights in family labour [is] an important determinant shaping and restricting their social action. It is also the characteristic which peasants share with 'primitive agriculturalists', though not with capitalist farmers. For while the capitalist farmer may *appear* to depend upon his land, he is not *forced* to rely upon these in the last instance; he has alternative potential sources of security and investment. What the peasant does share, in general terms, with the capitalist farmer (though not with the primitive agriculturalists) is his integration into a complex social structure characterised by stratification and economic differentiation.

In Africa it is also possible to keep the term 'peasant' flexible enough to include pastoralists since they are 'subject to the same kind of political and economic forces as their predominantly agricultural brethren and since their productive economy (in as much as it involves rights to, and control over, family herds) is based on a similar kind of homestead principle'. And, more controversially, to include migrant labourers. The latter inclusion is justified by the stake which such migrants retain in, precisely, the family economy. While some peasants will seek to guarantee the surplus demanded by the broader social structure by means of attaching a cash-crop component to their basically subsistence-oriented cultivation, others will seek to do so by periods of time spent labouring in mines, plantations and urban centres. But they will do so without relinquishing their family's claim to an agricultural stake in the rural community. The logic of the migrant's position within the overall system remains the same as that of the cash-cropper—at least in the short run, while both remain peasants.

Note the latter phrase. It is important, for the logic of continued capitalist penetration should be, of course, to phase out the African peasantry even as it creates it. At the one end of the spectrum peasants who start to generate surpluses in the sphere of cash-cropping may become, in time, capitalist farmers. And migrants (as well as those who start to sell their labour power locally to supplement their subsistence agricultural activities) may become, in time, more definitively proletarianised. In short, these two tendencies 'can chip away at the peasantry, pulling it in different directions'. At the same time, the pace at which this apparent 'logic' now works itself out must not be overestimated. The realities of Africa's continuing dependence means that peripheral capitalism in Africa tends to produce merely further underdevelopment rather than a total capitalist transformation of countries there. As a result, and as Colin Leys has written in demonstrating the increased rate of peasantisation in Kenya (itself one of the most seemingly dynamic of dependencies in Africa):

> Analytically speaking, the peasantry in Africa may be best seen as
> a transitional class, in between the period of primitive cultivators
> living in independent communities and that of capitalist development
> in which peasants are restratified into capitalists and proletarians; but
> under the conditions of growth of neo-colonialism it seems clear that
> in Kenya at least the stage during which the peasantry itself goes
> through a process of development, and develops its own pattern of
> relationships with the elite, may be fairly prolonged.[17]

It could be argued, therefore, that the African peasantry is not composed of peasants quite like those in earlier, historically more progressive, capitalist systems (as analysed by Barrington Moore) 'over whom the wave of progress is about to roll'.[18] Perhaps this will give them more of an opportunity to shape their own futures.[19]

Two main points follow from the analysis thus far presented. There is a peasantry in Africa—large numbers of rural Africans caught, by international capitalism and colonial and post-colonial state structures, between subsistence cultivation and the fates which capitalism might eventually hold in store for them. In this reality of common 'peasant-hood', there is the potential grounds for 'shared consciousness and shared political action' against the broader structures which have come to dominate and exploit them. The multinational corporations and the national elites (along with their representatives in the rural areas themselves) would be the legitimate targets of action to redress such a situation. It is in this reality that there lies the promise of a peasant revolution and possibly the seeds of socialism—a promise to the analysis of which we will return in the next section.

But what we have said so far also suggests that there are *peasantries* in Africa— these representing the wide range of variation in the way the peasantised have become involved in the broader imperial system. Or, in terms used by Lionel Cliffe, the presence of varying 'articulation of modes of production': different ways in which 'historically and geographically specific and varied modes' of production in Africa have 'articulated', or interacted with, 'the increasingly dominant capitalist mode'. This variation means, in turn, as Woods and I wrote, that:

... in each territory we can distinguish a number of peasantries who are differentiated according to locality—some localities being labour exporting, some food-crop exporting, some cash-crop exporting and some with varying proportions of each ... [In addition] the dynamic of capitalist development tends to introduce a further element which cuts across the differentiation of peasants by locality with a differentiation based on the degree of involvement in the cash economy. This involves ... the possible movements towards proletarianisation of migrant labour on the one hand and toward capitalist agriculture on the other.

Since, unlike certain other parts of the globe, African territories lacked some broadly comparable pre-capitalist structure (eg. feudalism) spread over a large area, but instead comprised an extraordinary range of pre-capitalist social formations, it seems probable that the range of 'articulation of modes of production' which springs from capitalist incursion is, if anything, more varied in Africa than elsewhere. To elicit even a roughly common response and common level of consciousness from 'peasants' so diversified is concomitantly difficult.

Revolution in Africa

What of revolution, then? In Section 1 we quoted Malcolm Caldwell's general conclusion to his argument concerning 'the revolutionary role of the peasantry': 'In the world of today, the poor, the dissatisfied and the unprivileged are peasants. Therefore "the peasants alone are revolutionary, for they have nothing to lose and everything to gain"'. Significantly, the quotation which Caldwell uses here is from Fanon—and Fanon was writing about Africa.[20] But Fanon's enthusiasm is not fully shared by others—the late Amilcar Cabral, one of Africa's outstanding revolutionaries, for example. 'Obviously,' he says, 'the group with the greatest interest in the struggle is the peasantry, given the nature of the various different societies in Guinea ... and the various degrees of exploitation to which they are subjected'. However, this cannot merely be left to rest there, for 'the question is not simply one of objective interest'. Cabral then proceeds:

to broach one key problem, which is of enormous importance for us, as we are a country of peasants, and that is the problem of whether or not the peasantry represents the main revolutionary force. A distinction must be drawn between a physical force and a revolutionary force; physically, the peasantry is a great force in Guinea; it is almost the whole of the population, it controls the nation's wealth, it is the peasantry which produces; but we know from experience what trouble we had convincing the peasantry to fight.[21]

Leys, the academic observer, states a related point even more forcefully in concluding his analysis of Kenya and of revolutionary prospects there. For 'as writers such as Moore, Alavi and Wolf have shown, it generally requires a rare combination of tyranny and misery to produce a peasant revolt, let alone a peasant revolution; short of which the clientelist political structures characteristic of peasant society have a resilience that can easily be underestimated'.

Many of the grounds for scepticism about the revolutionary vocation of the peasantry, which were asserted in general terms earlier, I apply to Africa—in some instances with even greater force. In many parts of the world rural dwellers are, in effect, peasantised twice over, first by the workings of some form of feudal system, and secondly by the further structural subordination which arises from the insertion of that feudal system within a colonial-cum-international capitalist framework. However, exploitation and subordination are rendered more intangible in many (though of course not all) African settings because of the absence of landlords and quasifeudal relationships at the point of direct production. This can have the result of depersonalising and distancing the overall exploitative system, thus diffusing discontent.[22] Secondly, population pressure on the land has not been as great in rural Africa, relatively speaking, as on other continents, and the visible threat to peasant status (especially to prospects for guaranteeing subsistence) from that quarter not quite so pressing.

Thirdly, while it is true that few but the most isolated of Africans remain untouched by the peasantisation process, the unfulfilled nature of this process, its unevenness and its relative recentness, has left standing, perhaps more firmly than elsewhere, important vestiges of precapitalist social networks and cultural preoccupations—particularly a range of variations on kinship relationship and upon the theme of ethnic identification—which mesh closely with the survival of the subsistence agricultural core of the system. At the same time some of those who do begin to break more definitively with the attributes of peasanthood do so under the influence of burgeoning petty capitalist aspirations, rather than as moved by notions of the collective improvement of the rural dwellers' lot. In making links with the world beyond the village such elements may find their most natural allies among the new elites who control state power.

But this—the aligning of itself with energetic capitalists-in-the-making in the villages—is only one way in which the neo-colonial state defuses the possibility of peasant class consciousness. Equally important, the quasi-traditional attributes of peasanthood can also be warped in such a way as to service the functioning of Africa's neo-colonial systems by those who benefit from them. The key, as Leys has argued, lies in the politics of patron-client relationships, broadly defined. In the first instance, peasants can be tied into the system by links with others above them in the hierarchy (these often being more privileged kinsmen), and by such small benefits as trickle down to them in this manner. In addition, politicians operating in the national arena have often come to play what is, in effect, a similar role over a broader terrain—that of super-patrons with their tribes as their clients. For 'tribalism' (the politicisation of ethnicity which is all too characteristically a pathology of dependent Africa) does not spring primarily from the bare fact of the existence of cultural differences between peoples. Rather, it has been teased into life, first by the divide-and-rule tactics of colonialism and by the uneven development in the economic sphere which colonialism also facilitates and, secondly, by the ruling petty-bourgeoisie of the post-colonial period. The latter, too, seek to divide and rule—better from their point of view that peasants should conceive the national pie as being divided, competitively, between regions and tribes, rather than (as in fact much more clearly the case) between classes. Moreover, as individuals, they are moved to mobilise tribal constituencies behind themselves, using this as a bargaining counter in the struggle for power against other members of the ruling circles.[23]

Can African peasants come to be something more than mere pawns in the unattractive game of underdevelopment? Certainly peasants have not always been passive elements in recent African history. Their discontent often flared into overt action, revealing in the process ironies which Fanon has pin-pointed (and Kilson and others have documented):

> What is the reaction of the nationalist parties of this eruption of peasant masses into the nationalist struggle? . . . As a whole they treat this new element as a sort of manna from heaven, and pray to goodness that it'll go on falling. They make the most of the manna, but do not attempt to organise the rebellion. They don't send leaders into the countryside to educate the people politically, or to increase their awareness or put the struggle on to a higher level. All they do is to hope that, carried onwards by its own momentum, the action of the people will not come to a standstill. There is no contamination of the rural movement by the urban movement; each develops according to its own dialectic.[24]

Of course, the very diversity of peasantries also makes the 'putting of the struggle on a higher level' a crucial necessity. For different peasantries have felt, immediately, different kinds of grievances against the colonial system. The nationalist movements described by Fanon tended merely to accumulate the support of such aggrieved peasantries around the lowest common denominator of a demand for political independence, rather than generalising their grievances into a critique of imperial and capitalist reality more adequately defined. The leadership elements, so soon to inherit the established structures, had little interest in encouraging the development of a broader vision, of allaying fears and drawing peasants 'into the process of cooperative endeavour' (as Alavi suggested to be one possible denouement of peasant upsurge effectively politicised).

Instead the mere Africanisation of peripheral capitalism proceeded apace. Yet, as Nyerere has argued, this has had little, ultimately, to offer the vast mass of the peasantry:

> . . . sooner or later, the people will lose their enthusiasm and will look upon the independence government as simply another new ruler which they should avoid as much as possible. Provided it has been possible to avoid any fundamental upset in their traditional economic and social conditions, they will then sink back into apathy—until the next time someone is able to convince them that their own efforts can lead to an improvement in their lives.'[25]

Moreover, this latter possibility suggested by Nyerere has occasionally become a reality. The Congo of the mid-1960s providing an example—glimpsed in Pierre Mulele's activities in the Kwilu and in the People's Republic of the Eastern Congo. Of the latter Gerard-Libois has written:

> . . . the insurrections which led to the creation of the People's Republic were first of all a revolt of impoverished and exploited peasants for whom the enemy was not only the foreign colonialist but above all those Congolese who had monopolised all the fruits of independence, and also those policemen, administrators and even teachers who served the new class and sought to imitate its style of life . . . The rebellion was . . . for all its limitations, the hope of a new independence, fundamentally different from the first, and through which the wealth of the Congo would accrue to the poorest and in which a new, genuinely decolonised African society would come into being.[26]

Such activities easily lost focus, and the character of the Mobutist denouement in the Congo (now Zaire) is well known. Whether more recent attempts to revive a revolutionary challenge in that country (seen in the work of the Congolese Marxist Revolutionary Party, for example) will be any more successful remains to be seen, but something of the nature of the 'steam' which does exist at the base of contemporary African societies could be discerned in Kwilu. In addition, broad trends like the growth of population pressure may come, over time, to further exacerbate such tensions in rural Africa.[27]

At base, then, the contradiction between the peasantry and established structures, world-wide and continental/territorial, remains. We quoted Cabral at the outset of this section. It is worth continuing that quotation, drawn from his analysis of the Guinean peasantry: 'All the same, in certain parts of the country and among certain groups we found a warm welcome, even right from the start. In other groups and in other areas all this had to be won.' Nevertheless, it has been won: in Guinea-Bissau the peasants have become an active agency for a deep-cutting revolution. Of course, the overall structure within which the achievement of Cabral and his PAIGC has been realised is a particularly anomalous one. Portuguese 'ultra-colonialism', even more cruel and unyielding than other colonialisms in Africa, provided precisely that 'rare combination of tyranny and misery' which Leys mentioned as being an important prerequisite of a peasant revolt. Moreover, it is obvious that anti-colonial nationalism could be used as an initial ideological rallying cry for revolution in Guinea much more unequivocally than in a post-colonial situation; in Nyerere's words, it is 'another thing when you have to remove your own people from the position of exploiters'.[28] Yet Cabral emphasises again and again that, despite even these 'advantages' in Guinea hard *political* work has still been necessary in order to realise a peasant base for struggle. How much more is this likely to be the case elsewhere in Africa?

Cabral describes the nature of such political work carefully and suggestively in his writings. Particularly important have been the cadres who came to play the role of catalyst of the Guinean revolution. They were drawn initially from the petty bourgeois stratum and from semi-proletarianised urban hangers-on, beginning their work as what Gorz has termed an 'external vanguard' vis-a-vis the peasants. But they have become, with time and with the effective resolution of the contradiction between leadership and participation, much more of an 'internal vanguard',[29] a development which has also meant the sharing of authority with new leadership elements thrown up by the newly mobilised peasants themselves as the peasants' own confidence and commitment to the struggle has grown. Obviously, a number of further questions arise from this: How are the *different* peasantries likely to be geared into such struggle (note that some provided a 'warm welcome' to Cabral and his colleagues, others not)? What kind of 'piston box' of organisation and ideology, constructed by the revolutionaries themselves, can most effectively facilitate this process? By turning to an examination of the situation in Mozambique, similar in certain important respects to that in Guinea, we can begin (though only begin) to answer these questions.

Mozambique

The two questions just mentioned are not separate, however. The Mozambican case demonstrates the importance of examining both the nature of the peasantry as a potential base for revolution and the nature of the presumed revolutionary organisation—in this case, the Mozambique Liberation Front (FRELIMO)—in considering recent developments there. But it is probably even more essential to examine the dialectical relationship established between the two—between peasantry and political organisation—for it is this relationship which has defined the forward momentum of the Mozambique revolution.

That the peasants are an essential base there can be no doubt. Eduardo Mondlane, the first President of FRELIMO, who was assassinated by the Portuguese in 1969, made this point clearly.

> Both the agitation of the intellectuals and the strikes of the urban labour force were doomed to failure, because in both cases it was the action only of a tiny isolated group. For a government like Portugal's, which has set its face against democracy and is prepared to use extremes of brutality to crush opposition, it is easy to deal with such isolated pockets of resistance. It was the very failure of these attempts however, and the fierce repression which followed, that made this clear and prepared the ground for more widely based action. The urban population of Mozambique amounts altogether to less than half a million. A nationalist movement without firm roots in the countryside could never hope to succeed.[30]

More recently, Marcelino dos Santos, FRELIMO's Vice-President, has described that countryside along lines which are essentially similar to those elaborated upon in this paper. Beginning with a juxtaposition of 'two societies' and that of 'the traditional type—a sort of subsistence economy', he proceeds to dissolve this distinction in his subsequent discussion.

> But these two societies do not exist in isolation from one another; they are entirely linked. Why? Where do these people who work in the plantations come from? All those people who work within the capitalist sector come from the traditional sector. And most of them do not remain permanently outside the traditional sector because, for instance, many of them go to work on the plantations for a maximum of two years and they then come back to the village and to the traditional system. So that is the main link—going back and forth. Then there are those people who do not become absorbed into the capitalist system but who are nevertheless related to it. For instance, the people who produce for themselves must sell their produce in the market, mainly food like grain, cashew nuts. They are forced into the market system to find the cash for colonial-imposed taxes and to purchase commodities which they do not produce themselves. So these two societies are linked and on many levels the persons comprising the two societies are the same.[31]

It will be readily apparent that dos Santos is here discussing what we have seen to be the African peasantry.

It has been an African peasantry pitchforked into existence and sustained in its 'transitional' state by methods even more brutal than those employed by other colonialisms. Mondlane documents many of these methods in his book, discussing cash-cropping peasantries for whom the enforced cultivation of cotton and the rigging of government price schedules have introduced great hardship, and labour-supplying peasantries, even more mercilessly exploited over the years by a complex system of virtual forced labour. It is precisely the systematic nature of such repressive practices that led Perry Anderson to speak of 'Portuguese ultra-colonialism'.[32] Small wonder that peasants periodically had given expression to their grievances even before the mounting of a comprehensive political challenge to colonialism. Thus, in Mondlane's words, 'some developments in the countryside which took place in the period just preceding the formation of FRELIMO were of enormous importance'. In the northern region around Mueda, for example, such activity centred upon efforts to organise a cooperative and obtain better terms for produce delivered to the colonial government; when peasants demonstrated peacefully in support of this programme at Mueda town in 1960, 500 were shot down by the Portuguese.

Grievances there certainly have been and continue to be. Nor does it require any very elaborate proof to demonstrate that they provide tinder for peasant action. Nonetheless, my own experience in the liberated areas of Mozambique in 1972 permits me to speak with some added confidence on the subject.[33] Travelling among the people of Tete Province with FRELIMO guerrillas, I had the opportunity to attend a number of political meetings and to hear the themes stressed both by FRELIMO militants and by ordinary peasants. A pinpointing of the economic linkages mentioned above—forced labour, a prejudicial system of cultivation—was joined with a precise enumeration of the abuses directly perpetrated by the Portuguese administration. Of the latter, Portuguese taxation was a theme given particular prominence, its historically heavy role in the daily life of peasants being elucidated by FRELIMO cadres alongside an explanation of its importance in sustaining Portugal's ability to support economically its continued military presence. In effect, Mozambican peasants seemed themselves prepared to validate both Post's and Derman's earlier emphases—economic exploitation on the one hand, state power on the other—in defining their essentially subordinate position within previously established structures.

FRELIMO personnel also hinted at the existence of a range of variation in the response of different peasantries to revolutionary imperatives. In fact, it was obvious to me that this has been the subject of much serious analysis by the movement, since its strategy is precisely to establish deep political roots among the people of a given area by means of careful political work prior to launching armed activity. For this to be done, considerable knowledge of the stresses and strains in the local community under consideration is necessary. So much became particularly clear from discussions which I held with cadres who had long been active in such preparatory political work (as well as in the subsequent tasks of constructing FRELIMO-type social institutions in areas once they have been liberated). But, necessarily, concrete and detailed information on these matters was not forthcoming. It was suggested to me that the work of mobilisation had gone much more easily in Tete than in Cabo Delgado and Niassa 'because the people had had more experience of exploitation'—especially of the push of labour to other parts in Mozambique and to Rhodesia and South Africa.[34] This might seem to be evidence in support of Barnett's thesis that the 'labour-exporting peasantry' has a 'relatively high revolutionary potential' compared with the 'cash-cropping peasantry' and the 'marginal-subsistence peasantry'.[35] But one cannot be categoric in these matters. Certainly the revolution has also advanced dramatically in Cabo and in Niassa where the latter types of peasantry are much more prominent, as well as in the cash-cropping areas of Tete itself. Similarly, in more immediately political terms, some chiefs seem to have reconciled themselves easily to the novel situation created by FRELIMO's presence, presenting few obstacles to the political involvement of 'their people' on an entirely new basis, while others have defended themselves and Portuguese overrule with vigour. Historians will one day have important work to do in reconstructing more precisely such realities and the reasons for this range of variation.

Peasant 'spontaneity' has been important, then, and will probably become all the more important as peasants both respond negatively to such new and desperate last-ditch Portuguese strategies as the enforced strategic hamlet programme and respond positively to the promise which life in the liberated areas increasingly exemplifies for them. Nonetheless, peasant spontaneity has not been a sufficient driving force for revolution in Mozambique. It has also taken an effective movement—FRELIMO—to bring the potential peasant base into meaningful and effective existence. I have discussed elsewhere the evolution of FRELIMO itself which has determined its character as a revolutionary movement. It was not inevitably such: 'all those features characteristic of the brand of nationalism which has facilitated false decolonisation elsewhere on the continent have been present in the Mozambican context'.[36] There are elements in FRELIMO who were quite prone to aim primarily at their own elitist and entrepreneurial aggrandisement under the guise of nationalism and to refuse to integrate themselves with the peasant masses, preferring instead to demobilise the latter with ethnic and racial sloganeering.

However, from the point of view of conservative members of the petty bourgeois leadership of the Mozambican independence struggle, there has been just one flaw in all this: in the context of a genuine liberation struggle this kind of nationalism, quite literally, *does not work* as it did for African leadership groups elsewhere on the continent. Portuguese intransigence meant that a stronger link with the people had to be forged in order to undertake effective guerrilla warfare. It was with this reality in mind that Sebastiao Mabote, FRELIMO's Chief of Operations (with whom I travelled in Mozambique), could say that the Portuguese had given Mozambique an opportunity other African states had missed—the opportunity to have a revolution. And that Eduardo Mondlane could say, shortly before his death, and only half-jokingly, that it would be almost a pity if the struggle were to succeed too quickly, 'we are learning so much!'

Learning, for example, the necessity of enlisting the peasants more actively in conscious support of the movement so that they would willingly undertake such *positive* tasks as maintaining the secrecy of FRELIMO activities in the face of colonialist pressure, as carriage of material and supply of produce, as direct enlistment in the army, reconnaissance and militia support work. But the peasants will not embrace such tasks if the leadership does not appear to present a genuine and less exploitative alternative than does the colonial system itself. They thus exercise a kind of passive veto over the movement and over those who lead it. Moreover, the establishment of participatory institutions throughout the liberated areas has enabled the peasant also to play an active role in helping to arbitrate the issue of the movement's direction. This fact became particularly important in 1968–69 when the contestation within FRELIMO's petty bourgeois leadership—this group drawn initially from classes like those cited by Cabral with reference to Guinea—reached its boiling-point. Then the progressive elements closest to the popular base of the struggle carried the day for their conception of the direction which the movement should take.

The popular base was significant. At the Congress of 1968 it was the delegates representing the people in the rural areas and those representing the army working inside the country who supported Mondlane; similarly, in 1969, when Simango broke with the movement, his defection found little or no echo in the liberated areas. It became clear that it was those who could work with the peasant as cadres—resolving in their own methods of political and educational work the contradiction between leadership and peasants participation—who had been able to consolidate their positions within the movement while others dropped by the wayside. It was also such cadres who could be expected to carry the revolution forward. For in the very process of this contestation the movement was encouraged to develop a new ideology, to move from 'primitive nationalism', as Marcelino dos Santos had termed it, to 'revolutionary nationalism'.

In short, the popular, peasant base of the struggle has become the key both to FRELIMO's military success and to its own internal clarity as a revolutionary movement. And this, in turn, has encouraged its cadres to return to the people with even more searching solutions for the problems of the peasantry; not merely genuine democratic involvement at village, circle, district and regional levels, but also a comprehensive and practical programme of socio-economic transformation.

In our case the necessity to define a revolutionary ideology with greater precision emerged when we started to build the liberated areas, to engage ourselves in national reconstruction. As always, the task of building a society economically poses the problem of the type of production and distribution, and especially who is going to benefit from what the society produces. This life process also raises more sharply than in the classroom the deeper question of the type of ideology to embrace. So to summarise, there comes a stage when it becomes clear why everybody in the nation should accept the idea that the main aim of the struggle is to advance the interests of the working people. In the field or organising the people we follow collectivistic ways as is the case, for example, with our cooperative movement in the liberated areas.

It is precisely here that peasants begin to be drawn 'into the process of cooperative endeavour' (Alavi). The further radicalisation of the nationalist movement, and the need to consolidate its rural base, create this kind of momentum. In the words of Samora Machel, FRELIMO's President:

... we leaders, cadres, fighters and militants must work hard to make the masses adopt and live by the collective spirit, using collective methods of production, which will make it possible to enhance the spirit of collective living thereby increasing the sense of unity, discipline and organisation. Adopting a collective consciousness in work means renouncing individualism and considering that all the cultivated plots belong to us, that all the granaries and houses are ours, the people's. It means that I must unite with others in a cooperative, a production brigade. We will cultivate, harvest and stand guard together, and together we will protect that which belongs not to me or you, but to us. The field is not mine or yours, but ours. The pupil in the school, the soldier in the base and the patient and the nurse in the hospital all have collective consciousness. No one looks upon the school, the base or the hospital as their private property, and everyone therefore takes an enthusiastic interest in advancing the work in the school, base and hospital. As a result, progress is made, the work advances and the enemy cannot so easily attack. Where there is collective spirit we are more organised, there is better discipline and a proper division of labour. There is also more initiative, a greater degree of sacrifice and we learn more, produce more and fight better, with more determination.[37]

This step is in some ways more difficult than laying the initial bases of armed struggle. Joaquim Chissano of FRELIMO suspects that 'peasants are generally rather conservative and you have to go step by step. In our case there are traditional ways of cooperation, such as mutual help, and at the first stage we encourage them. Later we establish district committees to administer the area, and groups within this framework to look after agriculture. In their discussions within these committees, little by little the members come to understand the benefits of working collectively.'[38] In other words, given the quality of FRELIMO cadres and the general participative atmosphere in the liberated areas, striking results can be achieved. When, for example, I visited one village inside Mozambique where this process had been underway for only a year or two, I discovered division of labour which incorporated a significant proportion of collectively farmed fields, work on these being recorded in a log-book against eventual distribution of the proceeds. I found metal-workers and basket-makers who had originally worked as mini-entrepreneurs in the village, now working as part of this collective division of labour, their time spent also being recorded in the village book. Such dramatic developments may eventually inspire social scientists to write books like *Fanshen*; for the present we must rely on twentieth-century versions of travellers' tales. But the latter evidence is impressive and does begin to suggest that in such a peasantry, increasingly well-organised and now working self-consciously against various forms of exploitation, there can be seen some guarantee of the continued forward momentum of the Mozambican revolution, even after independence has been won. This is also the underlying thrust of dos Santos' comment in his recent interview:

I accept that [communal effort] is partly made easier by the demands of war. But does that mean that once we have independence the approach will be changed? In the particular conditions of fighting against Portuguese colonialism, revolutionary attitudes are not only possible but necessary. If we do not follow collectivist attitudes we will not be able to face the enemy successfully. In thi sense it is true to say that the internal dynamic of the struggle is such that the conditions generate collectivist thinking. But one should also say that even if the origins of such attitudes are partly pragmatic, it can, nevertheless, provide a basis for the growth of real social revolution. There is certainly a strong possibility that in the course of the collectivist effort a situation is created from which it will be difficult to withdraw. If our organisation maintains a true revolutionary leadership, the special circumstances of the process of our liberation open up real possibilities for an advance from liberation to revolution.

How to make certain that this is achieved?

The main defence must be to popularise the revolutionary aims and to create such a situation that if for one reason or another at some future time some people start trying to change these aims, they will meet with resistance from the masses.

Tanzania

For Tanzania, the future is now. In consequence, that country reveals much more clearly some of the problems of peasant-based structural transformation.

The absence of 'tyranny and misery' of the proportions offered by Portuguese colonialism means that those features which tend to divide and to differentiate the peasantry become far more prominent aspects of the terrain of struggle than in Mozambique. At the same time, the leadership which has emerged in Tanzania has not been moved to cleanse and rededicate itself to anything like the extent of that in Mozambique. Despite the Arusha Declaration and *Mwongozo* (The TANU Guidelines of 1971), it is the more conservative wing of the petty bourgeoisie which seems increasingly to be consolidating itself, with the result that the cadre-based methods of work which might serve to crystallise and focus peasant discontent and positive aspirations are not so well developed. From both points of view, Tanzania falls short; rather than a dialectic being established between leaders and led which reinforces forward movement, the gap between them seems to be growing.

Still, what is striking about Tanzania is that it can be discussed in these terms at all. In most of independent Africa the break between nationalist parties and peasantry was of a kind described above by Fanon, often from a point even prior to the winning of independence. In Tanzania, on the other hand, an attempt has been made to resolve such a contradiction within the framework of the country's policy of 'socialism and self-reliance'. 'Peasants' were to become (with 'workers') a crucial agency for transforming established structures from within—for a 'quiet revolution', in effect. I have traced elsewhere the background to this attempt, and some of its continuing strengths and weaknesses.[39] Here it is relevant to note three themes which have defined the rural dimensions of Tanzania's socialist project.

First, there has been President Nyerere's often repeated emphasis on the necessity that, territorially, the masses—'the workers and peasants'—become responsible for their own socialist development, distrusting their leaders and holding them firmly to account.[40] Though not always clearly defined in the language of class struggle, the point was thus being made that *the peasantry* has an interest in confronting those elements who might work to sustain its continued subordination.[41] Moreover, this aspiration found some reinforcement in subsequent policy initiatives. *Mwongozo* further called upon the people to check their leaders.[42] It is true that this invitation was, in the first instance, taken up most actively by the workers in the urban areas; nonetheless, *Mwongozo* confirmed the general emphasis upon the peasants' own positive role. And the whole process of decentralising planning processes closer to the villages in 1971–73, however much disfigured in practice, was designed to redress a situation where 'to the mass of the people, power is still something wielded by others'. With decentralisation, 'more and more people must be trusted with responsibility—that is its whole purpose'.[43]

Second, there has been a desire to pre-empt the further development of capitalist relations of production in the rural areas themselves:

> ... as land becomes more scarce we shall find ourselves with a farmers' class and a labourers' class, with the latter being unable either to work for themselves or to receive a full return for the contribution they are making to total output. They will become a 'rural proletariat' depending on the decisions of other men for their existence, and subject in consequence to all the subservience, social and economic inequality, and insecurity, which such a position involves.
>
> Thus we still have in this country a predominantly peasant society in which farmers work for themselves and their families and are helped and protected from exploitation by cooperative marketing arrange-

ments [*sic*]. Yet the present trend is away from the extended family production and society unity and towards the development of a class system. It is this kind of development which would be inconsistent with the growth of a socialist Tanzania in which all citizens could be assured of human dignity and equality, and in which all were able to have a decent and constantly improving life for themselves and their children.[44]

In this respect, too, socialism was seen as a way out of the peasant condition. By becoming 'socialists' peasants would avoid the other possible fates discussed above—their continued subordination as a peasantry or their destruction under 'the wave of (capitalist) progress'. Thirdly, there has been a desire to improve the quality of rural life by raising productivity and by slowly but surely making available necessary services and amenities. Implicit was an agreement with Raikes' formulation:

> It has been shown time and time again that tremendous resources of productivity and creativity can be released in peasants and other producers once they take control of their own production process and control democratically its planning and implementation.[45]

The mechanism chosen to realise these goals has been the 'ujamaa (socialist) village' policy—an attempt to structure collective agricultural communities at the base of the Tanzanian system which would give concrete expression to the peasants' involvement in the tasks of socialist construction. In working to build rural socialism, peasants could be expected to transform themselves. Moreover, ujamaa communities, once established, could also be expected to provide more effective rallying-points for critical action by an increasingly radicalised and organised peasantry, and hence the greater likelihood of a 'real, rather than a theoretical, check upon the petty bourgeoisie of party and bureaucracy, at local and national levels, by the mass of the population in the interests of socialist development'.[46] And this on a nation-wide scale. It is true that much of the original emphasis seemed to lie on the formation of brand-new villages in marginal-subsistence areas, but this was by no means an exclusive emphasis. Already, in the first major policy paper which launched the *ujamaa* approach, the President made clear that in established cash-cropping areas the move towards collectivism was equally to be fostered—even if, of necessity, by more subtle and graduated means:

> It must be accepted . . . that socialist progress in these areas will be more difficult to achieve, for when vacant land is not available there is only one way to create a community farm; that is by individual farmers coming together and joining their pieces of land and working them in common . . . .
>
> It may be that the way to start under these circumstances is to operate first on the basis of working groups, but with the individual plots retained—that is, on the basis of mutual help. This would be simply a revival, and perhaps an extension, of the traditional system of joint activity, making it applicable to existing farms and not just to land clearing or house building. By working together on their private farms, the farmers will be able to finish different jobs more quickly, or to do things which would be too difficult for any of them individually. They will then have time to do other useful things—either by themselves or cooperatively.
>
> This first step of mutual help can be followed by others. The farmers could buy certain essential goods cooperatively—things like fertilisers

for example—or they could together build a store for their coffee, or something else which is of use to them all. By doing such things together the farmers will be gradually moving towards an acceptance of ujamaa socialism.[47]

Reference was also made in that paper to the peculiar problems of bringing collective agriculture to 'animal husbandry' areas. In short, the initial formulation was not a crude one: it began with the firm recognition that Tanzania contained a markedly diverse range of peasantries.

The original guidelines for the policy seemed also strongly to emphasise peasant spontaneity as a key to progress. Thus Nyerere argued that 'any citizen who understands the principles of ujamaa is encouraged to take the initiative'[48] and stressed again and again that the transition to collectivism was to be a voluntary one. Discussing his paper 'Socialism and Rural Development', he noted that 'it is directed to all the people of Tanzania—or at least all of those who live in the rural areas. It is an outline of a policy of inter-linked, self-governing village communities which are *of* the people, and which therefore cannot be created for them or imposed on them. The paper, therefore, calls for leadership, but not for orders to be given; it directs the people along the socialist path, but excludes any attempt to whip them into it—saying clearly that you cannot force people to lead socialist lives.' But the call for leadership is equally crucial. Nyerere in fact sought the key to success in leaders who will be, arguably, those very cadres whose importance we discussed earlier, persons who 'will lead by doing'.[49] He specifies some of the methods of work of such people, and concludes:

The members of an ujamaa village must control their own affairs—I say it again! But the role of a leader is crucial and good leadership will make all the difference to the socialist success and the material success of such a community.

Spontaneity and leadership are required with cadres who will resolve that contradiction. Let us again check both terms of the equation. In Tanzania, peasant protest was an active ingredient in the nationalist movement; moreover, the party (TANU) which gave a focus to nationalism was linked more closely to this peasant base than other parties in Africa. This was one factor which facilitated the forging of the progressive programme of socialism and self-reliance by one wing of the territorial leadership in the post-colonial period. In addition, there have been some significant peasant actions subsequent to the winning of independence—not least the taking of a number of local initiatives to establish rural collectivisation in scattered parts of the country—notably in remote Ruvuma Region. In the latter case, the Ruvuma Development Association (RDA, with its small attendant organisation of cadres, the Social and Economic Revolutionary Army—SERA) was established formally under the umbrella of TANU, but more spontaneously than that fact might tend to suggest. In important ways it became a prototype for Nyerere when he moved to generalise this and other 'unofficial' experiments into a national ujamaa villages policy. Moreover, the potency of such rural collectives in institutionalising a peasant challenge to class formation—in particular, a challenge to those whose power and privilege had begun to crystallise around the apparatuses of state and party—can be seen in the history of the RDA's struggle with the bureaucracy and with local notables over a number of years in Ruvuma. It can also be gauged from the fact that the RDA was dissolved by the party, possibly against the President's better judgment, in 1969.[50]

Despite the example of the RDA, it is nonetheless clear that 'spontaneity' has been an inadequate source of rural transformation in Tanzania. A potential is there, but to trigger off peasant consciousness around a national programme of socialist reconstruction and to give this programme its local embodiment in collective units requires the sort of leadership identified by Nyerere. It could of course be argued that in the period after 1967, when Nyerere and his colleagues launched their overall project of transforming the economy and consolidating a progressive leadership, some of the preconditions for drawing peasants into the process of cooperative endeavour did exist.[51] Yet the inability of Tanzanian leaders to cope with the reality of a mobilised peasantry when it had sprung to life (witness the RDA experience) is suggestive of a lingering problem. Not surprisingly, they have been equally unsuccessful in becoming active agents for mobilising such a peasantry into existence and releasing its energies elsewhere in the country where this is necessary.[52] On balance, the trend towards the *bureaucratisation* of the leadership (or, more accurately, its crystallisation as a privileged class around the apparatus of the state) has begun to outpace any counter-tendency which would serve to transform it into a complement·of socialist cadres.[53] Raikes argues that this degeneration has in turn determined a running-down of the ujamaa policy into one marked by coercion, by the uneconomic and demobilising reliance upon solely material incentives, and by compromise with the locally privileged who have most to lose from collectivisation. Thus, even if other more radical alternative approaches existed in theory,

> It would be unrealistic to paint a picture of what 'might have been' in a political vacuum. The change in emphasis of ujamaa was not simply the result of a neutral judgement . . . . The ujamaa strategy was changed to conform more closely with the preconceptions and interests of the bureaucratic bourgeoisie who controlled its implementation. Similarly, their judgement cannot be considered neutral concerning the question of socialist transformation of the economy. Just as they tend to distrust the intentions and capabilities of peasants and are concerned to maintain their own status in relation to them, so do they distrust the major political changes which would have to occur before and during a socialist transformation. Large numbers of democratically controlled ujamaa villages would pose a real threat to their status, and should the next logical step be taken, to form democratically elected local councils of village leaders, this would go further to threaten their very reason for existence.

This at a territorial level. The consolidation of a more radical overall tendency there would, as in liberated Mozambique, have been reflected in more adequate methods of political work at the local level as well. For despite Nyerere's emphasis, cited above, on adapting the policy to suit the situation of diverse peasantries, little has been done to follow up on this insight. Yet the need to generate detailed knowledge both of political 'stresses and strains' at the local level, and of the realities of productive potential there, is at least as crucial to those engaged in facilitating the transition to collectivisation in Tanzania as it is to those engaged in mobilising a base for guerrilla warfare in Mozambique. If anything, it is even more important, for the range of variation of the articulation of modes of production is vast in Tanzania, while the necessity to give the struggle for socialism a concrete and meaningful expression at the local level is even more pressing in the absence of a direct, physical threat to the peasantry like that provided by the Portuguese colonialists.

Several writers have addressed themselves to these realities,[54] Woods discussing a range of 'area-based peasantries in Tanzania' and Cliffe pinpointing six different 'broad types of rural situation' which need separate consideration: highland high-density areas, medium density, cash-crop areas, marginal subsistence areas, frontier areas, settler/estate areas, pastoral and semi-pastoral areas.[55] Furthermore, Cliffe, in a number of his writings, has spelled out some of the implications for socialist construction of this range of variation by identifying differing strategies for engaging the peasants of each such area in collective activity. He finds one key, particularly in advanced areas, in premising strategies upon the opportunities for struggle offered by class divisions internal to the areas themselves. In the absence of such strategies, those peasants who have shifted furthest towards a capitalist posture may seize the day, as in Bukoba where, as Cliffe shows in his article on rural class formation, 'in the contemporary period when the Tanzanian government is attempting to restructure the modes of production into cooperative forms in order to avoid class differentiation, the policy was pre-empted by a coalition of bureaucrats and the locally privileged. They translated the policy into terms which safeguarded the existing positions of rich and middle peasants by removing poor peasants who had little or no land to so-called "ujamaa" villages in resettlement areas'.

Nor is the latter case an isolated one: Raikes would see it merely as a further example of a more general phenomenon—the class alliance of bureaucrat and 'kulak':

> Thus communal labour for ujamaa villages required communal landholding, something which required careful political education for peasants both large and small if they were to give of all or part of the private plots on which their livelihood depended. More particularly, of course, the larger farmers plainly stood to lose, and this could have led to some difficult choices in view of their considerable local political influence. The discomfort would have been the greater since by training, inclination and previous practice, the administrators were accustomed to work through precisely these local leaders and specifically through 'progressive' (ie. large) farmers. This had been a stated objective of colonial agricultural policy, and was largely continued through the first six years of Independence. Concentration of advice, credit and membership of cooperative and other local committees upon such groups had led, in many areas (and especially the richer ones), to the emergence of fairly small and tight groups of relatively wealthy and influential peasants and capitalist farmers whose relations to government staff were much closer than those of the mass of the peasantry.[56]

Is there added steam to be drawn upon in such a situation? The work of the Iringa Regional Commissioner, Dr Wilbert Klerru, in emphasising class contradictions in the Ismani area, isolating the 'kulaks', taking over holdings, and releasing the energies of poor and middle peasant strata might seem to suggest so, though in the event it led to Klerru himself being assassinated by a 'rich peasant'.[57] And Ismani is a frontier area where capitalist relations are the most fully developed in Tanzania and the least muted by quasi-traditional identifications and solidarities. Where 'middle peasants' are a more dominant proportion of the rural population than in Ismani, the precise blend of class struggle, exemplification of collectivity, and technical innovation to be encouraged would have to be a more nuanced one.[58] Of the need for such effective and militant local struggles, however, there can be no doubt.

But, to repeat, the methods of work which might generate such strategies have not been forthcoming. The one effort (in 1967) to develop, systematically, a core of cadres who could be expected genuinely to release peasant energies around the promise of collective action foundered on the reef of bureaucratic and political hostility to such a programme.[59] Instead, quite dubious alternative policies have been mounted, some of which have already been mentioned: a frontal approach directed by civil servants (generally themselves from more developed regions) towards backward areas least able to defend themselves and reduced in content to mere 'villagisation', rather than collective enterprise; a ceding of other ujamaa experiments (in tea and tobacco) to the purvue of World Bank experts little concerned to guarantee socialist relations of production; and so on. Meanwhile, amidst the degeneration of his policy, President Nyerere seems only to have become more shrill and desperate in an attempt to recover the ground which has been lost. His latest utterance on the subject has struck a particularly uncharacteristic note: 'To live in villages is an order', in the words of a *Daily News of Tanzania* headline.

> President Nyerere said yesterday that living together in villages is now an order. And it should be implemented in the next three years. This was a Tanu decision. And any leader who hesitated to implement it would not be tolerated because he would be retarding national development. Addressing a public rally at Endabashi, Mbulu District, Mwalimu [ie. Nyerere] said there was a need for every Tanzanian to change his mode of life if rapid progress was to be achieved. People who refused to accept development changes were stupid, if not ignorant and stubborn.[60]

There may be more promising counter-tendencies at the base of the system, though (as noted earlier) it is workers and students who have thus far responded most actively to *Mwongozo's* invitation to take power into their own hands.[61] Nonetheless, in a country so rurally-based as Tanzania it remains true, ultimately, that 'the only available class *base* for revolutionary transformation would seem to be a reconstructed peasantry—even if elements from other strata of society provide much of the leadership'.[62] Nor is it likely that the peasantry has been entirely unaffected by the experience of struggle over the direction post-colonial Tanzania will take. Difficult though it is to gauge, some measure of consciousness-raising has undoubtedly taken place in the rural areas, even if the ujamaa programme has yet to give it effective institutional expression. Indeed, Von Freyhold seems to argue that the advance has been substantial, though

> While society has changed, parts of the bureaucracy have not yet fully understood that the peasants have emerged victorious from colonial domination. The old vices of bureaucracy—commandism, hasty decisions without investigation, red-tape and superiority feelings—have survived and it will probably take a cultural revolution—including communal re-education through self-criticism—to readapt the superstructure to its new social base.[63]

Whence such a cultural revolution? In Handeni, Freyhold does see seeds of growing consciousness even in the rather compromised villages which have emerged from implementation of the ujamaa policy there. Furthermore, she feels that the struggle to determine the overall direction of the system is still sufficiently alive to make the opting for a cadre-based strategy—and a consequent strengthening of a rejuvenated party over and against the 'staff' or bureaucracy—a continuing possibility. This conclusion is controversial—some would argue that it is the bureaucrats and not the peasants who have emerged victorious—but her perception as to the need 'to change the structures of communication between the villages and the outside (in a way) which could bring more knowledge, more motivation and more self-assurance to the common members of the villages' is much less controversial. In the end she returns to familiar recommendations, recommendations which recall the dynamic of developments witnessed in Mozambique.

> The kind of recruitment, training and task-description needed for political cadres will in any case have to change as the party and the peasants gain more experience with each other and with ujamaa. What matters at the moment is that the necessity of cadres [should be] realised and that different ways of finding and educating the right kind of people be tried. Strengthening the party at its base would have to be a priority not only because peasants need political guidance but also because the party at higher levels cannot grow into a meaningful institution without confrontation with the real and concrete problems on the ground.[64]

Here would be a rejoining of the dialectic between leadership and peasantry that we have seen to be so important. Time alone will tell whether Tanzania still retains the capacity to reverse all those trends which suggest the running-down of its socialist experiment and whether it can begin again to consolidate a peasant-base for itself along the lines thus suggested.[65]

Conclusion

The two cases which we have discussed are important, but they are not entirely typical of the continent as a whole. Southern Africa is crucial in its own right; moreover, successful revolution in Mozambique (using the term revolution in its broadest sense to include a successful challenge both to colonialism and to any prospect of subsequent neo-colonialism) would also be a stimulus to developments in the rest of Africa. But, as we have seen, the colonial factor—Portuguese ultra-colonialism—has given a point and purpose to nationalism there which has fashioned it, ineluctably and in the pre-independence period, into a revolutionary ideology and a revolutionary movement—of peasants. Tanzania, though already an independent state, is also atypical in that some attempt has been made by those already in positions of authority to mobilise the peasants (and workers) to support, even to demand, radical structural transformation.

Even with reference to Tanzania, there are those who would suggest that a point has now been reached which demands a more root-and-branch, from-the-bottom-up challenge to established structures, and who argue, in effect, that a much less ambiguous revolutionary thrust is becoming a necessity there.[66] Whatever the answer to this difficult question, the fact remains that the situation elsewhere in independent (and neo-colonialised) Africa is far less ambiguous and the imperative of such a straightforward challenge to established authority more clear cut, if the peasants' plight is to be alleviated. There the time has arrived where 'someone' operating outside the established structures must attempt again to convince the peasantry, in Nyerere's phrase, 'that their own efforts can lead to an improvement in their lives'! Of course, a further exploration of this prospect is not our concern there. Yet if and when mass-based revolutions do become a more characteristic feature of other parts of Africa, there will be lessons, both positive and negative, to be learned by African revolutionaries from the experience of Mozambique and Tanzania—lessons about the precise range of peasantries which exist in Africa and, most important, about the methods which might facilitate these peasantries making the revolution their own. We have begun to touch upon some of these lessons in this paper. More generally, it has become obvious that additional scientific work on the question of African peasantries can be expected to make a positive contribution to the revolutionary process on the continent.

Notes

1 Karl Marx, 'The Eighteenth Brumaire of Louis Bonaparte', in Marx, *Surveys from Exile*, Harmondsworth, 1973, p. 239.
2 Nigel Harris, 'The Revolutionary Role of the Peasants-2', *International Socialism*, 41, December–January 1969–70.
3 Malcolm Caldwell, 'The Revolutionary Role of the Peasants-2', *Ibid.*
4 Quoted in Daniel Singer, *Prelude to Revolution*, New York, 1970, p. 1.
5 See Paul Sweezy's particularly strong statement of this point in his 'Workers and the Third World' in George Fischer ed., *The Revival of American Socialism*, New York, 1971: 'If we consider capitalism as a global systeml which is the only correct procedure, we see that it is divided into a handful of exploiting countries and a much more numerous and populous group of exploited countries. The masses in these exploited dependencies constitute a force in the global capitalist system which is revolutionary in the same sense and for the same reasons that Marx considered the proletariat of the early period of modern industry to be revolutionary. And finally, world history since the Second World War proves that this revolutionary force is really capable of waging successful revolutionary struggles against capitalist domination.', p. 168.
6 Eric Wolf, *Peasant Wars of the Twentieth Century*, New York, 1969, p. 276.
7 Lionel Cliffe, 'Rural Class Formation in East Africa', paper presented to the Peasant Seminar of the Centre of International and Area Studies, University of London, 23 November 1973, mimeo, p. 1.
8 Hamza Alavi, 'Peasants and Revolution', in Ralph Miliband and John Saville eds., *The Socialist Register 1965*, London, 1965.
9 Alavi's emphasis suggests an additional point of crucial relevance to our discussion of Africa: that 'the peasantry' is not uniform. Alavi's own distinction between 'poor' and 'middle' peasant is one of a number of possible differentiations to be made among various peasantries in any specific historical setting.
10 Mark Selden, 'People's War in China and Vietnam' in Lawrence Kaplan ed., *Revolutions: A Comparative Study*, New York, 1973, pp. 374–5.
11 L.A. Fallers, 'Are African Cultivators to be Called "Peasants"?', *Current Anthropology*, 2, 1961, pp. 108–10.
12 See William Derman, 'Peasants: The African Exception?', *American Anthropologist*, 74, 1972, pp. 779–82.
13 John S. Saul and Roger Woods, 'African Peasantries' in Teodor Shanin ed., *Peasants and Peasant Societies*, Harmondsworth, 1971.
14 For a general overview of this process see Walter Rodney, *How Europe Underdeveloped Africa*, London and Dar es Salaam, 1972.
15 Ken Post, *On 'Peasantisation' and Rural Class Differentiation in Western Africa*, ISS Occasional Papers, The Hague, 1970.
16 William Derman in his book, *Serfs, Peasants and Socialists*, Los Angeles and London, 1973, suggests, following Wolf, a very broad definition of 'rent' to encompass these varying realities while maintaining conformity with certain of the literature on peasantries on other continents.
17 Colin Leys, 'Politics in Kenya: The Development of Peasant Society', *British Journal of Political Science*, 1, 1970, p. 326.
18 Barrington Moore, *Social Origins of Dictatorship and Democracy: Lord and Peasant*

in the Making of the Modern World, Boston, 1966, p. 505.

19 This fact also demonstrates the urgency of a peasant-based revolution in Africa, for peripheral capitalism seems unlikely, by its further evolution, to produce an alternative agency, a fully developed proletariat, which could underwrite a socialist way out of the dead-end of underdevelopment.

20 Cf. Frantz Fanon, *The Wretched of the Earth*, Harmondsworth, 1967.

21 Amilcar Cabral 'Brief Analysis of the Social Structure in Guinea' in his *Revolution in Guinea*, London, 1969. Here he draws an explicit comparison with the Chinese case: 'The conditions of the peasantry in China were very different: the peasantry had a tradition of revolt, but this was not the case in Guinea, and so it was not possible for our party militants and propaganda workers to find the same kind of welcome among the peasantry of Guinea for the idea of national liberation as the idea found in China.' p. 50.

22 The 'crisis of feudalism' which is often attendant upon the incursion of capitalism and which intensifies a number of contradictions for the peasantry will not, therefore, be so prominent a feature.

23 See the analysis in my essay *The Dialectic of Tribe and Class in Kenya and Uganda*, forthcoming.

24 Martin Kilson, *Political Change in a West African State*, among others.

25 Julius K. Nyerere, 'Introduction', *Freedom and Socialism*, London and Dar es Salaam, 1968, p. 29.

26 Jules Gerard-Libois, 'The New Class and Rebellion in the Congo' in Miliband and Saville eds., *The Socialist Register, 1966*, London, 1966. Gerard-Libois goes on to note, significantly, that 'the rebellion did not find the united, effective and revolutionary organisation it required, and it is very doubtful whether the brief experience of the People's Republic made any contribution to its creation.', p. 278.

27 Moreover, it is also obvious that trends in the urban areas (the activities of workers and/or lumpen elements, for example) will be important in determining the nature and extent of peasant involvement in movements directed towards radical social reconstruction.

28 Julius K. Nyerere quoted in *The Nationalist*, Dar es Salaam, 5 September 1967, and cited in John S. Saul, 'African Socialism in One Country: Tanzania' in G. Arrighi and J.S. Saul, *Essays on the Political Economy of Africa*, New York, 1973, p. 248.

29 This distinction is developed, with reference to an advanced capitalist setting, in Andre Gorz, *Socialism and Revolution*, New York, 1973.

30 Eduardo Mondlane, *The Struggle for Mozambique*, Harmondsworth, 1969, p. 116.

31 'FRELIMO Faces the Future', an interview by Joe Slovo with Marcelino dos Santos in *The African Communist*, 55, 1973, p. 29.

32 In Perry Anderson, 'Portugal and the End of Ultra Colonialism', *New Left Review*, Nos. 16, 17 and 18, 1962.

33 For a brief account of my initial impressions, see the article 'Lesson in Revolution for a Canadian Lecturer' in *Mozambique Revolution*, 52, July–September 1972.

34 See also Jorge Rebelo's comment on the struggle in the province of Manica e Sofala: 'One of the most interesting developments in Manica e Sofala has been the response of the people, which has been even stronger than that in Tete, again, we believe, because of the experience of oppression which the people here have' (in 'Comrade Rebelo's Report to CFM on Current Developments in Mozambique, 19 June 1973', in *Committee for a Free Mozambique News and Notes*, mimeo, New York, 1973).

35 Don Barnett, *Peasant Types and Revolutionary Potential in Colonial Africa*, Richmond BC, 1973.

36 John S. Saul, 'FRELIMO and the Mozambique Revolution' in Arrighi and Saul, *op.cit.*, chapter 8.

37 Samora Machel, 'Sowing the Seeds of Liberation' in *Mozambique Revolution*, 49, October–December 1971, pp. 23–4.

38 'Chissano: within 5 years the liberated areas will be developed 10 times more than under colonialism', interview with Joaquim Chissano in *Ceres*, Rome, July–August 1973, p. 40.

39 John S. Saul, 'African Socialism in One Country: Tanzania', *op.cit.*

40 Thus 'President Nyerere has called on the people of Tanzania to have great confidence in themselves and safe-guard the nation's hard-won freedom. He has warned the people against pinning all their hopes on the leadership who are apt to sell the people's freedom to meet their lusts. Mwalimu (ie. Nyerere) warned that the people should not allow their freedom to be pawned as most of the leaders were purchasable. He warned further that in running the affairs of the nation the people should not look on their leaders as 'saints or prophets'. The President stated that the attainment of freedom in many cases resulted merely in the change of colours, white to black faces without ending exploitation and injustices, and above all without the betterment of the life of the masses.' This statement is from the newspaper account cited in note 28.

41 This includes some attack upon imperialism—the confrontation with the 'new class' of leaders/bureaucrats is implicitly this throughout, and a wide-ranging programme of nationalisations and self-reliance is part of Tanzania's broader socialist policy. Nonetheless, it seems fair to argue that the overall policy has not been sufficiently clear concerning the peasants' role in subordination to international capitalism— especially vis-a-vis the world market system. Strategies for the rural sector have been weak in linking peasant production to a new pattern of demand brought into existence by structural change in the industrial/urban sector, the latter in turn to be facilitated by a more decisive break with dependency. Cf. Saul, *op.cit.*, for a more detailed critique along these lines.

42 *Mwongozo/The TANU Guidelines*, Dar es Salaam 1971.

43 Julius K. Nyerere, '*Decentralisation*' in *Freedom and Development*, Dar es Salaam and London, 1973, p. 347. Nyerere adds that 'those who cause the new system to become enmeshed in bureaucratic procedures will, as they are discovered, be treated as what they are—saboteurs'.

44 Julius K. Nyerere, 'Socialism and Rural Development' in his *Freedom and Socialism*, *op.cit.* This is an important perception of trends in rural Tanzania, though Roger Woods, in his 'Peasants and Peasantries in Tanzania and their Role in Socio-Political Development' (in Rural Development Reseach Committee, *Rural Co-operation in Tanzania*, Dar es Salaam, 1974), argues that involution and stagnation may be an equally prominent feature in many such areas.

45 Philip Raikes, 'Ujamaa Vijijini and Rural Socialist Development', paper delivered to the Annual Social Sciences Conference of the East African Universities, mimeo, Dar es Salaam, December 1973. This is a particularly important recent appraisal of Tanzania's rural development policy and practice.

46 John S. Saul, 'Who is the Immediate Enemy?' in Cliffe and Saul eds., *op.cit.*, vol. 2, p. 357.

47 Nyerere, 'Socialism and Rural Development', *op.cit.*, pp. 361–2.

48 Nyerere, 'After the Arusha Declaration' in *Freedom and Socialism*, *op.cit.*

49 Nyerere, 'Implementation of Rural Socialism' in *Freedom and Development*.

50 R. Ibbott, 'The Disbanding of the Ruvuma Development Association, Tanzania', mimeo, London, November 1969.

51 For example, 'leaders' were sealed off from very gross 'conflicts of interests' vis-a-vis the private sector under the terms of the 1967 Leadership Code (although familial links to 'kulaks' often remained); moreover, given the stated attempt to undermine elite consolidation and to rally the masses as 'workers and peasants', the instrumentalisation of the peasants by manipulating tribalism has been significantly reduced, thus encouraging the latter to come into more direct, unmediated, confrontation with structural realities.

52 See Raikes, *op.cit.* Michaela von Freyhold, 'The Government Staff and Ujamaa Villages', paper presented to the Annual Social Science Conference of the University of East Africa, Dar es Salaam, December 1973; Lionel Cliffe, 'Planning Rural Development' in Uchumi Editorial Board, *Towards Socialist Planning*, Tanzanian Studies, Dar es Salaam, 1972. For example, as I have argued in my 'African Socialism in One Country: Tanzania', 'it is . . . in the rural areas that manifestations of the hectoring, bureaucratic style of such a leadership are most likely to have the predicted effect

of demobilising the mass of the population, thus choking off that release of popular energies which is the programme's ostensible aim', p. 292.

53 The strongest statement of this position which, in fact, sees the leadership as compromised from the outset as a 'bureaucratic bourgeoisie' is to be found in Issa Shivji, *Tanzania: The Class Struggle Continues*, Dar es Salaam, 1973: I have argued the existence of a struggle within the petty bourgeoisie over the direction of Tanzanian development, a struggle which nonetheless evidences the growing strength of conservative elements in 'The State in Post-Colonial Societies: Tanzania', *Socialist Register 1974*.

54 For an important historical perspective on rural development in Tanzania and on the emergence of a differentiated peasantry, see John Iliffe, *Agricultural Change in Modern Tanganyika*, Nairobi, 1971.

55 Lionel Cliffe, 'The Policy of Ujamaa Vijijini and the Class Struggle in Tanzania', in Lionel Cliffe and John S. Saul eds., *Socialism in Tanzania, op.cit.*, Vol. 2.

56 Raikes, *op.cit.* Freyhold, *op.cit.* even argues that kulaks can sometimes operate within so-called ujamaa villages to advance their interests, a point which is also developed in an interesting case-study by H.U.E. Thoden van Velzen in his essay 'A Case-Study of Ujamaa Farming in Rungwe', in Rural Development Research Committee, *Rural Co-operation in Tanzania, op.cit.*

57 For an excellent, detailed account of developments in Ismani see Adhu Awiti, 'Class Struggle in Rural Society of Tanzania', *Maji Maji* Special Publication, 7, Dar es Salaam, October 1972.

58 Some examples of such possible strategies are presented in the final section of Rural Development Research Committee, *op.cit.*, where both the alteration of relations of production and the expansion of productive forces are equally stressed in exploring the promise of rural collectivisation.

59 See the account of this episode in N. Kisenge, 'The Party in Tanzania', *Maji Maji*, Dar es Salaam, September 1971.

60 *Daily News of Tanzania*, 7 November 1973.

61 On the recent dramatic rise of worker activism, see Henry Mapolu, 'The Workers' Movement in Tanzania', *Maji Maji*, 12, Dar es Salaam, September 1973, and Mapolu, 'Labour unrest: irresponsibility or worker revolution?', *Jenga*, No. 12, Dar es Salaam 1972. For an attempt to theorise student unrest see Karim Hirji, 'School Education and Underdevelopment in Tanzania, *Maji Maji*, No. 12, *op.cit.*

62 Cliffe, 'The Policy of Ujamaa Vijijini and the Class Struggle in Tanzania, *op.cit.*, p. 197.

63 Von Freyhold, *op.cit.* This is of a piece with my earlier conclusion which, however, now may seem excessively sanguine in light of the analyses by Raikes and others: 'the horizon of really dramatic, cumulative change remains a distant one, but there can be little doubt that in the rural areas the ujamaa policy has given a content and structure to the struggle for progress in a non-revolutionary situation around which consciousness can crystallise and a popular base may form' (in my 'African Socialism in One Country', *op.cit.*).

64 Von Freyhold, *op.cit.* In addition, Von Freyhold sees this as a step towards facilitating the emergence of 'peasant-experts' from within the village who would carry the process of transformation further; presumably, these kind of village activists would be precisely those militants who would also feed into the party from the base, helping to transform it from within.

65 Unfortunately, there is little comparative material to go on, since many aspects of the Tanzanian situation are unique on the continent; moreover, despite its title and despite its many other virtues, Derman's book, *Serfs, Peasants and Socialists*, does not take us far in understanding processes in Guinea which might conceivably be comparable, beyond his concluding sentence: 'In my view, the transformation of peasants into socialists will be far more difficult than the transformation of serfs into peasants or the transformation of Guinea from colony to independent nation'.

66 This might seem to be a conclusion to be drawn from Shivji's essay for example.